I0890601

BVR Legal & Court Case Yearbook 2015

BVR
What It's Worth
1000 SW Broadway, Suite 1200, Portland, OR 97205
(503) 291-7963 • www.bvresources.com

What It's Worth

Copyright © 2015 by Business Valuation Resources, LLC (BVR). All rights reserved. Printed in the United States of America.

No part of this publication may be reproduced, stored in a retrieval system or transmitted in any form or by any means, electronic, mechanical, photocopying, recording, scanning or otherwise, except as permitted under Sections 107 or 108 of the 1976 United States Copyright Act, without either the prior written permission of the Publisher or authorization through payment of the appropriate per copy fee to the Publisher. Requests for permission should be addressed to the Permissions Department, Business Valuation Resources, LLC, 1000 SW Broadway St., Suite 1200, Portland, OR 97205, (503) 291-7963, fax (503) 291-7955.

Information contained in this book has been obtained by Business Valuation Resources from sources believed to be reliable. However, neither Business Valuation Resources nor its authors guarantee the accuracy or completeness of any information published herein and neither Business Valuation Resources nor its authors shall be responsible for any errors, omissions, or damages arising out of use of this information. This work is published with the understanding that Business Valuation Resources and its authors are supplying information but are not attempting to render business valuation or other professional services. If such services are required, the assistance of an appropriate professional should be sought.

Editor: Jan Davis

Publisher: Sarah Andersen

Managing Editor: Janice Prescott

Chair and CEO: David Foster

President: Lucretia Lyons

Vice President of Sales: Lexie Gross

Customer Service Manager: Retta Dodge

ISBN: 978-1-62150-047-6

Library of Congress Control Number: 2015933474

Table of Contents

Introduction

Dear Reader,

As this compendium shows, 2014 gifted business valuators with a host of interesting and educational cases in many areas of law. Although appraisers hear a lot about picking a niche and becoming an expert in it, there are great benefits to reviewing cases from areas other than one's own to see how different courts handle a particular topic. This yearbook allows you to do just that.

A perfect illustration of this point is personal goodwill, a perennial topic of discussion among appraisers. This year, personal goodwill took the spotlight in several noteworthy cases, including the Tax Court's much-discussed *Estate of Adell* decision. In a dispute over the value of the decedent's 100% interest in a C corporation, the court, while chastening the estate for its "conflicting expert reports," adopted the estate expert's valuation, calling his treatment of personal goodwill more credible than that of the IRS's expert. Earlier in the year, Judge Paris, the author of the *Adell* decision, ruled on another tax dispute, *Bross Trucking*, which hinged on the same issue. Both opinions appear in this book, and, when read together, provide valuable insight into this particular judge's thinking on goodwill.

The topic was also at the center of a fascinating dissenting shareholder suit, *Potok v. Rebh*, in which a state court drilled down on the economic and legal theories underpinning personal goodwill when it reviewed a buyout in which the CEO of the acquired company had designated over $10 million as personal goodwill for himself and three other officers. The question was whether the personal goodwill allocation was justifiable or self-dealing by the defendants, as the plaintiff claimed. In a divorce case, *Brave v. Brave*, featuring spouses who co-owned a very successful restaurant, the issue took another turn. Two different appellate courts disagreed on the characterization of the goodwill present and on the larger question of whether to extend the scope of personal goodwill to businesses other than professional partnerships. Valuators working in the marital dissolution arena have noticed an effort by litigators to move courts to apply the concept of nontransferable personal goodwill to professions such as "chef." It will be interesting to see how receptive the courts are.

Valuation methodology is almost always a flashpoint in litigation. This year, courts in very different jurisdictions reminded appraisers of the limitations of the discounted cash flow (DCF) method. In this regard, perhaps the most attention-catching case was *Laidler v. Hesco,* a statutory appraisal action in which the Delaware Court of Chancery (J. Glasscock) found the DCF inappropriate because of the unique nature of the subject company's business and adopted the direct capitalization of cash flow (DCCF) analysis the parties' experts advocated.

Similarly, the Bankruptcy Court, in *Adelphia Recovery Trust v. FPL Group,* rejected the recovery trust's fraudulent transfer claim, finding the trust's expert was mistaken to base his valuation solely on the DCF analysis. "The DCF works best (and, arguably, only) when a company has accurate projections of future cash flows; when projections are not tainted by fraud; and when at least some of the cash flows are positive." This case was deficient in all regards, the court said. In a different bankruptcy case, *In re Genco Shipping & Trading Ltd.,* another expert advocating for the use of the DCF also fared poorly. This time, the Bankruptcy Court found that the nature of the industry precluded the possibility of achieving a reliable valuation by way of the DCF. Of course, as the reader of this book discovers, there were many more cases in which courts looked to the DCF method to produce a sound valuation.

As in the past, another issue that sparked discussion and litigation throughout the year was discounts—whether to apply them and what rate to use. Late in the year, two New York State courts presiding over fair value proceedings offered particularly rich decisions that centered on the discount for marketability, and also discussed other important valuation issues, that no expert worth his or her money will want to ignore. The cases are *Ferolito v. AriZona Beverages* and *Zelouf International Corp. v. Zelouf.*

There also was no shortage of *Daubert* cases, and we reported on those that added to the discussion of what admissible expert testimony looks like. This introduction only provides a sneak preview of the valuation cases and issues that have shaped the past year. Financial experts looking for a fuller picture of the litigation landscape will do well to dig into the *BVR Legal and Court Case Yearbook 2015.*

Sincerely,

Sylvia Golden, Esq.
Executive Legal Editor

Court Case Summary Table

Presented in order of case type, then by jurisdiction.

Case Name	Date	State/ Jurisdiction	Court	Summary	Page
Bankruptcy					
In re Flashcom, Inc.	12/4/13	Federal/ California	United States District Court	GAAP 'Relevant,' But 'Not Controlling' in Solvency Analysis	91
Stadtmueller v. Fitzgerald (In re Epic Cycle Interactive, Inc.)	6/6/14	Federal/ California	United States Bankruptcy Court	'Blurred' Solvency Analysis Diminishes Expert's Credibility	217
Mercury Companies, Inc. v. FNF Security Acquisition, Inc. (In re Mercury Companies, Inc.)	3/31/14	Federal/ Colorado	United States Bankruptcy Court	'Reasonably Equivalent Value' Analysis Is Not a Dollars-and-Cents Issue	151
Vision-Park Properties v. Seaside Engineering	3/27/14	Federal/ Florida	United States District Court	Debtor's Challenges Justify Bankruptcy Court's Emergence Risk Premium	244
In re Civic Partners Sioux City, LLC	10/7/13	Federal/Iowa	United States Bankruptcy Court	Plan Confirmation Hinges on Property Valuation	59
Dietz v. Jacobs	3/21/14	Federal/ Minnesota	United States District Court	Court Admits Solvency Analysis Lacking Specific Valuation of Debtor	72
Adelphia Recovery Trust v. FPL Group, Inc. (In re Adelphia Corp.)	5/6/14	Federal/New York	United States Bankruptcy Court	Court Finds Facts Back Expert's Value-Per-Subscriber Metric	15
In re Genco Shipping & Trading Ltd.	7/2/14	Federal/New York	United States Bankruptcy Court	Industry Characteristics Bolster Reliance on Net Asset Value	94
In re Residential Capital, LLC	11/15/13	Federal/New York	United States Bankruptcy Court	Creditors' Valuation Spoils Diminution in Value Claim	187
In re Tronox Incorporated	12/12/13	Federal/New York	United States Bankruptcy Court	Expert's Market-Based, 'Self-Contained' Solvency Analysis Crumbles	231
In re: LightSquared Inc.	7/11/14	Federal/New York	United States Bankruptcy Court	Regulatory Issue Causes Bankruptcy Valuation to Falter	140
Antioch Co. Litig. Trust v. Morgan	4/7/14	Federal/Ohio	United States District Court	Lost Value Opinion Using Untested Data Points Is No Go	27
Breach of Fiduciary Duty					
Marcus v. Quattrocchi	2/4/14	Federal/New York	United States District Court	Court Finds 'Market Value Concept' Requires Flexibility	149
Contract					
Leone v. Owsley	4/10/14	Federal/ Colorado	United States District Court	Buyout Agreement Short-Circuits Court's Scrutiny of Appraisals	134
Hardenbrook v. United Parcel Service, Inc.	2/7/14	Federal/Idaho	United States District Court	Courts Wrestle With Discount Rate for Future Stock Price Increase	105
Packgen v. Berry Plastics Corp.	9/12/14	Federal/Maine	United States District Court	Court Emphasizes Benefit of Hindsight in Evaluating Loss Period	165
Myservice Force v. Am. Home Shield	5/2/14	Federal/ Pennsylvania	United States District Court	Forecast's Assumption Imperils Conjoined Expert Opinions	159
St. Alphonsus Diversified Care, Inc. v. MRI Associates, LLP	8/4/14	Idaho	Supreme Court of Idaho	Usurped Opportunity Case Justifies Use of Defendant's Profits	202
Vega v. Fulcrum Energy, LLC	10/3/13	Texas	Court of Appeals	Expert's Disregard of ASB Guidelines Imperils Valuation	237
Mosaid Technologies Inc. v. LSI Corp.	2/28/14	Federal/ Delaware	United States District Court	'Stand-Alone' Lost Profits Claim Sinks, as Does Expert Opinion	155

Case Name	Date	State/ Jurisdiction	Court	Summary	Page
Estate of Tanenblatt v. Commissioner	11/18/13	Federal	United States Tax Court	Tax Court Foils 'End Run' Around Expert Rules	226
Washington Mutual, Inc. v. United States	2/10/14	Federal/ Washington	United States District Court	DCF Model Proves Unreliable Tool for Ascertaining Cost Basis	253
Intellectual Property					
VirnetX, Inc. v. Cisco Systems, Inc. (VirnetX v. Apple)	9/16/14	Federal	United States Court of Appeals for the Federal Circuit	EMVR Must Not Swallow Apportionment, Federal Circuit Says	240
Apple, Inc. v. Samsung Electronics Co., Ltd.(I)	11/12/13	Federal/ California	United States District Court	Apple Fails in Last-Ditch Effort to Offer Nonexpert Lost Profits Theory	29
Apple, Inc. v. Samsung Electronics Co., Ltd. (II)	3/28/14	Federal/ California	United States District Court	Samsung's About-Face on Off-the-Market Lost Profits Calculation	31
Dynetix Design Solutions, Inc. v. Synopsis, Inc.	8/22/13	Federal/ California	United States District Court	Finding 'Smallest Salable Unit' Does Not End Royalty Base Analysis	80
Volterra Semiconductor Corp. v. Primarion, Inc.	9/24/13	Federal/ California	United States District Court	Expert's 'Dollar-for-Dollar' Damages Theory Short of Factual Support	247
Robocast, Inc. v. Microsoft Corp. (I)	1/16/14	Federal/ Delaware	United States District Court	May Expert Use Valuation With Unknown Discounts for Royalty Analysis?	194
Robocast, Inc. v. Microsoft Corp. (II)	1/29/14	Federal/ Delaware	United States District Court	Nash Bargaining Solution a 'Non-Starter' for Royalty Analysis	196
Sloan Valve Company v. Zurn Industries, Inc.	3/26/14	Federal/Illinois	United States District Court	Abandoning 'Classic Way' to Royalty Analysis, Expert Gets Lost	209
Personalized Media Communications, LLC v. Zynga, Inc.	11/8/13	Federal/Texas	United States District Court	Plaintiff's Infringement Theory Constrains Apportionment	170
Rembrandt Social Media, LP v. Facebook, Inc.	12/3/13	Federal/ Virginia	United States District Court	Inexact Apportionment Invalidates Expert's Royalty Calculation	185
Judicial Dissolution					
Piche v. Braaten	2/3/14	Minnesota	Court of Appeals	May Court Disregard Shareholder Agreement In Judicial Buyout?	176
Surgem, LLC v. Seitz	10/16/13	New Jersey	Superior Court, Appellate Division	Expert's Calculation Report Fails to Yield 'Actual Fair Valuation'	224
Ferolito v. AriZona Beverages USA LLC	10/14/14	New York	New York Supreme Court (Trial Court)	Court Relies on DCF to Derive Value of 'Sui Generis' Company	82
Matter of Adelstein v. Finest Food Distributing Co. (I), (II)	4/16/14	New York	Court of Appeals	In Buyout, Court Extols Expert's Valuation and Legal Acumen	20
	11/3/11	New York	Supreme Court of New York (trial court)	In Buyout, Court Extols Expert's Valuation and Legal Acumen	20
Zelouf Int'l Corp. v. Zelouf	10/6/14	New York	New York Supreme Court (Trial Court)	Court Hitches DLOM Application to Probability of Sale	258
Marital Dissolution					
Brave v. Brave (I)	10/2/13	Arkansas	Court of Appeals	Can a Restaurant Have Personal Goodwill?	38
Brave v. Brave (II)	4/17/14	Arkansas	Supreme Court	Valuation Confirms Salability of 'Unique' Restaurant's Goodwill	41
Crews v. Crews	6/24/14	California	Court of Appeals	Court Nixes Murky Business Goodwill Determination	64
Finby v. Finby	12/18/13	California	Court of Appeals	Court Likens 'Book of Business' to Professional Goodwill	87
Burstein v. Burstein	2/13/14	Illinois	Appellate Court	Courts Decry Expert's Failure to Explore Different Ways to Develop FMV	49

Court Case Abstracts

Presented in alphabetical order.

Estate of Adell v. Commissioner

Citation: 2014 Tax Ct. Memo LEXIS 155
Date of decision: Aug. 4, 2014
Experts: Jeffrey M. Risius, C. Alex W. Howard (estate-petitioner); Francis X. Burns (IRS-respondent)
Judge: Paris
State/Jurisdiction: Federal
Court: United States Tax Court
Type of case: Estate and Gift Taxation
SIC code: 4899 Communications Services N.E.C.

Estate Valuation Can't Ignore Historical Data, Tax Court Says

In a lingering estate tax dispute, the estate and the Internal Revenue Service proposed numerous and wildly divergent valuations of the decedent's 100% ownership interest in a C corporation. In its fair market value determination, the court had harsh words for the estate, noting the latter's "conflicting expert reports and three different positions taken." Ultimately, the court adopted the valuation the estate submitted with its original Form 706 filing but rejected the estate's belated efforts to substitute it with a lower valuation. The opinion raises questions as to which party won or lost biggest in the fight.

Two-man operation. The decedent owned a for-profit cable company that provided uplinking services for one customer, a successful religious network known as "The Word." The Word was organized as a nonprofit 501(c)(3) entity. The decedent was the company's sole shareholder and in 2002 transferred his entire interest to a trust that he had set up on the same day. Before he died in 2006, he controlled the company and his son served as president. After the father's death, the son became CEO of the company, in addition to president, and also became the personal representative of the estate and trustee of the family trust. When his sisters sued him in probate court, he created a new company to provide The Word with the uplinking services it needed. The decedent's company ceased operations in 2010.

The son never had an employment agreement or noncompete agreement with the decedent's company. The Word was the son's brainchild. He developed contacts with influential religious leaders, including the Rev. Jesse Jackson; solicited content; and pursued broadcasting opportunities. Under a services agreement, The Word agreed to pay the company a monthly programming fee equal to "the lesser of actual cost or ninety-five percent of net programming revenue." In reality, the company received at least 95% of The Word's revenue each month and a few times as much as 100%. The company used the programming fee to pay its expenses, including a $20,000 rent payment to an S corp the decedent owned. But by far the largest expense was compensation to the decedent and the son. In 2006, the year of death, the decedent received over $7.3 million and the son almost $1.3 million.

The estate proffered three different values at three different times.

1. *The estate.* The estate's original estate tax filing (Form 706) stated a $9.3 million date-of-death value. It was based on a valuation report from an experienced financial expert, who considered historical data appearing in the company's financial statements, the services agreement between the company and The Word company's bylaws, a schedule of compensation to the company's officers, and management views regarding the business, industry, and prospects. His financial statement analysis showed a substantial sales increase during the historical period, from $7.9 million in 2002 to $15.9 million in 2006, and he found that there was an expectation that sales would increase from $18.5 million to $26 million during the projection period (2007 through 2011).

At the same time, the expert decided it was appropriate to adjust the company's operating expenses. Most important, he included an economic charge for the son's personal goodwill to reflect the company's dependence on the son's personal relationships with the board of directors of The Word. Also, the expert explained, since the company did not have a noncompete with the son, a hypothetical buyer would only buy the company to the extent it was able to retain him. The expert determined that the economic charge for the son's goodwill was anywhere from 37.2% to 43.4% of sales over the historical period and from 43.7% to 44.1% of sales over the projection period. In line with the company's overall growth, other operating expenses also would increase, he found. Taking into account the adjustments, the expert found that earnings before interest, taxes, depreciation and amortization generally increased over the historical period and projected they would reflect 12.1% of sales, or about $2.2 million in the first year of the projection period to $3.1 million in the residual period. The analysis led him to conclude that the company expected to produce positive cash flow in the future and should be valued as a going concern. He used the discounted cash flow method (DCF) to arrive at the $9.3 million value.

Reset button. At trial, some five years later, the estate submitted a different valuation prepared by the same expert that proposed a lower value, $4.3 million. This figure resulted from a change in methodology—using an asset approach instead of an income approach. The first valuation was done in error, the expert explained. Some two years after preparing his original report, he came to realize during a probate proceeding that he had failed to account for the limitation on the programming fee included in the services agreement. "Although [the company] has generated profits in the historical period a hypothetical buyer of a company would not place any weight on the historical performance of the company given the terms of the agreement with … The Word." His new understanding of the situation made it impossible for him to use the income approach, the expert said. Given the company's inability to generate profit from its only customer and its lack of any other source of income with which to generate revenue, the expert opted to perform another valuation based on an adjusted book value approach.

In addition, the estate submitted a second expert's opinion, prepared independently by an analyst working in the same firm as the first expert. This valuation also indicated a $4.3 million value based on the asset approach. In explaining his choice of methodology, the second expert echoed some of the reasons the first expert gave but added that the company's executive compensation model also restricted the company's earning potential. The services agreement, he said, provided that "any reduction in salaries would result in a dollar for dollar reduction in revenue for … the company." In other words, a hypothetical buyer could not hope to increase profits by cutting executive compensation nor by giving himself or herself a high salary. Also, projected cash flow was uncertain considering the son did not have a noncompete agreement and could set up a new company to service The Word. The goodwill between the son and The Word was personal, the expert explained. For all of these reasons, the income approach was unsuited to determining the company's fair market value.

In addition to the values in the expert opinions, the court says the estate claimed the stock value was zero in its original petition filed with the court. (The court's opinion is inconsistent as to the exact point at which the estate first set down the zero value; besides mentioning the original petition, the court also says that the zero value first appeared in the estate's second amended return.)

2. *The IRS.* The IRS, too, made significant adjustments to its values by the time the parties met at trial. After receipt of the estate's Form 706 filing, the agency issued a deficiency notice that proposed a value of $92.2 million for the company. As the dispute between the estate and the IRS took its course, the IRS adjusted the value to nearly $86 million.

IRS de-emphasizes goodwill. At trial, the IRS relied on an expert opinion that said the company was worth only about $26 million. This expert also used the DCF and in fact substantially relied on the estate expert's determinations in the estate's first valuation. The difference in value between two valuations based on the same methodology came down to the treatment of the son's personal goodwill. The estate's expert applied an economic charge for the son's personal goodwill—ranging from $8 million to $12 million over the projection period—that significantly increased the company's projected operating expenses and decreased the projected net cash flow. In contrast, the IRS expert concluded a hypothetical buyer would be able to retain the son by paying an annual salary of approximately $1.3 million—8.1% of sales in 2006. Consequently, the IRS expert's projected net cash flow and the resulting overall value were much higher.

3. *The court.* First, the court dealt with the estate's attempt to substitute the lower $4.3 million value in the two subsequent expert reports for the $9.3 million value it reported in its original Form 706 filing.

Court bears down on goodwill. The court pointed out that the original value was an admission by the estate. To replace it required the estate to show error, which it attempted to do by way of the expert's claim that he mistakenly had failed to consider the limiting provision of the services agreement. The court was not persuaded. Even if the expert subsequently realized he had made a mistake, he incorrectly assumed the company was not profitable, the court said. Reliable historical data and the expert's discussions with management showed that on the date of death the company was profitable and it expected to generate a profit in the future. And, even if The Word decided to enforce the programming fee limitation—which it had never done in the past—the company had equipment and expertise to augment the decreased sales revenue from The Word by providing uplinking services for other customers. If there was a risk, it lay in The Word's ability to choose another uplinking provider. But, said the court, this risk did not make the company not profitable. A valuator could adjust for it, as the estate's first expert had done by applying a 3% company risk premium in his original DCF valuation. Therefore, the court disregarded the proposed $4.3 million value.

But the court also found the IRS expert's valuation flawed. While the court approved of the use of the discounted cash flow approach, it disagreed with the IRS expert's handling of goodwill. The expert significantly undervalued the pivotal role the son played in operating both companies as well as the relationships he had forged with the ministers contributing to The Word. Many of the contributors did not even realize that there was a company that employed the son. They did business with him because they trusted him, not because of his affiliation with the company. He owned the asset of goodwill, the court said. There was no agreement that showed he had transferred his personal goodwill to the company. If he quit, he could compete directly with the company, the court pointed out. The estate expert's use of an economic charge to account for the son's personal goodwill was "high enough to account for the significant value of [the son's] relationships," the court concluded. For all these reasons, it adopted the estate's original $9.3 million value.

Based on the court's finding, it ruled that there was no underpayment—much less a substantial underpayment triggering penalty under IRC Section 6662—on the estate's part.

Adelphia Recovery Trust v. FPL Group, Inc. (In re Adelphia Corp.)

Citation: 2014 Bankr. LEXIS 2011
Date of decision: May 6, 2014
Experts: Israel Shaked, Michael-Shaked Group (recovery trust); Ralph Tuliano, Mesirow Financial Consulting (defendants)
Judge: Gerber
State/Jurisdiction: Federal/New York
Court: United States Bankruptcy Court
Type of case: Bankruptcy
SIC code: 4841 Cable and Other Pay Television Services

Court Finds Facts Back Expert's Value-Per-Subscriber Metric

In the protracted bankruptcy proceedings of Adelphia, once one of the cable industry's biggest companies, a $150 million stock buyback gave rise to a recent finding that merits attention from valuation professionals. The Bankruptcy Court's ruling on the trustee's fraudulent transfer claim discusses the pros and cons of the methodologies the parties' experts used. Discounted cash flow analysis, comparable companies analysis, and precedent transaction analysis were all in play.

No value from stock buyback. In June 2002, Adelphia Communications, then one of the country's largest cable television operators, and some 230 subsidiaries filed for Chapter 11 bankruptcy protection. The company's financial trouble came to light earlier that year when it disclosed that it had over $2 billion in unreported debt related to loans to its controlling shareholders, the Rigas family. Thereafter, a special committee investigating related party transactions between Adelphia entities and the Rigases determined the loans exceeded $3 billion. Members of the family subsequently faced prosecution on securities fraud, wire fraud, bank fraud, and criminal conspiracy and various convictions.

In connection with the bankruptcy, the Adelphia recovery trust sued in federal court (S.D.N.Y.) to recover, as a fraudulent transfer, $150 million Adelphia paid in January 1999 to repurchase its own stock from the defendants. In 1995, Adelphia and the defendants—a group of related businesses with cable properties—entered into a series of transactions that resulted in the defendants' owning over 3.4 million shares of Adelphia's common stock. Less than four years later, the parties decided to end their relationship. One step in the process was the Jan. 28, 1999, stock buyback. A second step occurred eight months later that year and involved Adelphia's redeeming the defendants' one-third interest in a joint venture.

One question in this case was whether the two transactions were interdependent. As the court explained, if they were, "any excess value received by Adelphia on its second purchase could be regarded as consideration to offset any value deficiency with respect to the first." Ultimately, the court found the transactions were separate and Adelphia's stock buyback "was indeed without consideration." But these findings, in themselves, did not make the stock buyback avoidable, the court explained. Under the "traditional fraudulent transfer analysis," it still needed to determine whether Adelphia was insolvent at the time it bought back the stock or was rendered insolvent as a result of the transaction.

Trust's expert relies solely on DCF. Both parties offered expert solvency opinions. First, the experts determined the value of assets Adelphia had at the time of the transfer by computing the company's total enterprise value (TEV). Next, they ascertained the business's liabilities and subtracted them from the assets.

In terms of TEV, the experts' approaches differed considerably, as did the resulting values. Even though both experts recognized that performing a discounted cash flow analysis (DCF) in this case posed a challenge, the trust's expert ultimately staked his opinion with the DCF alone. The problem was the lack of accurate management projections. Any existing management forecasts in this case likely were based on fraudulent information and not a reliable foundation for the DCF. Neither were third-party industry analyst projections that likely were based on the company's inaccurately reported information.

The trust's expert tried to circumvent the issue by developing his own projections of the company's cash flow for the following 10 years. To start with, he created assumptions as to the factors that would inform the company's cash flow for the upcoming years using contemporaneous third-party analyses. The factors included penetration rates and growth rates, as well as revenue per subscriber, EBITDA margins, and capital expenditures. To arrive at present value, he applied a 15.08% discount rate, which he believed to be the company's weighted average cost of capital (WACC). The WACC assumed a debt risk premium of 6.79% and an equity risk premium of 3.95% (no other premia are stated) and grew out of the premise that "both lenders and shareholders require a higher rate of return on their investment in a fraud-plagued company than in a company that is law abiding."

He used the perpetuity method to calculate the terminal value. He said it was inappropriate to base the terminal on a multiple of final-year EBITDA, as is common, because doing so here would "introduce market-based analyses into his non-market-based methodology." Instead, he assumed that, after 10 years, Adelphia would grow in perpetuity at a rate of about 4%, considering 3% inflation and less than 1% subscriber growth. He concluded that the company's unadjusted TEV was approximately $2.5 billion.

The defendants' expert considered preparing projections for the company but decided he lacked the necessary reliable data. He considered the process "speculative" and declined to perform an independent DCF analysis but critiqued aspects of the other expert's approach.

Defendants' expert uses market-based methods. For his part, the defendants' expert performed a comparable companies analysis and a precedent transactions analysis to compute the unadjusted TEV. For the comparable analysis, he selected six companies, using only their cable components to compute multiples. For each of the companies, he calculated TEV based on the market value of equity and debt interests in the company but excluding cash and equity investments. He next performed a value-per-subscriber analysis—dividing the respective TEV by a company's reported number of subscribers—to determine each company's multiple, i.e., value per subscriber. The multiples ranged between $2,462 and $3,835. He explained that the value-per-subscriber multiple was "commonly used in the cable industry and provides a highly reliable indication of the value of Adelphia's cable business."

He decided that $3,024 was the multiple applicable to Adelphia, based in part on the company's relative upgrade status compared to the other six companies. Ultimately, he found that the value of the company's cable assets on a marketable, minority, basis was nearly $4.5 billion. He decided in this case a 25% control premium ($376.4 million) was appropriate because the stock prices for the comparable companies reflected minority interests, "and here there was a controlling interest." Under the comparable companies analysis, Adelphia's assets were worth over $4.8 billion prior to adjustments. Adding cash yielded a TEV of over $5 billion before adjustments, he concluded.

The trust's expert rejected the comparable companies approach because it required "a measure of historical or forward earnings for the subject company and the comparable companies." But in this case such data were unavailable considering the misrepresentations related to the company's financial performance. And, even though the expert agreed that the value-per-subscriber multiple was often used and often appropriate, he considered it inappropriate in this case because it did "not account for the differences between companies relating to upgrade status and profitability."

The defendants' expert also performed a precedent transaction analysis—an analysis that generates the value of comparable companies from purchases prices in past mergers and acquisitions. Three criteria guided the selection of the transactions: (1) choose only transactions involving target cable systems with more than 300,000 subscribers; (2) use transactions that occurred within six months of the Jan. 28, 1999, stock buyback; and (3) exclude pure "system swaps," i.e., one cable company trading in a set of systems with another. He decided that four transactions met the requirements, including one that was part system swap and part sale for cash. In that case, he said, the cash portion did yield a "highly reliable indicator of value." Again, his sole metric was the value-per-subscriber multiple. The resulting range was between $3,234 and $3,667. Considering Adelphia's relative upgrade status, he settled on $3,277. He arrived at a TEV of $4.8 billion. Adding the company's cash, the TEV was just over $5 billion, prior to adjustments.

The trust's expert rejected the precedent transaction method for the same reasons he rejected the comparable companies analysis.

Adjustments widen value gap. Both experts adjusted their TEV calculations to account for Adelphia's interest in related entities—two of them acquired around the time of the transfer. The most noteworthy was a January 1999 acquisition of a cable TV company for which Adelphia paid $135 million. The trust's expert assigned zero value to it. As he saw it, Adelphia issued its own stock in exchange for the assets. If the stock turned out to be worth less than the assumed value, the company would be liable for issuing fraudulent stock. The defendants' expert considered any such liability "highly uncertain and inherently speculative" on the transaction date and credited the entire $135 million. He pointed out that the company also had "speculative assets," but, as long as speculative assets and liabilities were treated in a consistent way, they would offset one another.

In January 1999, Adelphia also had a two-thirds interest in a partnership in which the defendants owned a one-third interest that they later in the year sold back to Adelphia (the redemption transaction). The trust's expert valued the company's two-thirds interest at twice the price at which Adelphia later redeemed the one-third interest. Consequently, he added $216 million to his valuation. The defendant's expert also doubled the value of the one-third interest, but, instead of using the actual price Adelphia paid, he used a valuation a different expert for the defendants had proposed. Because Adelphia only had a 50% voting interest in the partnership, he did not apply a control premium. He also added a 5% marketability discount. He concluded Adelphia's two-thirds interest was worth $318 million, which he included in his valuation.

After adjustments and based on the DCF alone, the trust's expert concluded the TEV was $2.8 billion. The defendants' expert, averaging the values he obtained from his two analyses and making adjustments, said the TEV was $6.7 billion. The trust's expert assumed the company's net debt was $3.7 billion, slightly more than the company had reported on its 1998 Form 10-K. The defendants' expert assumed net debt was approximately $3 billion.

As a result, the trust's expert concluded that at the time of the transfer the company was insolvent by $1 billion. In contrast, the defendants' expert determined it was still solvent by about $3.7 billion.

Expert fails to do 'sanity check.' The court found that both experts' analyses had weaknesses, but, in the final analysis, the defendants' expert's assumptions and methods were more persuasive. It said that its own calculation yielded a starting TEV of between $4.4 billion and $4.8 billion and an adjusted TEV in the range of $5.722 billion and $5.725 billion. And it found the company's liabilities at the relevant date were about $3.2 billion. Therefore, it concluded that Adelphia had a net worth of between $2.494 billion and $2.497 billion at the time of the stock repurchase. These figures were closer to the defendants' expert's determinations and led to the conclusion that Adelphia was solvent at the time of the transfer.

The court made the following observations about the expert testimony:

- The trust expert's reliance on the DCF alone was problematic and surprising. "The DCF works best (and, arguably, only) when a company has accurate projections of future cash flows; when projections are not tainted by fraud; and when at least some of the cash flows are positive." This case was deficient in all regards.

- The data the trust's expert developed to create his own projections to "craft" a DCF analysis were filled with "uncertainties." He formulated assumptions based only roughly on projections for the cable industry or the "typical cable company," and he selectively used assumptions from third-party analyses, raising questions as to "whether his analysis unduly deflated Adelphia's value." Specifically, he used capital expenditure assumptions from one analysis that projected extensive upgrades, but he did not use that analysis's revenue assumptions, showing an attending increase in revenue. Instead, he used the lower growth rate from another analysis.

- The trust expert's failure to use an alternative valuation methodology as a "sanity check" for the conclusions based on the DCF amounted to a "material deficiency in the quality of his analysis."

- Under the circumstances, the defendants' expert was "wise" to rely on the comparable companies and precedent transactions. His value-per-subscriber metric used one of the company's most reliable historical metrics because, by the time Adelphia had completed its efforts to restate its financials and had ousted the Rigases, its count of subscribers was among the most accurate financial data set down. Moreover, in the cable industry, the subscriber number is widely used in valuations for mergers and acquisitions. Also, given the narrow range of the comparable companies multiples, the court was "comfortable" that Adelphia would have been able to sell its assets "roughly" within this range.

- The defendants' expert failed to do a "sanity check" by developing his own DCF analysis and, critically, by considering Adelphia's market capitalization (MarketCap). According to the court, the expert valuation was 19% over market price. How Adelphia's valuation could exceed its MarketCap was difficult to see, the court said, especially because there had been as yet undisclosed fraud. But even if one applied a 19% discount and assumed the adjustments the expert made to his comparable companies analysis, Adelphia would have been solvent by over $3 billion.

- In terms of adjustments, the court disapproved of the trust expert's decision not to attribute any value to the company Adelphia bought in January 1999 for $135 million. "The outcome of litigation that was never brought is too speculative to justify disregarding the entirety of the value of [the acquired company]." At the same time, liability was not "remote." If the acquired company had sued, it probably could have established some fraud. The most likely possibility was that Adelphia at the time was overvalued but not worthless. The difficult question, the court said, was whether to include the value "but with a haircut," i.e., a discount. Ultimately, since neither party argued for this approach, the court added $135 million to the assets.

- In terms of the second adjustment, the court agreed with the trust expert that the value of its two-thirds interest in one of the defendants' entities should align with the actual price Adelphia paid for the remaining one-third interest a few months after the stock buyback. Therefore, it included $216 million in its valuation.

- The defendants' expert produced a valuation that was "more closely tied to the market," offering a value that the company actually could get for its assets in a sale.

Conclusion. Besides finding that Adelphia was solvent at the time of the stock repurchase, the court determined the transaction did not leave the company with insufficient capital to keep operating and that it was not equitably insolvent. Accordingly, the trust's fraudulent transfer claim crumbled.

Matter of Adelstein v. Finest Food Distributing Co. (I), (II)

Citation: 2014 N.Y. App. Div. LEXIS 2542
Date of decision: April 16, 2014
Experts: Paul Marquez (petitioner); Brian Serotta (company/respondent)
Judge: Per Curiam
State/Jurisdiction: New York
Court: Court of Appeals
Type of case: Judicial Dissolution
SIC code: 5451 Groceries, General Line

Citation: 2011 N.Y. LEXIS 5956
Date of decision: Nov. 3, 2011
Experts: Paul Marquez (petitioner); Brian Serotta (company/respondent)
Judge: Kitzes
State/Jurisdiction: New York
Court: Supreme Court of New York (trial court)
Type of case: Judicial Dissolution
SIC code: 5451 Groceries, General Line

In Buyout, Court Extols Expert's Valuation and Legal Acumen

A New York appeals court recently affirmed a stock valuation that occurred in the context of an oppressed shareholder suit. While the appeals court decision is short, the underlying 2011 trial court decision provides invaluable insight into the factors courts consider when assessing the qualification and performance of appraisers. Solid valuation credentials, a thorough work product, and a demonstrated knowledge of valuation-related legal principles carried the day.

Backstory. In 1948, the petitioner and his brother started a business in Brooklyn, N.Y., buying and distributing pickles. In good time, a third brother joined the company, which eventually became the largest distributor of Caribbean food in the New York area. By 2006, the petitioner's two brothers gave their one-third interests to their sons and the petitioner held the remaining one-third ownership stake. In 2007, the petitioner fell ill and was absent from the business for a while. When he returned, the two nephews offered to buy him out. He refused, and the relationship deteriorated. Eventually, he filed suit, alleging they took oppressive actions to force him out and petitioning for a judicial dissolution of the business under New York Business Corporation Law (BLC) Section 1104-a.

After the New York Supreme Court (trial court) denied the nephews' motion to dismiss the petition, the company elected to buy the petitioner's shares pursuant to BCL Section 1118. In 2011, the court held a valuation hearing featuring the opinions of both parties' experts.

Company's expert uses one method. The company's expert was a CPA but not a credentialed appraiser. He stated he had performed about 50 valuations. He submitted a three-page report based on his review of the company's tax returns and "the sparse records he found." He also had conversations with the company's accountant and principals. He said he used a capitalized income method because he could not find any comparable businesses and the company was not a public corporation issuing stocks and dividends. He made adjustments to salaries, depreciation, and outstanding loans and weighted current earnings more heavily, arriving at average normalized earnings of $206,000. He determined a capitalization rate of 20%, translating into 5x earnings. It included company-specific risk factors, such as limited management and the company's large amount of business with the A&P supermarket chain, which was in jeopardy because of A&P's bankruptcy. He said he considered the company's growth in sales, which had doubled between 2004 and 2010, but found no "dramatic" growth in profits. He concluded the petitioner's one-third interest in the company was worth $230,000. Importantly, he also applied what he called a 20% discount for lack of marketability (DLOM). He said the DLOM accounted for the "difficulty finding somebody to buy a one-third interest. There's really no market. It's a privately-held company. Anybody who bought that one-third interest would conceivably have nothing to say about the company."

Petitioner's expert uses three methods. The petitioner's expert was a CPA and credentialed appraiser. He visited the company's premises and reviewed its books and records, which he found to be "minimal." In addition, he reviewed company tax returns for 2004 through 2010, the compiled financial statement trend that the company's appraiser had prepared, the general ledger, bank statements, and available truck manifests. He also took note of the petitioner's account that big stores paid by check through central billing, whereas small bodegas paid cash on delivery, which the truck driver collected. While the latter sales were not in the computer, they should appear in the salesmen's reports. According to the petitioner, smaller stores made up about 20% of the entire business.

The petitioner's expert became aware that from 2004 through 2010 the company's sales basically doubled and costs of goods sold increased commensurably, while the gross profit margin steadily decreased from a high of 27.5% to 24% in the last two years. During that very period, officer compensation went from zero to more than $500,000 per year for two officers. The only explanation, he concluded, was the existence of unreported sales. He performed a "stress test" on sales invoices and other available data and found the company had a gross margin of profitability of almost 35%, instead of the 25% appearing on the company's tax return. Based on this differential in profitability, he concluded that, for a company with gross sales of $10 million, the amount of unrecorded sales in 2010 was approximately $1 million. Accordingly, he imputed gross profit at the industrywide level of 35% rather than the 25% reported by the company.

He used the capitalization of earnings method, determining a weighted average net income of $486,000 and a capitalization rate of 12%, as opposed to the competing expert's 20%. Applying the cap rate to the earnings base, he calculated the company was worth $4,051,862 on a controlling, marketable basis. He assigned a 70% weight to this value.

As a cross-check, he also used a market-based approach—the merged and acquired company method—drawing on *Pratt's Stats* to determine valuation multiples of revenues, gross profit, and EBITDA. The resulting values ranged from $3,990,000 to $4,094,000 to $4,191,000, which he weighted at 10% each. All the weighted values resulted in a control, marketable value of $4,063,800. The expert applied a 5% discount for lack of marketability reflecting the lower range of transaction costs, which he said in a sale of a small business typically ranged between 5% and 10% of the sales prices. He concluded that the petitioner's one-third interest on a controlling, nonmarketable basis was worth $1,287,000.

One expert's contradictory statements. At the outset of its analysis, the trial court noted that the valuation "rests primarily on the credibility of the appraisers and the reliability of their valuation methods." It also pointed out that "the extent of the witness's qualifications has a bearing on the weight to be given to his testimony." Here, the court said the testimony and report of the petitioner's expert were "credible and reliable." It noted his extensive valuation and financial credentials and highlighted his thorough evaluation of the company, including making a site visit, developing an understanding of the company, learning about the industry, considering the economy, and selecting valuation approaches and valuation factors. "He methodically chose such critical factors in the evaluation process as the capitalization rate and lack of marketability discount based on studies in the evaluation field." Importantly, he demonstrated legal acumen: He knew that under New York law it was appropriate to discount for lack of marketability but not for minority status. He paid attention to the petitioner's testimony that considerable business took place in cash payments that did not appear on financial statements, and he explained how the financial statements indicated unreported sales. In sum, his valuation report was "clear, thorough, professional, and reliable."

In contrast, the trial court said, the company's expert lacked valuation credentials. He prepared a three-page report relying on the company's accountant. He failed to consider the existence of cash sales, and his discount rate leaned on the petitioner's minority status. He relied on one method of valuation, without doing a cross-check. He contradicted himself, acknowledging that the company's sales "had more than doubled" but saying profitability had been "basically flat." At the same time, he said the gross profit of the company also doubled during the relevant period. For all these reasons, the court gave "diminished weight" to his opinion.

No adjustment for shareholders' conduct. The petitioner wanted more. He asked for an upward adjustment of the valuation, arguing the two remaining shareholders had given themselves salaries, distributions, and benefits in the amount of nearly $864,000 to his detriment.

The trial court denied the request. This adjustment, it said, "functioned as a component of Petitioner's calculation of the fair value of his shares"—perhaps referring to the adjustments the petitioner's expert made to the financial statements. Also, this proceeding under BCL Section 1118 was only concerned with determining the fair value of the petitioner's shares. "Any misconduct or self-dealing by [the nephews] is not relevant to that determination." Moreover, the petitioner's expert did not state or suggest that the salaries represented "willful or reckless dissipation" of company assets.

No second-guessing. Both sides appealed. The company contested the trial court's valuation, and the petitioner objected to the trial court's denying his request for additional sums. The appeals court promptly disposed of the parties' arguments. The trial court's valuation was based on expert testimony. The sums related to salaries and disbursements to company officers were accounted for in the valuation the petitioner's expert performed, which the New York Supreme Court adopted. Therefore, the appeals court affirmed the $1,287,000 valuation.

Alli v. Commissioner

Citation: 2014 Tax Ct. Memo LEXIS 15
Date of decision: Jan. 27, 2014
Experts: Anthony Sanna (Appraisal 1, taxpayer), Darvin Jones (Appraisal 2, taxpayer)
Judge: Laro
State/Jurisdiction: Federal
Court: United States Tax Court
Type of case: Federal Taxation
SIC code: 6513 Operators of Apartment Buildings

Valuing a Hypothetical Asset Renders Appraisal 'Meaningless'

A taxpayer handed the IRS an easy victory when he challenged the government's denial of his claim for a charitable contribution deduction related to his S corporation's donation of a neglected apartment building. The dispute centered on meeting certain requirements of Section 170 of the Internal Revenue Code (IRC). The Tax Court found the taxpayer's petition leaned on two severely deficient appraisals from nonqualified appraisers and was rife with misrepresentations as well as omissions.

The taxpayer-petitioner was the sole shareholder of an S corp that owned two apartment buildings that he and his sister originally had bought at auction from the U.S. Department of Housing and Urban Development (HUD) by way of a HUD mortgage. In 1983, the total price was $353,000. In the 1990s and 2000s, the buildings failed every inspection HUD undertook to ensure that they were in a "decent, safe, and sanitary condition." A 1999 agency report said that they were in a "deplorable" state. Before HUD could complete foreclosure proceedings, the petitioner paid off the balance of the mortgage. About a year later, both sides sued each other, claiming a breach of the original HUD contract. In August 2008, the U.S. Court of Federal Claims found for the government. In September 2008, the petitioner donated one of the buildings to Volunteers of America (VoA) for nominal, $1, consideration. At that time, only six of the building's 34 units had tenants. VoA had a policy of finding a prospective buyer before accepting a donation to minimize its liability exposure.

VoA's real estate agent described the apartments as "pretty rough" and said most of them were "not rent-ready." He noticed a broken elevator, a leaking roof, "heav[ed] up" floors, missing kitchens, and one completely burnt unit. Ultimately, VoA sold the property quickly for $60,000 to the only interested buyer.

On their 2008 tax return, the petitioner and his wife claimed a noncash charitable contribution for $499,000. They stated that this was the appraised fair market value of the building; they also said it was a "34-unit apartment building" in "good condition" and maintained that they had acquired it in 2000 for $1.2 million. Besides other omitted things, their tax form did not identify the appraiser or include an appraiser declaration.

The IRS denied the claimed deduction, arguing, among other things, that the taxpayers were not entitled to it because they were not the owners of the building; the corporation was. Just as important, they failed to meet the qualified appraisal and other documentation requirements applicable under the IRC's section 170.

The taxpayers challenged the IRS's denial in Tax Court.

Deduction flows to shareholder. The Tax Court rejected the government's ownership argument. Although the corporation was the owner of the building at the time of contribution, the court found the petitioner, as the sole shareholder of an S corp, could still claim the deduction if he could satisfy the section 170 requirements. "Deductions for charitable contributions pursuant to *section 170* flow through separately to the shareholders, *sec. 1363(h)(2),* and are not allowed to the S corporation," the Tax Court stated.

Appraisal requirements. The IRC's section 170(f)(11) states that, if a taxpayer claims a deduction in excess of $5,000, he must secure a "qualified appraisal of such property" and attach to his return certain information about the property. Among other things, a qualified appraisal must be done not more than 60 days before the gift and signed by a qualified appraiser.

The applicable regulations require that the qualified appraisal provide a description of the property in sufficient detail so that the IRS is able to verify that the appraised property is the property that was donated, information as to the qualified appraiser, a description of his or her qualifications, the appraised fair market value (FMV) of the property on the date or expected date of contribution, a statement as to the method of valuation the appraiser used to determine the fair market value, and the specific basis for the valuation.

For a donation above $5,000, but below $500,000, the regulations require the donor to attach an appraisal summary (different from a qualified appraisal) to his tax return and keep information at hand, including identification of the donee organization, a reasonably detailed description of the property, the fair market value of the property at the time the contribution was made, the method used in determining the fair market value, and, if the valuation stemmed from an appraisal, a copy of the signed report of the appraiser.

Two appraisals, but no FMV. In this case, the taxpayer staked his claim on two appraisals that two different persons undertook nine years apart.

Appraisal 1: Almost a decade before the petitioner's company donated the subject building, an appraiser undertook a market rent survey of the two buildings. He used rental rates for five comparable buildings and concluded they had an annual gross income potential of about $390,800.

Appraisal 2: Approximately five months before the donation, a second person appraised the apartment buildings, ostensibly to update the 1999 appraisal. He said the "market value" of the first building was over $898,400 and the market value of the donated building was about $664,000, resulting in a total value of over $1.5 million. As he defined it, "market value" was "the highest price estimate in terms of money which a property Will [sic] bring, if exposed for sale in the open market, allowing a reasonable time of [sic] Find [sic] a purchaser who buys with knowledge of all uses of which it is adapted, and for which it was capable of being used."

The purpose of the appraisal was to establish the properties' values "after the renovation and remodeled [sic] condition," the appraiser went on to say. And, the "[v]aluation premise [sic] will assume a renovated market position. Also, assumption will be made that normal management will be implemented." As to the buildings' exteriors, he stated that "condition will be projected as good. Exterior painting, tuck pointing, and necessary repairs will be made [sic] good marketing position."

In terms of methodology, the second appraiser used the cost approach and the income approach. He said, "[T]he assemblage of sales was difficult for establishing market value." As to the cost approach, he assumed a $40,000-per-unit construction cost and 15-year life expectancy to arrive at a $718,750 value for the first building and a $531,250 for the donated building. Under this approach, the total value for both buildings was $1.25 million. As to the income approach, the appraiser determined the market rental rate using nine comparable apartment buildings, estimated expenses using 25 comparable apartment buildings, and assumed a 5% vacancy rate. Based on these figures, he determined that the two buildings could generate an annual net operating income of nearly $250,300. He then went on to determine the buildings' "market value," using the mortgage equity process and a capitalization rate of 16%. The latter was based on a heightened risk involved with real estate investments, a projected interest rate of 12%, and a projected loan term of 15 years.

In their petition, the taxpayers argued that the second appraisal updated the initial appraisal and that both appraisals were qualified appraisals. Put differently, even though the first appraisal was outdated, it was relevant to establishing the value of the donated building as of the date of contribution because the second appraisal was an update of the first appraisal.

None of the arguments carried weight with the Tax Court. First, it pointed out that, pursuant to the regulation, whenever a taxpayer relies on more than one appraisal, each appraisal must independently comply with the qualified appraisal requirements. For multiple reasons, in this case, neither of them did.

Appraisal 1 deficiencies. The first appraisal obviously was outdated and as such on its face did not reflect the property's value as of the date of contribution. By calling the second appraisal an update of the first appraisal, the petitioner conceded as much. Just as important, it failed to provide an FMV for the donated building. The appraiser used none of the three applicable approaches—income, asset, and market approach—but estimated the donated building's annual profit potential by using a projected income stream. "It did not perform a discounted cashflow analysis on the estimated profit potential" to arrive at the FMV, the court said. For all these reasons, it was not a qualified appraisal.

Appraisal 2 deficiencies. The most critical flaw of the second appraisal was that it did not appraise the contributed property, but a "hypothetical, fully renovated version of the contributed property," the Tax Court emphasized. At various points, the appraiser mentioned that the valuation assumed a "renovated and remodeled condition." At the same time, VoA's real estate agent testified that at the time of contribution the building was in poor condition and most of the apartments were uninhabitable.

Moreover, the appraiser did not determine the building's fair market value but provided a "market value." The FMV assumes a hypothetical willing buyer and willing seller. In regard to property, the FMV also reflects its "highest and best use as of the date of valuation."

In this case, the difference between FMV and market value was not just a matter of words, the court pointed out. The appraiser's definition of "market value" did not require that both the buyer and seller have "reasonable knowledge of relevant facts," as the regulation's FMV definition does. Further, the appraiser's definition of "market value" did not even include a reference to willing seller. As the Tax Court put it, the appraisal "determined the market value of a hypothetical [building], rather than the fair market value of the actual [building]."

The court also pointed to numerous inconsistencies in the appraisal report. For example, in its "Reconciliation and Conclusion" section, the report stated that the buildings combined were worth $1.5 million under all three approaches, resulting in a "reconciled" value of $1.5 million. At the same time, the body of the appraisal included only valuations based on the cost and income approaches. What's more, the body of the appraisal said the cost approach yielded a valuation of only $1.25 million.

Appraiser issues. Not only the appraisals, but also the appraisers failed to qualify under the regulations, the court found. It acknowledged that the first appraiser held a designation from the Appraisal Institute and regularly performed appraisals for compensation. But he failed the regulations' strict reporting requirements because he did not provide the necessary declaration that he was holding himself out as an appraiser, was so qualified, and understood the consequences of providing a fraudulent overvaluation on the petitioner's appraisal summary. The second appraiser did not include his qualifications in his appraisal report and also failed to furnish the declaration.

Problematic appraisal summary. Finally, the Tax Court found the petitioner's appraisal summary substandard. It included misrepresentations and omissions. For example, contrary to the record, the petitioner said he had acquired the building in June 2000 at a cost basis of $1.2 million. On the tax form, he said it was in "good" condition, when the record showed the conditions were "very poor."

Moreover, the petitioner claimed the appraised FMV was $499,000 when neither of the appraisal reports supported that figure. In fact, said the Tax Court, this number "smacks of manipulation." He likely chose it to avoid having to attach a qualified appraisal to the tax return for contributions valued at over $500,000.

For all these reasons, the petitioner was not entitled to the claimed deduction.

Antioch Co. Litig. Trust v. Morgan

Citation: 2014 U.S. Dist. LEXIS 47740
Date of decision: April 7, 2014
Experts: Mark A. Greenberg (plaintiff); unknown (defendants)
Judge: Black
State/Jurisdiction: Federal/Ohio
Court: U.S. District Court
Type of case: Bankruptcy
SIC code: 2732 Book Printing

Lost Value Opinion Using Untested Data Points Is No Go

A recent bankruptcy-related case illustrates how an experienced valuator made himself vulnerable under *Daubert* by agreeing to be a conduit for information the client wanted to place in evidence without investigating the source material. If the court's exclusion did not sting enough, the expert heard the client argue to the court that it could show damages without him because the calculation required only "simple arithmetic," which the jury could perform on its own.

Bungled sales process. The debtor was a privately held company that produced bookplates, bookmarks, book covers, and calendars. By 2007, it experienced financial trouble and determined it needed outside money to meet its obligations. The company's board of directors (the defendants) hired a financial advisor to guide the 2007-2008 sales process. Two credible buyers presented letters of interest (LOIs) that the board and its legal and financial advisors reviewed in August 2007. The values ranged between $148 million and $185 million. But, after doing due diligence on the company, in October 2007 the prospective buyers withdrew, citing the company's declining financial health. In May 2008, there was an offer from a venture capital firm, J.H. Whitney, to buy the company's assets for $54 million in a "363" sale that required the company to file for bankruptcy and reorganize. Ultimately that proposition came to nothing, and other efforts to pursue a sale also failed. In November 2008, the company petitioned for bankruptcy.

As part of the bankruptcy filing, the company submitted a disclosure statement that referenced a valuation of the company between $31 million and $38 million. The disclosure statement cautioned that the estimate "does not necessarily reflect, and should not be construed as reflecting, values that will be attained in the public or private markets." The Bankruptcy Court did not adopt the valuation in any of its findings or its confirmation order.

The litigation trust sued the defendants (D. Ohio) on a number of theories, claiming they mismanaged the sales process and committed waste by employing various professionals without receiving value in return. The trustee demanded lost value and professional fees damages.

'No way to know.' To testify to both sets of damages, the trust hired a financial expert with decades of experience in business valuation, deal structuring, and financial and investment analysis, who had dealt with "363" sales. However, he was not a qualified damages expert and had never given testimony on damages. He admitted he was not familiar with any damages methodologies and said he did not use any method to calculate damages for this case. He opined that the defendants' conduct "caused the Company to lose the opportunity to realize between $20 million and $30 million in value, and to waste $6 million on professional fees."

As to lost value, he said he arrived at his range by using the $54 million from the Whitney LOI as a "top-end value" and the $31 million-to-$38 million range appearing in the bankruptcy disclosure statement as a "bottom-end value"—subtracting the latter from the former. He did not perform a formal business valuation and also did no independent analysis of the LOI. He did not contend that the $54 million offer was reasonable. Rather, he believed that when it came to the value of the company "the worst it would have been would have been $54 million if there wasn't anybody else stepping up to the option of the 363 sale." Whitney, he believed, had done "substantial due diligence," and its offer would have been a "stalking horse" that would have attracted other offers. At the same time, he conceded that "there's no way to know that." He also stated that a letter of intent was nonbinding and was not the equivalent of cash; he noted there was only one way to know a deal was done: "when the money is in the bank." And "more value is lost between the time there is a signed letter of intent and a closing than anyone ever cares to admit."

Although his report said that the amount of waste on professional fees related to the unsuccessful sales process was $6 million, he admitted in his deposition that he had not reviewed any information related to the professional fees. This figure, he said, was an estimate he had received from plaintiff's counsel; he did not know which professional received what part, if any, of the amount and indeed did not know what part of the $6 million estimate actually represented waste.

Plaintiff at oral argument on the *Daubert* motion admitted the figure stemmed from just adding up invoices and subsequently said it would not rely on the expert's testimony for this damages claim.

Blind reliance on sources. The defendants filed a *Daubert* motion to strike both parts of the expert's damages opinion, arguing he had lifted his base values from the work of others without establishing the reliability of the source material. He admitted to having no experience with the computation of damages and to using no methodology or reliable principles. Therefore, the testimony was unreliable. Also, the plaintiff failed to commit to a damages calculation in the pretrial stage and should be precluded from introducing it for the first time at trial.

The plaintiff countered that the expert had experience in dealing with the transactions at issue in the contested sales process. He was qualified to testify to the reliability of the Whitney letter. His testimony combined with the bankruptcy court record sufficed to establish lost value damages. The damages methodology he used was "simple arithmetic." Once the top and bottom values were in evidence, the jury could subtract the two numbers itself.

The court found the argument seriously flawed. As to methodology, the expert did not do any independent analysis of the $54 million figure in the Whitney letter. Even if an expert's opinion need not be based on first-hand knowledge and he or she need not have performed his own valuation of the company, the expert must establish that he drew on reliable sources. Regarding the top value he used, he never suggested that it was a reliable data point. Also, no Whitney representative was deposed to speak to the letter of intent. Therefore, it was hearsay. And, although an expert may rely on hearsay, "s/he cannot do so blindly," said the court. Regarding the bottom value, the valuation range included in the disclosure statement also was not reliable. "It is a document prepared, sponsored and filed by a party soliciting votes to accept or reject a reorganization plan," the court pointed out. Therefore, "courts do not look to values set forth by a plan proponent in a disclosure statement as admissible evidence." Accordingly, even if the court were to allow the plaintiff to prove damages by "simple arithmetic," without a damages expert, the plaintiff lacked reliable sources providing the requisite base values.

The court swiftly dismissed the expert's opinion about the $6 million professional fees figure, noting he performed no independent review of the payment records and invoices related to professional fees.

In conclusion, the court not only excluded the expert's damages testimony, but it also denied the plaintiff's last-minute request to show damages without an expert. The court's finding was the end of the case.

Apple, Inc. v. Samsung Electronics Co., Ltd. (I)

Citation: 2013 U.S. Dist. LEXIS 162863
Date of decision: Nov. 12, 2013
Experts: Terry Musika, Julie L. Davis (plaintiff); Michael Wagner (defendants)
Judge: Koh
State/Jurisdiction: Federal/California
Court: United States District Court
Type of case: Intellectual Property
SIC: 4813 Telephone Communications, Except Radiotelephone (except resellers)

Apple Fails in Last-Ditch Effort to Offer Nonexpert Lost Profits Theory

On the weekend prior to the retrial on damages, Apple sought to increase the number of patents for which it could claim lost profits with a sketchy theory that ran counter to the damages model its own experts had constructed earlier. In an emergency motion, Samsung asked the court to preclude Apple's alternative lost profits theory.

Sidestepping its own experts. In 2012, a jury awarded Apple over $1 billion in damages, finding that Samsung had infringed critical components of Apple's iPhone and iPad. Damages included infringer's profits, lost profits, and reasonable royalties. Subsequently, the district court (N.D. Cal.) agreed with Samsung that irremediable errors related to Apple's damages calculation required it to reduce the award by some $450 million and order a retrial.

Poised for the new battle, Apple pursued nearly $380 million in additional damages. These included lost profits for a number of patents that its own experts earlier had found noneligible for lost profits because of a court-ordered shift in the start date for the design-around period. Specifically, Apple's two damages experts developed a lost profits model based on the four *Panduit* factors: (1) demand for the patented product; (2) absence of acceptable noninfringing substitutes; (3) the patent holder's manufacturing and marketing capabilities to exploit demand; and (4) the amount of profit the patent holder would have made. *Panduit Corp. v. Stahlin Bros. Fibre Works, Inc.*, 575 F.2d 1152 (6th Cir. 1978).

Panduit's Factor 2 was critical for their computation. The experts assumed that Samsung would design around Apple's three patents when Samsung first infringed on them, not when it received actual notice of the infringement, and thus would be able to return to the market with noninfringing products "well before the dates on which Apple first became eligible for infringement damages." At the same time, they assumed that Samsung's alternative products would be as attractive to consumers as the infringing smartphones and tablets and Samsung would sell them in similar numbers to the infringing products immediately after it had introduced them into the market. Therefore, Apple could not claim *any* lost profits for these patents.

Both of Apple's experts called their lost profits damages models "conservative" but did not present an alternative model.

However, "less than 48 hours before the retrial," Apple declared in court that it would pursue lost profits related to the disputed patents irrespective of its experts' theory. It claimed to have other evidence that indicated the number of Samsung's infringing sales, referring to "Apple's profits, demand, capacity, market share, 'competition,' 'injury,'" and "the unlikelihood that Samsung would have been able to design around Apple's patents." It proposed to present a variety of "fact and expert" witnesses who could testify "either to the individual *Panduit* factors or, perhaps, to a general standard of 'but for' causation." This evidence would enable the jury to "award an appropriate amount of damages to compensate Apple for lost profits," the company claimed.

In response, Samsung filed an emergency motion to preclude Apple from arguing for lost profits in connection with the disputed patents, claiming the alternative theory was "new and untimely"; moreover, it failed to satisfy the applicable evidentiary rules.

The district court sided with Samsung for a number of reasons:

1. The disclosure of the new, nonexpert theory was untimely and as such unfairly prejudicial to Samsung. Apple did not disagree that, under the models both of its experts had constructed, there was no claim for lost profits based on the patents at issue. In fact, said the court, Apple did not even contest that its new theory meant that it would have to disavow the very methodology its experts employed. It simply argued it could prove lost profits without expert testimony.

What's more, if the court were to admit Apple's proposed theory so late in the process, it would deprive Samsung of the opportunity to prepare a rebuttal to it.

2. Apple's nonexpert and non-*Panduit* theory was "entirely new." Neither of Apple's experts had ever said that Apple was entitled to lost profits under a methodology that did not rely on the *Panduit* test. Also, in none of the numerous submissions and oral arguments on the issue of the design-around start dates had Apple itself set down a different theory for lost profits related to these patents.

3. Apple failed to explain how exactly the retrial jury would be able to calculate lost profits for the patents considering the company did not intend to offer an actual lost profits figure. In a complex case that features many parties and hotly contested damages evidence, Apple offered no approach by which to ensure that the jury, left to its own devices, would not determine an award that was "wildly speculative or based on factors that have no place in a lost profits calculation," said the court.

For all these reasons, and in light of the court's doubts about Apple's ability to offer "sound economic proof of lost profits damages" under a previously undisclosed theory, it excluded the new theory.

Editor's Note. Not even a week later, on Nov. 20, 2013, a jury awarded Apple an additional $290 million in lost profits and reasonable royalty, bringing the total damages amount to about $930 million. The issue of when Samsung would have begun to avoid infringement of the patents in suit—when Samsung received actual notice of its infringement, as Apple claimed, or earlier, when it first infringed, as Samsung argued—is likely to figure prominently in post-trial motions and on appeal, which are certain to follow. As one commenter noted: "Things will really get interesting after the final judgment by the district court."

Apple, Inc. v. Samsung Electronics Co., Ltd. (II)

Citation: 2014 U.S. Dist. LEXIS 43907
Date of decision: March 28, 2014
Experts: Christopher A. Vellturo, Ph.D. (Apple); unknown (Samsung)
Judge: Koh
State/Jurisdiction: Federal/California
Court: U.S. District Court
Type of case: Intellectual Property
SIC code: 4813 Telephone Communications, Except Radiotelephone (except resellers)

Samsung's About-Face on Off-the-Market Lost Profits Calculation

As the tech giants Apple and Samsung litigated another infringement case, damages theories again took center stage. In a pretrial motion in federal district court, Samsung argued for the preclusion of an analysis that Apple's expert provided on off-the-market lost profits even though his calculation followed the very approach Samsung successfully advocated in a related prior case.

Prior case. In 2012, a jury awarded Apple over $1 billion in damages, finding that Samsung had infringed critical components of Apple's iPhone and iPad. Damages included infringer's profits, lost profits, and reasonable royalties. Subsequently, the district court (N.D. Cal.) reduced the award by approximately $450 million because of irremediable errors related to Apple's damages calculation.

A retrial on damages took place in November 2013, with Apple pursuing nearly $380 million in additional damages, including lost profits. The timing for calculating Apple's "off-the-market" lost profits was a source of contention. Apple claimed these damages for times when Samsung infringed but should not have been able to sell the infringing products because no noninfringing alternatives were available. The issue was whether the damages calculation must consider potential design-around products from the point of first infringement or the date of notice of the infringement. If the former, then Samsung could show that there were noninfringing alternatives before Apple first became eligible for infringement damages and thus Samsung was not liable for that period.

At the time, Samsung argued staunchly for the date of first infringement and prevailed in court. The court's ruling reduced Apple's damages demand by $305 million. Ultimately, Apple received a total of about $930 million in damages.

Lost profits ruling cuts both ways. In a second case in the same court, Apple claimed Samsung violated five of its mobile software patents and sought $2 billion in damages. Samsung, in turn, accused Apple of infringing two of its patents.

Initially, Apple's damages expert analyzed off-the-market lost profits based on the notice dates, not the infringement date. For four of Apple's five patents in suit, the infringement date preceded the notice date. But, since for one patent the notice date preceded the infringement date by over a year, he did not calculate damages for that fifth patent.

In a *Daubert* motion, Samsung successfully used the court's prior ruling to challenge the expert's calculation and force a revaluation for damages related to the four patents. The result was a decrease in the lost profits that Apple could demand from it. (The court redacted the precise amount.)

But, based on the ruling in the first case, Apple's expert prepared a supplemental report in which he included off-the-market lost profits for the fifth patent, concluding that the requirement to analyze noninfringing alternatives on the first date of infringement entitled Apple to additional damages (amount redacted) for that patent.

In response, Samsung tried to preclude the expert's calculation as to the fifth patent, arguing that the court's prior order *did not* apply to circumstances where the notice date was earlier than the first infringement date. All the while, Samsung contended that the ruling *did* apply to the computation of damages for Apple's four other patents.

Apple asserted that the court had decided the issue on design-arounds in the prior case in line with Samsung's argument for using the first infringement date. Samsung now "contradicts itself to reduce potential damages exposure for [the patent in suit]," Apple said. Even though Samsung had notice of the patent a year before infringement, Samsung decided to infringe rather than design around it, Apple alleged.

The court agreed with Apple. It explained that its earlier decision rested on Federal Circuit decisions to allow lost profits only "for the period of infringement, when the infringer made sales that would have otherwise gone to the patentee." And the infringement period was the "critical period for determining availability of an alternative." According to the court, Samsung's position as to the fifth patent was contrary to those principles—not to mention Samsung's earlier stance—in that it "would require analysis of potential design-arounds before the infringement period—in this case, on the notice date." Samsung failed to cite any authority for assessing noninfringing alternatives for a period "when no lost profits could have been available."

Moreover, there were policy reasons not to adopt Samsung's current position on design-around dates. It created a disincentive for the patent holder to provide early notice and for the alleged infringer to design around the patent early on.

For all of these reasons, the district court refused to strike the expert's calculation of additional damages related to Apple's fifth patent in suit.

Note: A discussion of *Apple, Inc. v. Samsung Electronics Co., Ltd.*, 2013 U.S. Dist. LEXIS 162863 (Nov. 12, 2013), is available in the January issue of *Business Valuation Update* and at *BVLaw*.

B & L Development LLC v. City of Norton Shores

Citation: 2014 Mich. App. LEXIS 1488
Date of decision: Aug. 14, 2014
Experts: Laurence G. Allen (taxpayers/appellees); Elden Nedeau (city/appellant)
Judge: Per Curiam
State/Jurisdiction: Michigan
Court: Court of Appeals
Type of case: Expert Testimony
SIC code: 6500 Real Estate

Expert's Tax Appraisal Weathers Frontal *Daubert* Attack

A city's appeal from a property tax assessment to the Michigan Court of Appeals is noteworthy because the appellant did not train its attack on the methodology the taxpayers' expert used for his prevailing appraisal but aimed squarely at the person of the expert. The overriding issue in front of the appeals court was whether the tax tribunal met its obligation as gatekeeper under the state's Rule 702 and the state's equivalent of *Daubert*.

The taxpayers owned a real estate company that developed a 56,000-square-foot strip mall in an area in which there was little development. Most of the property nearby was industrial. A larger mall and several "big" retail stores, such as Target, were some distance away. The developers believed that the bigger mall might increase traffic to their mall but came to find out from tenants that customers complained the site was difficult to see and access.

The city's original tax assessment found the property in 2009 had a true cash value—synonymous with fair market value under controlling law—of over $6.1 million and in 2010 was worth $5.9 million. In contrast, the taxpayers claimed the true cash value in 2009 was $3.8 million and in 2010 was $3.2 million. The taxpayers appealed to the Michigan Tax Tribunal (MTT), arguing the city's tax assessor valued the property in excess of 50% of the true cash value, in violation of the state constitution. The city subsequently lowered the value, claiming it was $5.3 million in 2009 and $5 million in 2010.

Experts agree on two methods. During a four-day hearing, both sides presented expert testimony. The proceeding was subject to the state rules of evidence, including Rule 702 governing expert testimony. The taxpayers' expert had worked as a real estate appraiser for nearly 40 years. Ninety percent of his appraisal work was in Michigan, and the work encompassed a variety of properties, including strip malls, regional shopping centers, and industrial properties. He said he appraised an average of 10 to 20 shopping centers a year. He had appraised the Target store in the area. He held an MBA and was a member of the Appraisal Institute, having held positions on its board of directors. He also was a CFA and had appeared as an expert on at least 30 occasions in front of the MTT.

Both he and the city's expert agreed on the use of the sales comparison and capitalization of income approaches to value the subject property, and both concluded the income approach was the more consequential method. In general, the taxpayers' expert found that the character of the property and its location resulted in a low valuation. In particular, when valuing the vacant land, he considered actual sales of properties that were in better locations than the subject but also considered a low sales offer that did not materialize. Specifically, in 2009 or 2010, the taxpayers hoped to sell an acre of excess vacant property that was part of the subject property to a business acquaintance for $70,000, but the prospective buyer declined the offer. The taxpayers' expert said he made adjustments for numerous factors, including size and location. He rejected the suggestion that he improperly used a value-in-use approach, considering the subject's submarket performance, as opposed to a market value approach. The value he tried to determine, he contended, was the value a prudent purchaser would pay for the subject property. "Obviously a prudent purchaser looking at the property with sixty-eight percent occupancy is not going to pay the same price as if the property had an eighty-five percent occupancy.... Any buyer would pay less for a property that has less than stabilized occupancy."

The city's expert, on the other hand, said the location and character of the property were fine and suggested the reason the taxpayers had trouble finding and retaining tenants was because of their poor management. The taxpayers' expert rejected that suggestion. He had inspected between 50 and 100 strip malls, he said, and found no evidence that the taxpayers' management was wanting. On cross-examination, he admitted that there were important differences between the taxpayers' style and the approach of typical professional operators of commercial property. But, he said, if the valuation assumed a prudent seller and prudent buyer, "who the seller is shouldn't make any difference in the valuation." Whatever the reason for vacant commercial space, the taxpayers' expert said, "a buyer is going to pay less for a less occupied building."

'Lowball defective appraisal'? Before the hearing got underway, the city urged the MTT, as the trial court, to exclude the opinion of the taxpayers' expert. The issue, the city claimed, was reliability, not the expert's qualification. The city pointed to two recent MTT decisions in which the tribunal had rejected the expert's "quality point methodology." Here, in calculating income, the expert improperly considered the subject property's vacancy rate and collection loss expense, the city stated. He also took a "stabilization" deduction from the value, and he ultimately produced a "double dip" lowball valuation. The MTT should use the occasion to make "a full and throaty announcement to the tax bar that reliability standards will be actively enforced by the MTT as a pre-condition for expert opinions being admitted in evidence."

During opening statements, the city resumed its attack, calling on the MTT to act as a gatekeeper, noting that in a third of the cases in which the expert had provided opinions his appraisals were found unreliable, and accusing him of advocacy. On the hearing's second day, the city wanted to voir dire the expert to demonstrate to the court why it should exclude the expert's testimony. The trial court rejected the calls for exclusion.

During trial, on cross-examination, the city wanted assurances from the appraiser that under the expert's methodology any qualified appraiser—no matter who—would come up "with the same result rather than a range of result." Was the process repeatable, was the appraisal 'falsifiable,' the city kept asking the appraiser and the court. State case law interpreting Rule 702 required the trial court to ensure that all expert testimony was reliable before being admitted, the city said. The trial court dismissed the city's objections. It found the case to which the city repeatedly referred dealt with a witness who was unqualified to appear as an expert but was erroneously permitted by the trial court to render a "faux" expert opinion. Subsequently, the state Supreme Court found the trial and appeals courts had failed to recognize the significance of the gatekeeper role.

In contrast, in this case, there was no question that the taxpayers' appraiser was qualified to value the property and did so using reliable principles and methodologies, the trial court stated. Moreover, it adopted the expert's valuation and determined the property's true value for 2009 was $3.8 million and for 2010 was $3.2 million.

Abdicating gatekeeper role? The city appealed. It alleged that the MTT made two critical errors: (1) it failed to perform its gatekeeper role under Rule 702 when it allowed the taxpayers' expert to testify; and (2) it failed to undertake an independent valuation but instead "rubber stamped" the expert's appraisal.

The court of appeals found neither argument was persuasive. It agreed with the trial court that the city relied on a case "whose primary focus was on the fact that the witness was not qualified to offer an opinion." That case did not deal with the data underlying the fake expert's opinion, the appeals court pointed out. Here, the city did not dispute the expert's qualifications. Therefore, the cited case did not bolster its claim that the trial court was required to conduct a searching inquiry into the expert's underlying data.

The appeals court also noted that the city wanted the trial court to scrutinize the expert's testimony before he was even able to give it. But its objections to certain comparables or adjustments for market conditions went to the weight of the evidence, not its admissibility. For the purpose of admissibility, the taxpayers did not have to show their expert's opinion was absolutely true and uncontested, the appeals court observed. Rather, "the focus was on the method, not the correctness, of his opinion." The MTT was well able to decide how relevant and credible the two valuations were, the appeals court concluded.

It also dismissed the "rubber stamping" allegation. Under case law, the MTT had no obligation to accept the parties' valuations, "split the baby," or come up with its own valuation. Since, in this case, the trial court accepted the taxpayers' expert's opinion and method, it was reasonable for it to also adopt his valuation. The expert's use of one failed sales offer did not make the valuation unreliable or the trial court's acceptance of it error. The trial court properly considered the conditions at the taxpayers' property because they related to the price a prospective buyer might pay under the income approach. Further, rent rates for the subject might signal how the market valued the subject. Also, the valuation of the taxpayers' expert was not merely based on the rates of the subject because the expert also considered comparables paid at other strip malls. In sum, the MTT did not commit error in admitting and adopting the valuation of the taxpayer's expert.

Barnes v. Barnes

Citation: 2014 Tenn. App. LEXIS 200
Date of decision: April 10, 2014
Experts: Unknown (wife); Unknown (husband)
Judge: Highers
State/Jurisdiction: Tennessee
Court: Court of Appeals
Type of case: Marital Dissolution
SIC code: 8021 Offices & Clinics of Dentists

For DLOM, Court Looks to Signs of Sale of Practice

A nasty divorce case centering on the dentist husband's practice offered up a number of interesting questions, including whether the final valuation was subject to a marketability discount and how to account for the goodwill value of two dentists in the absence of noncompete agreements.

In the parties' battle over marital assets, the valuation of the husband's dental practice most fueled the conflict. During the marriage, the husband set the practice up in a way that made a professional corporation the owner of the business and him the controlling owner of the company's stock. The practice had two dentists—the husband and an associate dentist—as well as nine other full-time employees. In 2003, the husband received an offer for $913,000, but he declined to sell the practice. According to the wife, the husband had listed it for sale for $1.2 million. In 2006, he signed a net worth statement that claimed the practice was worth $1 million. During 2005 and 2009, the corporation's net revenue ranged from $1.48 million to $1.74 million.

Debt matters. At trial, both parties offered extensive expert testimony on the valuation issue. The wife's expert used three methods—the summation of assets method, the gross revenue multiplier method, and the capitalization of earnings method—and averaged the resulting values to arrive at a recommended value. He then deducted the amount of goodwill that he determined belonged to the husband—as opposed to the business. He concluded the practice was worth $678,179 based on the value of its tangible assets and enterprise goodwill. He said he did not account for the entity's debts, its cash, or accounts receivable because "accounts receivable generally are not included in the value of a practice, as they are personal to the dentist selling the practice."

The husband's expert used both an asset-based approach and an income-based approach for the purpose of comparison. Ultimately, he settled on the income approach and specifically the capitalized cash flow method. He concluded the corporation was worth $50,000 but also noted that it actually showed a "deficit net worth" because debt exceeded assets. There was practically no enterprise goodwill, he found, because neither dentist had a noncompete agreement. The expert also applied a discount for lack of marketability (DLOM). Investors prefer liquid assets, he explained. Liquidating an interest in a closely held corporation required more time, and the cost was more difficult to estimate. Compared to other investments, such an interest was not liquid. Based on various studies and factors specific to the practice at issue, he believed a 15% DLOM was appropriate.

For its part, the trial court found the valuation the husband's expert proposed more credible. For one, said the court, "it takes into fuller consideration the debts of the practice and the value of the accounts receivable of the practice." Also, the expert supported his computation with "greater industry data" and more appropriate benchmarks. The court declared the opinion of the wife's expert "arbitrary in its approach to the standards applied to come up with the value of the practice." (The appellate court opinion does not specify whether "standards" refers to "standards of value" or business valuation standards.) The trial court also noted that the valuation of the wife's expert risked overstating the goodwill of the practice "given the tenuous nature of the practice and the lack of an agreement not to compete with the other dentist in the practice." The court gave little weight to the past offer for the business.

It ultimately valued the practice at $328,392—a value that was very close to 50% of the value the wife's expert had determined. Specifically, the court adjusted the proposed $678,179 to $677,796. (The appellate decision does not explain what necessitated the adjustment.) It then reduced the amount by the noncompete amount attributable to the associate dentist: 12/21 of the total value. This calculation generated an income approach value of $386,343. Finally, the trial court applied a 15% DLOM "via the Husband's expert opinion" to arrive at its final value.

One challenge sticks. The wife challenged the valuation at the state Court of Appeals for three reasons, two of which the reviewing court found without merit. First, she asserted the trial court failed to consider over $90,500 in accounts receivables due at the time of trial.

The appellate court called this a "cursory" argument. It pointed out that at trial the wife's own expert expressly declined to include the value of the accounts receivable in his valuation.

Second, the wife contended the trial court erred when it applied a 15% DLOM and thus reduced the value of the practice by $57,951. Under the applicable case law, it was improper to discount for lack of marketability where there was no need or desire on the interest holder's part to sell his interest.

This claim had traction with the appellate court. It noted that the controlling prior case centered on the husband's 90% interest in a partnership operating several McDonald's franchises. The husband challenged the trial court's decision not to apply a 20% marketability discount, but the appellate court affirmed. It found that, unless there were indications that a sale of his interest was necessary or desirable, the valuation "would not be impacted by the lack of marketability." *Bertuca v. Bertuca*, 2007 Tenn. App. LEXIS 690 (2007) (available at *BVLaw*).

The same principle applied in this case, the Court of Appeals said. Because the husband expressed no intention of selling his interest in the business, the value of the practice was not affected by the lack of marketability; therefore it was improper for the trial court to apply the 15% DLOM. Consequently, the $57,951 reduction should be added back into the value for a total value of $386,343. Based on the trial court's statement that it intended to divide the marital estate equally, the wife had a right to half of this amount. The appellate court left it to the trial court to decide on remand how to compensate the wife.

Third, the wife asserted the trial court's valuation was "extremely low given the amount of income produced by the company on an annual basis." The husband countered that the trial court expressly stated it found his expert's valuation more convincing. He even proposed that the Court of Appeals reduce the trial court's valuation to the $50,000 amount his expert had calculated. The appeals court rejected both sides' positions. Neither had made a "cogent argument" that the trial court erred when it came to valuation methodology or the figures it used. Leaving aside the DLOM-related error, the trial court's valuation was valid, the Court of Appeals held.

Brave v. Brave (I)

Citation: 2013 Ark. App. LEXIS 570
Date of decision: Oct. 2, 2013
Experts: Unknown (plaintiff); unknown (defendants)
Judge: Walmsley
State/Jurisdiction: Arkansas
Court: Court of Appeals
Type of case: Marital Dissolution
SIC: 5812 Eating Places (full-service restaurants)

Can a Restaurant Have Personal Goodwill?

For over 25 years, Arkansas courts recognized a tight "professional license goodwill" exception in divorce cases. It applied primarily in cases involving professional partnerships such as medical and dental offices and treated the professional spouse's personal goodwill as his or her separate property for the purpose of dividing marital property. But a recent appeal in which the co-owner and chef of a successful restaurant claimed that the business's goodwill was personal to him and, therefore, nonmarital property sought to expand the scope of the exception.

Conflicting goodwill testimony. After marriage, the husband and wife opened a restaurant, in which both were 50% shareholders. They had equal legal power to make decisions, cut checks, and run the business. The husband was a trained chef and created and executed the menu, whereas the wife handled the "front end" of the business. She was responsible for staffing, dealing with financial matters, and holding the establishment's liquor license. She received a salary from the restaurant, but over the next 10 years her involvement diminished and she worked there sporadically. The restaurant achieved great success.

At trial, the spouses presented two "nationally-certified business appraiser experts" who valued the restaurant using various methods, including the income approach. (The opinion provides no further details about their testimony.) In addition, the husband offered testimony from a business consultant who was "admittedly not a business valuation expert," but an employee of the restaurant in charge of accounting and payroll. He professed to use the income approach "to value the goodwill associated with [the couple's] business." He said he based his calculation on the restaurant's value as an ongoing business with a replacement chef for the husband. He determined the business was worth slightly more than $819,000 and stated it had no equity without goodwill.

He admitted he could not determine whether the goodwill was corporate or personal. At the same time, he maintained the husband was the business. "The whole business is his personality." He described the restaurant as "a unique operation in a hard-to-find location" and the husband as irreplaceable. On direct examination, he said that stating a replacement value "was my most difficult decision to make, what number do you plug in there to replace [the husband]." Yet, on cross-examination, he agreed that the restaurant would not suffer if the husband were absent for "two weeks"; he subsequently increased the period to two months. When asked what would happen to the goodwill if the husband were gone for two years, he said "goodwill is something that is an intangible asset and it depreciates over time." Buyers look at the goodwill number and know "they can't maintain that necessarily over a period of time," he added.

The record also showed that the husband had trained other employees to manage the kitchen and "mimic everything wonderfully," which allowed him to vacation for weeks at a time.

The trial court found that the real estate of the business entity was worth $495,000, and the restaurant's value—including furniture, fixtures, goodwill, and equipment—was $895,000. Deducting debt of $550,000, the court found the business had a net value of $840,000, including real property. The wife's one-half interest in the restaurant was worth $420,000, it declared. The court did not expressly mention the opinions of the business appraiser experts in its order or divorce decree.

As to goodwill, the court considered the opinion of the business consultant, acknowledging that the loss of the husband to the business would be "very, very damaging." It noted that the husband "has built up goodwill" and that, if he were to leave the business, "it would not be the same." But the court concluded that, as long as the restaurant still had its name, "was still there," and "still had the menu, people would come for a while."

In a subsequent hearing on the husband's post-trial motion for additional findings, the trial court found the restaurant had corporate goodwill that was marital property. It considered the valuation testimony he had offered "not helpful … to the [personal] goodwill argument." Even though the court understood the husband's argument that some of the goodwill "might be personal," it said it had no "way to allocate it."

An 'essential' ingredient to success. The husband appealed the order to pay the wife $420,000 to the Arkansas Court of Appeals. The principal argument was that the trial court erred when it failed to recognize that the restaurant's goodwill was personal to him and thus was nonmarital property.

On review, the Court of Appeals noted that goodwill was marital property only if it belonged to the business and was not dependent on the presence or reputation of a particular individual. "Any value that attaches to the entity solely as a result of personal goodwill represents nothing more than probable future earnings capacity, which … is not a proper consideration in dividing marital property in a divorce proceeding."

Until now state courts had not recognized personal goodwill in a nonprofessional business, the appellate court pointed out. However, "under the unique facts of this particular case, we are extending the concept to [the restaurant] because [the husband's] presence is essential to the success of the restaurant." According to the appellate court, the trial court itself had recognized that there was personal goodwill in the restaurant and also had acknowledged that the restaurant's success was in large part due to the husband's hard work. The trial court simply stated it had no basis on which to allocate how much of the goodwill was personal and how much was corporate. Finding that the trial court had erred, the appellate court remanded, ordering it to perform the very allocation it earlier had been unable to make.

Dissent wonders about 'utility' of remand. The opinion triggered two strong dissenting opinions. Both judges agreed that the majority was mistaken when it expanded the scope of the "professional license goodwill" exception to include other commercial enterprises. "What does 'under the unique facts of this particular case' mean?" one of the dissenting judges asked. Under existing law, the exception never applied beyond a licensed professional practice, specifically a medical or dental practice. But, considering the majority's language, the exception now could easily reach '"every small business with a key man."

The second dissenting judge noted the contradictions in the testimony the business consultant gave. He was not a business valuation expert but a tax advisor, the dissent pointed out. It also said that the majority practiced "selective reliance" on his testimony. It emphasized that the majority failed to take proper note of his statement that his computation rested on the restaurant's value with a *replacement* chef for the husband. The majority also did not mention the witness's changing testimony about how long the husband could be absent before the restaurant would suffer. "A main aspect of personal goodwill associated with a business, however, is that the personal goodwill is not saleable and the business cannot survive if the so-called key person is cleaved from it." Here, the witness's own testimony "directly undermined" the husband's personal-goodwill argument, the dissent found. Finally, it wondered about "the utility and fairness" of requiring the lower court to determine what part of the restaurant's value was personal goodwill. "How is the circuit court to do now what it could not do before?" the dissent asked.

Brave v. Brave (II)

Citation: 2014 Ark. LEXIS 232
Date of decision: April 17, 2014
Experts: Unknown (wife); Unknown (husband)
Judge: Hoofman
State/Jurisdiction: Arkansas
Court: Supreme Court
Type of case: Marital Dissolution
SIC code: 5812 Eating Places

Valuation Confirms Salability of 'Unique' Restaurant's Goodwill

What a difference a court makes! A divorce case involving a successful restaurant made news several months ago when the state Court of Appeals extended the scope of personal goodwill to businesses other than professional partnerships, requiring the trial court to exclude the value of the husband's personal goodwill from its calculation. To block a revaluation, the wife appealed to the state's highest court, which reviewed the trial court's determination as if the appeal had been filed with it in the first case.

EBITDA valuation. At divorce, the husband and wife vigorously contested the value of their successful restaurant. Both were 50% shareholders, but in the course of the marriage the husband, as the chef and creator of the menu, had come to play the greater role in its day-to-day operations. At trial, the spouses presented two "nationally certified business appraiser experts" who valued the restaurant using various methods, including the income approach, but their testimony proved inconsequential to the trial court's valuation. Instead, the court looked to a valuation the husband's business consultant, who was not an accountant or financial expert, offered. He said he did an "EBITDA valuation of the business" and determined the restaurant was worth slightly more than $819,000. When asked how much of it was goodwill, he replied "[t]he goodwill part is the value of the business." This value excluded fixtures, furniture, equipment, or anything in it, all of which had a fair market value of over $82,000. At the same time, he also included a $120,000 value in his calculation; he said it represented the value for a new owner to replace the husband.

The trial court ultimately found the testimony "not helpful ... to the argument that we should recognize personal goodwill." But, it said, unlike most testimony in divorce cases that was developed solely for the purpose of litigation, this opinion tried to get at what the business would sell for. "The person that comes in to say this is my belief based on my assessment of what this would sell for in the open market. So that was good testimony." The trial court valued the real estate of the business entity at $495,000 and the restaurant at $895,000, including fixtures and equipment. Deducting debt of $550,000, it determined the business had a net value of $840,000, including real property. The wife's half interest in the restaurant was worth $420,000.

The husband challenged the valuation at the state Court of Appeals. The trial court was wrong not to recognize that the restaurant's goodwill was personal to him and thus nonmarital property, he contended. The appellate court noted the difference between corporate and personal goodwill and pointed out that, up to the present, state courts had not recognized personal goodwill in a business that was not a professional practice, such as a medical or dental office. But, "under the unique facts of this particular case, we are extending the concept to [the restaurant] because [the husband's] presence is essential to the success of the restaurant." It remanded the case to the trial court, ordering it to perform an allocation between personal and corporate goodwill. The opinion spurred a strong dissent from two judges who said the majority "selectively relied" on the witness's statements that supported its finding of personal goodwill while ignoring others that disproved it and who cautioned that the court's vague language risked allowing the exception to apply to "every small business with a key man." (An extended discussion of the Court of Appeals decision and the court's opinion appear in the February edition of *Business Valuation Update* and at *BVLaw*.)

No extension of personal goodwill. Subsequently, the wife appealed the Court of Appeals decision to the state Supreme Court, which reviewed the trial court's ruling as to goodwill as if the appellate decision had never happened.

To assess whether the trial court erred in finding no corporate goodwill, the Supreme Court homed in on very different aspects of the consultant's testimony than the Court of Appeals had done. The high court did not adopt the husband's position that there was personal goodwill in nonprofessional practices, such as the restaurant at issue. Also, even if there was, the Supreme Court said, there was no evidence that the trial court erred in finding corporate goodwill only in this instance. The witness said he valued the restaurant as if sold on the open market and this valuation included goodwill. Moreover, his valuation took into account the replacement for the husband. "Goodwill is characterized as corporate goodwill ... if the evidence establishes the salability or marketability of the goodwill as a business asset," the court pointed out. Therefore, the trial court did not err in assigning the goodwill to the business. The state Supreme Court set aside the Court of Appeals' decision; there was no revaluation.

Editor's Note: It is worth reading both appellate decisions to compare the reviewing courts' differing selection of valuation-related facts either to affirm or deny the existence of personal goodwill. This exercise supports the dissent's critique as to selective reliance.

Bross Trucking, Inc. v. Commissioner

Citation: 2014 Tax Ct. Memo LEXIS 109
Date of decision: June 5, 2014
Experts: N/A
Judge: Paris
State/Jurisdiction: Federal
Court: United States Tax Court
Type of case: Federal Taxation
SIC code: 4213 Trucking, except local

Devoid of Goodwill, Corporation Escapes Income Tax Liability

A Tax Court decision that came out earlier in the year commands attention because of its thorough discussion of personal versus corporate goodwill. The case, which was decided by Judge Paris, is not strictly about valuation but explores the nature of goodwill as property that is transferrable and the tax consequences resulting from the transfer. Financial experts may know that Judge Paris is also the author of the more recent *Estate of Adell* decision—an estate tax case in which personal goodwill played a central role in the valuation of a closely held corporation. Together the cases provide valuable insight into the judge's thinking on goodwill.

Regulatory clean slate. The taxpayer started in the road construction business in 1966. In 1972, he formed a construction company to undertake a number of construction projects. As the projects expanded, he organized a series of companies to provide services and equipment to the numerous construction projects. He was in charge of arranging and seeing to the completion of the projects, cultivated personal relationships in the road construction industry, and was responsible for maintaining those relationships on behalf of the family business. The family business's umbrella included Bross Trucking, which the taxpayer founded in 1982 and owned 100% directly or through his revocable living trust. Bross Trucking hauled construction-related materials and equipment for construction projects. It leased most of its equipment from another wholly owned family entity. Most of its drivers were independent contractors, and its main customers were entities whose owners were family members with whom the taxpayer-owner had close relationships.

In the late 1990s, Bross Trucking became the target of audits and investigations by a number of government agencies. Fearing the effects of negative attention and a possible shutdown of the business, the taxpayer and his three sons met with an attorney to discuss the best way to ensure the family business had a suitable trucking provider. They decided to form a new company, ostensibly to ensure a clean regulatory slate. The new company was majority owned by the sons, who had had no involvement in Bross Trucking, and it provided more services than Bross Trucking did. The taxpayer played no role in managing the new company. At the end of 2003, Bross Trucking recorded nearly $263,400 in assets; in 2004, it continued to collect accounts receivables and had cash assets, which it never distributed but used a few years later to pay litigation expenses.

The new company hired about half of the employees that had worked for Bross Trucking. When the new company started out, some of its trucks still displayed the Bross Trucking logo. But since the trucks attracted unwelcome attention from the government, the company quickly used magnetic signs to cover up the old name.

Income tax and gift tax liabilities combined. In 2011, the Internal Revenue Service sent Bross Trucking a notice of deficiency, claiming the latter had distributed an appreciated intangible asset to the taxpayer for which the company should have recognized gain for 2004 under IRC Section 311(b)(1). Subsequently, the IRS sent three deficiency notices to the taxpayer and his wife alleging the taxpayer gave the asset to his three sons and, therefore, owed gift tax. The alleged total amount of liability, including accuracy-related penalties, was over $2.6 million. The court consolidated the cases; the remaining case, therefore, combines corporate income tax and gift tax issues.

Section 311(b)(1) provides that "if a corporation distributes appreciated assets to a shareholder, the corporation recognizes gain as if the property were sold to the shareholder at its fair market value. Gain is recognized to the extent that the property's fair market value exceeds the corporation's adjusted basis." The law aims to capture the asset's appreciation and prevent a corporation from avoiding tax on the inherent gain by distributing such property to its shareholders.

At the start of its analysis, the Tax Court noted that the IRS was less than clear in identifying the distributed asset for which it claimed the corporation was liable. The government's opening brief, the court said, suggested it was goodwill, which included numerous attributes, including established revenue stream, developed customer base, established workforce including independent contractors, and others.

'Antithesis of goodwill.' The outcome of the case turned on what "regime" of goodwill was in play: personal goodwill or corporate goodwill. "A business can only distribute corporate assets and cannot distribute assets that it does not own," the court stated, referencing *Martin Ice Cream Co. v. Commissioner,* 110 T.C. 18 (1998). By extension, it cannot distribute intangible assets that the shareholders own individually. Such was the case here, the court found.

Even assuming Bross Trucking once had corporate goodwill, it had lost most of it by the time of the alleged transfer due to various regulatory infractions. Regulatory agencies were "hounding" the company to such an extent that the new company immediately took steps to remove the Bross Trucking name from its leased trucks. Under threat of losing the trust and patronage of customers, the taxpayer decided to establish a new entity. If trade names and trademarks are the embodiment of goodwill, the court said, this action showed that any transferred corporate goodwill was not valuable and may in fact have been detrimental to the new company. According to the court, the reputational situation was "the antithesis of goodwill."

The only aspect of goodwill Bross Trucking could point to at the time of transfer was a workforce in place, including several mechanics and administrative staff, but it did not transfer it to the taxpayer. The new company, the court found, assembled its own workforce. The new company's key employees, including the taxpayer's sons who had no role in Bross Trucking, had nothing to do with the old company, and the new company offered services that the old one did not, including GPS service and truck maintenance for third parties. If the new company hired employees from

Bross Trucking, they appear to have been hired on their own merit rather than transferred, the court concluded.

Also, there was no organized transfer of customers between Bross Trucking and the new entity, the court found. To the extent customers of Bross Trucking became customers of the new company, it was the customers' choice to use a trucking company with an unblemished reputation and record.

Nearly all the goodwill Bross Trucking had was attributable to the personal ability of the taxpayer, the court determined. The company's customers chose to do business with Bross Trucking only because of the efforts of the taxpayer. During his many years in the business, he had developed invaluable relationships with Bross Trucking's major customers. The customers hired Bross Trucking for the taxpayer's expertise and reputation.

Critically, the taxpayer did not transfer his personal goodwill to Bross Trucking, the court continued to say. It had no employment contract with the taxpayer and had no right to his future services. It also had no noncompete and could not expect to benefit from his personal goodwill once he left the business.

In sum, the court found that, since Bross Trucking had no corporate goodwill and no right to the taxpayer's personal goodwill, it did not transfer goodwill to the taxpayer and, therefore, was not liable for income tax related to it. Since the taxpayer did not transfer corporate goodwill to his sons, he was not liable for gift tax.

Editor's note: The case leaves a related issue open. What, if any, tax consequences are there if the taxpayer transfers his personal goodwill to the sons' new trucking business? All the cases discussed above are available at *BVLaw*.

Browne v. Browne, Jr.

Citation: 2014 Tenn. App. LEXIS 521
Date of decision: Aug. 27, 2014
Experts: Shannon Welsh Farr (wife); Randall Benjamin Hebert (husband)
Judge: Frierson, II
State/Jurisdiction: Tennessee
Court: Court of Appeals
Type of case: Marital Dissolution
SIC code: 2899 Chemicals and Chemical Preparations N.E.C.

Valuation Combines Elements of Rival Experts' Cash Flow Analyses

Another instance of "splitting the baby"? In a divorce proceeding, both experts used the capitalization of cash flow method but reached vastly different results in valuing the husband's closely held company. One key difference was the cap rate, which they both generated with the build-up method. The trial court used the cap rate from one expert and applied it to the cash flow analysis of the other expert. On appeal, the wife contested the valuation, arguing that this kind of mixing and matching was inappropriate and objecting to the trial court's application of a minority discount.

Minority or controlling interest? The husband was the president of a closely held chemical treatment company. Both he and a business partner—the company's vice president—each held a 44.837% interest. The husband's father, who was the original founder of the company, owned the remaining interest in the business but was selling his shares monthly to the other partners equally. The agreement specified a purchase price of $13,000 per 1.25 shares. There was evidence that the husband's father wanted to leave the business and set a "take-it-or-leave-it" price for his shares based on the amount he believed he needed to obtain. Except for one month or two, both partners bought the stock since the agreement had gone into effect; the completion of the buyout would likely be April 2003.

The husband and his business partner jointly made business decisions, but they played different roles in the operation of the business. The husband testified that, notwithstanding his title as president, he did not have unilateral authority to liquidate any part of the business.

The wife filed for divorce in 2010, but trial took place in fall 2012. A few years earlier, the husband had indicated in a financial planning document that the company was worth $1.5 million and subsequently in a loan application that his total net worth was $2.1 million.

At trial, the parties presented expert testimony. Both experts valued the company under an income approach, performing a capitalization of cash flow analysis. The wife's expert also conducted a transaction analysis based on the stock option agreement. She determined that, under the $13,000-per-1.25-shares price in the stock purchase agreement, each share was worth $10,400. The value resulting from the transaction approach did not increase the value of the company's overall equity, she explained, because ultimately the value of equity derived from the transaction method was less than that resulting from the income approach. She averaged the values from the two methods. In contrast, the husband's expert rejected the transaction method, noting that the price in the stock option agreement "grossly overvalued the company." He valued each share at slightly below $2,300. Both experts agreed that the asset approach was inappropriate in this instance because the husband lacked the power to liquidate assets unilaterally.

The wife's expert determined that the husband's interest in the corporation was about $863,000. The husband's expert originally set the value at over $186,000 but prior to trial amended his report because an item that was an expense was counted throughout the original valuation as income. The revised value for the husband's interest was about $146,000, the expert determined.

Cap rate based on BUM. The experts differed on key inputs, including the time frame they used for the single-period estimates and the capitalization rates. Specifically, the wife's expert considered the latest 12 months (LTM), whereas the husband's expert reviewed a five-year period (2007 through 2011) and removed the two highest earning years, 2009 and 2010. The wife's expert estimated that the amount of ongoing cash flow to invested capital was almost $257,000, whereas the husband's expert arrived at an amount of over $195,000. The wife's equity rate was 17.81%, and the resulting capitalization rate was 12.23%, yielding a capitalization multiple of 8.18. In contrast, the husband determined the total equity rate was 25.27%, which resulted in a capitalization rate of 18.46% and a capitalization multiple of 5.42.

Both experts used the build-up method (BUM) to generate their capitalization rates. Their source for bound market capitalization was Morningstar, but they disagreed over the applicable subcategory. The husband's expert chose "10z," saying it was designed for companies such as the subject company—"the smallest of the small." But the wife's expert explained that, based on her understanding of valuation literature, it may not be necessary to use "10z" when valuing a small company because companies within "10z" may be riskier than the company that is being valued. She selected "10b," she said, "primarily because it does include a large number of companies." As a result of their differing selections, the husband's expert applied an 11.77% size risk premium, while the wife's expert used a 6.1% premium.

Moreover, when testifying, the wife's expert characterized the husband's interest in the company as a controlling interest. She recognized that the husband and his business partner were equal decision-makers but said a provision in the stock option agreement provided that the husband eventually would inherit any shares that his father still had in the company at his father's death—notwithstanding the near completion of the buyout. The husband's expert, on the other hand, said both partners were minority interest holders and applied a 25% minority discount as well as a 28% marketability discount. The wife's expert stated that experts differed on the use of a minority discount in the capitalization of cash flow method:

> Many believe apples to apples that you should make controlling or normalizing adjustments to the cash flows and then also use the discount rate, which is based on the build-up method and ... could result in a control or a marketable minority interest.

Finally, both experts agreed to submit to a test of reasonableness. Specifically, the respective valuations should be a multiple of four to nine times EBTIDA for companies similar to the subject company. The valuation from the wife's expert resulted in a 4.8-to-5.0 multiple. The amended valuation the husband's expert proposed produced a 3.5 multiple and as such fell below the 4.0 mark.

The trial court generally adopted the amended valuation the husband's expert submitted, including his capitalization of cash flow calculation and the minority and marketability discounts, but it directed that the capitalization rate the wife's expert determined be applied to the calculation (the opinion does not explain why). The recalculation yielded a total value of $277,000 for the husband's interest.

The trial court agreed with the husband's expert that the stock option agreement was not indicative of the value of the company since it did not result from an arm's-length transaction. The court also expressed concern that the wife's expert valued the equity on a controlling interest basis. A 44.837% interest in a company does not amount to a controlling interest, "especially when the co-partner has exactly the same ownership interest," the trial court pointed out.

Split on minority discount. The wife appealed the trial court's findings to the state's Court of Appeal. She objected to the valuation for a number of reasons.

First, she claimed that, in giving greater weight to the valuation of the husband's expert, the trial court failed to abide by the "Delaware Rule," which requires the use of three methods—market value, asset value, and investment of earnings value—to determine the fair value of a dissenter's shares in a closely held corporation.

The Court of Appeals noted that divorce was different. Whereas the Delaware Rule applied when it came to valuing a dissenting minority shareholder's shares, there were other acceptable ways to value a party's interest in the context of divorce, including use of the nine-factor test that appears in Revenue Ruling 59-60. Here, the husband's expert specifically referenced the factors in his valuation and the valuation from the wife's expert's showed she considered comparable factors. Both experts rejected the asset approach. Consequently, the appeals court rejected this argument.

Second, the trial court erred when it decided to apply the capitalization rate the wife's expert determined to the cash flow analysis the husband's expert performed, the wife stated. Moreover, she claimed that, even though the wife's expert characterized the husband's interest as controlling, she did not apply a control premium. It, therefore, was improper for the husband's expert to apply a 25% minority discount because the minority interest was assumed in the expert's capitalization of cash flow analysis.

The appeals court deferred to the trial court's assessment of the weight and credibility given to each of the experts. The lower court specifically credited the cash flow analysis the husband's expert had performed and specifically stated that the capitalization rate the wife's expert calculated was the most appropriate rate, the appeals court said.

As for the minority discount, it was "undisputed" that the husband's interest was not a controlling interest on its face because it was less than 51%. As for the minority interest, the husband's expert "purposefully" chose to apply a minority discount with his cash flow analysis and the wife's expert allowed that this approach had support among many valuation experts, the appeals court observed.

Third, the wife argued that the trial court erred when it failed to consider the price the husband and his business partner paid to buy the founder's shares under the stock purchase agreement.

The appeals court disagreed. The trial court specifically noted that the husband's father was able to "operate in a vacuum" and that the buyout was "no where close to an arm's length transaction." There was no record that a buyer other than the two partners was willing to pay that amount, the appeals court pointed out.

Fourth, the wife claimed that the husband's valuation failed the test of reasonableness.

The appeals court said there would be merit to this concern if the trial court had adopted the valuation of the husband's expert in its entirety. Instead, the lower court required a recalculation that resulted in a higher overall valuation. The final $277,000 value was a 5.71 multiple of the expert's amended capitalized value of invested capital, almost $1.6 million, and met the reasonableness test. Moreover, the trial court had discretion "to place a value on a marital asset that is within the range of the evidence submitted."

Finally, the wife maintained that the trial court erred by not taking into account the husband's prior statements as to the value of his ownership interest in the business. That claim also had no traction. The self-reporting statements took place years before the filing for divorce, they were vague, and they did not support either expert's valuation, the court pointed out. For all these reasons, it affirmed the trial court's valuation of the husband's ownership interest.

Burstein v. Burstein

Citation: 2014 Ill. App. Unpub. LEXIS 245
Date of decision: Feb. 13, 2014
Experts: Joseph Modica (wife); Donald Fontana (husband)
Judge: Zenoff
State/Jurisdiction: Illinois
Court: Appellate Court
Type of case: Marital Dissolution
SIC code: 8011 Offices & Clinics of Medical Doctors

Courts Decry Expert's Failure to Explore Different Ways to Develop FMV

Experts don't just disqualify themselves under *Daubert* by making egregious technical errors. Short-circuiting an analysis because of litigation snags can also get the appraiser in trouble, as a recent ugly divorce case illustrates. When the wife's expert based his calculations of the husband's interests in several businesses only on the companies' buyout provisions but said the resulting values did not meet the applicable fair market value standard, he provoked the trial court's impatience. "If I had something else from your expert other than 'I don't know what the fair market value is,' then you'd be in a better position, but that's not what I got," the court said to the wife. She appealed.

The husband was a urologist who owned interests in a clinic, a related limited liability company, and a medical center. For three years, the wife issued subpoenas to the businesses for documents that would enable her financial expert to value the husband's interests. In June 2011, four months before trial, the companies for the most part complied. The documents at issue included annual financial statements, income tax returns, general ledgers, fixed asset registers, accounts receivable and payable, lists of subsidiaries, shareholder agreements, buy-sell agreements, major sale or purchase contracts, and details of any litigation.

Under the clinic's shareholder agreement, shareholders had to be medical doctors and active employees of the company. The buyout price of the shares was based on a formula that adjusted a "legacy amount" for inflation at the time of the shareholder's departure; the "legacy amount" was the shareholder's initial investment. The clinic's CFO testified that, during his eight-year tenure, he never saw any distributions of equity to shareholders other than buyouts using the formula. He said that, under the formula, the value of the husband's 100 shares just prior to trial was $49,500. Also, shareholders had no personal ownership interest in the entity's assets, but, if the business were sold to a third party, any profit would be distributed to the shareholders, he added. No negotiations for a sale or merger were underway.

In 2008, the clinic's shareholders established the LLC. Its only assets were the 70,000-square-foot medical building in which the clinic operated and the land on which it stood. The husband was one of 21 members in the LLC but had no financial investment in it. The clinic's CFO, who also served as the accountant for the LLC, said the company was a "fully debted entity at the time it began." Its asset value was zero, he claimed. Since its formation, the entity had made no distributions to members and no member had become eligible to transfer his or her membership interest.

In addition, the husband also owned 14.82 membership interests of a medical center. That entity's operating agreement provided that in a buyout the price would either be a lump sum to which the departing member and the company's managers agreed or an amount equal to the distributions the member would receive in the 24 months following the sale. In any event, the buyout price would not exceed the amount the member would receive in the 24 months prior to the sale.

At trial, the parties contested the value of all three entities. The wife presented expert testimony and the husband a rebuttal witness.

Experts fail to state FMV. The wife's expert was a CPA and certified valuation and financial forensic analyst. As to valuing the clinic, he said he had reviewed its audited financial statements from 2005 through 2009, as well as documents from two of its subsidiaries. But, he said, he was unable to obtain documents pertaining to transactions in 2010 concerning the company's stock and a strategic plan. He also believed it would have been helpful to meet with the clinic's management. He said he had listed all the documents he requested but did not receive in his report. For some reason, however, the report was not made part of the trial record.

Based on the documents, the expert calculated the buyout price of the husband's 100 shares. Their original value, he said, was $32,500. Under the agreement, that price "would be multiplied by the change in the consumer price index from August 1, 1994, [date of initial investment], to whatever date the buyout took place." But he did not say what the price was for any date. When asked in trial whether the buyout price "truly and accurately" stated the value of the husband's interest, the expert replied: "Well, on some levels, yes, but certainly not under a standard value of fair market value, no." He explained that the fair market value (FMV) emerged from an arm's-length transaction that took place in the open market. A shareholder transaction was not an arm's-length transaction, he added. When asked why the FMV was important, he replied that state law required it in business valuations.

For the LLC, he used the entity's operating agreement to calculate that the husband's interest was worth about $359,000 as of December 2009. The buyout formula used the husband's percentage of ownership interest (5.5%), multiplied by the year's net operating rents of $545,000 and divided by an 8% capitalization rate. The expert noted that this calculation also did not reflect the FMV of the ownership interest because it did not consider the FMV of the building, which was the entity's primary asset. When asked whether the FMV could be zero, he hesitated. He was not sure, he said; the answer would depend on the FMV of the building and the debt owed on the building.

For the medical center, he used the available operating agreement to determine a buyout price for the husband's 14.62 membership interests of $260,400—or $17,811 per membership interest. It was based on the distributions that the husband had received for 2008 and 2009. He again stated that this price did not reflect the FMV of the ownership interest.

The husband's rebuttal expert was also a CPA and certified valuator. He noted that there were three methods with which to value businesses: asset, income, and market approach. As to the value of the ownership interest in the clinic, he lacked the information necessary to apply the asset or income approach, he explained. Moreover, he pointed out that his inability to find sales of comparable medical practices precluded his using the market approach. Therefore, he looked to prior sales of company stock and concluded that the husband's shares were worth $482 each—$48,200 in total.

In terms of the LLC, he claimed he used the "net asset value method" but never said what value he had arrived at. Moreover, he used the buyout provisions of the entity's operating agreement and "approximated" that the husband's interest was worth $818,000.

Finally, he testified that he lacked the requisite information to value the third entity, the medical center, under the income or asset approach. However, he did perform a calculation looking to 18 prior transactions involving the center's membership interests, but he did not state his valuation conclusion.

Where are the alternatives? The trial court was troubled by the stunted analyses that both experts presented. It said that it was "not a big fan of using the buyout agreements ... because ... there are other issues that can affect [value.]" It asked "why they chose not to look at alternative ways to value businesses." It pointed out that, even assuming there were missing documents, the wife's expert never even discussed valuation methods that would have been preferable to the buyout provisions. For example, he did not talk about the availability of sales of comparable medical practices, which, said the court, was information he could have obtained on his own, without cooperation from the clinical and medial center. The expert never mentioned the income or asset approach. He only discussed the buyout provisions and the fact that any value resulting from their formulas might not accurately reflect the FMV of the husband's interests. The court said that, if left without a valuation, it would "come up with a way to allocate the assets that protects both sides."

Ultimately, the trial court valued the husband's interest in the clinic at $49,500, based on the value the clinic's CFO had stated. The marital interest of the husband's membership interests in the medical center was worth $130,185, it found, valuing the interests at $18,081 each—$270 more per membership interest than the wife's expert determined based on the buyout formula. The LLC's value, the court said, was zero. The company was too new to hold title to a newly constructed, fully mortgaged building. However, it ordered the husband to pay the wife 50% of any income or proceeds that he received from his shares in the company in the future.

Discovery dispute is no excuse. The wife appealed the trial court's ruling on various grounds but particularly objected to the valuations of the clinic and medical center. Case law, she argued, made it clear that a value stemming from a buyout provision did not reflect the fair market value of the ownership interests in the businesses. Therefore, it was improper for the lower court to base its valuations on them.

Her arguments got no traction with the appeals court. It found that this case was different from the one she had cited—*In re Marriage of Gunn*, 598 N.E.2d 1013 (1992) (available at *BVLaw*). In the latter, the trial court received at least some evidence of a transaction that did not occur pursuant to the buyout provision. Not here. On the contrary, the CFO of the clinic stated he knew of no transactions outside the provisions. The same lack of evidence applied to the medical center.

More importantly, said the appeals court, the trial court only heard about valuations resulting from the buyout formula. Notwithstanding the wife's claim that the protracted discovery dispute left her expert with insufficient information to use any other valuation method, in his testimony, the expert never even discussed "the availability or viability of any other valuation method." When asked why the FMV was important, he mentioned that state law seemed to require it, but he did not attempt to explain how an expert "would have accurately determined the fair market value" of the husband's interests in the two medical practices. With no alternative valuations in front of it, the trial court made its determination "in the only manner it could," the appeals court concluded.

Moreover, the appeals court dismissed the wife's argument that her expert was unable to obtain the documents he needed to properly value the husband's interests. With the exception of a few documents, the expert at trial did not specify what other pertinent information he required, the court noted. Instead, he referred to a list in his report, which, for purposes of the appeal, was meaningless since the report was not admitted into evidence. Also, the entities ultimately did produce many of the documents the wife had demanded before trial. Considering that her expert was unable to perform valuations based on those, "it would be tenuous to assume" he would be able to do so with any additional documents.

For all these reasons, the appellate court affirmed the trial court's valuations.

Cavallaro v. Commissioner

Citation: 2014 Tax Ct. Memo LEXIS 189
Date of decision: Sept. 17, 2014
Experts: Timothy Maio, Ernst & Young; John Murphy, Atlantic Management Co. (petitioners); Marc Bello, Edelstein & Co. (IRS/respondent)
Judge: Gustafson
State/Jurisdiction: Federal
Court: United States Tax Court
Type of case: Estate and Gift Taxation
SIC code: 3599 Industrial Machinery NEC

Gift Tax Case Pivots on Key Assumption Informing Valuations

Hardworking taxpayers who built a successful business turned to estate planning professionals for advice on how best to transfer the value in their company to their children via another family business. Some 15 years later, the IRS scrutinized the structured merger between the two companies and found the taxpayers were liable for tax on a $46 million gift to their offspring. The dispute turned on the valuations of three companies and ended in Tax Court.

'A few embarrassing facts.' In 1979, the taxpayers founded Knight Tool Co., an S corporation that built custom tools and machines. The husband owned 49%, the wife 51%. One of their three sons was working at the company in sales and marketing. When they looked to expand beyond contract manufacturing, Knight engineers and employees collaborated with the husband and son to develop an automated liquid-dispensing machine—CAM/ALOT—that they hoped to sell to a larger market. In December 1987, the three sons formed another company (also an S corp), Camelot Systems Inc., whose purpose was to improve the CAM/ALOT technology and market it. No contemporaneous documents showed a transfer of the rights to the machines from Knight to Camelot.

In essence, Knight manufactured the machines and Camelot sold and distributed them to third parties. Documents described Knight as "the sole provider of machines sold by Camelot Systems, Inc." Knight funded the operations of both businesses, and, in financial transactions that included guaranteeing loans, Knight consistently assumed the risk. Also, the two companies operated out of the same building and shared payroll and accounting services.

In 1994, when the companies showed some promise of success, the taxpayers consulted a big accounting firm as well as a well-known law firm for estate planning advice. Initially, the professionals had differing ideas as to which entity owned the value of the CAM/ALOT technology and how to pass that value to the three sons in a way that minimized estate tax liability. During an earlier engagement, the accountants had determined that Knight was the owner and could claim research and development (R&D) tax credits based on work its engineers had done. In contrast, the attorney decided to construct a narrative in which the value transfer started in 1987 with the incorporation of Camelot. He dismissed objections that real events did not bear out this story, saying that in any history one had "to squeeze a few embarrassing facts into the suitcase by force." Eventually, the accountants fell in line and the two sets of professionals structured a merger based on the premise that no gift tax was due because, in 1995, on the merger date, Camelot already owned the CAM/ALOT technology. To fit the narrative, the accountants filed an amended tax return in which Knight disclaimed the R&D tax credits and Camelot claimed them. Based on the narrative, the taxpayers accepted a 19% interest in the new entity, while the three sons claimed the remaining 81% in equal measure. This meant that Camelot had four times the value of Knight. Six months later, in 1996, the merged company was sold for $57 million in cash with a contingent additional amount that was never paid. The petitioners received a total of $10.8 million, and the three sons each received nearly $15.4 million.

In 1998, during an investigation into the 1994 and 1995 income tax returns for Knight and Camelot, the IRS became alert to a possible gift tax liability related to the merger and sued, successfully, for discovery of relevant documents, including documents the accountants had prepared prior to and around the time of the merger. In 2010, the government issued a deficiency notice claiming the premerger Camelot had zero value and the merger resulted in a roughly $23 million gift from each parent to the sons. The taxpayers petitioned the Tax Court for a redetermination.

The case turned on what the fair market value of Knight, Camelot, and the combined entity was around the time of the merger and by extension whether the petitioners received an unduly low interest and the sons an unduly high interest in the new entity.

Different premise, different methods. The taxpayers offered appraisals from two experts in business valuations. The first expert worked for the accounting firm and valued the two companies in preparation for the merger. He visited both companies, reviewed relevant company material, and interviewed the principals of both companies. He said he had complete access to information and relied on relevant financial information the accountants from Knight and Camelot furnished.

Using a market approach, he was able to find company comparables for Knight and the new entity but said he could not find any suitable comparables for Camelot as a stand-alone company. He concluded the merged entity was worth between $70 million and $75 million and Knight's portion of that value was between $13 million and $15 million. His valuations were based on the assumption that Knight had transferred the value of the technology to Camelot at the time of the merger and that it was the contract manufacturer of the machines.

The taxpayers engaged a second expert for trial. He also used a market approach. He, too, said he could not find any appropriate comparables for the premerger Camelot and, consequently, did not value it as a stand-alone company. In terms of Knight, he said he looked for companies "that are similar in nature," assuming Knight at the time of the merger was not the owner of the technology. Instead, he viewed Knight as a machine shop to which Camelot "outsourced the assembly of the product line." He also said he considered companies that had a similar "net profit" as Knight. His calculation included a royalty adjustment to account for Knight's owning the right to the CAM/ALOT trademark and the taxpayer husband owning the patent to a component of the technology in some CAM/ALOT models. This expert concluded the merged entity was worth $72.8 million, slightly more than the first expert had proposed, of which $13.7 million—18.8%—was Knight's share.

Neither expert prepared a valuation based on the assumption that Knight owned the technology and manufactured the machines.

In contrast, the IRS's trial expert assumed Knight owned the technology. He based his valuation on an income approach, using the discounted cash flow method. In essence, he used the companies' 1995 annualized pretax earnings and adjusted for cash flow items to arrive at adjusted net income amounts. Because he believed that the companies' financial documents included irregularities and Camelot's revenue numbers were inappropriately high considering Knight owned the technology, he used Risk Management Association data (then Robert Morris Association) and data from the *Almanac of Business and Financial Ratios* as benchmarks for normalizing adjustments to the ongoing after-tax cash flows of both companies. He subsequently calculated cash flows for four years following the merger, assumed a terminal value, and applied a discount rate. He concluded the merged entity was worth $64.5 million—less than the taxpayers' experts stated. And he determined that 65% of that value, $41.9 million, belonged to Knight.

The taxpayers objected to the valuation. It was based on the mistaken assumption that Knight owned the value of the technology, they argued. Moreover, the IRS expert improperly used RMA data—selecting an improper SIC code for analyzing the companies' financials—and made improper normalizing adjustments. Further, his valuation failed to be unbiased because IRS counsel improperly informed the expert that the taxpayers had submitted false statements regarding ownership of the technology. Also, the expert failed to interview executives at either company or visit the site.

The IRS replied that the expert's value conclusions signaled his independence. He arrived at a value for the combined entity that was considerably below the values the taxpayers' experts proposed. The expert himself countered that there was "negligible" value to visiting a company that had been sold to a third party 16 years earlier. Also, there was enough documentation related to the owners and background information on the company to render owner interviews unnecessary.

IRS concession. The court found the IRS in effect had made a concession based on its expert's valuation, lowering the taxable gift from $46.1 million to $29.6 million. This meant the petitioners, not the government, had the burden of proving that the transfer of stock by way of the merger was not a gift, subject to Section 2512 of the Gift Tax Regulations.

The petitioners failed to meet their burden, the court determined. For one, the 1995 merger was not an arm's-length transaction. It was inconceivable that a hypothetical buyer, with no connection to the owners, would buy Camelot without demanding documentation that it owned the CAM/ALOT technology. However, no such documentation existed. Most likely a prospective buyer would have walked away from the deal.

At the same time, it was unreasonable to assume that, if Knight had dealt with an unrelated party that sold the machines Knight developed and manufactured and for which it owned the intellectual property, Knight simply would have abandoned its ownership claim and let the third party take its technology. In reality, the transfer took place for estate planning purposes and involved parents who agreed to the arrangement for the benefit of their sons.

The court dismissed the valuations from the petitioners' experts, finding that both rested on the false premise that Camelot owned the technology and had a right to most of the income the machines generated. Since the petitioners did not proffer a valuation based on the accurate assumption that Knight owned the technology, they had no evidence to counter the IRS valuation.

The court adopted the IRS's conclusion that the petitioners were liable for making a $29.6 million gift based on the IRS's expert valuation. At the same time, it acknowledged that the expert's analysis might have been flawed when it came to determining the value attributable to each of the companies, but it declined to correct the IRS's figures. "It would serve no useful purpose to review ... each and every aspect of the experts' opinions," the court concluded.

The court found the petitioners had a reasonable cause defense and were not subject to an accuracy-related penalty. They had no formal training in accounting, law, or business and in good faith had relied on a team of estate planning professionals. "The fault in the positions [the taxpayers] took was attributable not to them but to the professionals who advised them," the court noted.

Chattree v. Chattree

Citation: 2014 Ohio App. LEXIS 479
Date of decision: Feb. 13, 2014
Experts: Robert Ranallo (wife); Bernard Agin (husband)
Judge: Celebrezze, Jr.
State/Jurisdiction: Ohio
Court: Court of Appeals
Type of case: Marital Dissolution
SIC code: 8049 Offices and Clinics of Health Practitioners, N.E.C.

Court Proscribes Litigant's Efforts to Foil Expert's Valuation

Experts working on a lawsuit may be targets in the play of litigation. The key to surviving with one's reputation intact is to dot one's i's and cross one's t's every step in the process. In an ugly divorce case, the wife's expert took all the necessary precautions and succeeded in protecting his work product against a series of attacks from the husband at the trial and appeals levels.

The husband and wife had been married for 48 years, when, in 2008, the wife filed for divorce. A highly contested issue was the valuation of a business that the husband had started in 1995 and that provided mental health services to patients through various providers and agencies. Although a May 2009 court order required the husband to provide the wife with funds to retain an expert, he did not do so until November 2009. Subsequently, he limited the expert's access to critical tax returns and other corporate documents and refused to allow the expert to visit the site and conduct management interviews. As a result of the impediment, the wife's expert was unable to complete his report ahead of a March 4, 2010, deposition and declined to appear. Instead, he submitted his report after trial began on March 8, 2010, which prompted the husband to file a pretrial motion asking the trial court to preclude the expert's report and testimony for untimeliness. The court declined; it found there was sufficient time to reschedule the deposition ahead of the expert's trial testimony. The husband never did so.

At the same time, the husband did not disclose his expert and submit the latter's report until six and a half months into trial, in September 2010. (Due to delays, the entire trial took seven months.) The trial court decided to exclude the portion of the report that concerned the business's valuation but permitted the husband's expert to give limited rebuttal testimony as to the methodology the wife's expert used.

Expert report includes caveats. The wife's expert used the "capitalization of earnings method" to value the business at $1.9 million as of the end of December 2008. He said he made a "normalized adjustment" to add back the annual cost of the business's defined pension plan and the cash surrender value of its officer life insurance policies. He explained these were nonoperating or nonrecurring assets that were "discretionary in nature." Specifically, he found that adjusting for the pension plan yielded a value of $1.5 million "on a marketable, controlling interest basis." However, adjusting for the life insurance policy produced a "controlling, marketable interest value of … approximately $2,132,000." He said he applied a 10% discount for lack of marketability to arrive at the $1.9 million figure.

In his expert report, he noted that, since he only had limited access to information and management, his analysis "was not subject to the development or reporting standards" of the AICPA's Statement of Standards for Valuation Services No. 1 (SSVS) nor the valuation standards of NACVA.

He further explained what additional information he had requested but did not receive from the husband and said it could have affected his valuation. The missing information included:

(1) Access to management or the opportunity to interview management;

(2) Detail of certain balance sheet and income statement accounts;

(3) Corporate governance documents, significant contractual relationships, and other relevant business information;

(4) Details of previous ownership transactions;

(5) Budgets and/or projections for the company; and

(6) Organizational chart depicting corporate structure.

Ultimately, the expert relied on the company's tax returns and financial statements from December 2005 through December 2008. At trial, he said that the valuation was based on a "reasonable degree of accounting certainty."

On cross-examination, the opposing counsel asked him to hypothesize about the difference in value if he did not make a normalized adjustment for the pension plan. The expert expressed reluctance to answer hypothetical questions. But ultimately he said the business would have had a hypothetical value of about $231,000. When counsel pressed him about whether the difference was "231 versus 1.9 million," he replied it was "231 against a million five thirty." He tried to explain that this was the value before adjusting for the life insurance policy—"I'm trying to be real clear"—but was cut off by counsel before he could finish his statement.

The husband claimed that, given the business's liabilities and limited access, it had no fair market value.

Trial court adopted the opinion of the wife's expert but used the cross-examination statements to rule the expert had modified his opinion based on assumptions the opposing counsel put to him and that applied to the case, and it determined the business was worth $1.5 million.

Inaccurate interpretation of expert's statements. Both parties appealed the trial court's valuation. The husband claimed multiple errors: (1) the trial court should have excluded the report and testimony of the wife's expert given his failure to appear at the scheduled deposition; (2) it should have excluded the opinion because of the untimely delivery of the expert report to the husband's counsel; (3) it was wrong to exclude the report of the husband's expert; and (4) it erred when it credited the valuation of the wife's expert, which was unreliable under the state's rule of evidence 702. The expert exhibited an "unfamiliarity with [the business] and its business structure." Specifically, he did not know about "relevant aspects" of the business, including Medicare and Medicaid regulations, the funding requirements for its defined pension plan, or even just its day-to-day operations.

The wife claimed the trial court abused its discretion in valuing the business at $1.5 million when evidence indicated its market value was $1.9 million.

None of the husband's arguments gained traction with the appeals court. It agreed with the trial court's attributing any delay in producing and submitting the expert report to the husband's conduct. Also, the husband himself produced his expert report late, which explained the trial court's limiting the scope of the testimony by the husband's expert, the appeals court found.

In terms of the valuation itself, it noted that the expert's lack of knowledge about "the intricacies" of the business stemmed from the husband's refusal to provide the information that the expert had requested and his refusal to consent to a site visit or management interview. The appellate court agreed with the trial court that the husband should not be rewarded for his conduct, which aimed "to prevent [the wife] from establishing a crucial part of her case, the value of the business." Under the circumstances, if there was an error in the basis of the expert's opinion, it was "invited," the appeals court added. Moreover, "within the confines of the information provided to him," the wife's expert developed a reliable opinion; he considered relevant literature in his field and any available financial data.

On the other hand, the appellate court found the wife's cross-appeal persuasive. At no point during the cross-examination did the wife's expert say the hypothetical questions "reflected the financial realities of [the business]." He also never agreed that the value should be reduced to $1.5 million. To the contrary, while the expert attempted to explain that neither hypothetical value included the adjustment made for the life insurance policy, the opposing counsel stopped him, the appeals court pointed out. Therefore, it concluded that the trial court's interpretation of the expert's responses did not accurately reflect "the context of his testimony" and remanded to the trial court to decide whether the $1.9 million value was appropriate.

In re Civic Partners Sioux City, LLC

Citation: 2013 Bankr. LEXIS 4225
Date of decision: Oct. 7, 2013
Experts: Steven Shaykett (creditors); Fred Lock (debtor)
Judge: Collins
State/Jurisdiction: Federal/Iowa
Court: United States Bankruptcy Court
Type of case: Bankruptcy
SIC: 6512 Operators of Nonresidential Buildings (except stadium and arena owners)

Plan Confirmation Hinges on Property Valuation

After declaring Chapter 11 bankruptcy, the debtor, a developer, asked the Bankruptcy Court to confirm the latest version of its reorganization plan in a "cram down" proceeding. Two key creditors objected, arguing that the plan rested on an improperly low valuation of the building complex that represented most of the collateral securing the claim. To resolve the issue, the court considered expert testimony on the value of the property.

Road to bankruptcy. In the early 2000s, Sioux City, one of the creditors involved in the case, invited proposals to revitalize a historic district. The debtor, a California real estate developer and his company, won the contract. The plan included building a movie theater complex with related retail spaces, including restaurants, bars, and similar services, as well as a hotel complex on an adjacent property. As part of the development agreement, the city offered cheap land and significant tax increment financing. The debtor received construction financing from a major bank, the other key creditor. The bank took a first mortgage and assignment of rents on the property in the amount of its loan whose principal sum was $5,625,000. Under the loan agreement, the city guaranteed the debtor's payments up to $300,000 per year to the bank. In addition, the debtor borrowed almost $2 million from the city. All parties agreed that the arrangement between the debtor and the city were subordinate to the debtor's obligations to the bank. The city had a second mortgage on the property.

The debtor only built the theater complex. It settled the city's claim that it had failed to perform on the hotel development. In 2004, it leased the theater space to a regional movie theater operator under an agreement that the tenant would pay "several categories of payments totaling $1.2 million in annual rent" and the debtor would fill up the vacant retail spaces with complementary tenants. Essentially, the theater operator was financing the debtor's whole project; its annual rental payment covered the debtor's debt service payments to the bank and the city. But construction on the site continued after the theater opened, and it had difficulty attracting moviegoers. Ultimately, its operator was unable to make even one full rent payment.

Relations between the debtor and the tenant deteriorated. The debtor never whipped the vacant retail space into ready-to-rent condition, and by 2009 it had decided not to put any more money into the project. Subsequently, an expert from the city testified about significant water and structural problems plaguing the building and requiring prompt fixing. Eventually, the debtor fell behind on its own payments to the bank, the city, and other lenders. Attempts among all the parties to restructure the entangled financial arrangements in mediation failed when the city decided not to support a proposed new arrangement because of the prior agreed-upon tax assessment and loan guarantees.

Among other things, the parties had contemplated an amended lease that lowered the annual rent payment to $900,000 to address the tenant's complaints, with one immediate $200,000 payment to make the new lease effective. Before it knew about the city's decision, the bank had taken steps to effect the loan modification for the debtor, and the debtor and the tenant had executed the amended lease. Once apprised of the city's decision, the bank cancelled its agreement and filed for foreclosure. The debtor initially adhered to the amended lease and collected on the $900,000 annual rent. But 12 days before declaring Chapter 11 bankruptcy, in April 2011, it reinstated the original lease, without obtaining the required consent from the bank. It never offered to pay the movie house operator back the $200,000 upfront payment or any of the $900,000 rent. For its part, the city sued the debtor for breach of contract based on its failure to pay on the city's additional loan. The debtor countersued and transferred all the actions to the Bankruptcy Court (N.D. Iowa).

Three reorganization plans. The debtor's first plan was based on reinstatement of the original lease. The debtor claimed that the tenant owed $3.2 million in back rent and it wanted equitable subordination of the creditors' claims. The bank called the plan "impossible to confirm," as it wrongly assumed that the tenant could afford to pay back rent or even was responsible for it and that the creditors did anything to justify equitable subordination.

Eventually, the debtor filed an amended plan that generated the same resistance from the creditors and the movie house operator. It contained a "new value" contribution from the debtor for $150,000, which the creditors found "woefully inadequate" to move the development ahead. In addition, it required reinstatement of the original lease, recovery of back rent, and equitable subordination.

When the lease issue took on urgency, the court ruled that the amended lease governed the case. Subsequently, the debtor filed a second amended plan—the subject of this case—under which it would continue to use the property that served as the bank's collateral. The latest plan sought to reduce the bank's secured claim and leave the city unsecured. At the same time, it contemplated full satisfaction of any smaller debt the debtor company's owner had guaranteed personally. Further, by way of a "new value" contribution in the amount of $150,000, the owner would keep an ownership interest in the reorganized business.

Not surprisingly, the bank and the city requested denial of the confirmation and dismissal of the case. Meanwhile, the movie house operator, satisfied about the lease ruling, backed off on most of its objections. In fact, at the time of the confirmation proceeding, its business was profitable. It was able to pay rent under the amended lease and wanted to stay in the space.

In response to the objections, the debtor asked for confirmation under the Bankruptcy Code's § 1129(b)(2) "cram down provisions."

Valuation of property. The bank and city's objection ultimately boiled down to one argument: that the plan was not feasible under the code's § 1129(a)(11). Specifically, it significantly undervalued the bank's secured claim. Proper valuation would leave the debtor unable to pay the secured claim in full as the applicable law required. (The bank submitted a total claim of over $6.2 million.) Also, the creditors argued, the plan was based on unreliable and unrealistic cash flow projections, and the debtor proposed to continue the same futile course with the same ineffectual management.

Because the bank had a first mortgage on the property and the property made up a large part of the total value of its security interest, valuation of the building was pivotal in determining the total value of the bank's secured claim. Both sides retained experts, who agreed that the discounted cash flow (DCF) method was the appropriate valuation technique but disagreed about variables that figured into the computation, including the length of time appropriate to measure cash flow and inputs for future cash flow.

1. *Debtor's expert.* Both experts used the seven years of annual rent that remained under the amended lease to project future cash flow. The debtor's expert used a 10-year holding period with a projected sale after 10 years. He said he believed the amended lease was substantially "above market" because it was paying off back rent from the original lease.

Fair market value rents would drop "precipitously," in years eight through 10. This decline in rent, in turn, would drive the property's resale value down sharply.

As comparables, he used an older movie theater project, as well as other commercial rent properties that did not function as movie houses.

He valued the property at $4.2 million, excluding repair-related deductions. As he saw it, no buyer would take the property without the requisite structural and drainage repairs, which amounted to $290,000, lowering the property's value to $3.91 million. He subsequently raised the repair costs by an additional $400,000 and decreased the property's value to $3.51 million.

2. *City's expert.* In contrast, the city's expert used a seven-year holding period with a projected sale after seven years. As he saw it, a prospective buyer would be more interested in the cash flow for the known and definite seven-year period than in adding three years of estimates. This was the most accurate forecast of how a buyer would determine value, he said. But he did give an estimate of Year 8 rent, which helped provide the proper reversion value for his calculation. For that value, he assumed the annual lease payment would be similar to the projections for the seven-year existing lease. But he applied a "generous discount" to account for the possibility—small, he believed—that the amount could drop after the seven-year period.

For comparables, he looked to one similar movie theater complex in Sioux Falls, S.D. This theater was geographically close to the one at issue; also both movie houses were similar in age and were part of economic development areas in their locations. They became the leading movie theaters in cities "that function as regional population centers." Moreover, he noted that, if the building's vacant spaces were improved to vanilla shell quality and the rent was lowered to $10 per square foot, the entire space could see full occupancy in three to four years. Avoiding a delay in building out the space, he believed, would improve the project's financial situation significantly. "[N]ewer dollars are worth more than future dollars."

He concluded the property was worth $5.54 million, including a downward deduction of $290,000 for the necessary repairs to the building. His valuation exceeded the debtor's appraisal by over $2 million.

3. *Court.* The court found several aspects of the debtor's valuation "entirely unpersuasive." For example, in assessing rent under the amended lease, the debtor's expert did not use a similarly situated movie theater. Even though he had more comparables than the competing expert, his selected properties were "less 'comparable.'" Moreover, he and the debtor strained to explain away the contradiction in the debtor's position as to the amended lease. On the one hand, the debtor had spent most of the case claiming that it had a right to reinstatement of the original lease, which provided for $1.2 million annual rent, and to $3.2 million in back rent under the original lease. On the other hand, its valuation expert testified that the amended lease was significantly above market value. "The Court finds those arguments hard to square."

All the evidence supported the city expert's central assumption that the current rents would continue. To show that the amended lease was near fair market value, he properly relied on a theater that was "a good comparable and good indicator of market value." Also, the theater operator had experienced an increase in revenue and had been able to pay the rent under the amended lease. If anything, the city expert's generous discount to account for a possible drop in lease payments may have produced too low an estimate. For these reasons, the court adopted the city expert's valuation.

However, it agreed with the debtor that the downward deduction for repairs should have been $600,000, not $290,000 as the city expert assumed. This modification resulted in a $5.23 million valuation for the property.

Effect of post-petition payments on secured claim. The bank received post-petition payments from the debtor because of its secured position. The parties reasoned these were appropriate because the case qualified as a "single asset real estate case" under the Bankruptcy Code, § 362(d)(3). In essence, the provision seeks to compensate secured creditors for the use of their collateral. (The court noted that none of the parties had ever asked it for a determination of whether the case indeed qualified as such.)

The valuation-related issue was how the payments affected the bank's secured claim. As the court noted, if the payments reduced the bank's secured portion of its claim, the amount the debtor had to pay in full to the bank would decrease, which would make the debtor's plan more feasible. Conversely, if the payments did not reduce the bank's secured portion but only the overall claim value, there would be no reduction in the amount the debtor had to pay, and the plan would be even less feasible. Courts have divided over the treatment of such payments: Some have added the post-petition rents to the secured portion and reduced the creditor's claim from the unsecured portion first; others have subtracted the payments from the secured portion and reduced it before affecting the unsecured portion.

Here the court concluded that the "addition approach" was more appropriate. In applying the approach, it found that the bank's post-petition security interest in rents increased its collateral, bringing the total value to over $5.5 million. This claim did not include any value the bank claimed for its security interest in "general intangibles," the court added.

The court's finding added yet another layer of support to its overall conclusion that the debtor's reorganization plan did not provide enough funds to fulfill its obligations. Under the plan, the debtor would likely "wind up in a future reorganization or liquidation," the court said.

Problematic cash flow projections. The court also agreed with the creditors' claim that there was no way that the debtor could pay off all its obligations over the life of the plan through its cash flow projections. For one, the projections were based on the undervaluation of the bank's secured claim. But other aspects of the projections were equally questionable.

Even though it was clear that the debtor needed to spend significant amounts of money immediately to turn the project around, until now, it had failed to put that value into it. Testimony showed that repair costs amounted to a minimum of $600,000 and certain defects demanded immediate attention. But the projections deferred most of the maintenance and repairs, without factoring in the greater future costs that would result from the delay. The projections also did not "realistically" address costs related to building out the vacant retail space. By the bank's "most persuasive" estimate, these exceeded $500,000. "That money simply does not appear in the near-term projections," the court found.

Repair and build-out costs were likely to rise above $1 million, said the court. But the debtor's plan only provided for a new value contribution of $150,000 augmented by $148,000 in the tenant improvement account. Even assuming all of these funds were available now, the debtor would still be short. The projections "simply reflect a hope that what did not work in the past will work in the future—without any new ideas or concepts for how that will happen," the court concluded, finding the debtor's reorganization plan not feasible and declining to confirm it.

Crews v. Crews

Citation: 2014 Cal. App. Unpub. LEXIS 4415
Date of decision: June 24, 2014
Experts: Tony Yip, CPA (court-appointed); Karen Kaseno, forensic expert
Judge: Irion
State/Jurisdiction: California
Court: Court of Appeal
Type of case: Marital Dissolution
SIC code: 1531 Operative Builders

Court Nixes Murky Business Goodwill Determination

Goodwill is a complicated concept and one that comes into play frequently in divorce cases involving a community interest in a spouse's business. Determining goodwill where a business is essentially a one-person operation presents an extra challenge for valuators. A recent California case illustrates just how confused experts can get when it comes to allocating and quantifying goodwill and how their confusion can transfer to the trial court, causing it to make findings that go against its own understanding of controlling case law.

Unsteady business. The husband was a real estate developer in the San Diego area who had almost three decades of experience building homes at the time of the divorce trial. Shortly before getting married, in 1998, he and the wife set up a company that they owned in equal shares. The wife ran the company's marketing department, and the husband ran the rest of the business. For years, the company grew steadily. In 2002, it recorded sales of about $17 million; in 2005, sales amounted to about $39 million. But debt also rose, from $6.4 million in 1999 to $25 million in 2004. In 2006, the company owed $26 million in construction loans and its sales dropped to $29 million. Aside from the jointly started business, the husband pursued a host of other business interests—judging from the appeals court's opinion, there were as many as 18 additional entities, but they seemed less central to the case. The couple's income also grew and fell drastically. In 1999, their adjusted income was about $1.5 million. In 2004, it climbed to $12.4 million and in 2005—when the real estate market in San Diego reached a peak—it was $18.9 million, including the sale of land. By 2006, it had fallen to $5.3 million.

Also, in 2005, the couple entered into a post-nuptial written agreement (PMA) that provided that all of the parties' property represented community property regardless of when the spouses acquired specific assets and whether the property was in the name of one spouse, both spouses, or a business. The PMA also specified that, in the event of divorce, the parties could request a separate property distribution that had to occur "forthwith." The husband could unilaterally transfer $5 million from the community estate to himself as separate property and the wife $126,000. The husband waited until October 2008 to request the $5 million. By then, the community assets had shrunk considerably in light of the crisis in the building industry and the real estate sector. Early in the divorce proceedings, the court gave the husband control of the business interests until there was a resolution of the case, finding that he "anchored" the enterprises. By the time of trial, he had received some $14 million in community assets for various business purposes, in addition to the $5 million PMA amount.

Straining to find goodwill. The parties stipulated to the appointment of an appraiser as the court's expert. He was a CPA, who brought in a forensic expert. The two experts valued the various business interests and analyzed incomes to determine spousal and child support. A major valuation concern was how to characterize and quantify the goodwill that went along with the various business operations, particularly the jointly owned business. The appraiser proposed a value of $474,000, which the trial court adopted. In his report, the appraiser talked about the "goodwill of Crews entities" ("Crews" was the parties' last name). In trial testimony, he said he determined the goodwill based on the husband's reputation for building quality houses in the past, his vendor relationship with subcontractors, his "know-how," and contacts. According to the appraiser, "all these would put him into a position such that *at the time when the market rebounds*, he would be able to leverage and capitalize on that to again get back into the business and generate profit. (emphasis in trial court's statement of decision) The appraiser assumed the husband would capitalize future business and invest $523,000 per year. But he also testified that "I cannot ... say I know for sure as of a *certain time in the future* when [the husband] would have the amount available." (emphasis in trial court's statement of decision) Moreover, the expert assumed that the husband would attract an equity partner—unidentified—and that "90 percent of the equity capital that's required would be kicked in by the financial partner who returned it at 50 percent profit." The husband's share would be 10% of the equity capital, "plus some seed money to secure loans."

The trial court found the appraiser's report and testimony problematic. "There are no entities," the court pointed out to the expert. "So you're really talking about his personal goodwill, are you not?" it asked. And it acknowledged that it had "trouble conceptually with this because it seems like we're talking about [the husband] personally." If so, then the appraiser's goodwill determination contradicted the controlling state case, which has held that, where the goodwill belongs to the natural person, as distinct from a business, there is no divisible goodwill. Based on precedent, the definition of "business" does not include "a person doing business" but refers "to a professional, commercial or industrial enterprise with assets, i.e., an entity other than a natural person." See *In re Marriage of McTiernan*, 2005 Cal. App. LEXIS 1692 (2005) (available at *BVLaw*). The *McTiernan* case involved a successful movie director; a majority of the court found that the "goodwill" the wife's expert found in the director's business was simply a prediction of the husband's future earnings capacity. According to the *McTiernan* court: "Something that cannot be ... sold has no value on the market. Dividing such a non-transferable quantity" would create an obligation without ensuring a source of funds.

In the case at bar, the expert explained to the trial court that he saw the husband and his businesses as the same. The jointly owned company may be going out of business, he explained, but "*later on when the market rebounds* we have [a successor company]." He added, "in my mind it's a continuum of a business that [the husband] has been in for ... 20, 30 years." (emphasis in trial court's statement of decision)

The forensic expert initially said the goodwill was attributable to the entities. When the trial court asked her if it was the husband's personal goodwill, she said it was goodwill "in the form of several entities at the moment." She explained that the husband was "capable of doing all of these tasks and all of these things that he clearly has been doing over the last few years in a bad market, and he has maintained relationships. He has … the knowledge and expertise to be able to in the future earn money at a level most people can't." The expert resisted the use of the term "personal goodwill": "I don't want you to use that term because I know that there's … case law that says personal goodwill versus other types. This is in an entity right now." The trial court responded it knew the entity had no goodwill. "I mean, I can look at that and see—what goodwill does an entity have that is defaulting on its debts, that is in trouble with the banks, and so forth? It clearly doesn't—to my way of looking at goodwill, it doesn't have it." On further questioning from the trial court, the forensic expert admitted that she was not defining the goodwill but instead was showing that the husband could earn money above the average real estate developer—which was the basis of her excess earnings analysis.

Notwithstanding its comments, the trial court accepted the appraiser's goodwill valuation of $474,000 and his underlying calculations and awarded the goodwill to the husband as a distinct asset. To add to the confusion, in its statement of decision, the trial court referred to the goodwill as "Husband's goodwill." In the subsequent judgment, it referred to the goodwill as "business goodwill." At the same time, the appraiser did not include goodwill in his calculation of the value of the jointly owned company or in valuing any of the other business entities.

Finding violates precedent. Both parties contested the trial court's property division in the Court of Appeal for various reasons. The husband particularly challenged the goodwill award saying there was insufficient evidence to support the court's $474,000 business goodwill. The wife claimed there was evidence that the trial court awarded business, as opposed to personal, goodwill to the husband.

The appeals court reviewed under the higher "abuse of discretion" standard. Unless the lower court's finding was "wholly unsupported" by the record, it would be upheld. The appeals court found two problems with the trial court's goodwill award: (1) the trial court awarded the husband personal goodwill, rather than the goodwill of any of his business entities; and (2) it improperly based the goodwill valuation on an expectation of future earnings. Both of the trial court's steps violated the principles of *McTiernan*,

In fact, the appeals court said, this case was analogous to *McTiernan*. Here, the expert's testimony and the trial court's statement of decision with its italicized language made clear that the goodwill determination was based on the husband's future earning capacity as a real estate developer. Like in *McTiernan*, the expert here focused on the husband's personal skill, reputation, and experience to find there was goodwill that was a divisible asset. The trial court itself recognized the problems with this approach when it suggested that the expert's goodwill valuation was subject to reversal under *McTiernan*. Yet, it adopted the expert's valuation, noting the husband's ability to generate excess earnings in the future to the extent he had done before the downturn once the market improved. A spouse's "skill, reputation and experience are not community property and may not be divided in a dissolution," the Court of Appeals pointed out. Further, goodwill must exist at the time of the dissolution and "that value must be established without dependence on the potential or continuing net income of the professional spouse," that is, relying on the spouse's future earnings.

According to the appeals court, even if the husband's potential future earnings were the proper basis for valuing his business interest, the expert's calculation in this case was too speculative to qualify as substantial evidence. The appraiser assumed that the husband would capitalize future business and would invest a certain amount per year but could not say when that would happen. He speculated that the husband would attract a business partner who would contribute 90% of the equity capital but did not identify anyone. He assumed the real estate market would recover in two or three years, but the husband estimated it could take three to five years. The expert admitted that the longer the recovery period, the smaller the goodwill number.

The appeals court noted that the testimony of the forensic expert regarding the nature of the goodwill "was ambiguous at best." Her assertions that the goodwill was in one or more business entities were conclusory. And, like her colleague, she based her goodwill calculation on the husband's ability to earn a substantial income in the future based on his skill and reputation as a real estate developer. Neither testimony represented evidence that there was goodwill in any of the community's business entities at the time of trial, the appeals court concluded. For all of these reasons, it was an abuse of discretion to award goodwill to the husband as a community asset.

Editor's note: There were other, related reasons, why the appeals court remanded the case. For example, the trial court awarded all of the "remaining" business interests to the husband at zero value rather than making specific findings as to their present value. The appraiser had in fact assigned a negative value to some of the interests, but the trial court assumed that the husband might be able to restructure their debt and turn them into positive assets. If that were the case, he would be fairly compensated for his continuing efforts, the trial court said. The appeals court rejected this approach. Also, it found the wife had a claim to damages for the husband's breach of the PMA since he did not request the $5 million "forthwith." His delaying meant the depletion of what little remained of the community assets, the wife argued. The appeals court remanded for a proper calculation of damages resulting from the delay. Stay tuned.

Crider v. Crider

Citation: 2014 Ind. App. LEXIS 416
Date of decision: Aug. 26, 2014
Experts: Thomas Sponsel, Brian Madden, Wayne Johnson (wife); Steven Riddle, Leo Lichtenberg (husband)
Judge: Barnes
State/Jurisdiction: Indiana
Court: Court of Appeals
Type of case: Marital Dissolution
SIC code: 1500 Building Construction General Contractors and Operative Builders

High Valuations Complicate Division of Sizable Marital Estate

In a recent divorce case involving a series of family businesses in which the husband owned interests, the trial court faced considerable hurdles to arrive at a valuation of the marital estate. A small army of experts gave conflicting opinions on how to account for a corporation's union pension liability and machinery and equipment and how to value the land and bond anticipation notes held by two other businesses. Moreover, the trial court had to devise a way to give the wife her share of the husband's ownership interests. It mandated an equalization payment that proved more of a problem than a solution, considering the illiquid nature of the husband's assets. The husband appealed the trial court's decision.

The husband, his father, and his brother owned a large number of businesses, the primary being a closely held S corporation that did road and other construction work. Both brothers held approximately 42.25% of the stock and the father the remaining 15.5%. The other companies were LLCs that seemed to develop real estate; two of these companies owned property in a planned unit development (PUD) site. The husband held a 33% interest in the two entities. All of the companies had agreements that restricted the transfer of shares or membership interests to other persons. The wife filed for divorce in 2006 and for legal separation in 2007, but these actions did not go forward. She filed another divorce petition in 2009. The husband's finances were "complicated." Although in the divorce proceedings he talked about the $72,000 salary he received from the S corp. as his only income, there was evidence that he earned much more. For one, the corporation regularly made sizable annual distributions to the three shareholders through 2007. In 2007, it distributed nearly $6.3 million on gross profits of $8.1 million. In 2009, the year of the divorce petition, its gross profits were over $8.9 million, but it made no distributions; instead, the shareholders loaned it nearly $3.4 million. They later explained that they did so at the request of the bonding companies. Other evidence suggested that the bonding companies made no such request and considered the company financially very sound.

For valuation purposes, the most controversial issues at trial and on appeal arose in connection with valuing the S corp. and the two land-owning LLCs. The valuation date was 2009.

1. Corporation valuation.

Pension obligation. One of the major disagreements among the experts in regard to the corporation was whether to reduce the company's value to account for what the husband claimed were unfunded union pension liabilities that amounted to $4.5 million. The husband's expert said he based the deduction on information from a construction industry group representative who said the amount reflected "estimated unrecorded economic liability associated with [the company's] portion of the unfunded pension plans." The expert's report also referred to a federal requirement that employers withdrawing from a multiemployer pension plan pay their proportionate share of the pension fund's vested but unfunded benefits. And the report pointed to a general problem of pension plan underfunding and employers having to account for an underfunded pension plan in the future when retires may withdraw more money than the plan can bear. The expert said the company's liability was "real" and it "will have to come out of the company's future cash flows, one way or another."

The wife's expert acknowledged that unfunded pension liability was a "major issue" in high-profile cases such as the General Motors bankruptcy but found it was not a concern in terms of valuing the company at issue. Although in 2009 the company's accountants stated funded pension liabilities, they did not mention unfunded liabilities. The wife's expert also mentioned that he had valued other construction companies and the issue of pension withdrawal liabilities under federal law "has never been even brought up in a single issue." Also, the two events that would trigger the federal law requirements—switching from union to nonunion labor or ceasing operations in the near future—were unlikely to occur here.

A second expert for the wife also said he had never seen a valuation report handle the issue in the way the husband's expert proposed. According to the second expert, it was inappropriate to show potential liability under federal law as an actual liability in 2009. He allowed that the issue might come up in negotiations around the sale of the company, but if it did it would be dealt with in the sales agreement, he said.

Machinery and equipment. The husband's accounting expert used appraisals based on sales of comparable equipment and machinery at auction and found the value ranged from about $9.6 million to $10.2 million. But the appraisals excluded equipment the company had owned in 2009 but gotten rid of before the appraisal occurred. In contrast, the wife's expert relied on an appraisal that used a "desktop" method and concluded the machinery and equipment was worth $20.1 million.

Ultimately, the wife's expert concluded the company's total value was $15.6 million and the husband's interest was worth over $4.3 million. The trial court largely accepted the valuations the wife's experts offered. In terms of the pension obligations, it declined to reduce the company's value by the $4.5 million the husband's expert set down. As for the machinery and equipment, the trial court noted there were flaws in each expert's report. It rejected the "desktop" approach that informed the value of the wife's expert, but it also found the husband's expert had failed to appraise all the equipment the company owned on the valuation date. Therefore, the court set the value at $11 million. It concluded that the corporation had a total value of about $10.1 million and the husband's interest was worth over $2.8 million, including discounts for lack of marketability and the nonvoting nature of many of the husband's shares.

2. Land-owning entities.

Land. The experts had serious disagreements as to how to value two LLCs that owned over 291 acres in the PUD site. In 2009, the land was only partially developed. The wife's expert was an experienced real estate appraiser with extensive knowledge of the area in question. He said the presence of a major university insulated the area's economy somewhat from the economic downturn. He tried to obtain estimates from the husband's brother about estimated costs of improving the land in compliance with the PUD requirements but was unable to do so. He made an educated guess that costs would amount to about $2.5 million. Also, in 2006, there was a sale of 84 acres to a major hospital in the area for $150,000 per acre. Applying a discount for the costs of development, the real estate appraiser concluded the land was worth approximately $9.6 million. He based his valuation on the highest and best use of the land as development property.

The husband's expert said that in 2009 real estate development was in bad shape. Many properties similar to the land at issue were abandoned to lenders because of the poor economic outlook. Also, the likelihood of further development was slim particularly given the PUD requirements. By his calculation, the total value of land was $1.8 million.

The trial court accepted the value the wife's real estate appraiser offered. This meant the husband's one-third interest in the two companies amounted to approximately $4.5 million.

BANs. A related issue was how to value bonds the company held. They were bond anticipation notes (BANs) the county had issued in 2005 in anticipation of the issuance of $7 million in tax increment financing (TIF) bonds in 2010. The county in fact issued the TIFs. Before it did so, its financial advisor cautioned the county not to guarantee repayment of the bonds through its full faith and credit and general taxing power. He mentioned the slow progress in developing the area and said the total assessed valuation of the land was far below the original projections.

In 2009, the company listed the BANs as an asset with a book value of nearly $5.8 million on its balance sheet. At issue for the valuators was what the likelihood of the county's repaying the TIF bonds was.

The wife's valuation expert used the $5.8 million book value given that this value appeared on the company's financial statements. Even if the county ended up not repaying the TIF bonds in full, any loss would show up in the company's 2021 financial statements, not its 2009 statements, he said. Also, the wife's real estate appraiser in appraising the land saw strong development potential in the area in 2009.

The husband's valuation expert contended the BANs' fair market value in 2009 was much less than the book value, as the testimony from the county's financial advisor proved. He concluded the BANs were worth $1.1 million.

The trial court considered the BANs an asset and used the $5.8 million book value.

3. Equalization payment. Ultimately, the trial court determined the total value of the husband's business interests was $11 million. There was little marital debt. Dividing the estate evenly in two meant that each spouse would receive $5.5 million. Because the wife received few liquid assets, the court prescribed an equalization payment to the wife in the amount of $4.7 million. To ensure payment, the court gave her a security lien on all of the husband's shares and ownership interests in the various entities if the husband failed to pay the judgment in full within 180 days.

The husband did not pay but filed an appeal with the state's Court of Appeals. He contested various aspects of the trial court's valuation of the corporation and LLCs and the equalization payment.

FMV not required. The Court of Appeals affirmed the lower court's valuations. As for the pension obligation, the appeals court said the trial court had testimony from two experts disfavoring a $4.5 million deduction in valuing the company in 2009, as opposed to one opinion from the husband's expert. Therefore, there was evidence that supported the trial court's accepting the treatment the wife's experts proposed. The appeals court also found support for the trial court's $11 million machinery and equipment value. It accepted the method and value the husband's appraiser chose but increased it to account for the "extra" equipment the husband's appraiser did not count.

As for the land appraisals, the appeals court said the case "highlights just how inexact property valuation is." Both experts in front of the trial court presented extensive reports and reasoning to support their valuations of the LLCs' real estate. The trial court had discretion to decide which opinion to accept. Concerning the BANs, there was no legal obligation that the trial court had to use the fair market value as opposed to book value or the original purchase price. The court's favoring the way in which the wife's expert treated the notes was not an abuse of discretion.

But the appeals court strongly disagreed with the trial court's use of a security lien against the husband's business interests to enforce the equalization payment. It recognized the difficulty of dividing interests in closely held businesses, particularly in this case, where the husband's net worth was tied up in his stock and membership interests in the various entities. There were not enough liquid assets to award the wife her share of the marital estate and completely avoid "some continued entanglement" of the spouses in the businesses, the appeals court noted. But it also said that the trial court should have done more to limit the entanglement. One way to do this, the appeals court suggested, is to give the wife an equitable interest only in the husband's nonvoting stock in the corporation. As a result, she would receive distributions, but she would not be able to participate in the management of the company. Consequently, the appeals court upheld the $4.7 million equalization payment and the underlying valuations but ordered the trial court to develop a less draconian method with which to enforce the equalization payment.

Dietz v. Jacobs

Citation: 2014 U.S. Dist. LEXIS 37144
Date of decision: March 21, 2014
Experts: Arthur C. Cobb (solvency-defendants); unknown (trustee)
Judge: Ericksen
State/Jurisdiction: Federal/Minnesota
Court: United States District Court
Type of case: Bankruptcy
SIC code: 3732 Boat Building and Repair

Court Admits Solvency Analysis Lacking Specific Valuation of Debtor

In a bankruptcy proceeding, the trustee filed a pretrial *Daubert* motion attacking the adjusted balance sheet and discounted cash flow analyses that the defendants' expert submitted to show solvency. As the court considered the arguments, it discussed the significance that the AICPA's valuation standards assume in a solvency analysis.

The debtor, a parent company and numerous subsidiaries, manufactured marine yachts sold to various dealers. On June 1, 2009, the companies filed for Chapter 11 bankruptcy, which subsequently became a Chapter 7 bankruptcy. The appointed trustee brought suits against various individual defendants to avoid preferential and fraudulent transfers under the Bankruptcy Code's Sections 547 and 548. Ultimately, the consolidated case wound up in federal district court (D. Minn.) for a jury trial.

Balance sheet a 'starting point.' To succeed under either Section 547(b) or Section 548, the trustee had to show that the debtor was insolvent at the time of transfer.

The defendants' expert was a CPA who concluded that during the relevant period—two years before bankruptcy—the parent company was a going concern and its assets were greater than its liabilities. His primary solvency analysis took an adjusted balance sheet approach. In his report, he explained that he started with the company's balance sheet as of May 30, 2009, which, he said, complied with GAAP. He acknowledged that GAAP-conforming balance sheets "do not include all assets, property, and liabilities, debts, and do not include assets at fair valuation." He called them a "starting point."

He then adjusted the numbers in two asset categories: (1) land, buildings, and operating equipment; and (2) trade names, trademarks, and intellectual property. Specifically, he added over $21.5 million to the first category and approximately $142.6 million to the second category to "reflect their 'fair' rather than 'book' value," he explained. Under the bankruptcy schedules, the company's liabilities exceeded its assets by over $68.2 million as of the petition date. Owing to the adjustments, the expert's analysis showed that assets exceeded liabilities by nearly $95.9 million.

The expert's report also noted that for the other categories the "fair value is estimated to be the reported value." And it included a separate section discussing "Unreported Liabilities" but did not state a definitive figure for those items. Moreover, even though the analysis focused on the May 30, 2009, balance sheet, the report stated that in general the company's assets decreased and its liabilities increased from June 2006 to June 2009. It concluded that, since the company was solvent on May 30, 2009, it likely was solvent during the relevant prior years.

In the report's brief section called "Valuation," there was scant reference to a discounted cash flow (DCF) analysis. Without providing specific numbers or inputs, the expert concluded that "representative estimates of prospective cash flow" indicated an equity value for the parent company of approximately $50 million as of May 30, 2009. In his deposition, the expert declared he developed numerous projections "that varied by the top line revenues" and he discussed several considerations (missing from the court's opinion). He did not remember what discount rate he had used.

Regarding the solvency of the related debtor entities, the report listed the subsidiaries' reported numbers for stockholder equity and intercompany balances for 2008 and 2009. In his deposition, the expert admitted he only "generally" analyzed the entities' solvency situation but said the numbers showed that the entities' assets exceeded the liabilities. In his words, "as went [the parent company], I believe so go the subsidiaries."

Vital DCF information missing. The trustee filed a *Daubert* motion to preclude the expert from testifying on solvency. Although the trustee did not challenge the expert's going concern analysis, he claimed that the valuation part of the analysis was unreliable and thus inadmissible.

1. The adjusted balance sheet analysis was deficient for two reasons:

(a) Violation of SSVS No.1. The trustee contended that the expert's approach did not meet the professional standards of the American Institute of Certified Public Accountants (AICPA). The standards (SSVS No. 1) require a financial expert to reach a "conclusion of value," which the defendants' solvency expert did not do. Specifically, he did not reach "a specific conclusion about the amount by which he believed" the parent company's assets exceeded its liabilities but only concluded that they exceeded them.

The court saw this issue differently. Here, the expert was not on the case to provide a valuation opinion for the parent company but to determine solvency under the Bankruptcy Code. Although the AICPA's standards list bankruptcy as one situation in which a valuation may occur, they do not indicate that solvency determinations under the Bankruptcy Code must result in a definitive valuation number, the court pointed out. The trustee failed to cite any other authority to the contrary.

Here, the court observed, the defendants' expert took the position that the "magnitude of excess" resulting from his two adjustments made other variations immaterial and allowed him to conclude that the company was solvent. The court agreed that there were weak areas in the report, but they did not render the testimony inadmissible. Rather, they were targets for cross-examination. For example, the report stated that for the other categories the reported values equaled the fair values but did not explain why; it also did not give a determinative number for the unreported liabilities.

(b) Improper use of book values. Next, the trustee claimed the expert used book value rather than fair market value because he only adjusted two asset values.

The court disagreed. True, the expert only performed two adjustments, but he analyzed the other categories and concluded that the reported values represented the fair value, said the court. Even if his conclusions were open to challenges, his opinion was admissible.

2. Details about the DCF were too sketchy.

The trustee claimed the expert failed to provide any of the numbers he used for his DCF analysis or data sources that resulted in his finding that the parent company's equity value was at least $50 million.

The court explained that a DCF analysis required:

> [E]stimating the periodic cash flow that a company will generate over a discrete time period, determining the "terminal value" of the company at the end of the period, and discounting each of the cash flows and terminal value to determine the total value as of the relevant date.

Here, said the court, the expert's report lacked the projected periodic cash flows, the terminal value, and the discount rate that led the expert to his conclusion. At his deposition, the expert could not recall the discount rate he had applied. His actual calculations were not available anywhere. According to the court, the trustee had no opportunity to explore and counter the specifics of the expert's analysis. It went on to say that "the omission cannot be overlooked," particularly since the expert claimed the DCF analysis stated the company's value as of the date that the company was poised to file for bankruptcy.

Accordingly, the court precluded the expert from discussing the DCF analysis and his conclusion resulting from it.

3. Missing solvency analyses for subsidiaries.

The trustee also objected to any statements regarding the solvency of the related debtor entities because the expert did not analyze those businesses separately from the parent company.

The court agreed that a particularized analysis was appropriate under the Code's provisions for preferential and fraudulent transfer claims and under case law: "Moreover, a parent company's solvency does not necessarily imply solvency of its subsidiaries."

Here, the defendants' expert admitted he only "generally" analyzed the solvency situation of the subsidiaries and his report only quoted financial statement numbers without any explanation as to why it was unnecessary to make further adjustments. Also, the defendants failed to show that the solvency of the parent company implied the solvency of the subsidiaries.

Therefore, the court also precluded the expert from testifying on solvency as it related to the subsidiaries.

Diez v. Davey

Citation: 2014 Mich. App. LEXIS 2041
Date of decision: Oct. 23, 2014
Judge: Hoekstra
State/Jurisdiction: Michigan
Court: Court of Appeals
Type of case: Expert Testimony
SIC code: 3728 Aircraft Parts and Auxiliary Equipment N.E.C.

Court Deems Treatment of S Corp Undistributed Income 'Problematic'

How does the law treat undistributed income from a parent's S corporation for purposes of determining child support? This was the central question in a recent child custody case. The lower court relied on expert testimony that attributed to the owner parent income based on a CPA expert's "excess working capital" approach. Industry data indicated the owner parent could have taken more money out of the company than he had done in the past while still maintaining a viable business, the expert said. The parent appealed.

Capital-intensive industry. The plaintiff was the sole shareholder of a business that manufactured precision gears used in the aerospace industry. It was organized as an S corp. The plaintiff explained that the industry was "majorly capital intensive" and required the company to purchase new equipment regularly to stay competitive. The purchases, which occurred almost every year, could range from a few hundred thousand dollars to over $2 million per machine. The company needed to have cash on hand.

The owner and his partner had three children and were together for 16 years. After they separated, the owner sued for custody. Child support was one of the contested issues. It first came before the Friend of the Court (FOC) referee, who held an evidentiary hearing that featured three CPAs testifying as experts on the available income for child support from 2008 through 2011. They reached different conclusions. Ultimately, the referee adopted the opinion of one expert.

Conservative business model. The expert estimated the business owner had an average income of $723,000 over a three-year period and an average income of nearly $1.1 million over a four-year period. He reviewed the plaintiff's W-2 statements, interest and dividends, actual distributions, perks, and "additional monies available for income, or for payment of child support, that aren't in any of the other four categories." He also included sums the company distributed to the owner for the payment of taxes on corporate earnings retained by the company.

The "additional monies" category included a portion of what he called "excess working capital." The expert determined the amount of "excess working capital" by using the "Bardahl formula." He first calculated "working capital" and then determined how much the company required to pay for operating expenses. Any amount beyond this was "excess." In his opinion, 60% to 65% of the company's excess working capital was available for distribution in any given year. He admitted that his percentage determination was not based on any existing studies. Rather, the numbers seemed reasonable to him when compared with the company's requirements. He also said he compared the company to other businesses and found it followed a more conservative business model. Specifically, it had more cash and less debt than other companies in the same industry. Twenty-two percent of its total assets were in cash, and it had a zero debt-to-capital ratio; in contrast, other companies kept 6% of their total assets in cash and had an average debt-to-capital ratio of 20%. He maintained that a distribution of additional capital would not hurt the company because it could assume debt to finance new machinery, rather than following its historical practice of paying with cash.

The referee adopted the expert's opinion and recommended child support based on the determination that the plaintiff's average monthly gross income for 2010 and 2011 was approximately $74,000. This amount included distributions to the plaintiff to meet the company's tax liability, which the referee concluded were the plaintiff's liability.

After the plaintiff objected to the recommendation, the trial court reviewed the matter anew. The issue, it said, was whether the FOC referee had erred when it credited the expert's testimony. State law treats "the income of an S corporation as the income of the S corporation's shareholders," the trial court noted. Therefore, the expert properly considered the income of the plaintiff's company as the plaintiff's income. According to the court, because the expert only considered "excess working capital," rather than all of the corporation's income, as available for distribution, the expert's analysis actually worked to the plaintiff's advantage. The trial court found no error and accepted the conclusion that 60% to 65% of excess working capital was available for distribution. However, it used a three-year, rather than a two-year, average, which yielded a net monthly income of over $35,700. The trial court did not discuss the tax liability payment.

'Historical patterns.' The plaintiff appealed the findings to the state's Court of Appeals, which reviewed the trial court's order under the abuse of discretion standard.

The starting point for the appeals court was the state's child support statute and the formula it prescribed for determining a parent's net income. The income calculation under the formula was not the same as take-home pay or net taxable income, the court clarified. The purpose was to establish "how much money a parent *should* have available for support," the court stated with emphasis. The formula provides a list of forms of compensation that courts trying to calculate the income of a business owner, executive, or self-employed person should consider closely. The concern underlying the statute is the potential for manipulation. Since business owners or executives have more control over their compensation, they may be able to "arrange compensation to reduce the amount visible to others looking for common forms of income." The statute required courts to consider "historical patterns" when it came to making distributions to determine whether a parent used the business to shield money from child support consideration.

The Court of Appeals first found that the statute did not identify undistributed corporate profits as income available to a parent where there was no evidence that the owner parent reduced distributions in a departure from historical practices. According to the court, "it would be inappropriate to adopt a bright-line rule including undistributed earnings retained by an S corporation within the calculation of a parent's income ... in all circumstances."

The court rebuffed the expert's "excess working capital" analysis, which, it said, would attribute income to a parent based on industry averages. While the statute does seek to uncover what income a parent has or *should* have available, it does not require a parent owner to "revamp … reasonable and historical business practices in favor of alternative methods" of running the company to make more funds available.

The expert's opinion was "problematic," the court said. He disregarded the company's historical practices and substituted his own judgment for that of the plaintiff as to how to manage the company. Instead of focusing his analysis on how the company was run, he focused on how the company *could* be run. He failed to show that the plaintiff's management was outside the realm of the reasonable or that the undistributed profits were for unnecessary or illegitimate business expenses or ran counter to the company's historical distribution patterns. There was no basis for his conclusion that 60% to 65% was "excess working capital," the appeals court said. By the expert's own admission, it simply represented his business judgment.

Further, the appeals court found the expert's calculation of income wrongly included funds distributed by the business to the taxpayer for the payment of taxes on earnings retained by the corporation. Electing S corp status was a tax strategy, the court noted. The child support statute was clear that funds distributed for the payment of taxes under this corporate model were not indicators of what the parent had or should have available for child support and must not be attributed as income to the shareholder parent. Based on these errors, the Court of Appeals remanded the matter to the trial court for a redetermination of income available for child support.

Dominion Liquid Technologies, LLC v. GT Beverage Co., LLC

Citation: 2014 U.S. Dist. LEXIS 87075
Date of decision: June 26, 2014
Experts: unknown (plaintiff); Daniel E. McMackin (defendants)
Judge: Litkovitz
State/Jurisdiction: Federal/Ohio
Court: U.S. District Court
Type of case: Damages
SIC code: 2086 Beverages, soft drink (including artificially carbonated waters), manufacturing

Failure to Specify Offset Value Does Not Preclude Expert's Admissibility

In a breach of contract action, the defendant used expert testimony to argue for an offset regarding the damages it owed. The plaintiff attacked the expert opinion in a *Daubert* motion, saying it was irrelevant and thus inadmissible since the expert failed to quantify in dollars and cents the benefit it allegedly received from installing a piece of equipment it did not really need but bought in reliance on the contract. The court took a broader view.

The plaintiff was a beverage blending, bottling, and packaging plant. The defendant (and its successor in interest) developed and marketed beverages including the proprietary "Sportastic" line of drinks that it sold in a patented spherical bottle. The parties agreed that the plaintiff would become the defendant's Midwest bottling company. To accommodate the unique design of the Sportastic bottle, the plaintiff had to install a new bottling line (Line 3), which had two components: a "front end," or "wet end," which mixed, bottled, and capped the Sportastic product, and a "back end," or "dry end," which packaged and wrapped the product. Ultimately, the defendant cancelled the contract. The plaintiff sued (S.D. Ohio), and the court found the defendant liable for breach of contract and ordered reliance damages. At trial, the issue was the damages amount.

Potential for significant production value. By way of expert testimony, the defendant sought to show that the plaintiff received a monetary benefit from the newly installed line whose value would offset some or all of the damages it owed to the plaintiff. The expert had degrees in business and economics and 30 years of experience in the field of beverage production equipment. He currently was the president of an engineering firm specializing in the manufacture and engineering of food and beverage production lines and had done work for the beverage giants PepsiCo and Coca-Cola.

The expert reviewed documents reflecting purchasing and installation costs and the deposition testimony of the plaintiff's president. He also met with the president, inspected the Line 3 equipment, and reviewed proposals from equipment manufacturers. He determined that the front-end portion had "significant value" to the plaintiff because it allowed the plaintiff to produce diverse products and also significantly increased flexibility in production by adding tankage and blend area capacity.

He said that components of Line 3 were worth $303,000; the entire line's liquidation value ranged from $250,000 to $300,000. The cost of duplicating the line as it sat in the plaintiff's facility was over $1 million. By his calculation, the value of Line 3 was greatest to the plaintiff as a going concern as opposed to its value to another bottling facility. Based on variables related to line efficiency and production rates, he explained that Line 3 could generate production values to the plaintiff of $1.2 million to $1.68 million, depending on the margin per 12-pack case. He concluded the "going concern potential value" was $1.5 million.

The expert pointed out that the valuation of Line 3's front end was based in part on the fact that the plaintiff had used this component. It represented running equipment. In contrast, he valued the back-end portion as offline equipment. He determined its "in place value replacement cost" was $400,000. If this component were used to provide variety packages, he said, it would be worth $250,000 to the plaintiff "after a $50,000 to $100,000 reconfiguration investment." He concluded it would be "unwise to liquidate the [back end] equipment since so little demand exists for it." In his deposition, he allowed that another appraiser could reach entirely different conclusions.

What about 'reasonable certainty'? The plaintiff attacked the opinion in a *Daubert* motion, contending the proposed testimony was irrelevant and based on an unreliable methodology. As to relevancy, the expert's going-concern valuation failed to quantify the benefit the plaintiff derived from using Line 3; also, he failed to address the plaintiff's need for the line. Simply put, the plaintiff was able to maintain its production levels without using Line 3; therefore, the technology had no value to the plaintiff. As to reliability, the expert's opinion represented prohibited ipse dixit. In assessing the value of Line 3's front end, he merely relied on his experience and he admitted that someone else working in the field could come up with a totally different appraisal of Line 3's value.

The plaintiff countered that the defendant's claim that it had no need for Line 3 was irrelevant. The plaintiff had used the front end of the line and consequently had received a financial benefit from it; this value had to offset the damages amount. The expert's opinion was relevant since it assisted the trier of fact in assessing the benefit to the plaintiff and in calculating the award. His capacity-based going-concern valuation was a "logical method" for estimating the value of the front end, which, unlike the back end, was used in the plaintiff's production. In general, the expert's valuations were based on his specialized knowledge of similar bottling lines and were admissible.

The court sided with the defendant. There was no question that the expert's knowledge, experience, and education qualified him as an expert under *Daubert*. As for the expert's failure to provide specific dollar amounts of the benefit the plaintiff had realized from its use of Line 3 in his report and deposition, the court acknowledged that case law required the defendant to show the offsetting benefit with reasonable certainty. But, said the court, the inquiry for the purpose of determining relevance under *Daubert* did not hinge on whether he "has put forth precise damages calculations." It was whether the testimony assisted the court in understanding the evidence or determining a fact at issue. Here, the expert's specialized knowledge and his opinion as to costs and values of bottling production line equipment were "certainly relevant."

The court also was not persuaded by the plaintiff's ipse dixit argument. Here, the expert's opinion rested on more than "he, himself, said it." The expert reviewed pertinent documents, met with the plaintiff's president, and inspected Line 3. He also based his findings on his decades of professional experience in the field. There was a reliable foundation for his opinion. Saying that another appraiser could arrive at different conclusions did not make the expert's opinions ipse dixit. The court concluded that under *Daubert* the plaintiff's attacks went to weight, not admissibility, and allowed the valuation testimony in.

Dynetix Design Solutions, Inc. v. Synopsis, Inc.

Citation: 2013 U.S. Dist. LEXIS 120403
Date of decision: Aug. 22, 2013
Experts: Dr. William H. Black (plaintiff); unknown (defendant)
Judge: Grewal
State/Jurisdiction: Federal/California
Court: United States District Court
Type of case: Intellectual Property
SIC: 7372 Prepackaged Software (mass reproduction of software)

Finding 'Smallest Salable Unit' Does Not End Royalty Base Analysis

Patent litigation is a little like football, where "new schemes come and go faster than teenage fashion trends," said the court in a recent *Daubert* ruling. *Daubert* motions once were rare, but a few high-profile successes have made it obligatory for trial lawyers to challenge the other side's patent damages expert, despite the "exceedingly small" success rate. But every so often the challenge has traction, the court went on to say. "This case presents just such an instance."

The plaintiff developed design verification tools, and the defendant was a leading company in the electronic design automation industry. One of the defendant's verification products contained a protected design-level parallelism (DLP), among numerous other features. The plaintiff sued for patent infringement, initially based on two accused features. During the course of litigation (N.D. Cal.), only the DLP feature remained in the case and formed the basis of the plaintiff's damages claim. The plaintiff retained an expert to calculate reasonable royalty damages resulting from a hypothetical negotiation using the *Georgia-Pacific* factors as a framework.

As to the royalty base, the expert used the sales data from the defendant's entire verification product, reasoning that this was the smallest salable unit that included the patented component. He made no further apportionment to account for the product's many nonpatented parts.

As to the rate, he relied on the assumption that the patent was valid and there was liability, but there was no other information. His experience, he said, suggested that a "starting point for a reasonable royalty rate is half of the gross margin of the infringing products." This meant "divid[ing] the gross margin of the product between the parties." Accordingly, he split the 76.7% profit margin he had calculated into half and applied the *Georgia-Pacific* factors to the remaining 38%. Concluding that (1) there were no other similar licenses he could consider, (2) a hypothetical license would be nonexclusive, and (3) the plaintiff was willing to sell a license, he reduced the rate to 19%. Next, he found that the plaintiff lacked a successful product, which prompted him to cut the rate in half again, to 9.5%. However, based on "strong evidence of the value of the parallel simulation technology of the patent," he increased the rate to reach a final 14.25%. When he multiplied the royalty base by the royalty rate for the relevant period, he obtained a reasonable royalty of about $156 million.

To account for the exclusion of one of the two accused features from the case, he apportioned 75% of the royalty to the feature that remained in suit and 25% to the nonaccused part, leading to a $117 million royalty claim.

Worse than 25% rule of thumb. The defendant argued the testimony was inadmissible as to the royalty base and royalty rate under Fed. R. Evid. 702 and *Daubert*. The court agreed that both aspects of the expert's analysis were problematic.

1. *Royalty base analysis.* At the outset, the court acknowledged the difficulty in calculating a royalty base in a product where one component has patent protection, while other components do not. "Courts—including, to be fair, this one—have struggled with whether and how to evaluate an apportionment of the royalty base in this scenario." The court looked to precedent for guidance. Under the Federal Circuit's decision in *Lucent*, absent evidence that the infringing feature drives demand, the patent holder must apportion the royalty base to isolate the value of a patent-related feature. But *Lucent* did not deal with the critical issue "of exactly how one is to apportion the base," said the court in this case.

Under Chief Judge Rader's holding in *Cornell*, a patent holder must use the smallest salable unit as the starting point for the royalty base analysis. However, this principle, said the court here, did not imply that apportionment necessarily stopped with the smallest salable unit; rather, *Cornell* expressly rejects the use of the entire market value where the patented feature is not driving consumer demand for the product that contains it. Put differently, there is no logical basis to drop the apportionment requirement in a case "where the alleged smallest salable unit plainly is *not* closely tied to the patented feature," the court in the case at bar concluded. It also noted that *LaserDynamics*, another precedent, supported its conclusion. There, the Federal Circuit emphasized that if the smallest salable unit were an entire computer, the "exceedingly difficult and error-prone task of *discerning the [protected feature's] value relative to all other components* in the laptop" still remained.

In the case at bar, the protected component, DLP, was an *optional* feature in the defendant's product, and it was just one component, the court stated with emphasis. Instead of pinpointing DLP's value relative to the product's other components, the plaintiff's expert made a blanket assumption that his analysis ended with his determination that the defendant's entire product was the smallest salable unit. Because the expert "improperly skipped this task of apportionment," his royalty base was fundamentally flawed and the opinion was inadmissible on this basis alone, the court said.

2. *Royalty rate analysis.* The expert's rate analysis also violated a patent law principle, the court noted. Specifically, his presumption that a 50-50 split of the gross margin for the infringing product between the parties would be "one reasonable starting place" runs afoul of *Uniloc*. In that seminal case, the Federal Circuit emphatically rejected the "now-infamous 25% 'rule of thumb' (i.e., an assumption that 25% of the profit margin was a reasonable place for starting a royalty rate determination)." The rule of thumb was based on studies of previous, unrelated commercial licenses.

Here, the court pointed out, the plaintiff expert's choice was, if anything, "more arbitrary" because he simply relied on his own experience and judgment on how to apportion profits where there was no other information. He did not point to any evidence that might support his conclusion that a 50% starting place applied to components such as DLP in the industry in which the parties operated. Notwithstanding the difficulty in arriving at a proper baseline where there are no prior licenses for the DLP patent, "the analysis must be based on industry evidence and must consider the relationship between the patented feature and the accused products to determine a case and party specific starting point." Because the expert failed even to account for the small and optional role DLP played in the accused product, the royalty analysis, too, was inadmissible.

Referencing *Cornell* again, where Chief Judge Rader showed leniency, the court said it was "loathe" to strip the plaintiff of all damages expert testimony and gave it one more opportunity to present a new expert report on the issue.

Note: All of the cases the district court cites are available at *BVLaw.*

Ferolito v. AriZona Beverages USA LLC

Citation: 2014 N.Y. Misc. LEXIS 4709
Date of decision: Oct. 14, 2014
Experts: Z. Christopher Mercer, Christopher Stradling (plaintiff); Richard S. Ruback, Shannon Pratt (defendant)
Judge: Driscoll
State/Jurisdiction: New York
Court: New York Supreme Court (Trial Court)
Type of case: Judicial Dissolution
SIC code: 2086 Bottled and Canned Soft Drinks and Carbonated Waters

Court Relies on DCF to Derive Value of 'Sui Generis' Company

Only a week after a New York trial court issued its contentious discount for marketability ruling, another New York court discussed DLOM when it presided over a fair value proceeding that featured an "extremely successful company," extremely combative business partners, and extremely well-known valuators. This appraisal case is also noteworthy for its sole reliance on the discounted cash flow method and its analysis of the variables underlying the DCF.

Backstory. In 1992, the plaintiff and the defendant founded AriZona, by now the largest privately owned beverage company in the United States. The company encompasses multiple businesses that produce beverages and food- and beverage-related products. AriZona is also a leader in the ready-to-drink (RTD) tea market and noncarbonated beverage market.

Both partners were equal shareholders. The company's EBITDA, including normalizing adjustments to its financial statements for management fees, officer compensation, and nonrecurring expenditures, for the last 12 months ending Sept. 30, 2010, was approximately $173 million. Since the company's foundation, the plaintiff and the defendant have received over $500 million per side in distributions.

Expressions of interest. A few years into the business venture, the plaintiff and the defendant were falling out but for the good of the business decided that the defendant should take control of the day-to-day decisions. The partners also made a "One Captain" agreement under which the defendant would have final authority over the company's business. Pursuant to a second contract, the owners' agreement, they limited the transfer of shares in AriZona to a designated class of transferees.

At one time or another, two rivals in the beverage industry expressed interest in acquiring part or all of AriZona. One was Tata, a global conglomerate that, due to its ownership of Tetley Tea, was the second largest tea manufacturer in the world. In 2005, Tata estimated AriZona might be worth as much as $4.5 billion, and it has come up with similar estimates over the past 10 years. But Tata never performed due diligence on AriZona and never obtained board approval for pursuing an acquisition.

The other potential acquirer was Nestle, which recognized AriZona's high growth rate and superior distribution system. But Nestle said it was unable to obtain "good financial data," calling AriZona's information "woefully inadequate for a proper due diligence." There were no audited financial records. Also, Nestle wanted to secure a "path to control" on which both partners agreed. In July 2010, Nestle expressed interest to buy the plaintiff's shares for $1.3 billion conditioned on its ability to conduct due diligence, to eventually acquire the defendant's shares, and to reach an agreement with both partners to control the company. After the plaintiff rejected the proposal, Nestle increased the amount to $1.45 billion. Ultimately, discussions foundered. There was no binding offer, and Nestle's board of directors never authorized any acquisition of AriZona.

At some point, the plaintiff himself offered to buy the defendant out for $2 billion, but it was not clear how serious this offer was and whether there was funding behind it.

In the end, the transfer restriction in the owners' agreement and the plaintiff's failed attempts to sell his shares prompted him to sue for the dissolution of the company in October 2010. In return, the defendant decided to pursue a buyout under New York Business Corporation Law Section 1118.

A trial on the valuation issue took place from May 2014 to July 2014 and featured a gaggle of witnesses, including illustrious business appraisers whose contributions to the field the court noted. The instant ruling represents the New York Supreme Court's (trial court's) determination of the fair value of the plaintiff's shares.

No synergistic value. Investment value is often the most appropriate method to value a closely held corporation, the court said at the start of its analysis. This method allows for the use of DLOM, for the purpose of recognizing that "a potential investor would pay less for shares in a close corporation because they could not readily be liquidated for cash," the court explained, citing *Friedman v. Beway Realty Corp.*, 87 N.Y.2d 161 (1995) (available at *BVLaw*).

Although the court may consider a company's past performance and future events "known or susceptible to proof," it must not consider "strategic" or "synergistic" value to a hypothetical buyer, the court went on to say. To include synergistic elements in the valuation—as the plaintiff urged—would be speculating about the future. Accordingly, the court decided to use the "financial control" measurement absent any expectation of synergies.

Lack of comparable transactions. Both parties used a discounted cash flow (DCF) analysis and both agreed that the net asset value (NAV) approach was inappropriate in this case. But the plaintiff's experts also militated in favor of using a comparable transaction analysis, albeit weighting the resulting value at only 20% and assigning the remaining 80% to the DCF value.

The defendant objected that the proposed comparables were not sufficiently similar in size, timing, and products and were "synergistic market transactions" that the controlling case law did not recognize.

The court agreed with the defendant. AriZona, it said, was "truly *sui generis*, and thus any attempts to find comparable companies are truly lacking." The court gave numerous reasons that distinguished the company, including its "extremely advantageous position in the RTD tea market"; its uncertain S corp status; its difficulty in achieving audited financial statements, due in part to the partners' constant battles; and open questions as to how an acquirer would gain control of AriZona.

But even assuming there were comparable companies, there were no comparable transactions around the valuation date, the court added. The transactions on which the plaintiff's experts relied not only preceded the valuation date, but also preceded the 2008 recession, which caused the economy to reel even years later. There were few mergers in any industry, not to mention industries comparable to the market in which AriZona operated around the relevant date, involving companies with sales or EBITDA of the size of AriZona's, the court concluded.

The court also found the expressions of interest from Tata or Nestle unreliable indicators of the value of AriZona. Those companies made preliminary statements that left critical issues open. Neither company had access to audited financials or was able to do due diligence, and neither company's board of directors had approved an acquisition.

In sum, the only method that could provide a reliable value calculation was the DCF, the court decided.

DCF input issues. The parties' experts differed on a number of variables.

1. *Projections.* One of the plaintiff's experts was the founder of a consulting and marketing research organization focusing on the global beverage industry. He determined that the RTD market in the U.S. grew at a compounded annual rate of 2% in the five years prior to 2010. AriZona, in turn, grew at a greater rate and outpaced its competitors. He predicted continuing growth due to the company's short, two-month, "innovation timeline—its ability to quickly conceive and market a new product." The court found him credible and adopted his domestic growth projections. It also found reliable his prediction that AriZona could capture part of the international market, considering its success domestically against Nestea and Lipton.

The court dismissed the bleak opinions the defendant's experts gave as to the company's future prospects. The company recorded a 25% increase in sales from 2008 to 2010, which contradicted the grim view, the court pointed out. It noted that it served the defendant's interest to paint as dim a picture as possible about the company's future, "lest the value of the company (and thus [the defendant's] obligation to [the plaintiff]) increase."

By extension, the court credited the revenue forecast the plaintiff's business valuator developed based on the growth projections. It found the projected 10.2% compounded annual growth (CAGR) rate was consistent with, and perhaps even conservative in comparison to, the company's 13.9% CAGR from 2006 to 2010.

2. *Costs.* Given the company's "unique ownership and financing structure," AriZona's EBITDA margins were consistent with its sales. The plaintiff's valuator based his estimate of future costs on the company's past costs. The defendant's expert assumed total costs would track inflation. He said his forecast was a "reasonable simplification." The plaintiff's expert criticized this approach because it relied on a business plan that had no support in the historical data. It assumed the defendant and the company's management were incompetent and not capable of adjusting to changing business conditions, the plaintiff's expert said. The court credited his testimony.

3. *Terminal value.* The plaintiff's expert projected the company would grow at a 4.5% rate based on expected inflation and real growth in domestic product. The court credited the testimony, while also noting it might be overly conservative considering the significant growth the expert anticipated and the court credited. At the same time, the court rejected the defendant expert's terminal value, which, it said, unreasonably assumed a company in decline.

4. *Tax amortization benefit.* Based on a directive from the plaintiff's tax attorney, the plaintiff's valuator included a tax amortization benefit in his calculation while admitting that he had never done so in valuing similar companies.

The defendant's expert, an accountant, attacked the application of this benefit as an "unjustified windfall" to the seller. The court agreed with the criticism, noting that including the benefit would make an S corp. more valuable than a C corp. when there was no evidence that buyers pay more for the former than for the latter.

5. *"Key man" discount.* Based on the defendant's significant contributions to the success of the company, the court found that some form of key person discount was applicable in this case. AriZona employees testified to the defendant's great work ethic and business acumen. One of the defendant's experts acknowledged that such a discount might be appropriate and said that a "key person discount can be reflected in adjustment to a discount or capitalization rate in a DCF." Nevertheless, the defendant's valuation did not include it.

The plaintiff's expert, on the other hand, "quantified" the defendant's role by incorporating the calculation into his discount rate. The court adopted his assessment.

6. *DLOM.* The court noted another trial court's recent ruling against the application of DLOM where there was no real liquidity risk because the business at issue probably would never be for sale. See *Zelouf Int'l Corp. v. Zelouf*, 2014 N.Y. Misc. LEXIS 4341 (Oct. 6, 2014) (featured in this issue of *Business Valuation Update*).

The question was how this court would rule. The defendant's expert advocated in favor of a 35% DLOM. The owners' agreement was proof that the partners could not easily liquidate their shares, the expert said. There were other obstacles, including the lack of audited financial statements for the years prior to the valuation date; the fierce court battles between the parties; and the uncertain S corp status.

The plaintiff's expert maintained there was no justification for a DLOM. The company had been successful, and major companies had expressed an interest in buying part or all of it.

The court swiftly distinguished the circumstances in this case from those confronting the *Zelouf* court. Here the liquidity risk was real, it said. None of the expressions of interest ever led to a bona fide offer. The stalled Nestle negotiations exemplified the plaintiff's difficulty in liquidating his shares. But even though a DLOM was appropriate, the court rejected the 35% rate the defendant's expert proposed. The difficulties were not insurmountable, it said. For one, the defendant's expert acknowledged that many closely held private companies did not have audited financial statements; also, the litigation would come to an end once one partner's interest was acquired, and reasonable minds could differ over the company's S corp status.

The court found a 25% DLOM was appropriate, noting that the defendant's expert, a recognized authority on valuations, allowed that "smaller discounts are often appropriate for large and growing companies." This described AriZona, the court said.

7. *"Bad acts."* The defendant accused the plaintiff of compromising the company's success with his numerous "bad acts." Accordingly, he urged the court to reduce any payout to the plaintiff.

The court rejected this argument. The plaintiff's conduct resulted from his growing frustration of not being able to sell his shares in the company, it noted. According to the court, he was not a "sophisticated, urbane businessman." For example, he signed the owners' agreement without fully understanding the consequences of his consent. While some of his actions might have been "immature," his motivation was consistent: "to get appropriate value for his share of the company," the court explained.

Further, the defendant failed to show a causal connection between the plaintiff's conduct and damage to the company. By many accounts, the company actually was thriving while the plaintiff performed his "bad acts."

Vague valuation. The court acknowledged that a precise value of the partners' shares was not yet available due to a host of necessary adjustments to the DCF analysis. The court's "back-of-the-envelope" calculation suggested the company's value was approximately $2 billion in October 2010, the court said. After applying a 25% DLOM to the plaintiff's share and adding a 9% prejudgment interest, the value of his share currently was around $1 billion and "may well exceed $1 billion on the date that the Court enters judgment." Future proceedings also would deal with the company's ability to pay and the conditions and terms of a payout, the court added.

Finby v. Finby

Citation: 2013 Cal. App. Unpub. LEXIS 9097
Date of decision: Dec. 18, 2013
Experts: Andrew Hunt, CPA (wife); Quinton Ellis, Industry Analyst (wife); Stephen Zamucen, CPA (husband); Howard Buchler, Industry Analyst (husband)
Judge: Rylaarsdam
State/Jurisdiction: California
Court: Court of Appeals
Type of case: Marital Dissolution
SIC code: 6282 Financial Planners & Investment Advisors

Court Likens 'Book of Business' to Professional Goodwill

A California divorce case in which one spouse was a financial advisor with an impressive client list raised a host of conceptual and technical valuation questions as to the community's interest in her "book of business" and several sizable conditional bonuses she received when she transferred to a new employer about a year before separation.

Lucrative career transition. During her career as a licensed financial advisor, the wife developed a list of clients—her book of business—owning over $192 million in investments and generating over $1.8 million in commissions and fees as of January 2009. That month, she signed an employment contract with Wells Fargo under which she would work there as a financial advisor and the bank's managing director of investments. The agreement's "offer summary" included several bonuses:

- A transitional bonus exceeding $2.8 million as consideration based on her book of business. To receive the entire amount, she had to remain employed for 112 months and generate commissions and fees of over $1.12 million annually.

The wife chose to receive the entire amount when she transferred over and signed a promissory note under which Wells Fargo agreed to forgive roughly $27,700 each month over 112 months. Should she stop working for the bank earlier, she would owe the entire unpaid balance; should she fail to make the production quota, the bank could reduce the amount of the monthly payment it normally credited to her.

- A deferred recruitment award bonus of nearly $187,000. Eligibility depended on her remaining employed until January 2016.

- Production bonus 1 in the amount of $374,000 based on her output from February 2009 to March 2010. The wife achieved the goal and received the entire amount in April 2010; this payment also came in the form of a 10-year loan.

- Production bonus 2 required meeting higher productions goals, which she failed to achieve.

- A level 4front bonus of $890,000 based on maintaining her client's investment profile; the wife qualified and received it in mid-2010, again in the form of a loan.

The husband and wife separated in February 2010.

Questions as to how to deal with the book of business and how to characterize and value the conditional bonuses dominated the trial proceedings, with both parties presenting expert testimony in support of their positions.

The wife's expert, a CPA, used a "time rule" to determine the character of the bonuses and loans. He said the transitional bonus was a "mixed-type asset," of which approximately 13.5% (on an after-tax basis) was community property and the rest was the wife's separate property. The wife's first production bonus and the level 4front bonus were her separate property because they were earned over a period of years and received after separation.

The wife's financial industry analyst called the transitional bonus a "kind of pay for the book of business … coming over," which was calculated as a "multiple of the value of … the [recruitee's] production credits of the trailing 12 months before they were to join [a] firm." Typically, the hiring firm expected to receive "a nine-to-ten-year commitment to earn [it]." By contrast, the production bonus was a "back-end bonus," an incentive to "work extremely diligently in bringing their book over, as well as continue to seek new business and continue to be successful." The level 4front bonus required the wife to perform analytical work and financial plans for her clients.

According to the husband's CPA, all the bonuses the wife received were community property. They were either based on her book of business (transitional bonus) or had been agreed to before separation (deferred recruitment award) or based on the wife's preseparation production (production bonus 1 and level 4front bonus).

The husband's industry expert agreed that the transitional bonus was compensation for the wife's bringing her book of business to Wells Fargo. The brokerage industry "now recognizes that brokers own their book of business," he said. As to value, it would "range anywhere from one to three times the gross … commissions generated by the book of business." As to the question of whether there was a market in which a financial advisor could sell her book, he responded, "the market for it would be … [moving to] another [firm]."

No value, no community interest. The trial court recognized that the wife's high compensation correlated to the value of the investments her clients held, but it did not find that the husband's role in enabling her transfer to Wells Fargo gave him any interest in her book of business. It said that "there was no expert testimony given as to the value of" the client list, and, citing prior case law, it found that the book of business "cannot be transferred to another party for a price." Consequently, it awarded the book of business to the wife.

Regarding the bonuses, it held that the community had a $380,000 interest in the portion of the $2.8 million transitional bonus the wife had earned during the 11 months she worked for Wells Fargo before separation. It divided this amount between the parties.

But it said the balance of that bonus and all the other bonuses were the wife's separate property because they were not paid or not due until after the couple's separation. Moreover, retention of the bonuses depended on the wife's continued employment and her meeting production requirements.

Ways to divvy up contingent rights. The husband attacked the trial court's rulings on the book of business and the conditional bonuses accompanying the wife's transfer to Wells Fargo in his appeal with the state Court of Appeals.

1. *Book of business.* The husband claimed there was a community interest in the book of business. It could be valued even if there was no market for it; what's more, the wife in fact was able to sell hers when she transferred from the previous employer to Wells Fargo. He also contended that the wife's status as a licensed financial advisor who had developed the ability to persuade clients to follow her to a new firm was similar to the goodwill other professionals—lawyers and doctors—are able to build up during their years of practice and marriage.

The wife objected that Wells Fargo paid her a significant sum of money "because she is successful at her job" and her success "is primarily measured by the amount of assets she manages."

The appellate court found the husband's goodwill argument persuasive. At the start of its analysis, it explained that under controlling case law an employer's customer lists represented part of the goodwill of the business. However, it explained that there was no precedent in California on the issue of whether a licensed professional's list of clients was an asset subject to division in a divorce case. Other jurisdictions have held that a client list may represent a marital asset, it added.

In this case, the wife acquired her book of business during the marriage. Both sides' industry experts verified that financial advisors qualified as professionals in that they had to obtain and maintain one or more licenses. Industry protocol also allowed them to take their client lists with them when changing firms.

The trial court erred when it found that the wife's book of business had no value, the appellate court said. The offer summary in her employment contract and expert testimony for both sides made it clear that the book of business was a valuable asset. Wells Fargo paid $2.8 million in consideration for her transferring her clients to the firm. It did not merely pay her for her high standing in the securities industry. Even the wife's expert conceded that, without her book of business, Wells Fargo likely would not have paid the transitional bonus.

Although the trial court found that the community had a right to a portion of the transitional bonus, its limited valuation was an abuse of discretion, the appellate court noted. This approach curtailed the right to the payments the wife earned during the 11 months between the date of her hire and the parties' separation. But the wife's right to the entire bonus arose when she signed the offer summary, received payment for all of it, and began working for Wells Fargo. Also, it was within her control to satisfy the requirements and thus ensure she could keep the entire bonus.

At the same time, the appeals court was careful to say that "[t]his does not mean the court must simply award one-half of the $2.8 million to husband." It found the wife's conditional right to the entire bonus, leaving the possibility that she may have to pay back any unearned portion, was analogous to a nonvested or unmatured pension right or "other contractually contingent interests."

Under the applicable case law, there were two solutions to dividing the community's interest in a contingent benefit: (1) the trial court must determine the present value of the rights or obligations that are community property and make an equal division or adjustment; or (2) if the court finds that the uncertainties surrounding a right or liability make a division impossible, it can award each spouse an appropriate portion of each payment as it is paid or each obligation as it is due.

Accordingly, the appeals court remanded, directing the trial court to calculate the community's interest in the transitional bonus and decide which of the two options it wanted to apply.

2. *Remaining bonuses.* The husband also objected to the trial court's characterizing production bonus 1 and level 4front bonus as the wife's separate property and its making no finding on the deferred recruitment bonus because it did not become due until 2016 and then only if the wife still worked for Wells Fargo. According to the husband, none of these bonuses compensated her for future employment but for the book of business she was able to assemble during the marriage. Instead, her post-separation salary represented compensation for any obligation she had to maintain a certain level of production and remain in good standing.

The wife responded that the payments related to the bonuses were "unearned income until the condition[s are] met."

The appeals court outright rejected the husband's claim as to the deferred recruitment award. Even though it was in the offer summary, under the terms of the contract, the wife would not receive it unless she remained an employee until 2016. Before such date, the bonus was not an enforceable right but merely an "expectancy."

The appeals court said it owed deference to the trial court's determination that only the transitional bonus was consideration for the wife's book of business because the finding was based on sufficient evidence: testimony from the wife's expert.

However, it also remanded as to the first production and the level 4front bonuses, cautioning: "The critical question here is when wife's right to each bonus accrued, not her receipt of them." Specifically, although she received both payments a few months after separation, she not only had a contractual right to them, but also made efforts to qualify for them before the separation. Accordingly, the appellate court ordered the trial court to perform the same analysis and computation necessary for the transitional bonus for these two bonuses.

In re Flashcom, Inc.

Citation: 2013 U.S. Dist. LEXIS 171266
Date of decision: Dec. 4, 2013
Experts: David Hahn (trustee-appellant); Randy Sugarman (defendants-appellees)
Judge: Olguin
State/Jurisdiction: Federal/California
Court: U.S. District Court
Type of case: Bankruptcy
SIC code: 4813 Telephone Communications, Except Radiotelephone (resellers)

GAAP 'Relevant,' But 'Not Controlling' in Solvency Analysis

After an Internet business collapsed, the bankruptcy trustee unsuccessfully sued its venture capital investors and directors over a $9 million transfer to one of the company's founders. The Bankruptcy Court found that the trustee failed to prove insolvency, by relying on a problematic valuation. The expert who performed it failed to value the business as a going concern and slavishly followed generally accepted accounting principles in analyzing assets and liabilities. The trustee attacked the ruling in an appeal with the district court.

Interlocking transactions. In the late 1990s, a wife and husband formed an Internet service provider that resold digital subscriber line (DSL) service to consumers and businesses. Several venture capital (VC) funds invested $15 million to buy preferred stock and obtained the right to appoint three of the company's five-member board of directors; the husband and wife occupied the other two seats. When the majority of the board decided the wife's management style interfered with customer, vendor, and strategic partner relations, she demanded a substantial amount of money in exchange for her withdrawal. Eventually, she threatened litigation against the company, the VC investors, the directors, including the husband, and management. To raise money and resolve all disputes with the wife, the VC funds arranged for another round of financing. They committed to buying $5.7 million in Series B shares but insisted that settling matters with the wife was vital to proceeding with the financing. They also made bridge loans in the amount of $9 million to the company, as short-term working capital to keep operations going before the financing.

Ultimately, the investors, the company, and the wife executed a stock purchase agreement under which the company would repurchase some of the wife's common stock for $9 million. Relatedly, under a settlement and release agreement, the wife would abandon her claims against the various parties. The $9 million transfer, in turn, was conditioned on the company's ability to raise at least $40 million through a Series B offering. This condition was satisfied. On Feb. 23, 2000, the company raised $84 million in an offering that actually was oversubscribed; the same day, it bought out the wife by way of a $9 million wire transfer and reaped $75 million in proceeds. Subsequently, it even contemplated an IPO but was unable to secure additional financing. Ultimately, the economic downturn contributed to its filing for bankruptcy at the end of 2000.

Going concern or barely standing? The bankruptcy trustee pursued various legal strategies and theories to recover the $9 million from the VC funds and directors, the defendants-appellees. In a pretrial motion in Bankruptcy Court (C.D. Cal.), she argued that the transaction was a constructive fraudulent transfer because the company received nothing in return for the redemption of the wife's stock in exchange for the $9 million payment.

The Bankruptcy Court disagreed, finding that the transfer left "no negative effect" on the company's estate. It was appropriate to consider the entire context in which the transaction occurred. Without the wife's relinquishing all claims against the company, investors would not have completed the Series B financing. The wife, however, would not have released the company without receiving a $9 million payment for her stock. In the final analysis, the company benefited from the exchange by securing $75 million of new financing and an end to the threat of litigation.

At trial, the trustee tried to avoid the $9 million transfer by showing that the company was insolvent at the time of the transfer, February 2000. Both parties presented valuation experts to shore up their arguments.

The company's expert determined that the company was worth approximately $400 million on a going-concern basis just prior to the transfer. The calculation included $21.9 million for subscriber contracts as of the transfer date based on book value. He explained that, if the company had put up its subscriber contracts for sale at that time, the market would have considered them "very valuable" and "there would have been a bidding war to purchase [the] contracts."

In contrast, the trustee's expert said he had not valued the company "as an entire entity on a going-concern basis." In determining assets and liabilities, the expert believed the $5.7 million of funds from the investors should not be treated as assets under generally accepted accounting principles (GAAP) because they had not closed at the date of transfer. At the same time, he testified that at that date it was more likely that 100% of the legally committed Series B proceeds would be received than the projected 90% of the company's accounts receivable that he did include as assets in his solvency analysis. He also counted $6.7 million in bridge loans as a liability, even if they were not absolute, because "liabilities include debts that are contingent or disputed." Further, relying on the opinion of the trustee's subscriber valuation expert, he determined the contracts would only generate approximately $3.3 million in an orderly sale.

The Bankruptcy Court gave numerous reasons why the company should be valued as a going concern, including: (1) it was able to raise $84 million in an oversubscribed Series B financing; (2) its vendors were willing to extend it substantial credit; (3) investors seemed uniformly optimistic about its prospects; and (4) it received 1,500 new orders for subscriber lines each week.

It discredited the trustee expert's valuation, finding it should have counted the $5.7 million in Series B proceeds as an asset because the "investors were contractually committed to fund their obligation to purchase Series B shares, and [the company] would have had a claim against these investors if the payment was not made." At the same time, the valuation incorrectly included $6.7 million in bridge loans as a liability. Under controlling case law, "[t]o determine a contingent liability, one must discount it by the probability that the contingency will occur and the liability will become real." In this case, the promissory notes for the loans stated that they automatically would convert to equity once the company received at least $30 million in Series B proceeds. There was an "extremely low" probability that the company would have to pay for the notes," the court found. The trustee's expert had failed to consider this eventuality in his analysis. As for the value of the subscriber contracts, the court noted that the trustee's expert relied on a subscriber valuation expert who by his own admission had not considered all of the testimony key members of the company's management and board had given. Further, other trial witnesses described his data as unreliable compared with the data the competing subscriber valuation expert used.

Adopting the company expert's valuation, the Bankruptcy Court found the company was solvent on the date of transfer.

Subscription value dispute. The trustee next appealed the Bankruptcy Court's decisions with the district court (C.D. Cal.). First, the trustee argued error as to the ruling that there was no fraudulent conveyance.

The District Court dealt with that claim quickly. At issue in the case was an "integrated transaction," whose effect was a net financial gain for the company of $75 million in new equity, it said. Consequently, the company did not receive less than a reasonably equivalent value in exchange.

Second, the trustee challenged the Bankruptcy Court's insolvency ruling, honing in on three errors. Were it not for these errors, the Bankruptcy Court "would have had no choice but to conclude" that the company was insolvent at the transfer date, the trustee contended.

At the outset of its analysis, the district court noted that a "fair valuation" in the context of the Bankruptcy Code involves a two-step process: First, the court determines whether the debtor company was a "going concern" or "on its deathbed." Second, the court values the debtor's assets based on the status it assigned in the first part of its analysis. If it designated the company as a going concern, it determines the fair market price of its assets; if it finds that the company is barely alive, it determines the liquidation value.

Here, the Bankruptcy Court correctly held that the company should be valued as a going concern. Because the trustee's expert "declined to provide a [going concern] valuation," the $400 million valuation the company's expert presented was uncontroverted evidence and by itself "enough for the court to conclude that the Trustee did not meet her burden" of showing insolvency, the reviewing court concluded.

Next, the district court addressed the three errors the trustee alleged.

1. Under the GAAP, it was error to include cash—specifically the $5.7 million in Series B funds—as an asset because it arrived after the $9 million transfer to the wife.

The reviewing court found no error. "GAAP is not controlling in determining the fair market value of assets or the insolvency of the debtor," it said. To find otherwise "would make accountants and the board which promulgate GAAP the arbiters of insolvency questions." But the Bankruptcy Code "clearly" left the decisions to judges. Moreover, no rationale existed "why judges should not be allowed to consider subsequent events … in valuing assets and determining liabilities." Here, the Bankruptcy Court correctly found that the investors had a contractual obligation to buy Series B shares. "In any event, the Series B proceeds arrived two days later." Also, the trustee's expert testified to the strong likelihood that 100% of the Series B proceeds would be received as opposed to only 90% of accounts receivable, which he designated as assets.

2. It was error not to count debts—that is, the bridge loans, which the company owed at the transfer date—as liabilities. Even if the loans were not an absolute liability, they were a contingent liability, which "must be reduced ... to its present or expected amount before a determination on insolvency can be made."

According to the reviewing court, the Bankruptcy Court correctly assessed the probability—extremely low—that the liability would become real by looking at the provisions in the related promissory notes. Accordingly, it properly determined not to include them as a liability in its analysis.

3. It was error to value the DSL subscriber contracts in place, not as if sold.

"Book value does not necessarily prove fair market value," the district court acknowledged, but nonetheless "is competent evidence." Here, the company's expert testified to the high value the contracts would have held in the market had they been offered for sale at the time of transfer. His statements suggested that the contracts were valued as if sold, said the court. Also, statements from the trustee's contracts valuation expert and other witnesses supported the Bankruptcy Court's decision not to give great weight to the much lower estimate the trustee's valuation assigned to the contracts.

For all these reasons, the district court affirmed the Bankruptcy Court's ruling.

In re Genco Shipping & Trading Ltd.

Citation: 2014 Bankr. LEXIS 2854
Date of decision: July 2, 2014
Experts: Timothy Coleman, Blackstone (debtors); Neil Augustine, Rothschild Inc. (equity committee)
Judge: Lane
State/Jurisdiction: Federal/New York
Court: U.S. Bankruptcy Court
Type of case: Bankruptcy
SIC code: 4731 Freight Transportation Arrangement

Industry Characteristics Bolster Reliance on Net Asset Value

In a prepackaged Chapter 11 case, the fight came down to the debtors' proposed reorganization plan. The dissenting equity committee objected to the debtors' use of the net asset value (NAV) for determining the value of the debtor shipping company, claiming NAV undervalued the going-concern company and left equity holders without adequate recovery. While the court found legitimate reasons for relying at least in part on NAV, it saw none for using the discounted cash flow (DCF) method the equity committee pushed forward.

The debtor company was one of the world's largest dry bulk shippers, with a fleet of 53 shipping vessels. It was seriously overleveraged and sought to implement a consensual debt conversion restructuring that the majority of its lenders supported. Under an agreement, approximately $1.2 billion of the over $1.3 billion senior secured debt would convert to equity in the reorganized company and there would be new liquidity through a fully backstopped $100 million rights offering. Pursuant to the reorganization plan, the existing equity holders would receive warrants in exchange for the surrender or cancellation of their equity interests. The warrants covered 6% of the new equity. The U.S. trustee appointed an equity committee, which rejected the plan. Consequently, the debtors sought confirmation under the Bankruptcy Code's "cramdown" provision, Section 1129(b)(1), arguing the plan was fair and equitable and did not unfairly discriminate against the equity holders. At the confirmation hearing and trial, both sides presented extensive valuation testimony to support their positions.

To determine the "fair and equitable" requirement, the court had to decide whether the company's total enterprise value (TEV) exceeded $1.48 billion—the value underlying the plan. The debtors established that this amount represented the payments due for claims that had to be paid before the equity holders could recover.

Three 'useful' methods. Valuation experts for the two sides used four methods, but the debtors' experts urged the court to adopt a NAV analysis, which, they said, was best suited to value a dry bulk shipping company and resulted in a range between $1.36 billion and $1.44 billion. In contrast, the equity committee proposed using the results from all four methods but assigning different weights to the values. Specifically, the DCF and comparable companies values should weigh 37.5%, whereas the NAV value should account for 15%, and the precedent transactions value should only account for 10%. Under the equity committee's approach, the company's value ranged from $1.54 billion to $1.91 billion—thus leaving enough money for recovery by the note holders.

The court agreed to assign considerable weight to the NAV valuation but declined to rely on it exclusively. The comparable companies analysis was "equally useful," it said, and there even was "limited utility" to the precedent transaction method. The only approach the court rejected was the DCF.

1. *NAV.* The debtors retained four third-party firms to perform fleet appraisals. An expert on vessel valuation testified that "[m]arket valuation is undoubtedly the dominant and most widely accepted approach [to ascertain vessel price] in the industry." His calculation of the total market value of the vessels relied on three approaches: econometric modeling approach, time series analysis approach, and last done approach. He analyzed each of the 53 vessels separately, considering each method as it related to each vessel. He also took into account an array of other factors bearing on value, including historical cargo routes, chartering history, detentions and deficiencies, class of vessel, and engine make and model. He concluded that the "charter free market value" of the debtors' vessels was $1.21 billion.

The debtors' valuation expert added the value of the company's other assets to this value to arrive at the $1.34 billion-to-$1.44 billion range, with a median of $1.39 billion. All the values confirmed that equity was "out of the money."

The equity committee did not challenge the debtors' vessel expert or his methodology but contended NAV was inappropriate when it came to valuing an ongoing business. It failed to account for the value of the debtors' management and other business-related intangibles, the committee's valuation expert contended.

The court found merit in the debtors' valuation expert's claim that the dry bulk shipping industry required a different treatment. The expert said the industry was similar to the classic economic model of "perfect competition." It was fragmented, competitive, and had low barriers of entry. Investors come in when rates are attractive, which increases supply and forces rates down. This situation puts strain on vessel owners and operators to produce returns in excess of the cost of capital, the expert explained.

The court rejected the equity committee's "dismissive attitude regarding NAV," finding it ignored the nature of the industry and the committee's own evidence: two fairness opinions related to the SEC filings of other shipping companies, which acknowledged that NAV was a legitimate valuation method in this industry.

2. *Comparable companies.* At the same time, the court saw no reason to disregard the traditional methods, particularly the comparable companies valuation.

Both sides' experts used essentially the same method and data from the same sources to perform a comparable companies analysis. However, they disagreed over the makeup of the peer group and over EBITDA adjustment for fleet age. Specifically, the debtors' expert identified six similar companies and performed two comparisons for the peer group set: a TEV/NAV analysis and TEV/EBITDA analysis. He computed TEV by adding each company's market capitalization, financial liabilities, and preferred stock and subtracting the nonoperating assets. He calculated the comparables' NAV by using an automated ship valuation service, "VesselsValue," and the TEV by using publicly available information. He explained that the first analysis intended to determine "whether market participants assign value to pure play dry bulk operators in excess of the value of the assets." He produced values ranging from $1.2 billion to $1.32 billion, leaving no money for the equity holders.

In the second analysis, the debtors' expert adjusted each EBITDA multiple to account for the difference between the debtor company's average fleet age and the comparable companies' average fleet ages. When he applied the adjusted EBITDA multiples to the debtor company's 2015E EBITDA of $175 million, he arrived at a total value ranging from $1.17 billion to $1.41 billion; consequently, equity was out of the money.

The equity committee's expert excluded two companies from the peer group set. One, he said, was not truly comparable because it was smaller and had significant transparency and governance issues. He found the second company was a bad fit in terms of size and specifically because of its much lower TEV.

The court agreed that the first comparable's governance issues could affect its financial situation and make it dissimilar to the other peer group companies. But it found no support for excluding the second company. It also adopted the "overall comparable analysis" the debtors' expert presented. Excluding the first comparable did not materially change the conclusions resulting from the debtors' analysis, the court found. In contrast, inclusion of the second comparable had a drastic effect on the equity committee's expert's numbers, the court found. Performing what it called a "common sense check," the court found that, if it took the committee's expert's prior data and included the comparable, there would be a considerable reduction in value. The low range would be about $1.21 billion—thus, closer to the debtors' expert's values.

The court also agreed with the debtors' expert's claim that EBITDA did not account sufficiently for the different ages of the comparable companies' fleets and that "some" adjustment was appropriate.

3. *Precedent transactions.* Experts for both sides agreed that there were very few change-in-control transactions in the industry. Instead, almost all of the transactions took the form of vessel sales.

The debtors' expert proposed six comparable "fleet sale" transactions but admitted on cross-examination that five of the six transactions were fleet acquisitions. Using this method, the expert concluded the company was worth from $1.29 billion to $1.4 billion, thus leaving no money for the note holders. The committee's expert opposed this approach, saying it assumed that, "[b]y definition, fleet value acquisitions tend to be at or around NAV because NAV is established by broker estimates of fleet value, which is driven by the last vessel sale." A proper precedent transactions method would have to consider "what buyers would pay for a full business, inclusive of an operating platform, management, and expected future cash flows, not simply the value of the assets," he said. He calculated the company was worth $1.54 billion at the low end and $1.62 billion at the high end. The midpoint was $1.58 billion. All the amounts allowed for recovery by the note holders.

The court found only three "actual" change-in-control transactions—compared to over 4,400 dry bulk vessel sales—in the last 10 years. They took place in 2008, 2011, and 2014. "Tellingly," the court said, "these three transactions took place at or extremely close to NAV." In other words, the "NAV for comparable transactions confirms use of NAV as a reliable source of valuation."

The court also pointed out that only one of the transactions was above NAV; it took place at the height of the dry bulk shipping rate boom, prior to the financial crisis. According to the court, this transaction received undue weight in the equity committee's expert's calculation. Ultimately, the court concluded that the limited number of qualifying transactions meant the precedent transactions method was of limited use. But, said the court, the precedent transactions method served to justify the debtors' expert's advocacy of the NAV valuation and further confirmed that "valuation in the dry bulk shipping industry is vastly different from other industries."

'Many good reasons' to reject DCF. The equity committee put considerable weight on the DCF valuation, and the results its expert achieved with it were significantly higher than the values resulting from the other three methodologies. Specifically, the low range was $1.66 billion and the high range was $2.27 billion, resulting in a midpoint of $1.96 billion. The debtors' expert contended throughout that the DCF was an unreliable and inappropriate method with which to calculate the debtor company's value; however, he performed a DCF to "stress test" his conclusions. His DCF analysis showed the company was worth between $1.1 billion and $1.3 billion.

The court agreed with the debtors' expert that there were "many good reasons" not to use the DCF in this case. For one, there were no accurate projections. All parties agreed that dry bulk shipping rates were extremely volatile and difficult to predict. The debtors' expert explained that rates varied day by day based on supply and demand. A company's ability to make long-term revenue forecasts was "severely constrained."

The equity committee's expert used flawed data, most critically when it came to shipping rates forecasts, the court found. The debtors' expert relied on a reputed and established industry risk evaluation system, Marsoft, and an expert working for it. In contrast, the equity committee's expert relied on an expert who had shipping industry experience but not much experience in the specific area of forecasting rates. To forecast rates from 2014 to 2016, the latter took an average of 10 shipping industry equity analysts and the Marsoft projected rates. He chose the analysts because he considered them "thoughtful industry participants with deep knowledge of the shipping business," he said. The court found his selection criterion problematic, but it found the expert's taking a straight average of the reports without testing the data or adjusting it even more troubling. He also failed to consider any upward bias common among equity analysts. According to the court, the analysis the committee's rate expert performed the court could perform itself if it received the analysts' projections. Although the court admitted the testimony under Federal Rule of Evidence 702, it found the expert's methodology unpersuasive.

In discussing the future of the industry, the equity committee's valuation expert relied on a survey of 13 equity analysts. The court pointed out that of those analysts only five relied on the DCF for their assessment.

Appraiser's troubling record. Moreover, the equity committee's expert and his firm left a record of prior statements that undercut their reliance on the DCF at trial. For example, the court pointed to written materials the firm had presented to an equity holder in which it noted that financial experts in two recent shipping cases eschewed traditional methodologies in favor of fleet valuation and market indicators of value.

Also, in making a pitch to serve as the debtors' financial advisor prior to the bankruptcy filing, the equity committee's appraiser allowed for a shortfall in collateral value based on his preliminary analysis. When it did not get the job, the appraiser changed its viewpoint.

There was evidence that the valuation fight was part of a strategy the appraiser proposed to an equity holder for gaining leverage and taking control of the restructuring process without actually contributing money to the restructuring. One such step, the appraiser said in its pitch, was to "demonstrat[e] equity value ... by arguing for the use of forward multiples, highlighting the cyclical nature of the industry in recovery mode and pointing towards debt trading levels at or above par." This record, the court said, "creates a troubling impression" that the equity committee's valuation firm was tied to the strategy and its valuation was a "forgone conclusion."

Finally, the court pointed up the debtors' remark that none of the hedge funds on the equity committee showed any interest in investing their own money in the debtor, notwithstanding the high valuation the committee's expert produced. At the least, the equity holders' reluctance supported the debtors' views on value, the court noted.

There was no undervaluation, the court concluded. The debtors acted in good faith and arrived at the plan by engaging in an arm's-length process. Accordingly, the court confirmed the plan.

Hamelink v. Hamelink

Citation: 2014 Minn. App. Unpub. LEXIS 1175
Date of decision: Dec. 30, 2013
Experts: Arthur Cobb (wife); Stephen Hosch (husband)
Judge: Kirk
State/Jurisdiction: Minnesota
Court: Court of Appeals
Type of case: Marital Dissolution
SIC code: 3400 Fabricated Metal Products

Appeals Court Tiptoes Around Tax Affecting in Divorce Setting

Since *Bernier v. Bernier*, a Massachusetts divorce case in which the state's highest court required that a valuation for equitable distribution purposes use a hybrid tax-affecting model to account for an S corporation owner's personal taxes on company profits, few marriage-dissolution decisions have followed up on the tax-affecting issue. Recently, the Minnesota appeals court entered the debate, and its opinion shows a court that seems both receptive to adopting the technique and noncommittal.

Some 30 years before the husband and wife separated, which was in 2010, he founded a company designing and manufacturing custom metal gas-burner equipment for use in fireplaces, grills, furnaces, and commercial ovens. The business was organized as an S corp, and he was the sole owner. Accordingly, the company did not pay corporate taxes, but he was liable for personal taxes on any corporate profits.

At trial, the question of whether to tax affect or not in valuing the business became a major bone of contention between the parties. Both sides offered expert testimony to bolster their positions.

Wife's expert cites case law. The husband's expert computed the fair market value of the company by using a single-period capitalization method while tax affecting estimated future earnings. In other words, he quantified the effect of the personal tax liability on a hypothetical buyer by determining and applying a hypothetical tax rate to estimated earnings. This approach reduced the projected future earnings and the resulting fair market value (FMV). By his calculation, the business was worth nearly $2.3 million.

The wife's expert used the discounted cash flow (DCF) approach without tax affecting and obtained a $6.5 million value. He based his decision not to tax affect on the *Gross* U.S. Tax Court decision. In *Gross*, the taxpayer's expert tax affected the company's earnings by an assumed 40% corporate rate, as if the company were a C corporation, even though it was an S corp. The Tax Court rejected the approach, noting "the principal benefit that shareholders expect from an S corporation election is a reduction in the total tax burden imposed on the enterprise ... and we see no reason why that savings ought to be ignored as a matter of course in valuing the S corporation." See *Gross v. Commissioner,* T.C. Memo 1999-254, *aff'd,* 272 F.3d (6th Cir. 2001) (available at *BVLaw*).

In addition, he referenced a Minnesota district court decision related to a forced buyout in which the trial court rejected tax affecting for a different reason: Assuming a hypothetical sale, the company most likely would be sold to another S corp not to a C corp.

Here, without explaining its position on tax affecting, the district court adopted the method that the wife's expert used but adjusted some of its components to settle at a value of $3.7 million. (The appellate opinion says the adjustments were of no consequence to the appeal.)

Appeal advocates for *Kessler* model. The husband appealed the decision at the Minnesota Court of Appeals. The district court erred in refusing to use the after-tax value for its valuation of the company and overvalued the company by approximately $700,000, he contended. For one, the cases the wife's expert cited in support of not tax affecting were not divorce cases. "[N]ational case law makes clear that in order to arrive at an accurate value, the [c]ourt must tax affect the business," the husband claimed. He advocated for the hybrid tax-affecting approach that the Delaware Court of Chancery developed in *Delaware Open MRI Radiology Assocs. v. Kessler* and that the Massachusetts Supreme Court applied specifically in the marriage dissolution context in *Bernier.*

At the start of its review, the appellate court noted that the district court's opinion was based on admissible expert testimony and the expert's methodology had support in the record. Accordingly, the appeals court was unable to say with "definite and firm conviction that the district court's valuation fell outside a reasonable range of figure."

However, the reviewing court acknowledged that no Minnesota appellate court had decided the tax-affecting issue in the divorce context, and it allowed that the husband's position had "some weight," even though he "overstates the level of support" for it.

Kessler, the court explained, also was not a divorce case but a combined appraisal and fairness action. Asked to assess the fair value of company stock, the Delaware Court of Chancery assumed a dividend rate of 15% and a personal income tax rate of 40% to impute a "predividend" rate of 29.4%. Applying this rate to the earnings of the pass-through entity measures "with the greatest practicable precision" the fair value of the going concern, the Chancery concluded.

The Massachusetts Supreme Court subsequently adopted the *Kessler* model in the *Bernier* divorce case, the appeals court explained. Specifically, in *Bernier,* the trial court had adopted the husband's valuation, which tax affected at a hypothetical full corporate rate of 35%. The Supreme Court found this approach unreasonable since it significantly undervalued the businesses, two supermarkets.

At the same time, the failure to tax affect an S corp at all would artificially inflate its value by overstating the retaining shareholders expected rate of return. (The decision did not resolve *Bernier* because a change in the federal income tax treatment of corporate dividends raised issues the Supreme Court initially failed to address.)

No categorical rejection of tax affecting. Where did these cases leave the Minnesota appeal? The Court of Appeals agreed that they provided support for the tax affecting the husband's expert did. But, the court continued, this was not the end of the discussion. As an error-correcting court, it had to decide whether the district court's refusal to tax affect was an abuse of discretion. It was not. For one, the husband's expert admitted, "the issue of tax affecting is an open debate." Also, the difference between divorce and nondivorce cases that the husband highlighted was "superficial" and of no consequence to the heart of the issue: how to determine the value at which a business would change hands between a hypothetical willing buyer and a hypothetical willing seller.

The husband's argument that ignoring the personal taxes of an S corp owner would result in overvaluation was not persuasive. Referencing comments from Nancy Fannon and Keith F. Sellers on pass-through entities, the court noted that, in valuing C corps, the courts, the IRS, and the valuation profession for decades have accepted the practice of ignoring the effect of personal tax liability. Therefore, the appeals court continued, "we do not find it unreasonable to employ the same practice for the valuation of S corporations in a hypothetical transaction." Finally: "Whether to do so is for the experts to explain, the parties to prove, and the district court to decide."

In a last-ditch effort, at oral argument, the husband cautioned that a failure to adopt a pro-tax-affecting stance meant the wife's expert would continue to testify in upcoming divorce cases and "no district court would ever find tax affecting to be appropriate." The appeals court disagreed. Litigants should not read its decision to stand for the proposition that "tax affecting should never be considered." The *Gross* case did not set down a bright-line rule. "Indeed, *Gross* actually advocated for tax affecting under the right circumstances," the Court of Appeals maintained. It cited with emphasis the Tax Court's statement: "If ... the discount rate is assumed to be an after-shareholder-tax rate of return, *then the cash-flow should be reduced ('tax affected') to an after-shareholder-tax amount.*"

Note: Digests and the court opinions for the cited cases are available at *BVLaw*.

Hanusin v. Hanusin

Citation: 2013 Ill. App. Unpub. LEXIS 2618
Date of decision: Nov. 20, 2013
Experts: Mary Miller (wife); Thomas Kammerait (husband)
Judge: Schostok
State/Jurisdiction: Illinois
Court: Appellate Court
Type of case: Marital Dissolution
SIC code: 8742 Management and Consulting Services

Should Dated Buyout Set Value of Stock in Closely Held Corporation?

How relevant and reliable is the price that the future owners of a closely held corporation paid under a 2004 stock purchase agreement to a 2012 divorce proceeding? This was a critical issue for the purpose of equitable distribution. The wife's expert relied on it when valuing the husband's interest in the company, and the trial court agreed with her approach. The husband appealed, claiming that the court's consideration of the buyout as an indicator of value was one of several harmful errors undermining the valuation.

In 2004, the husband and four colleagues bought a "manufacturer's rep" company from its owner under a 10-year stock purchase agreement (SPA). The company brokered contracts for manufacturing companies and obtained 90% of its business from military contracts. Four of the new owners, including the husband, acquired a 23% interest each; one person bought the remaining 8%. The husband served as the company president. Under the SPA, the former owner received 10% of the company's annual gross receipts for a 10-year period ending in January 2014. At the time of trial, the husband's share of past payments amounted to approximately $373,700.

In 2012, four of the owners settled a lawsuit with the fifth owner (8% shareholder), paying her $12,000 or $15,000 (the court noted there was conflicting testimony on the amount) in exchange for her surrendering her interest. The husband called the payment a "nuisance value."

Experts have unequal access to financials. During the divorce proceedings, a discovery dispute between the parties developed when the company stymied the wife's access to financial information.

The company's valuation became a focal point of contention. Both sides retained experienced business valuators; what's more, the husband's expert had extensive experience in valuing manufacturer's rep firms.

The husband's expert relied on information the company's principals had provided about the company and its contracts. He declined to consider the price the shareholders paid under the 2004 SPA, arguing that the buyout occurred years ago and failed to factor in the effects of the 2008 Great Recession. Instead, he relied in part on the amount the fifth shareholder received under the 2012 settlement; this arrangement, he believed, represented an arm's-length transaction.

He calculated the company's book value at $75,000 and its commission business at around $154,400 to arrive at a total gross value of some $229,400. He applied a 35% discount to account for nonmarketability and the minority interest and a 25% discount to account for expiring contracts. He concluded the husband's share was worth nearly $19,000.

For her valuation, the wife's expert used an income—capitalization of excess earnings— approach. Since she had no access to the company's principals or financial statements, she relied on a review of the last five years of the company's tax returns. Moreover, she considered the price per share resulting from the 2004 SPA, projecting a 10% increase in revenue for the final two years of the SPA, that is, 2013 and 2014. In normal circumstances, she would examine 10-year financial records for a valuation, she said.

She applied a 28% discount to account for nonmarketability and the husband's minority position. Based on all of these considerations, she found the husband's shares were worth $324,000.

The trial court recognized that the wife's expert lacked experience valuing manufacturer's rep companies and that she was not able to develop her analysis as fully as she and the court would have liked because of the company's refusal to provide access to financial information. Regardless, the court found her calculations as to the total price paid under the SPA through the year 2012 "reasonable." At the same time, it found that, in light of the federal budget sequestration in late 2013 and its effects on defense spending, it was not reasonable to project a 10% increase in revenue for 2013 and 2014. Rather, said the court, revenues in those two years likely would be 10% lower than in 2012. It concluded that the amount paid for the shares over the entire 10-year period pursuant to the SPA would be approximately $2 million and the husband's 23% share would be worth approximately $469,000. To this amount the court applied a 35% discount for nonmarketability and minority and an additional 10% discount to account for the fact that payments occurred over a 10-year period. In the final analysis, the husband's interest was worth nearly $275,000, the trial court determined.

Settlement represents 'nuisance value.' The husband appealed various aspects of the trial court's stock valuation. The appellate court addressed his objections in order.

1. *Wrong methodology.* He contended that under relevant case law the value of a closely held company equals its book value and goodwill.

The reviewing court disagreed, noting that applicable prior cases approved three valuation methods, including the income approach and market approach that figured into the valuation by the wife's expert and the trial court.

2. *Improper use of SPA.* The husband claimed that the trial court erred when it took into account the price paid under the 2004 SPA; a 1979 case specifically found that an earlier stock price was not reliable because, "[u]nlike land, which has a fairly stable value, the value of stock fluctuates freely with the operation of the business."

The appeals court saw it differently. The referenced case cited no authority for its proposition. To the contrary, the leading divorce case on the valuation of a closely held corporation emphasized the importance of using previous arm's-length sales of the company's stock to make the process more objective. See *Grunsten v. Grunsten*, 709 N.E.2d 597 (1999) (available at *BVLaw*). Here, the 2004 SPA involved a willing seller and willing buyers and, therefore, was relevant to the value of the company's stock. On the other hand, the appeals court found the use of the 2012 litigation settlement problematic. The payment to the fifth shareholder was a nuisance value intended to conclude litigation and did not seem "a purely voluntary transfer of the shares." The trial court's reliance on the SPA was not error.

3. *Improper reliance on projected revenues.* The husband argued that the proper valuation date for marital assets was the date of the dissolution. Consequently, it was error for the trial court to rely on projected company revenues for 2013 and 2014.

The appeals court noted that the lower court could have avoided reliance on the projections if it had simply treated the amount paid through the end of 2012 as 80% of the value of the shares under the SPA. But had it done so, the share value would have been higher than it came out to be under the trial court's methodology, considering the latter discounted the projected income to account for federal defense cuts. Accordingly, the trial court's calculation did not harm the husband.

4. *Omitted deduction.* Finally, the husband argued the trial court failed to deduct the amounts the company would have had to pay the former owner in 2013 and 2014—10% of its gross earnings.

This argument also lacked merit, the appeals court said. The lower court in effect based its calculation on the amounts the company shareholders paid for the stock, not the company's gross revenues.

For all of these reasons, the appellate court refused to upend the trial court's valuation of the husband's interest.

Hardenbrook v. United Parcel Service, Inc.

Citation: 2014 U.S. Dist. LEXIS 15830
Date of decision: Feb. 7, 2014
Experts: Dennis Reinstein (plaintiff-employee); Cornelius Hofman (defendant)
Judge: Lodge
State/Jurisdiction: Federal/Idaho
Court: United States District Court
Type of case: Contract
SIC code: 4215, Courier Services Except by Air

Courts Wrestle With Discount Rate for Future Stock Price Increase

In an involved retaliation suit against UPS, which the employee won, one of the flash points was the calculation of lost future benefits, specifically the question of what the applicable discount rate was to compute the present value of the company's restricted stock units. This issue came before the district court after trial, the 9th Circuit on appeal, and the district court again on remand. The present resolution may provoke more consternation and discussion.

In 2007, a UPS employee sued the company for wrongful termination (D. Idaho) and prevailed in trial. The jury awarded him over $1.4 million in front pay and $40,000 in back pay. Damages for future lost benefits were based on future lost wages, UPS restricted stock unit grants, and the company's pension and health benefits plan for the remainder of the employee's work life—27 years. The district court denied UPS's subsequent motion for a new trial but found the award was grossly excessive, not supported by the evidence, and speculative. Therefore, it reduced the front-pay amount to $673,000 and kept the $40,000 in back pay.

A critical part of the front-pay analysis was the calculation of the value of the UPS restricted stock. Both sides retained experts who, for the most part, agreed on how to compute it but disagreed on the applicable net discount rate to calculate the present value of the stock.

The employee's expert was a CPA, as well as a certified business valuator and appraiser. The starting point of his analysis was what the employee had received in the two years before his termination; he assumed that the award would have remained the same going forward. He then calculated the net discount rate by taking the anticipated cost of capital of the company and subtracting it from the expected rate of return. Under the "capital asset pricing model" (CAPM), the cost of capital to UPS would range between 7% and 8%, he determined. At the same time, he arrived at an expected rate of return of 8% to 9% based on the past performance of the stock, five-year projections, and stock increases for large capitalized companies. Specifically, UPS stock had increased at a rate of 18% over the previous 12 months, and projections from Yahoo Finance estimated growth of 23% to 24% for the next 12 months and around 8% for the next five years. A review of the last 50 years of stock increases for UPS peer companies—large capital companies—showed the average rate of return was between 8% and 9%, he said. Accordingly, there was a difference of 1%, which actually would lead to a negative net discount rate, he explained. To be conservative, he chose zero as the applicable net discount rate.

UPS's expert had an MBA in economics and finance. His role, he said, was to testify to the future valuation of stock. According to him, "the higher the risk of an asset you are valuing, the higher discount rate you use, meaning the lower the present value will be because it is more risky that you won't get that money in the future." The asset in this case—the UPS stock—had a higher risk than government Treasury securities or bonds, he added, and that risk was an important factor in determining the future value of the stock.

He called the competing expert's use of a 0% net discount rate "unsound" because it neither properly valued the risk adhering to the UPS stock nor discounted the future money to present value. He said he developed the applicable discount rate based on "the UPS discount rate" figure of between 10.4% and 11.5% that appeared in the competing expert's earlier report. Averaging the two numbers, he subtracted 0.3% to account for the historical growth of UPS stock and obtained a 10.5% net discount rate. He did not know what the competing expert's basis for "the UPS discount rate" was. In his role as critic, he simply "reviewed the plaintiff's own record and their own opinion on what the discount rate is…. I took their own discount rate at face value and said, well, you should have applied it, and they didn't." He admitted he did not account for any future projections of UPS stock but contended that they would not have generated a zero discount rate. By his calculation, the present value of the UPS stock was around $79,500 for the relevant period.

The employee's expert subsequently defended the rate, explaining again how he arrived at it. He claimed that the present value calculation "has nothing to do with how risky the stock might be."

What about 'time value of money'? The district court found the employee expert's conclusion troubling. It "seems to ignore the time value of money when the expert also calculates a substantial growth rate in the value of the UPS stock in the future." The court went on to say that this discount rate calculation did not align with "basic economic principles and/or methodologies which would normally be used by economists in determining the present value of money to be earned in the future." Also, the court suggested, the expert might have overstated the future growth rate for UPS stock considering the historical stock growth since the company had gone public.

But ultimately the court had an overriding concern that prevented it from calculating a different discount rate. UPS's economist expert failed to "articulate how to properly calculate a discount rate for stock growth in this particular case," said the court. While the employee's expert presented some evidence to buttress his claim, UPS's expert simply critiqued the approach as "not a normally accepted calculation method" for discount rates on future stock price increases over a significant number of years. At the same time, he used a figure from the employee expert's prior report without identifying where that figure came from or what its basis was. Since the expert reports were not in evidence, neither the jury nor the court could determine whether the use of that figure was sound. Further, the UPS expert did not give enough weight to the future growth projections for the stock. Because the court lacked credible evidence with which to calculate its own discount rate, it adopted the 0% rate.

Two problematic discount choices. UPS appealed the amended judgment to the 9th Circuit, arguing among other things that the district court failed to discount the restricted stock to present value. The 9th Circuit sent the case back, asking the lower court to reconsider its decision, particularly in terms of whether the employee as the plaintiff had proven the correct discount rate. In a partial dissent, one of the judges found no error with the district court's ratification of the jury's use of the 0% rate. When the employee's expert proposed the rate, UPS did not try to strike the evidence as irrelevant because it was absurd. Instead, it put on the stand its own expert who offered an alternative 10.5% rate. The jury had two choices, said the dissent with emphasis: Choose either the employee expert's rate, which "seems implausible but was at least supported by *some* evidence, however unconvincing that evidence seems to all judges who have now considered the matter," or the alternative 10.5% rate, which had no testimony or evidence to support it. It chose 0%. The plaintiff employee carried the burden of proof here, the dissent found.

'Appropriate value.' On remand, UPS asked for permission to present additional testimony on the present value adjustment issue, but the district court refused to take new evidence. It said that its review of the trial record and the parties' briefs on the issue confirmed that the employee's expert provided the "appropriate value" for the UPS stock, notwithstanding the court's earlier reservations. The expert's testimony "amply supported his valuation figure and the basis for the rate applied to the stock value." In its verdict, the jury adopted his calculation based on credible evidence in the record. Consequently, the court's second amended judgment included a front-pay calculation applying the 0% discount rate.

Harrison Mfg, LLC v. JMG Mfg., Inc.

Citation: 2014 U.S. Dist. LEXIS 57782
Date of decision: April 25, 2014
Experts: David A. Parks (plaintiff); unknown (defendant)
Judge: Walton-Pratt
State/Jurisdiction: Federal/Indiana
Court: U.S. District Court
Type of case: Tort
SIC code: 2510 Household Furniture

Do Lost Profits Represent Diminished Value or Double Recovery?

After a business collapsed because of misrepresentations from the defendant, the court held a hearing on damages. What makes the case noteworthy is the court's acceptance of the plaintiff expert's methodology: "identifying" lost profits as part of the total financial loss he calculated.

Tort, not breach of contract, suit. The plaintiff's predecessor manufactured baby and children's furniture. It started as a family business in 1921 and at its pinnacle in the 1990s employed over 1,200 workers. But by 2008 its fortune had turned and it was sold. In August 2008, the acquiring company, the plaintiff, received $1.9 million in starting capital.

The defendant was the owner and president of a company that acted as a consultant for furniture manufacturers. When the plaintiff sought a manufacturer for a new line of high-end furniture, the "Vogue Line," it decided to use the defendant as a broker for obtaining wood subassemblies for cribs and "case goods" (dressers and night stands) from a manufacturer in Indonesia. The defendant knew the plaintiff worked under a tight deadline and depended on the manufacture of the cribs for the success of its new line.

The deal went sour. Despite repeated assurances from the defendant that the parts coming from Indonesia met the plaintiff's specifications, the latter did not receive any usable cribs and was unable to sell any products under the Vogue Line. By February 2009, the plaintiff had used up its available cash and required an additional $2 million to stay in business. By June 2009, it had depleted all of its operating capital and went out of business.

Although the defendant did not have a contractual relationship with the plaintiff (his company, which was no longer a party in the suit, did), the plaintiff was able to sue for damages under a tort theory of negligent misrepresentation. Had it known of the problems in February 2009, it would have been able to switch to a different supplier in Vietnam. Instead, it relied on the defendant's assurances and remained with the Indonesian manufacturer, it argued. In the first phase of the trial, the court found the defendant was liable.

Challenge to steady rate of sales. The issue in the damages phase was how to quantify the losses stemming from the defendant's wrongdoing. The plaintiff retained an expert whose report discussed causation: Because the plaintiff did not receive workable parts from the defendant, it was unable to fulfill its customer orders and suffered lost sales, which, in turn, resulted in the plaintiff's complete loss of business. He projected what the business would have looked like had the defendant performed as promised, starting with the company's actual financial position in November 2008. Next, he forecast profits and losses, cash flows, and ending balance sheets for December 2008 and annually from 2009 to 2016. He capitalized projected annual cash flow in the terminal period beyond 2016. Besides the November 2008 balance sheet, he considered the company's business plan and its own forecast, as well as information on the children's furniture market and the terms of the company's loans. He arrived at present value by using a 50% discount rate, which he said accounted for risk in the business and the bad economy in 2008. Moreover, he assumed restricted cash flow until the company paid down its debt. He concluded the total financial loss was nearly $4.3 million before interest and fees on the loans.

He also determined that the present value of the future cash flows was about $770,000, which, he said, represented the plaintiff's equity value as of December 2008, just prior to the defendant's misrepresentations and failure to provide usable products. Adding the two figures up, he arrived at total losses of over $5 million.

He "identified" lost profits from the sales of the Vogue Line. Assuming the plaintiff would sell two cribs to each of 100 stores for five years, as well as make sales for case goods, and using a 20% discount rate (not explained in the opinion), he computed the present value of lost profits was nearly $2.3 million. He said his approach was conservative since the plaintiff's own forecast assumed an increase in sales volume.

The defendant attacked the expert's forecasting methodology, arguing that one of the plaintiff's representatives had stated in his deposition that a product line typically only has strong sales for two years. Also, given the uncertain economic climate in 2008 and beyond, the expert's use of a steady rate of sales for five years made his calculation unreliable.

The court found there was no evidence about the two-year strong sales statement on record, but it was receptive to the economic climate argument. It was more reasonable to assume sales would taper off and not remain constant, the court said. Consequently, it reduced the amount of the present value of the lost profits by $1 million and awarded a total of about $4 million.

Editor's Note: The case raises a question about double recovery—an argument the defendant did not make. Did the expert's calculation include both damages for loss of business value and lost profits? State law precedent allows damages for diminution in value of the business, where the diminution may be measured by lost profits. But it does not allow both. In commenting on the expert's damages calculation, the court twice pointed out that lost profits in this case represented "a subset of the total damages … not an additional amount."

Hartline v. Hartline

Citation: 2014 Tenn. App. LEXIS 7
Date of decision: Jan. 13, 2014
Experts: Corinne Henderson (wife); no expert (husband)
Judge: Frierson
State/Jurisdiction: Tennessee
Court: Court of Appeals
Type of case: Marital Dissolution
SIC code: 8021 Offices & Clinics of Dentists

Court Questions Idea of Goodwill in Solo Practice Valuation

Does it make sense to distinguish between professional and personal goodwill in valuing the medical practice of a sole practitioner? This was the issue at the heart of a divorce case in which the husband appealed the trial court's adoption of the valuation that the wife's expert prepared.

The husband was a dentist who, for more than 30 years, operated a solo practice in Tennessee. Its value became an issue of contention between the parties at trial. The wife retained a CPA, who was also what the court called a "Certified Evaluation Analyst." The husband did not use an expert but presented his own valuation.

Expert uses guideline transaction method. As to her qualifications, the wife's expert stated that she had valued medical and other professional practices, but not a dental practice, and that she had testified in "less than a dozen" other cases. She explained she used the guideline transaction method, "a market approach." Specifically, the "measurement used to calculate the value of the company was annual clinical production. The value multiple applied to the company's annual production was derived from guideline transactions." In terms of a dentist, "production" meant the number of patients he treated, she stated. For her calculation, she assumed all collections actually "hit the books" and analyzed the numbers from January 2011 until June 2011, when the parties filed for divorce.

Moreover, she said that in determining the market value of the practice it was an important consideration that if the husband were to sell it, the buyer would obtain a going concern: "You're buying something that's already operating." According to her, a part of the practice's value was "that you've got an in-place, existing, going-concern business." While this included having patients "in place," she considered it equally important that the practice was already set up in a particular location. That fact attracted the patients. By way of differentiating between business and personal goodwill, she maintained that her valuation did not depend on the husband's continuing the business.

Finally, in response to questioning about her methodology and whether it assumed the husband would continue to practice as a dentist, she said: "I'm going to say sort of." If the husband asked her what the practice was worth because he wanted to sell, she would say: "You should get $468 to half a million." This amount—"between $468,000 and $500,000, excluding real estate"—was the fair market value of the practice, she determined. But if the husband sold the practice she assumed he wouldn't continue to practice.

Because she assumed "the proprietor of the company is not willing or interested in liquidating the company at this time," she rejected the asset approach, liquidation value. The latter "can only be established by the actual sale of assets and the payment of all outstanding obligations." She also declined to consider the debt owed by the practice because "debt is not included in a market-based approach."

In contrast, the husband advocated for the asset approach. By his account, the practice was worth negative $100,000.

The husband's office manager testified that accounts receivable historically were collected at a high rate—99.9% in 2011—and the amount for current accounts under 30 days old was over $43,600.

Husband's valuation full of gaps. In a pretrial motion, the husband attempted to exclude the wife's expert under the state's rules of evidence, Rule 702. He claimed she did not qualify as a business valuator and her valuation was the result of a methodology that improperly incorporated the husband's goodwill as a practitioner.

The trial court expressly credited the testimony of the wife's expert. It determined that the practice was worth $468,000. But the court, unlike the wife's expert, subtracted debt in the amount of approximately $165,700 to arrive at a net value of nearly $302,300. In so doing, it implicitly denied the husband's Rule 702 motion. It also denied his subsequent motion to alter or amend the judgment, explaining that the wife's expert had testified that she had not considered personal goodwill in her valuation and had rejected the asset approach because it was not standard for the industry when it came to valuing this type of dental clinic. The husband "failed to value his patient charts, his accounts receivable, and the fact that this is an ongoing business," found the court. Also, he employed several people, the court added.

'Fine line' separates types of goodwill. The husband challenged the decision with the state Court of Appeals, claiming the trial court erred when it failed to disqualify the wife's expert under the state's Rule 702 and when it adopted her valuation resulting from a methodology that improperly considered the practice's goodwill.

The Court of Appeals disagreed as to the qualifications but agreed as to the goodwill argument. There was evidence for the trial court to conclude that the expert had the specialized knowledge that could assist the court as trier of fact. Further, she explained her approach and applied it to the data she had obtained from the husband's practice. There was no abuse of discretion in finding her "a qualified expert in relation to business valuation," said the appellate court.

The valuation itself was problematic, the appeals court concluded. The practice was a marital asset, but the expert's testimony "illustrates a fine line previously noted by this Court between the personal goodwill of a practitioner and the business goodwill of a practitioner's business, complete with staff, equipment, and a location that could be assumed by another practitioner." The court referred to *Smith v. Smith*, 709 S.W. 2d, 588 (Tenn. Ct. App. 1985) (available at *BVLaw*). The expert's analysis showed she tried to distinguish between personal and enterprise goodwill to bolster her claim that the valuation did not inappropriately include the husband's personal goodwill and, therefore, his future earning capacity. This distinction, said the court, might be relevant when valuing a practice with one or more partners or "pre-established contracts that could be assumed by another practitioner" in terms of including business goodwill. But, considering that the husband here was the sole practitioner of an unincorporated practice, it was speculation to assume his business could continue without him. Therefore, the valuation should not include any goodwill, whether associated with him personally or with his practice. For this reason, the Court of Appeals remanded to the trial court for a new valuation of the practice. It pointed out, however, that the trial court was correct in considering the practice's debt and the testimony on collection of accounts receivables in its earlier valuation. These pieces of the record should factor into its revised valuation.

Hill v. Hill

Citation: 2014 Tex. App. LEXIS 292
Date of decision: Jan. 9, 2014
Experts: Mike Hill (wife); Bryan Rice (husband)
Judge: McCoy
State/Jurisdiction: Texas
Court: Court of Appeals
Type of case: Marital Dissolution
SIC code: 8721 Accounting, Auditing, and Bookkeeping

Murky Goodwill Testimony Makes Partner Agreement Best Indicator of Value

What happens to the commercial goodwill of a big accounting firm when a principal gets divorced? In a recent Texas appeals case, the wife accused the trial court of failing to account for commercial goodwill in valuing the subject interest by relying on a partnership agreement that did not address compensation under a divorce scenario.

Shortly after getting married, in 2008, the husband joined KPMG as a Class B principal. The company is one of the Big Four auditing and accounting firms and has approximately 1,900 partners and principals in the U.S. division. A 2008 partnership agreement provided that a principal's sole interest in the firm was his required contribution to a capital account. In case of "separation," by which the agreement meant death, withdrawal, or retirement, the member would receive the balance of his capital account, excluding any amount he owed under a loan he took out to fund his interest in the firm. At year-end 2010, the amount in the husband's capital account was $715,000, and the loan amount was $700,900.

KPMG's 2003 offer letter stated that compensation depended on satisfactory performance, that is, meeting "mutually agreed upon goals." It went on to say: "If you cease to be a member of KPMG, you will be entitled only to the compensation that has been earned and accrued through the date you cease to be a member of the firm."

'Incomplete and nonstandard' valuation? The parties retained experts to value the husband's interest—a flashpoint in the case. In an August 2011 "letter," the wife's expert (an ASA) explained: "This Letter does not constitute a valuation report as defined by the Uniform Standards of Professional Appraisal Practices" and said that his submission was not a complete valuation report. He acknowledged that his calculation did not mention the partnership agreement, and, while it referred to tangible value, it did not discuss goodwill or distinguish between commercial and personal goodwill. He also ignored language in the offer letter as to the conditions applying if the husband were to end his employment at the firm. Further, he did not speak to the husband.

He essentially performed an excess earnings analysis. He determined that the husband owned approximately a tenth of one percent partnership interest in KPMG. A comparison of the husband's position with similar positions led him to conclude that reasonable compensation amounted to no more than $700,000; therefore, $800,000 of the husband's $1.5 million average income was attributable to his KPMG ownership interest. Applying a cap rate of around 33.3%, he determined the fair market value of the interest was $2.4 million. Because the $800,000 was excess income, he said, "it requires a higher rate of return than, say, normal income-based salary and so forth." The market for the husband's share was "a specific type of buyer that would have the skill set to be able to step in and receive the salary plus the excess income." Also, since the valuation covered a single period and not a discounted cash flow period "out a number of years," he did not adjust for present value.

The husband's expert acknowledged that a large professional practice might possess commercial goodwill "when the firm is marketed and operated as a collection of individuals as opposed to a group of individual practices." In this type of practice, owners usually hold a minority interest, he said; when one of them leaves, it "is generally not devastating to the entirety of the firm." He emphasized that "corporate governance" was critical to valuing interests in a firm such as KPMG. He decided to base his valuation on the partnership agreement and the offer letter. According to him, "the only way to obtain value for your partnership interest is to sell it back to the firm.... You get the capital account, you pay off the debt, and that's what you get." Here, the interest was $14,100, the value of the capital account, minus the loan against it.

He also critiqued the report that the wife's expert had submitted. For one, it was not "incomplete and nonstandard." It also contained errors, he said. For example, the expert determined the interest was a minority interest but failed to apply the standard discounts for lack of marketability or lack of control. The competing valuation basically came down to normalizing compensation, the husband's expert believed. But "you don't make normalizing adjustments when you are appraising a minority interest because the owner of the minority interest has no power to enforce those types of normalizing adjustments." He also contended the wife's expert overstated value by applying "the typical 33% cost of capital applicable to post tax benefit streams to [the husband's] pretax benefit streams." Finally, the wife's expert failed to take into account the outstanding debt against the partnership interest and the offer letter, which indicated that compensation was performance-driven.

'Impossible to access.' Texas is a community property state, and the community's interest in the value of a spouse's interest in an entity depends on the form the entity takes. Generally speaking, if the asset is an interest in a partnership, any increases in the asset's value that accrue during the marriage may be a community asset, whereas increases in a corporation's net worth are not an asset of the community of each of the corporation's shareholders. *Mandell v. Mandell*, 310 S.W.3d 531 (2010) (available at *BVLaw*).

Against this background, the wife in her closing argument claimed KPMG was a partnership, not a corporation, and fair market value was the applicable standard of value. In contrast, the husband characterized the interest as a "set of contractual rights defined and limited by the agreement." Those rights were not salable, transferable, or assignable, he reminded the court.

"I don't find that the contract controls," the trial court stated at the outset of its analysis of the valuation issue. At the same time, the court only found professional goodwill, even though "[l]ogic tells me there is some [commercial goodwill]." Also, "it's probably impossible to quantify." Most importantly, even if there were a way to assign a value to commercial goodwill, the husband could only access it by remaining employed in the future. Perhaps, the court added, if the company went out of business in the future, "he might get some piece of the value." Prior case law required valuing the partnership as a going concern, which neither of the experts did, the court emphasized. Assuming that is done, the court would consider other facts, including partnership goodwill, in determining the value of the interest at issue. In light of the evidence in front of it, it concluded that the husband's interest was worth $14,000.

It denied the wife's motion for reconsideration, emphasizing that the wife's expert did not use the appropriate method to determine fair market value.

'Goodwill is key factor.' The wife attacked the trial court's ruling in an appeal with the Texas Court of Appeals. Goodwill, she argued, was "the key factor in valuing the [husband's] partnership interest," and it was error to use the partnership agreement as the only method with which to establish the value.

To value goodwill subject to division upon divorce, there has to be evidence that commercial goodwill exists, the appeals court noted. In this case, the trial court heard expert testimony that was "vague and conflicting" as to the existence and availability of commercial goodwill. The wife's expert admitted he did not distinguish between personal and commercial goodwill; the husband's expert acknowledged that commercial goodwill could exist in a multiowner professional practice but found the partnership agreement controlling. And even though he admitted that the husband received "some interest" on his capital account besides guaranteed payments for services rendered, he considered it "minimal" and subject to offset against outstanding debt.

Another complication confronting the trial court was the lack of any provisions in the partnership agreement for accessing the value of a spouse's interest in an ongoing partnership at the time of divorce, the appeals court stated. Ultimately, the reviewing court brought back its analysis to an established principle: Whether a business possesses goodwill and what that value consists of were questions for the trier of fact, here the trial court. The latter could choose to credit the testimony of the husband's expert as to the status of the partnership interest and reasonably come to the conclusion it reached. Therefore, the appellate court affirmed the trial court's valuation of the husband's interest.

Hipple v. SCIX, LLC

Citation: 2014 U.S. LEXIS 113198
Date of decision: Aug. 13, 2014
Experts: Wayne D. Geisser (plaintiff); unknown (defendants)
Judge: DuBois
State/Jurisdiction: Federal/Pennsylvania
Court: U.S. District Court
Type of case: Expert Testimony
SIC code: 5010 Motor Vehicles and Motor Vehicle Parts and Supplies

Court Trusts Process to Test Expert's Calculation of Value

Calculation reports periodically become a point of contention in litigation in trial and appeals courts. Courts have responded in different ways to questions about their usefulness and reliability. A recent case explores the issue of whether expert testimony based on a calculation of value is admissible under *Daubert.*

Prior to marriage, the husband founded a company that marketed and sold Steel Seal, a car repair product that sealed blown head gaskets. The company had three patents related to the product. Subsequently, the husband transferred his membership interest to his son. During the marriage, the wife made two loans to the company, totaling $350,000. The company books later showed additional creditors—the husband and companies he had set up—for loans in the amount of $210,000. After the divorce, the husband caused the son to sign an agreement designating the husband as a secured creditor, which the husband used to take possession of the company's assets. The son later died.

The wife sued the husband and his entities alleging fraudulent transfer of the company's assets and the proceeds of the assets. Specifically, she claimed that he took the business's inventory, which was worth over $490,000; the husband claimed it was $110,000. She also accused the husband of orchestrating the fraudulent transfer of licensing rights to sell and produce Steel Seal to one of his companies such that he continues to benefit from the proceeds of the fraudulently transferred assets. In contrast, by the time the company went out of business, the wife had recovered only about $53,500.

Although the court found the transactions had "badges of fraud," it denied the wife's summary judgment motion because there was an issue for trial as to what assets were transferred and what their value was. The wife's summary judgment motion included expert testimony on the value of the company's assets on the transfer date, which the defendants challenged in a pretrial *Daubert* motion.

SDE-based calculation. The proposed testimony was based on an expert report in which the wife's expert stated that he prepared a calculation of value of the company—as opposed to a more extensive opinion of value resulting in a conclusion of value. During his deposition, he explained that he had had limited information about the company's financial records and, therefore, was unable to do a full appraisal. He explained that one way to value an asset or a company is to examine the sale of comparable businesses to determine a multiplier based on the annual seller's discretionary earnings (SDE) of each business. In this case, he was able to calculate the total personal withdrawals from the company and a related company that had acquired the licensing rights to Steel Seal for the relevant years. He classified the withdrawals as SDE. He also found that comparable businesses were valued at an average of 2.92 times the annual SDE generated by the companies. To value the subject company, he applied the 2.92 multiple to the average SDE he had determined for the two companies at issue. He concluded that a reasonably equivalent value for the transfer of the company's assets was approximately $1.8 million.

The defendants claimed that, since the expert merely completed a calculation report, the testimony failed two of the *Daubert* requirements: reliability and fit (or relevance). Therefore, they asked the court to preclude it.

The court disagreed. It defined a calculation of value as an engagement in which the appraiser and the client agree on the valuation approaches and methods; the work performed does not include all of the procedures an opinion of value requires, the court noted. Also, an opinion of value allows the appraiser to decide which valuation methods and approaches are appropriate under the circumstances and results in a conclusion of value, the court went on to say.

The court found that both types of engagement are approved by the American Institute of Certified Public Accountants (AICPA) and there was no reason to prevent the trier of fact from hearing the expert's testimony. According to the court, he explained why he could not perform a full valuation, and his methodology and assumptions were clear. Any questions as to the specifics of the testimony went to its weight and should be the subject of cross-examination. The testimony based on the calculation of value was admissible under *Daubert*, the court concluded.

Huff Fund Investment Partnership v. CKx, Inc. (I)

Citation: 2013 Del. Ch. LEXIS 262
Date of decision: Oct. 31, 2013
Experts: Robert Reilly (petitioners); Jeffrey Cohen (respondent)
Judge: Glasscock
State/Jurisdiction: Delaware
Court: Court of Chancery
Type of case: Dissenting Shareholder
SIC: 4833 Television Broadcasting Stations

DE Chancery Prefers Use of Merger Price to Determine Fair Value

In a statutory appraisal action arising from the sale of a media company, the petitioners' expert determined that the stock was worth more than twice the sales price, relying on discounted cash flow (DCF) and "guideline" analyses, whereas the company expert's DCF generated a value below the sales price. In something of a departure, the Delaware Chancery rejected all of these methodologies and looked elsewhere—the merger price—for the fair value.

Asset of debatable value. The sales target (respondent) was a publicly traded company that owned and managed "iconic" entertainment assets, including a business that owned rights to "American Idol" and "So You Think You Can Dance." The company's name was shorthand for "content is king," signaling management's philosophy that the acquisition of content, rather than distribution channels, was the key to increasing returns. A major issue for the company—and the case—was how to handle "the maturation" of the "American Idol" franchise. After the show peaked in the ratings in 2006, declined for five seasons. Also, around the time of the merger, the contract with the show's network distributor, Fox, was about to expire. The company had only limited leverage in the negotiations because Fox owned a perpetual license to renew its exclusive contract to broadcast the show. True, the company could refuse to produce programming in excess of 37 hours in a given season if it did not like the amount in fixed licensing fees Fox was willing to pay. But, as the court put it: "[The company] could extract meaningful concessions from Fox only if it could convince Fox that [it] was willing to cut off its nose to spite its face."

On the plus side, despite the general trend of declining ratings in the network television industry, advertising revenue actually was increasing for many years. Company management believed that, with fewer shows that had mass appeal on offer, the value of "American Idol" was still going up, and, therefore, the company might extract a higher license fee from Fox in the future.

Between 2008 and 2011, the company made it known that it was for sale and made numerous confidentiality agreements with strategic and equity bidders that had shown interest. Initially, one bidder offered $4.50 per share, another $4.75 per share, and the future buyer proposed $5.00 per share. Management decided to act swiftly to avoid sending negative signals to the market and retained a financial advisor to run an auction among interested buyers and also generate interest from third parties. To obtain a bid exceeding $5.50 per share, it promised additional compensation to its financial advisor. Even though one buyer did offer $6.50, the company ultimately agreed to the future buyer's proposed $5.50 because there was uncertainty as to the alternative bidder's financing and the actual buyer agreed to specific performance on certain provisions. The financial advisor considered the price fair.

The petitioners were stockholders who decided not to take the cash-out price resulting from the sale but instead asked the Delaware Court of Chancery for an appraisal.

'Optimistic' management projections. When potential buyers expressed an interest in the company, management created five-year projections. The CFO instructed the preparer to assume that revenues under the to-be-negotiated "American Idol" contract would increase by some $20 million each year.

Subsequently, the parties in the case disagreed whether the additional $20 million per year was a "genuine prediction" of future revenue or merely a "marketing ploy" with which to generate a high bid. The CFO testified that, to his mind, this assumption was not a prediction of the most likely outcome of the negotiations with Fox but reflected "the most optimistic" possible outcome for the company to put it in "the best possible negotiating position with potential buyers." Other witnesses agreed that this increase in payments represented "the very outside best scenario" resulting from the negotiations.

In arguing for a higher per-share price than the merger price, the petitioners claimed that the optimistic nature of the projections was "entirely consistent" with their argument that it was management's best estimate of the company's future financial performance. Also, even before the auction, top executives were bullish on the Fox negotiations. For example, they noted in emails that industry estimates suggested the show had revenues of $800 million to $900 million per season, commanding 2.6 times as much per half hour of advertising sales as the next highest rated prime-time broadcast show. In deposition, Fox's COO confirmed management's confidence that the increasing value in content would generate an increase in licensing revenues. What's more, a new Fox contract could bring with it an increase in payments other than the licensing fee, including rights to profits from Internet sales of the show's content.

Effect of 'just a few different assumptions.' To determine the fair value of the company's stock at the time of merger, both sides retained reputed experts.

For his valuation, the petitioners' expert used the DCF method, as well as a "guideline" publicly traded company approach and a "guideline" merged and acquired company method. He concluded the stock was worth $11.02 per share. This figure represented a $9.03 value resulting from the various analyses and a $1.99 addition to account for "unexploited opportunities."

As to the comparative analyses, he testified that his use of the term "guideline" reflected his inability to find companies that were truly comparable to the target. None of the guideline companies were comparable in size, none owned assets similar to the target's assets, and none were competitors of the target or used a similar business model. In the end, he weighted the two "guideline" analyses to make up 40% of his value estimate.

In contrast, the company's expert relied solely on the DCF method to compute a value per share of $4.41, which was $1.09 below the sales price.

"The gulf between the two estimates is wide," said the court, but it was the outcome of "just a few different assumptions."

1. In terms of the cash flow element in the DCF analysis, the petitioners' expert wholly adopted the revenues appearing in the management projections, whereas the company's expert ignored the projected $20 million annual increase and instead assumed Fox's fees would grow at a 4% rate for five years.

2. The petitioners' expert used a long-term nominal growth rate of 4%, whereas his counterpart used a 0% rate.

3. Both experts used different (not specified) values for the company's weighted-average cost of capital (WACC), which the court said, resulted from differing betas and size premia.

For its analysis, the Chancery first disposed of the two "guideline" analyses, noting that the guideline companies the petitioners' expert had chosen were not comparable. The petitioners' expert had admitted as much. That he accorded their results 40% of the weight of his estimate made his fair value conclusion unreliable.

The experts' DCF analyses were equally problematic, the court concluded. "DCF, in theory, is not a difficult calculation to make…. However, without reliable five-year projections, any values generated by a DCF analysis are meaningless." It pointed out that the Chancery frequently considers projections that were created outside the ordinary course of business, i.e., within in the context of litigation or a merger, unreliable. In this case, the projections included a $20 million increase in Fox's licensing fees that lacked a consistent rationale. Most of the testimony suggested management made "optimistic" projections not to indicate the most likely outcomes of the contract negotiations but to get short-term gains in the form of lower interest rates or a potentially higher merger price.

The petitioner expert's use of the projections made his DCF valuation speculative.

At the same time, the court acknowledged that there was evidence that the economic benefit to the company under the contract could have improved, which it could not simply ignore, as the company's expert had done. But there was no way to predict whether and to what extent the cash flows under the contract would have changed. "Unlike normal projections … management attempted to account for a single superseding event beyond the company's control involving idiosyncratic actors making decisions that would have a large effect on the company's future value." And it did so in an "offhand, almost casual manner," which suggested that "this was not a serious estimate," noted the court.

For all these reasons, the Chancery also found the DCF method unreliable. Ultimately, it looked to the merger price as "the best and most reliable indication" of the company's value. In so doing, it expressly rejected the petitioners' argument that U.S. Supreme Court precedent and decisions from the Chancery itself suggested that price was irrelevant and had no role in the appraisal context. On the contrary, the Chancery had "an obligation to consider all relevant factors and … no per se rule should presumptively or conclusively exclude any of those factors from consideration," the court said.

Here, the merger price was the outcome of a sales process that was "thorough, effective, and free from any spectre of self-interest or disloyalty." There were multiple bids, and the company immediately employed a respected financial advisor to maximize the price. The company had a rationale for expediting the sale, and there was no indication that the tempo deterred any bidder.

The Court of Chancery concluded that the evidence showed there was little, if any, synergy value embedded in the sales price, but it gave the parties an opportunity to discuss "this limited issue," if they so desired.

Huff Fund Investment Partnership v. CKx, Inc. (II)

Citation: 2014 Del. Ch. LEXIS 82
Date of decision: May 19, 2014
Experts: Robert Reilly (petitioners); Jeffrey Cohen (respondent)
Judge: Glasscock
State/Jurisdiction: Delaware
Court: Delaware Court of Chancery
Type of case: Dissenting Shareholder
SIC code: 4833 Television Broadcasting Stations

DE Chancery Plumbs Merger Price for 'Speculative Value Elements'

This statutory appraisal action made news last year because the Delaware Court of Chancery found that the merger price, rather than the value resulting from the discounted cash flow (DCF) analysis, was the most reliable indicator of the fair value of the subject company. At the time, the court (Judge Glasscock) allowed the parties to present additional arguments for downward or upward adjustments related to synergies and business opportunities not reflected in the merger price. This case represents the court's final ruling on the share price.

Backstory. The subject company (respondent) was a publicly traded company that owned and managed "iconic" entertainment assets, including a business that owned rights to "American Idol" and "So You Think You Can Dance." A major issue for the company—and the original case—was how to handle "the maturation" of the "American Idol" franchise. After the show peaked in ratings in 2006, it began to decline for five seasons. Around the time of the merger, the contract between the show's network distributor, Fox, and the company was about to expire. The company had only limited leverage in the negotiations because Fox owned a perpetual license to renew its exclusive contract to broadcast the show. When the company was ready for sale, management retained a financial advisor to run an auction among interested buyers and also generate interest from third parties. Even though one buyer offered $5.60 per share, the company ultimately accepted the future buyer's proposed $5.50 per share because there was uncertainty as to the alternative bidder's financing and the actual buyer agreed to specific performance on certain provisions. The financial advisor considered the price fair. But certain stockholders (petitioners) decided not to take the cash-out price resulting from the sale, and they instead asked the Chancery for an appraisal.

At trial, the valuation turned on the reliability of management's five-year projections, which assumed that revenues under the to-be-negotiated "American Idol" contract would increase by some $20 million each year. The parties disagreed as to whether that amount was a "genuine prediction" of future revenue or merely a "marketing ploy" with which to generate a high bid. For his DCF analysis, the petitioners' expert included the amount. He also developed comparable analyses and ultimately arrived at a price of $11.02 per share. In contrast, the company's expert excluded the amount in his DCF calculation and computed a value per share of $4.41, which was $1.09 below the sales price.

The Chancery first dismissed the petitioner expert's comparable analyses, only to find both experts' DCF analyses were also unreliable. Even though the DCF is not a difficult calculation to make, it may produce meaningless values when there are no reliable five-year projections, said the court. This was the case here. "Unlike normal projections … management attempted to account for a single superseding event beyond the company's control involving idiosyncratic actors making decisions that would have a large effect on the company's future value." Here, management acted in an "offhand, almost casual manner" when it came to the projections. All of these factors led to the conclusion that "this was not a serious estimate."

In contrast, the court considered the merger price to be the outcome of a sales process that was "thorough, effective, and free from any spectre of self-interest or disloyalty." There were multiple bids, and the company immediately employed a respected financial advisor to maximize the price. Although the court found little, if any, evidence that there was an improper synergy value embedded in the sales price, it gave the parties an opportunity to discuss "this limited issue," if they so desired. *Huff Fund Investment Partnership v. CKx, Inc.*, 2013 Del. Ch. LEXIS 262 (Oct. 31, 2013) (available at *BVLaw*).

Exclude cost savings? At the root of the court's willingness to entertain adjustments to the merger price was the statutory requirement to determine the fair value of the shares "exclusive of any element of value arising from the accomplishment or expectation of the merger or consolidation" in order to generate the company's going-concern value, as opposed to third-party sale value. In other words, the law prohibits an appraisal award that includes "speculative elements of value" arising only from the merger. Here both parties argued in favor of adjusting the merger price but disagreed over the direction of the adjustment.

The respondent claimed the price should be lowered from $5.50 per share to $5.21 per share because it contained "synergistic elements of value." Specifically, prior to the merger, the acquirer identified some $4.6 million in cost savings it hoped to realize by converting the subject from a publicly held corporation to a privately held firm. As primary support, the respondent referred to a 2011 budget the acquirer developed when performing due diligence that identified corporate overhead expenses for the past four years and savings the subject's management and the acquirer identified. The petitioners objected to lowering the price because the cost savings were not value "uniquely available to the acquirer … as a result of its ability to operate the acquired company as part of a larger corporate organization."

The court declined to answer the larger question as to when cost savings might represent excludable synergies. Instead, it found that in this case there was no evidence that the acquirer arrived at its $5.50 bid based on cost savings that the subject might not have realized if it had continued as a going concern. Also, documentation from the acquirer did not on its face support a finding that it believed it would realize *merger-specific* cost savings, said the court with emphasis.

What did market participants know? For their part, the petitioners wanted an upward adjustment to account for the value resulting from a post-merger acquisition and "unexploited revenue opportunities," which, they claimed, were part of the subject's "operative reality" at the time of the merger but whose value was not captured in the merger price. Specifically, about a month before the company effected the merger, it began to explore buying a television production company, Sharp, specializing in reality and event-based programming that was expected to generate $11 million in operating income in 2011, double the amount of its 2010 earnings. As for the unexploited revenue opportunities, the petitioners pointed to merchandise and music purchasing during "American Idol" over-the-phone voting; a permanent "AI" event in Las Vegas; an international "Idol" competition; an "AI" website that a third-party provider would host ("Internet Idol"); and "So You Think You Can Dance" "dance clinics." The petitioners admitted that the acquirer became aware of those opportunities during due diligence, prior to the merger.

According to the court, in this case, the issue was not whether future cash flows would have to include revenue stemming from projects the company had in the works, if it had continued as a going concern. Case law was clear that when a company begins to implement business plans, revenues related to the plans must be considered in an income-based valuation method. Here, the court pointed out, the valuation method was a market-derived sales price. Therefore, the Chancery emphasized, the issue was whether *market participants* were aware of the opportunities the acquirer and the subject identified such that the value related to these opportunities made its way into the merger price.

Contrary to the petitioners' claim, the record indicated that the buyer knew of several acquisition targets, including Sharp, when formulating its bid for the subject company. It did so based on diligence information from the subject's management. It also knew of the "unexploited revenue opportunities"; in fact it referred to them as "low-hanging fruit." The court added that there was no evidence that other market participants did not receive the same material when doing diligence.

The Chancery quickly dismissed the petitioners' objections that, since the buyer's offer rested on a "base case" that did not break out value for the Sharp acquisition and other revenue opportunities, the subject's shareholders did not obtain value for them. The process leading to the $5.50 bid was an arm's-length transaction, with the goal of achieving the highest price for the stockholders, the court noted. Under this circumstance, it made no sense to determine whether the price incorporated the value of certain opportunities "by considering only the idiosyncratic weight attached to that information by any particular bidder, even the winning bidder." In other words, the subjective valuation the bidder put on the opportunities was not relevant.

Further, the court pointed out that the petitioners did not try to quantify the difference between: (1) how the market would have valued the acquisition of Sharp at the time the buyer submitted its $5.50 bid when that acquisition was one acquisition among several possible acquisitions; and (2) how the market would have valued that acquisition after the company let it be known it was in "advanced discussions," but the transaction was still not a done deal.

The petitioners also claimed the merger price did not capture the value of side agreements the acquirer made with two stockholders to ensure approval of the merger. The respondent objected that this was asking for a share in a control premium to which the petitioners were not entitled as an element of going-concern value. The court declined to rule on whether the side agreements amounted to a control premium. Instead, it found that the petitioners had failed to offer a reasonable method with which to value those transactions.

The petitioners' final argument was that the acquirer's $5.50 bid was not the highest bid. The court noted it had rejected that argument in its earlier decision, when finding the merger was an arm's-length transaction. For all of these reasons, the Court of Chancery declined to adjust the $5.50-per-share price.

Hugh v. Hugh

Citation: 2014 Va. App. LEXIS 222
Date of decision: June 3, 2014
Experts: Mark Vogel (wife); none (husband)
Judge: Alston Jr.
State/Jurisdiction: Virginia
Court: Court of Appeals
Type of case: Marital Dissolution
SIC code: 3674 Semiconductors and Related Devices

Can You Trust a Valuation That Falls Short of AICPA Standards?

What type and quantity of evidence does a trial court need to make a meaningful valuation of a business? This was the central question in a hard-fought divorce case featuring questionable financial records, problematic expert testimony, and a range of values from zero to $1.4 million. After the trial court decided not to classify, value, or distribute the business at issue, the parties appealed.

During the marriage, the husband owned a business that he regularly dissolved and subsequently reincorporated under different but similar names. According to the appeals court, a "rather convoluted and strained record" made it impossible to discern the exact nature of the business and the husband's work; however, there was some evidence that he worked as a broker for the semiconductor industry. When, in mid-2011, the husband dissolved a predecessor company and incorporated the business in suit, the wife owned 51% and the husband 49%, but he ran the company. On the record, he was the 100% owner of the successor business. Valuing that company became a focal point of contention during the divorce proceedings.

Drastic decrease in income. The wife presented expert testimony, but the husband did not. Instead, he himself testified about the company. He said it did business "everywhere" and had no inventory at the time of trial. He offered past tax returns into evidence, including a 2010 return that showed revenue for the predecessor company of $9.3 million, total income of just over $700,000, and total profit of just under $400,000. In 2011, eight months prior to its dissolution, the predecessor company showed revenue of $6.8 million, total income of just over $400,000, and total profit of $50,000. The tax return also stated officer compensation in the amount of $240,000. The successor company's 2011 tax return accounted for four months and listed revenue of $155,000, total income of just over $136,000, and total profit of minus $12,929. Its 2012 tax return stated revenue of about $1 million and $150,000 in losses. The company's bank account also listed debits totaling $335,000 for personal expenses.

The husband explained that the company's poor performance in 2012 was the result of "the bad economy." He added that "the semiconductor business was not doing well at all." Also, "I was not in a situation to run the business." He concluded the company was worth nothing.

The wife's expert was a CPA and business valuator who reviewed the company's website, tax returns, financial statements, deposition statements the husband and the husband's CPA gave, bank statements, invoice and purchase orders, depreciation and amortization schedules, and corporate charter documents. He received "scant" information from the husband. For example, he only had access to the company's 2010 financial statement; he said there were discrepancies between that statement and the relevant tax return in that the statement showed more than double the income the tax return listed. He expressed "some doubts about the correctness of the tax returns as filed," pointing out that a lot of personal expenses were run through the business and concluding the tax returns were "prepared in a very taxable motivated fashion." He never received general ledgers or QuickBooks files and was unable to interview management or perform a site visit. Also, he said that he preferred to look at five years of financial statements but in this case was unable to obtain a complete set of bank and credit card statements. From the information available to him, he believed the company was reselling and refurbishing semiconductor manufacturing equipment. He noted that on its website the company announced equipment for sale and claimed it had "the world's largest inventory of semiconductor and manufacturing equipment parts."

For his valuation of the company, the expert decided not to use the asset approach because he "didn't see much" in the balance sheet or in cash. The balance sheet as reported on the tax return showed "little to no inventory," he said, adding he was unable to determine why that was. He explained he could not use the income approach because he was unable to create cash flow projections or determine with accuracy the company's income. Ultimately, he relied on the market approach, which he described as a generally accepted method among experts in the field and as a "sound and reasonable" approach for valuing closely held businesses. To this end, he reviewed 31 comparable companies. He said he did not consider companies older than 10 years and for each company considered size and industry to ensure those selected were similar to the subject company. On cross-examination, he admitted no companies were "exactly like" the company at issue. He said this happened frequently, and when it did he looked to "the industry and gross profit margins to find comparable transactions." He concluded the goodwill value of the company that was attributable to the husband was 30% of its $2 million value. Applying that discount rate, the company's intrinsic value was $1.4 million, the expert concluded.

The expert acknowledged that, in light of the limited data the husband made available to him, his valuation did not meet the standards of the American Institute of Certified Public Accountants (AICPA). But, he said, his calculation was based on "sound foundation and fact and accounting theory." His work product for trial was "useful and … a reasonable estimate of the value of the company as it [was]."

The trial court said there was insufficient evidence for valuing the company. It referred to the husband's testimony that the value was zero and found that "almost all of what [the expert] relied upon to form his opinion was not in fact correct." In its written opinion, the court pointed out that the husband had obstructed expert discovery; but for the latter's stonewalling, "the expert witness would have been able to value the business." Therefore, the trial court ordered the husband to pay $25,000 in expert fees.

Mixed signals on ability to value. Both parties appealed the trial court's decision not to value the company and not to make an equitable distribution of this asset. At the outset, the state Court of Appeals recognized the obstacles to valuation facing the trial court. "At best, husband's testimony regarding [the company] was vague, indefinite, and confusing," it said. Further, the husband provided "scant and indefinable" information to the wife's expert. The appeals court also noted the expert's caveat to his valuation. It said that, "to no great surprise," the trial court decided it had insufficient evidence to place a value on the business.

At the same time, the appeals court concluded that the trial court's refusal to value the company was error. Under state law, "the type or quantity of evidence required to enable the trial court to value a business is not fixed," the court said. Citing precedent, it noted that tax returns showing a business's gross income may be sufficient evidence as "[a]ssuredly, a business that has gross income can be valued." Also, conflicting evidence or a range of values was not necessarily an impediment to valuation. In fact, the appeals court said, here the trial court "had a relative wealth of information" with which to value the company. Both the husband and the wife's expert placed a value on the company. The wife's expert reviewed corporate financial documents and used an accepted valuation method. He also determined a discount rate for the husband's goodwill. Even though the expert did not have all the information necessary to produce an AICPA standard value, he himself called his result "a reasonable estimate" of the company's value as it was. Moreover, the record provided the trial court with the relevant tax returns.

For all these reasons, the appeals court remanded for a valuation and equitable distribution of the business.

Kahn v. M&F Worldwide Corp.

Citation: 2014 Del. LEXIS 115
Date of decision: March 14, 2014
Experts: Evercore Partners (defendants)
Judge: Holland
State/Jurisdiction: Delaware
Court: Supreme Court of Delaware
Type of case: Dissenting Shareholder
SIC code: 6790 Miscellaneous Investing

Valuations Underpin DE Chancery's Ruling in Going-Private Merger

After the controlling stockholder effected a going-private merger, the plaintiff shareholders sued in the Delaware Court of Chancery for post-closing damages. The defendants contended two procedural safeguards ensured that the transaction replicated an arm's-length transaction in terms of protecting the interests of minority shareholders. Finding the case presented a "novel question of law" as to the applicable standard for review, the Chancery applied the business judgment rule and granted the defendants' summary judgment motion. The plaintiffs asked the Delaware Supreme Court for review. Valuation issues played a central role in both rulings, as did the plaintiffs' failure to provide an expert valuation.

Going private. The 43.4% stockholder (an individual and his company) in the target company set out to take it private. The target was a holding company with four business segments. It had a 13-member board; three of the members were officers of both the target and the controlling shareholder.

In May 2011, the target's stock traded in the $20-to-$24-per-share range. The controlling shareholder contacted a financial advisor, which, based on projections the target had given to lenders in April 2011 and May 2011, valued the company in the $10-to-$32-a-share range. In June 2011, its shares closed on the New York Stock Exchange at almost $17 per share. The next business day, the controlling shareholder proposed to buy the remaining common stock for $24 a share in cash.

The merger proposal came with two up-front conditions: (1) it required the directors to appoint a special committee to negotiate and approve the merger; and (2) it required the approval of a majority of stockholders that had no affiliation with the controlling stockholder. The proposal also made it clear that the controlling shareholder had no intention of selling its block of shares or support an alternative sale, merger, or similar transaction. At the same time, it promised there would be no adverse consequences if either one of the conditions was not met. The controlling stockholder would remain a long-term stockholder.

Range of valuations. In response, the target's independent directors formed a special committee, which interviewed four potential financial advisors and ultimately retained Evercore Partners; the committee also hired its own legal advisors. The committee and Evercore asked management for updated projections to reflect current thinking on the target's prospects. Executives from the majority shareholder as well as "dual" executives did not participate in preparing the new projections.

One business segment informed Evercore that its projections remained the same, but the other businesses submitted new forecasts that Evercore used to construct a valuation model. The revised forecasts indicated a downward trend: Where the original projections stated EBITDA for the target of $535 million in 2015, the revised projections only showed $491 million.

Evercore used various valuation methods, including the discounted cash flow (DCF) and comparable company analyses. Valuations based on the updated projections indicated a range of $15 to $45 per share. The DCF valuations generated a range of fair value of $22 to $38 per share; a premium paid analysis indicated a range of $22 to $45 per share.

Even though the proposed $24-per-share price fell within these ranges, the special committee asked Evercore to undertake additional analyses and investigate alternative strategies that might produce more value for the minority stockholders than the proposed sale, notwithstanding the majority stockholder's clear unwillingness to sell. Ultimately, the special committee concluded that none of them would top the offer. Still, it rejected the $24-a-share price and countered with $30 per share, a price the majority owner rejected. Ultimately, the parties settled on a $25-per-share "best and final" offer. Evercore opined the price was fair based on generally accepted valuation techniques.

As to the second procedural safeguard, following the special committee's recommendation, the minority stockholders received a proxy statement that described the committee's efforts, including its collaboration with Evercore and the thinking that informed the updated projections underlying the valuations, as well as Evercore's fairness opinion. More than 65% of the holders of the minority shares approved the merger.

A number of shareholders disapproved and initially wanted to enjoin the merger in the Delaware Court of Chancery. Subsequently, they pursued post-closing relief instead against the majority shareholder, the board of directors, and members of the special committee for breach of fiduciary duty. The defendants asked for summary judgment. The merger, they claimed, from the outset had two procedural protections—the independent special committee and the approval of a majority of the disinterested shareholders—that replicated an arm's-length merger. Therefore, the court should review the transaction under the business judgment rule, not the entire fairness standard, which was the highest level of scrutiny in corporate law. Under the former standard, the transaction was fair and there was no issue to be tried, they concluded.

Chancery makes a new rule. The Court of Chancery said the dual procedural safeguards that were built into the going private merger raised a novel legal issue. What standard of review should apply to ensure adequate protection of the minority investor: entire fairness, as applied in transactions involving self-dealing by a controlling shareholder, or business judgment. It adopted the latter and ruled in favor of the defendants.

As to the special committee, the Chancery noted the plaintiffs did not even contend that it had failed to meet its duty to make an informed decision as to what terms would be most advantageous for the minority stockholders in the proposed sale. It retained independent legal and financial advisors. The interview process for the financial advisors "lets the client consider a number of qualified advisors and, one hopes, therefore get better financial terms from the winner because the winner knows it has competition." It also serves another purpose, said the court:

> [W]hich is that each of the pitching firms present "pitch books" relevant to the potential engagement, and give the committee a chance to hear preliminary thoughts from a variety of well qualified financial advisors, a process that therefore helps the committee begin to get fully grounded in the relevant economic factors.

The court recognized that despite its power, the special committee did not have the practical authority to market the target to other buyers. Considering the controlling shareholder's declaration that it was not open to selling, it was unlikely that any potentially interested party would incur the costs and risks of exploring a purchase of the target.

But, the court concluded, the special committee was empowered to say no to the merger and had a financial advisor with which to evaluate other options; and it did negotiate with the majority holder over the terms of the offer. The merger resulted in a 47% premium to the closing price preceding the offer. The court emphasized that the financial advisor considered the price fair in light of various analyses, "including a DCF analysis, which mirrors the valuation standard applicable in an appraisal case."

The plaintiffs, the court pointed out, did not produce a valuation from an expert that declared the merger price was unfair. They rationalized their omission by saying that the defendants' motion was not about the issue of fairness but about the business judgment rule. But, said the Chancery, the plaintiffs had to realize that to survive summary judgment they would have to show the merger imposed terms that a rational fiduciary could not accept in good faith. Without a countervailing expert opinion, they "have not come close to meeting that burden."

Similarly, there was no issue as to the legality of the majority-of-the-minority vote. The noncontrolling shareholders received adequate disclosure of the background to the merger and were not coerced into voting for it. Yet they did.

Record supports acceptance of merger terms. The plaintiffs next appealed the Chancery's decision to the Delaware Supreme Court, arguing that under the business judgment standard there was evidence that the special committee was not independent and effective and the majority-of-the-minority provision was not enough protection to deviate from entire fairness review.

The Supreme Court disagreed. First, it affirmed the Chancery's decision to apply the business judgment standard to controller buyouts whenever the dual protections are established prior to trial. Next, it applied the standard to the case at hand and, like the Chancery, found the special committee had real negotiating power and authority to reject the offer and it exercised due care by, among other things, hiring Evercore and asking it to perform a series of valuation analyses, all of which showed the proposed price fell into the range of the generated values. Moreover, the Supreme Court stated with emphasis, "Evercore opined that the $25 per share *price was fair* based on generally accepted valuation methodologies, including DCF and comparable companies analysis."

In this case, said the high court, there was no credible argument—let alone a conclusion—that no rational person would find the merger favorable to the minority stockholders. Consequently, it affirmed the decision of the Court of Chancery.

Laidler v. Hesco Bastion Environmental, Inc.

Citation: 2014 Del. Ch. LEXIS 75
Date of decision: May 12, 2014
Experts: Thomas Frazee (petitioner); Curtis Kimball (respondent)
Judge: Glasscock
State/Jurisdiction: Delaware
Court: Delaware Court of Chancery
Type of case: Dissenting Shareholder
SIC code: 344 Fabricated Structural Metal Products

Lack of Cash Flow Projections Compels Use of DCCF

In a statutory appraisal action arising out of a short-form merger, the Delaware Court of Chancery (J. Glasscock) adopted the direct capitalization of cash flow (DCCF) analysis the parties' experts advocated because of the unique nature of the target's business and factors affecting the transaction. This was a less common approach than the discounted cash flow (DCF) analysis, the Chancery noted. Since there was wide agreement over the inputs and calculations to be used, the court focused its role on resolving value disputes.

One minority stockholder holds out. The merger involved a group of related entities in the United Kingdom and the United States operating under common control and being players in the flood barrier industry. When the British inventor of the proprietary sole product ("Concertainer units," see below) that launched the enterprise died in 2010, he had a controlling interest in the entities, which subsequently transferred to his estate. The petitioner was the company secretary, general manager, and managing director of the U.K. corporation, who was terminated in 2011 in connection with fraud allegations. She and two other individuals each owned 10,000 shares of the target company, which amounted to a 10% interest per person. Under a shareholder agreement, the petitioner could force the target company to repurchase her shares. Anticipating she would exercise her right, the company in November 2011 requested a fair market opinion from Willamette Management Association (Willamette), which then valued the stock at $180 per share. The petitioner chose not to sell at that price.

In January 2012, the two other minority stockholders tendered their shares to the entity acquiring the target—the respondent—for $207.50 per share. This meant that, on the merger date, Jan. 26, 2012, the acquiring entity owned 90% of the target and the petitioner 10%, which allowed for a short-form merger that did not require a stockholder vote. The petitioner rejected the $207.50-per-share offer and requested a statutory appraisal—i.e., a determination of the fair value of the target on the merger date—from the Delaware Court of Chancery.

Factors affecting revenue. The target company assembled the proprietary Concertainer units, which are rapidly deployable barriers that function as giant sandbags to protect against storms or floods. Its customers were architecture and civil engineering firms, as well as governmental organizations. Its revenue was hard to predict since sales depended on natural disasters and similar weather-related events. As one commenter said, "The bigger the disaster, the more revenue." Given fluctuating demand, the company never created forward-looking projections.

Three events played a significant role in the company's revenues in 2009, 2010, and 2011 and later became flashpoints in the suit. First, in 2009, revenues reached $8.5 million; $1.7 million of that amount stemmed from the Howard Hanson Dam project in Washington state. Because of structural damage to the dam and flood warnings from the United States Army Corps of Engineers, several major companies in the area, including Boeing, contracted for Concertainer units to protect their assets, driving sales up. Second, in 2010, the target achieved $7 million in revenues, in large part because of the experimental use of its Concertainer units to assist with the cleanup of the BP oil spill, one of the largest marine oil spills in history. Third, in 2011, the target generated some $22.5 million in revenues resulting primarily from the "500-year flood," a federal disaster affecting three states. The Concertainer units served as flood barriers throughout the flooded areas, but many sales also stemmed from "premitigation" efforts. There was uncertainty as to how revenues from these years prefigured future revenues.

There were other factors creating uncertainty. For instance, the record showed that on the merger date there were plans to open a company for manufacturing components of the Concertainer units in South Carolina. But it was not clear whether this project was a part of the target's business plan or of the controlling U.K. entity. Moreover, the target was about to lose a license and the patent covering its sole product.

Expert valuations. The petitioner retained an expert who performed a DCCF-based valuation and concluded the fair value of her shares was $515 per share on the merger date.

The respondent obtained a post-merger valuation that was a combination of a DCCF analysis and guideline companies and guideline transaction analyses. It stated a $322-per-share price. Subsequently, an executor of the estate disapproved of the valuation. It "did not adequately reflect particular issues around normalized earnings," he believed. In testimony, he said he had not instructed the expert as to how to do the valuation but had told him that there were "extraordinary events" that he should have factored into the calculation but did not. Subsequently, the expert backed out revenues related to "nonrecurring" events," including those connected to the dam project, the BP oil spill, and the 500-year flood. Based on the revised "normalized" revenues, he decreased the per-share value to $250.30.

For its value determination, the court considered the petitioner expert's valuation and the respondent expert's revised valuation: $515 per share versus $250.30 per share.

Unreliable indicators of value. At the start of its analysis, the court quickly disposed of the respondent's arguments in favor of considering the merger price and its expert's market analyses. As for the merger price, it dismissed the respondent's suggestion that this transaction was comparable to the situation in *Huff Fund*, where the court (also J. Glasscock) leaned on the merger price for its valuation because the target's unique assets and circumstances surrounding them made it next to impossible to predict future cash flows. (*Huff Fund Inv. P'ship v. CKx, Inc.*, 2013 Del. Ch. LEXIS 262 (Nov. 1, 2013), is available at *BVLaw*.) *Huff Fund* involved a true arm's-length transaction, said the court, whereas, in this short-form merger, the 90%-controlling shareholder determined the price it would pay to the petitioner minority shareholder and went through with the merger without the latter's consent.

The Chancery also declined to adopt the respondent expert's comparable transaction and comparable companies analyses. He failed to make a persuasive argument that the companies or transactions on which his analyses relied were truly comparable. In his deposition, he himself admitted that "there is no ideally comparable company in this particular case" and, regarding the four he selected, "[n]one of these were great comps or even necessarily that good a comp." Further, the petitioner's expert pointed out that the selected companies made building products: "They are not in the business of anything close to flood control barriers."

DCCF is a two-step process. Both experts relied primarily on an income approach and agreed that the commonly used discounted cash flow (DCF) method did not work in this case because the target's management had never made cash flow projections in the ordinary course of business. Therefore, both primarily relied on the DCCF analysis, which the court adopted.

The Chancery described the DCCF as a method that "estimates a normalized level of cash flows in perpetuity and divides those cash flows by a capitalization rate to estimate the present value of the business." In other words, the court explained, it involves a two-step process: (1) determine the normalized cash flow figure; and (2) calculate a capitalization rate. It noted that it was "unfamiliar with the methodology typically employed in a DCCF analysis." But since the experts agreed as to the necessary inputs and calculations, the court would use the methodology to resolve disputes as to the values for each.

The main issues were:

1. *Cash flows.* The disagreements focused on the appropriate cash flows to use in a DCCF analysis. The petitioner's expert derived his cash flow figure from weighting the target's actual revenues in 2010 and 2011 at 40% and 60%, respectively. He then multiplied the resulting figure by a projected 55% profit margin and subtracted $1.5 million in estimated overhead expenses.

The respondent's expert weighted actual and "normalized" EBITDA figures for 2009, 2010, and 2011; the "normalized" figures backed out revenues resulting from the Howard Hanson Dam project, the BP oil spill, and the 500-year flood. He used the 2009 figures to represent poor years, the 2010 figures to represent typical years, and the 2011 figures to represent active years, he explained. The actual results made up 25% of the target's cash flow estimate, and the normalized results represented 75%.

The experts disagreed over the effect on future cash flows of the proposed plant in South Carolina, the expiration of patents, and the termination of licenses, but the court noted that neither expert quantified the value of these events. Consequently, it declined to accord them major significance for its analysis. The other cash flow issue was how reliable past cash flows were considering that revenues in the crucial previous years in part stemmed from what the respondent called "nonrecurring events."

The plaintiff contended that the respondent expert's revised valuation was "litigation-driven and self-serving." The respondent's expert's original fair market value opinion adjusted the growth rate down for 2011 to account for the unusually large sales related to the 500-year flood but did not treat revenues related to the dam project and the oil spill as extraordinary. Management never considered revenues "nonrecurring" until the petitioner sued, and then it did so to depress the target's value, the petitioner argued.

The "nonrecurring" event argument carried no weight with the Chancery. Considering the company was in the business of providing protection in anticipation of natural disasters, there was no evidence that it would not in the future be able to sell its products to protect against different dam breaks, floods, or other disasters. It was not unlikely, said the court, that some future "nonrecurring" event would occur considering those extraordinary events occurred every year the entity was in existence. At the same time, the court pointed out that the petitioner's expert failed to justify his 40%-to-60% weighting. Indeed, it was suspicious that he placed a 60% weight on the 2011 cash flows when 2011 was the highest grossing year.

The court concluded that the best predictor of future cash flows was the past cash flows for the three years, weighted equally. Considering EBITDA in 2009 was nearly $5.9 million, in 2010 $5.3 million, and in 2011 $11.3 million, the average was $7.5 million, which was the court's estimate of future cash flow.

2. *Capitalization rate.* Both experts arrived at their capitalization rate by multiplying the company's weighted average cost of capital (WACC) by its long-term growth rate. Both agreed the growth rate was 4% but disputed the various inputs with which to compute the WACC.

Concerning the cost of equity, they both used a build-up model but disagreed over the Ibbotson deciles for the industry risk premium and size premium. They also argued over the appropriate capital structure.

a. Industry risk premium. The petitioner's expert said he used "something that was roughly consistent with the average" of three SIC codes over several years. The codes were 34 (Fabricated Metal Products, Except Machinery and Transportation Equipment) and two subsets of the category, 344 (Fabricated Structural Metal Products) and 3499 (Fabricated Metal Products, N.E.C.). However, in his deposition, he cautioned that code 34 and code 3499 were not very good, and in testimony in front of the court he said that code 344 was not comparable to the target.

In contrast, the respondent's expert used only code 344 for 2011. He said, with emphasis, that he had contacted Morningstar, the publisher of the *Ibbotson Valuation Yearbook,* and learned that "the appropriate use of their statistic is to use the latest available data, *not* to average codes over a period of years because a code of the latest year already incorporates statistical data for previous years."

The court found the respondent expert's approach more persuasive and determined that using code 344 for the year 2011 led to a 5.91% industry risk premium.

b. Size premium. The petitioner's expert used decile 10a, whereas the respondent's expert used decile 10. Decile 10a, he argued, "includes companies with market capitalization between $144 million and $236 million," but the target was worth much less than companies in that range. The petitioner's expert countered that "using Decile 10 will result in the inclusion of premiums derived from companies that fall in 10b"; this was undesirable because "10b includes a disproportionately large number of highly leveraged or poorly performing companies that have low equity values, not because their business operations are 'small,' but because their equity valuations are low."

Both experts had good arguments, said the court. The respondent's expert said 10a was inappropriate because it included companies with market capitalizations that were too high and the petitioner's expert said 10b was inappropriate because it included companies with too much debt. Therefore, the court used decile 10. The resulting risk premium was 6.10%.

c. Cost of debt. At the time of the merger, the target had no debt. However, both experts agreed that as a going concern it would be expected to take on some debt. The petitioner's expert used a ratio of 85% equity-to-15% debt, whereas the respondent's expert determined a ratio of 90% equity-to-10% debt.

The court pointed out that neither of them provided supporting evidence for his choice, but it decided the respondent's ratio was more conservative and adopted it. The cost of debt, it explained, was from Moody's rating of a Baa company as of the merger date. It was 5.24%. Based on the formula with which to calculate WACC, the Chancery arrived at a figure of 21.83%. Subtracting the long-term growth rate (4%) from the WACC yielded a 17.83% capitalization rate, with its inverse, 5.6, as the capitalization multiple.

Result. In sum, the Chancery's DCCF analysis resulted in a fair value of $364.24 per share. The court held the respondent owed the petitioner $3,642,400, plus statutory interest for her 10% interest in the target.

Leone v. Owsley

Citation: 2014 U.S. Dist. LEXIS 49700
Date of decision: April 10, 2014
Experts: Mitchell Hoffman (plaintiff); St. Charles Capital, LLC; Intrinsic (defendants)
Judge: Brimmer
State/Jurisdiction: Federal/Colorado
Court: U.S. District Court
Type of case: Contract
SIC code: 6282 Investment Advice

Buyout Agreement Short-Circuits Court's Scrutiny of Appraisals

Did the defendants provide inaccurate information to the appraisers or otherwise manipulate the valuation, and does it matter? These were questions at the heart of a buyout suit involving a limited liability company (LLC) that managed several hedge funds. The case illustrates the court's deference to an existing operating agreement as to how to appraise the interest of a departed shareholder and its reluctance to "second-guess" the valuators' judgments.

The plaintiff and the two defendants were members of a registered investment advisor that was created in 2004. The firm had six members altogether and earned profit from managing investor assets. From 2005 until August 2012, the plaintiff was a principal, holding a 19.75% interest in the company, and the defendants were managers. An operating agreement provided that, if a member's status as a principal ended, the company had the right, but not the obligation, to repurchase the departing member's interest in part or in whole. If the company decided not to do so, the individual members could elect to buy the stake. Critically, the repurchase price was to be the fair market value, "as determined in good faith by the Managers." The agreement did not prescribe a valuation method.

In 2009, Duff & Phelps prepared a valuation, but it did not purport to provide a fair market value. The appraiser's report concluded that the company then was worth between $50 million and $65 million.

In the spring and summer of 2012, the defendants indicated they wanted to terminate the plaintiff's employment. Before they took that step, in early August, the plaintiff resigned as a principal and alleged in his resignation letter that the defendants had mismanaged the company. Since the company did not choose to buy the plaintiff's interest back, the defendants made moves to do so. For this purpose, they hired two independent valuation firms that had no prior relationship with the company.

St. Charles Capital was the first financial expert the defendants contacted. They described their partner's departure from the firm as "not amicable" and said they wanted a valuation to "facilitate a buyout." They portrayed the company as struggling, even though it had been in business for eight years and had no debt. It also was managing $150 million in assets, but the defendants emphasized it had managed as much as $450 million in 2008 and told St. Charles to consider the decline. They also suggested that the decline had to do with the plaintiff's taking business from the company—which was not true. They asked the appraiser to take into account the poor performance of other small hedge funds in the current market, but they did not disclose to the appraiser monthly newsletters the company sent out. A July 2012 newsletter stated that the firm's portfolio had posted a net gain of 2.65% since the start of the month. But it did discuss the possibility of a "very choppy and volatile investment climate for the balance of the year." It did not suggest the company was "struggling."

Spin on valuation-related facts. St. Charles said it based its valuation on the information the company provided, publicly available information, and its expert assessment of the company's likely future performance. It relied on the 2011 total revenue, which was nearly $5.9 million, and the total net income, which was $2.21 million. These figures were lower than those listed in the company's internal profit and loss statement—which stated $7.2 million in revenue and $3.4 million in net income for 2011. St. Charles' report concluded that the plaintiff's interest in early August 2012 valued between $126,400 and $158,000.

The second appraiser was called Intrinsic, and it received instructions from the defendants to do a "back-of-the-envelope" valuation or a calculation report. A valuator for the company described this type of appraisal as a "rougher" financial assessment that does not provide a valuation opinion. Intrinsic, too, learned that its report was to serve as a tool in a potential conflict and that the defendants were "looking for a valuation metric that they [could] use to make the negotiation smoother." The defendants also mentioned "adverse developments" surrounding the firm, including the plaintiff's departure, all of them signaling to the market that things "aren't going right." They did not provide the appraiser with the company's tax returns.

The defendants asked that Intrinsic use a "Monte Carlo" option approach, which a member of the appraiser firm described as a "stochastic method where you apply some randomness to each variable and … you play it out within a range of possibilities in an iterative manner and you wind up with … the Brownian motion outcome." Intrinsic initially used a 10-year time frame, but the defendants had it revise the report using a two-year time frame because they were not sure the company would be around for longer than that.

Intrinsic's calculation report arrived at a range of values between $109,000 and $150,000. The appraiser also provided the defendants with an electronic spreadsheet that allowed them to use different numbers for different variables to see firsthand how the changes altered the company's value.

Based on the two appraisals, the defendants set the repurchase price at $135,850, the average of the midpoints of the two ranges.

The plaintiff retained his own expert whose initial calculation in the fall of 2012 indicated the plaintiff's interest was worth $1.5 million. After he gained access to some of the company's financials, he prepared a report that increased the value to $2.1 million. (The court's opinion provides no further details.) He also critiqued both of the defendants' valuations, but his rebuttal received little attention in the court's analysis and ultimately was of no consequence to the outcome of the case.

In an e-mail one of the defendants sent within a month of informing the appraisers that the company was not doing well, he said that "for once in a long time the firm is on stable grounds." Some nine months later, an analysis of the company appearing in an industry publication put the firm in the top 50 out of 400 hedge funds for value-weighted returns in the second and third quarters of 2012. An October 2012 performance review in another journal said the company's investment funds were up 19.18% for the year.

In November 2012, the plaintiff sued in federal court (D. Colo.). The crux of his argument was that the defendants breached the operating agreement by failing to value the plaintiff's interest in good faith and trying to force the plaintiff to sell his stake for less than fair market value. The defendants responded with a motion for summary judgment, arguing that under the operating agreement the plaintiff had no case.

Tainted valuation process? The case turned on good faith. Since the plaintiff had agreed to the operating agreement, the court said it would only consider the "substantive accuracy" of the experts' valuations if there were evidence that the defendants acted in bad faith—for example, by blindly relying on obviously unreasonable expert advice or by providing the appraisers with false financial information.

In this case, there was no problem with blind reliance, the court concluded. The defendants retained two qualified appraisal firms to do an analysis and "provided reams of financial information" about the company. The values the two appraisers generated were similar, "despite the lack of any evidence that the firms collaborated or reviewed each other's reports."

In this context, the court also dismissed the plaintiff's contention that commissioning a calculation report instead of a valuation report was in itself an act of bad faith. The operating agreement did not mandate a particular valuation method, said the court. In fact, the defendants were not obligated to obtain a third-party valuation report, let alone two. Had they only obtained one, from St. Charles, they would have met the agreement's condition as long as they acted in good faith. Also, even if Intrinsic's calculation report was not as "thorough or robust as it could have been," it states a buyout figure that finds support in the St. Charles valuation report.

The court also found the plaintiff's various claims that the defendants "wrongfully influenced" the appraisers were too weak. For example, even though the defendants lied to St. Charles about the firm's losing business when the plaintiff left, a St. Charles analyst said the defendants did not tell him how much business disappeared and he "measured the loss in [the company's assets under management] based on the financials and the detail I had." In other words, said the court, it was not reasonable to infer that the defendants' lie "materially impacted St. Charles' report." The plaintiff emphasized that some of the numbers in the St. Charles valuation report differed from those appearing in the company's profit and loss statement and tax returns. According to the court, this discrepancy did not prove impropriety or the appraiser's reliance on inappropriate financial documents. In fact, a St. Charles appraiser testified that when he does an analysis "I try to find GAAP financials. Tax returns are not GAAP.... For that reason alone, we would never use a tax return and then compare those financial returns to a GAAP financial statement."

Further, there was no evidence that the defendants' failure to provide the investor newsletters to the valuators negatively affected the appraisals; for one, it was not clear that the information in the newsletters was relevant to valuation of the company as opposed to valuation of the assets the company managed or that the information was not available in the other financial information the defendants did provide. Moreover, the fact that the defendants had a motive to undervalue the plaintiff's ownership in the company did not mean they did undervalue his stake in it, the court noted. It added that post-valuation information regarding the company's performance was by definition not available at the time the valuations took place and was not evidence about the company's prospects on the valuation date.

The court concluded that there was no evidence that the defendants tainted the valuation process by providing material misinformation, pressuring the appraisers to arrive at a particular result, or imposing unreasonable assumptions on the firm's calculations. Consequently, the court refused to go behind the valuators' financial calculations and dismissed the plaintiff's claims.

Editor's Note: The plaintiff's appraiser raised a series of technical questions about both appraisals in his own report, but the posture of the case was such that he never got the chance to elaborate on his objections. For example, he said the St. Charles valuation: (1) was based on an unreasonably applied equity discount rate; (2) was based on an unreasonable discount for lack of marketability; (3) was based on unreasonable near-term new customer and market value growth assumptions; (4) was based on an inappropriate choice and application of guideline company multiples; and (5) failed to do a "waterfall" analysis to estimate future fees. These were substantive issues for a *Daubert* challenge, but the plaintiff's case crumbled before it could file the requisite motion.

LightLab Imaging, Inc. v. Axsun Technologies, Inc.

Citation: 2014 Mass. LEXIS 585
Date of decision: July 28, 2014
Experts: Roy Weinstein (plaintiff); unknown (defendants)
Judge: Spina
State/Jurisdiction: Massachusetts
Court: Court of Appeals
Type of case: Damages
SIC code: 3826 Laboratory Analytical Instruments
NAICS code: 334516 Analytical Laboratory Instrument Mfg.

Use of Reliable Method Does Not Assure Admissibility

Readers may remember the *Manpower* case in which the 7th Circuit struck down the trial court's decision to exclude expert testimony based on what it considered questionable data underlying the expert's generally accepted methodology. A recent state appellate decision in a lost profits case offers another take on how far the trial court can go in its role as "gatekeeper" to ensure that expert testimony meets the reliability requirement of *Daubert.*

Until recently, the plaintiff was the only company to manufacture and sell optical coherence tomography (OCT) systems used to image human coronary arteries. There was a competitor, but it used another process. Since the plaintiff's technique relied on lasers, it made an agreement with one of the defendants, a leading manufacturer of industrial lasers, to develop a laser that would improve the existing OCT technology. A second confidentiality agreement gave the plaintiff the exclusive right to the new lasers and imposed a ban on the defendant that prohibited the sale of all lasers to the competitor until April 2014, with subsequent nonexclusive rights. During the course of the agreement, the plaintiff's competitor acquired the defendant laser manufacturer and, during sales negotiations, gained access to some of the plaintiff's trade secrets. The plaintiff sued both companies alleging breach of contract and the covenant of good faith and fair dealing, misappropriation of trade secrets, and tortious interference with contractual and advantageous business relations. It argued that the misconduct prevented the development of next-generation product featuring the jointly developed laser and robbed the plaintiff of its "first-mover advantage" in the OCT market.

The plaintiff was a startup and made no profit during the contract term with the defendant laser manufacturer. It also could not point to any lost sales stemming from the defendants' misconduct.

Significance of first-mover advantage. A jury found the defendant companies liable. In the damages phase of the trial, the court questioned the plaintiff's designated expert, a well-known economist, on his lost profits calculation, particularly future lost profits and profits for any future generation of products featuring the laser.

The expert used the discounted cash flow method (DCF) to quantify damages up to and some 20 years beyond the expiration of the confidentiality agreement. (The court's opinion is confusing as to the end date: 2034 or 2038.) He assumed that the plaintiff would be able to grow its customer base until 2014, when its contract with the defendant expired. He surmised that demand subsequently would level off and profits would decline until 2038 and become negligible. He also assumed that beginning in 2014 the plaintiff's customers would replace the OCT product they owned with one of the plaintiff's new-generation products every six years, until 2038. He did not perform a market study to support the assumption or evaluate likely products of potential future competitors. Instead, he relied on the concept of brand loyalty. Moreover, he acknowledged that he did not have information as to what direction the plaintiff would have taken to develop next-generation OCT products and did not know whether the plaintiff had the sales and marketing infrastructure to support the assumed future system.

His calculation leaned on the first-mover advantage principle, but he was equivocal as to whether this principle was part of the economic theory he used to calculate lost profits or whether he treated first-mover advantage as an assumption with which to evaluate the reasonableness of the company's projections. He acknowledged, however, that nothing in the economic literature supported quantifying lost profits based on first-mover advantage.

The trial court precluded the testimony as to lost profits after April 2014 and for future generation product. It found: (1) the expert's opinion was not based on a demonstrated reliable methodology and as such did not meet the requirements of *Daubert* and its state case equivalent; and (2) the calculation was too speculative.

In determining that the expert failed to use a reliable methodology, the trial court placed great emphasis on his use of "first-mover advantage." It said the expert used it to quantify loss rather than just as an assumption about market behavior. Use of the principle, however, made the expert's methodology incapable of being validated and tested, as required under *Daubert* and related cases.

The court also found that numerous factors made the opinion speculative. There were no lost sales. The plaintiff had not received regulatory clearance for its product in the U.S., Japan, South Korea, and China. There was no solid evidence that the plaintiff would have had the funding necessary to expand its business. The expert failed to identify "precisely the type of hypothetical new product" for which the plaintiff sought and for which the expert calculated damages.

As a result of the trial court's conclusions, the plaintiff had no lost profits evidence to present at trial. Instead, the parties stipulated to non-lost-profits damages in the amount of $200,000.

Call for other damages model. The plaintiff subsequently appealed. The expert used a generally accepted methodology, the DCF, to calculate damages. The trial court should have stopped its inquiry into reliability there, the plaintiff argued. Under *Daubert,* it was the jury's role to decide whether the assumptions underlying the expert's opinion were valid. The plaintiff further claimed that the first-mover advantage was not a loss-quantifying methodology but an assumption about market behavior that found support in scholarly articles and in the expert's own professional observations. The scholarly articles consisted of one Supreme Court case that did not deal with lost profits but in which a justice observed that "firms that innovate often capture long-term benefits from doing so, thanks to various first-mover advantages."

The appeals court affirmed the trial court's decision as to methodology. *Daubert,* the court said with emphasis, requires an assessment "of whether the reasoning or methodology underlying the testimony is scientifically valid *and* of whether that reasoning or methodology properly can be applied to the facts in issue." It went on to explain that ensuring "reliability" did not just mean the trial court's determining the reliability of the methodology used but was part of a broader determination of the admissibility of expert testimony. Trial courts had considerable leeway in deciding how to determine whether an opinion was reliable. Here, the trial court had discretion to find that the expert's use of "first-mover advantage" was part of his methodology and rendered it unreliable.

The appeals court also upheld the trial court's separate conclusion that the testimony was speculative, noting the plaintiff had no history of profitable sales, only losses, and could not show it lost sales because of the defendants' misconduct. Also, its expert's future lost profits depended on as-yet undeveloped new products for which the plaintiff had not even conducted market research.

In concluding, the appeals court cautioned that "traditional lost profits analysis as a measure of damages may not be an adequate model for analyzing harm caused by misappropriation of the trade secrets of a 'start-up' business." Just because such businesses often operate for years without profit should not make them "damage proof," the court said. It added that it was aware of other damages theories that could be useful in misappropriation of trade secrets cases and "they may be ripe for testing in our courts."

In re: LightSquared Inc.

Citation: 2014 Bankr. LEXIS 2984
Date of decision: July 11, 2014
Experts: Mark Hootnick, Moelis (debtors); J. Soren Reynertson, GLC (dissenting class)
Judge: Chapman
State/Jurisdiction: Federal/New York
Court: United States Bankruptcy Court
Type of case: Bankruptcy
SIC code: 4899 Communications Services N.E.C.

Regulatory Issue Causes Bankruptcy Valuation to Falter

In the notorious fight over LightSquared, a Chapter 11 satellite and broadband services provider, the debtors and affiliated entities sought confirmation of their third amended reorganization plan. All significant parties in interest supported the plan, except for the largest secured lender—a special purpose entity owned and controlled by Charles Ergen, the founder of LightSquared's direct competitor, DISH. Plan confirmation ultimately centered on the valuation of LightSquared's assets. Ergen retained an expert who only had three weeks to deliver his report. On the upside, he was paid $1.25 million for his work. The Bankruptcy Court (S.D.N.Y.) recently decided how good the testimony was.

Backstory. LightSquared owned several satellites and licenses to use mobile satellite service spectrum issued by the Federal Communications Commission (FCC). It provided voice and data services to mobile devices that were used by the military, first responders, safety providers, and others throughout North America. In May 2012, the company filed for Chapter 11 bankruptcy, but it continues to operate as debtor in possession. Ergen's special purpose entity (SPSO) held approximately $844 million of the face amount of the outstanding LightSquared LP prepetition secured debt. The way in which SPSO acquired its claims and Ergen's conduct in particular fueled litigation in which the debtors alleged inequitable conduct, fraud, tortious interference with prospective economic advantage, and other wrongdoing. According to the debtors, SPSO impermissibly acquired LP debt with the ulterior motive of facilitating DISH's acquisition of LightSquared's assets. The debtors also claimed they were the victims of a "bait and switch" strategy under which Ergen and his affiliates would offer a high bid price for LightSquared's wireless spectrum to find out whether anyone else showed interest in the assets and replace the offer with a lower bid if there were no competing bids, which is what happened. Earlier in the year, the Bankruptcy Court found that Ergen indeed violated the spirit of a credit agreement when he purchased his debt and ruled that some of his debt would be paid after other claims against LightSquared.

Given the connection among SPSO, Ergen, and DISH, after the failed auction, the debtors came up with a reorganization plan that sought to place the SPSO claim in a separate class where it was the sole classified claim and would receive markedly different treatment than the claim of other holders of LightSquared LP prepetition secured debt. SPSO rejected the plan. The debtors argued that, even if the court recognized SPSO's rejection vote, it should confirm the plan. First, there were business reasons for the separate classification: The holder of SPSO was a competitor with noncreditor interests. Also, the plan was fair and equitable because it ensured that SPSO received the "indubitable equivalent" of its claim. As it stood, SPSO received plan consideration in the form of cash payment equal to the amount of its allowed claims; under the proposed treatment, consideration would be in the form of a note, which would have a seven-year maturity, payment of interest in kind, and a silent third lien. Since SPSO would not be paid in cash, the plan required almost $1 billion less in financing than the debtors' prior plans.

Valuation assumes FCC approval. To show the plan was feasible as well as fair and equitable to SPSO, the debtors relied heavily upon the valuation of LightSquared's spectrum and satellite assets. A collateral valuation showed that the contemplated third-lien note more than sufficiently protected the full principal value of SPSO's claim, they maintained. The premise of the debtors' valuation was that LightSquared would be able to obtain critical FCC approval of its license modification application for augmented spectrum rights. The debtors offered expert testimony from a former FCC commissioner about the chances and time frames for approval. Although the witness had not had contact with any FCC staff regarding the pending application, he said he was certain, "based on his thirty years of experience," that the agency would grant the application by the dates the debtors' used in their projections. He said he had examined and discounted a number of factors that could impede the approval process.

The debtors' valuation expert had "stellar" credentials. His firm had a telecommunications practice, and he had worked on several spectrum deals. He performed extensive research and analysis over the almost two years in which he served as LightSquared's financial advisor and also relied on his experience with other valuation exercises of similar assets. He said he discussed a range of topics with management throughout the Chapter 11 proceedings, including "regulatory issues," the company's "business plan," and its "liquidity forecast." By his calculation, LightSquared's assets were worth somewhere in the range of $6.2 billion at the low end to $9.1 billion at the high end, with a midpoint of $7.7 billion. He explained that he relied on a methodology that was widely accepted in the industry: using a market multiple comparable based on the price per MHz/POP. He explained that it reflected the market price as a function of the size of the band of spectrum and the number of people it covered. He also considered spectrum characteristics, saying LightSquared had an "attractive low-frequency spectrum with strong propagation and inbuilding penetration." Critically, he relied on the FCC expert's opinion regarding the license modification process. His calculation assumed that the FCC would grant LightSquared the desired spectrum license and would do so in the time the debtors counted on.

The valuation expert repeatedly pointed out that his firm's valuation aligned with two earlier valuations Ergen undertook when he contemplated a low-band acquisition bid for LightSquared's assets, both in terms of the methodology and the outcomes. Ergen analyzed the aggregate value of LightSquared's assets to DISH by determining: (a) the value resulting from LightSquared spectrum and satellites themselves; and (b) the incremental value DISH would receive based on the additional value that LightSquared's spectrum would bring to DISH's existing spectrum. He concluded the range of value for the former was $3.3 billion to $5.2 billion; the range of value for the latter was $5.1 billion to $8.9 billion.

In addition, the DISH special committee also retained Perella Weinberg Partners (PWP) to issue a fairness opinion and valuation in connection with a potential $2.2 billion bid for LightSquared's assets in July 2013. PWP's analysis stated "the cumulative value … is estimated to be $4.4 billion to $13.3 billion." The range included the stand-alone value of LightSquared's spectrum and an estimate of how LightSquared's spectrum would enhance the value of DISH's existing and planned businesses.

'Methodology is all over the place.' SPSO's expert had not previously valued satellites or spectrum. From the date of hire, he had about three weeks to prepare a valuation in the case, receiving $1.25 million for his work. He first saw the Ergen and PWP valuations at his deposition, a day after completing his report. He later admitted that reviewing the earlier valuations would have been "informative" and would "have helped [him] understand how other sophisticated investors have looked at this spectrum."

At the plan confirmation hearing, the debtors tried to disqualify the expert under *Daubert*, arguing he lacked the necessary qualifications. However, the court then rejected the claim, finding the debtors had not given notice of the challenge and the exclusion was inappropriate on the merits.

SPSO's expert said he relied "100 percent" on the opinions of SPSO's technical expert with respect to the amount of spectrum available to and usable by LightSquared. At the same time, the valuation expert used his own judgment to reduce the value of the spectrum based on his assessment of the risk associated with obtaining FCC approval for use of the spectrum. He also concluded there were technical—interference—problems that either were insurmountable or would reduce the value of LightSquared's spectrum considerably. (The court's opinion does not provide figures for this valuation.)

The court discounted the SPSO expert report as "an unimpressive piece of work." His lack of experience valuing satellites and spectrum was noteworthy. He applied faulty and arbitrary assumptions in valuing the assets. Although he was not an FCC expert, he reduced the value of LightSquared's spectrum based on his risk assessment. He purported to rely on SPSO's technical advisor but drew conclusions on interference issues. Also, the technical expert did not speak to those technical issues until the confirmation hearing. The court concluded: "Simply put, his methodology is all over the place. Paid $1.25 million for his work, [the valuation expert] delivered a superficial analysis that was not even informed by a review of the valuations prepared by Mr. Ergen and PWP."

In contrast, the court extolled the debtor's expert and his work. He brought "broad and deep" experience to the job, and the methodology he used was "clearly consistent with industry standards." But, said the court, none of it mattered because his valuation rested almost entirely on unsupportable assumptions about the certainty and timing of FCC approvals. The debtors had no evidence that their FCC expert had any knowledge of how and when the responsible agencies would act on LightSquared's application. The court called the FCC expert's opinion "an educated guess" to which it could not attribute significant weight. Since the debtors' valuation expert used the FCC expert's unsupported conclusions, his valuation was unsupported.

That the debtors' valuation aligned with the Ergen and PWP valuations did not change the court's view. The latter valuations may support the proposition that LightSquared's assets were of "tremendous value in the hands of DISH," the court said, but this did not mean they bolstered the debtors' plan and proposed treatment of the SPSO claim.

Ultimately, the court declined to accept any valuation and found the plan was not fair and equitable because Ergen neither retained a first lien nor received the indubitable equivalent under the plan. Separately, the court also found that the intended treatment of the SPSO claim discriminated against SPSO "in ways that far exceed those necessary to address the legitimate concerns attendant to SPSO's competitor status and connections to DISH."

MacDermid Printing Solutions, Inc. v. Cortron Corp.

Citation: 2014 U.S. Dist. LEXIS 79940
Date of decision: June 12, 2014
Experts: James A. Levinsohn (plaintiff/counterclaimant); John H. Kramer (defendant/counterclaimant)
Judge: Shea
State/Jurisdiction: Federal/Connecticut
Court: U.S. District Court
Type of case: Damages
SIC code: 2759 Commercial Printing N.E.C.

A Time Limit on Use of Destruction of Business Method?

May an expert use the destruction of business method to calculate damages where there is a lengthy delay between the alleged misconduct and the alleged collapse of the claimant company? A federal court recently examined the question in the context of a *Daubert* attack that the opposing side launched against the expert's testimony.

The parties in this case were at once claimants and counterclaimants. The original plaintiff was a printing company that designed thermal flexographic processing machines for labeling commercial packaging such as potato chips bags. At the time it entered the thermal processing business, its only rival was DuPont, which had developed its own technology several years earlier. In November 2004, the printing company entered into a contract with the defendant-counterclaimant manufacturer to produce a certain number of machines, known as LAVA machines, a year. However, the parties' relationship disintegrated when, in April 2008, DuPont filed a patent infringement suit against the manufacturer. That suit led to a settlement in which the manufacturer agreed to cease producing the technology. In connection with the settlement, it also gave DuPont technical information related to thermal processing and erased the data from its computers. Sometime after DuPont announced the settlement in a press release, the manufacturer ceased operations. It had been in business for 20 years before entering into the agreement with the printing company. DuPont, in exchange, agreed to indemnify the manufacturer against claims from the printing company.

In 2008, the printing company sued (D. Conn.) the manufacturer, alleging antitrust violations, breach of contract, misappropriation of trade secrets, and other misconduct. (It also sued DuPont regarding the settlement agreement.) The manufacturer counterclaimed, alleging fraud and misrepresentation, breach of contract, misappropriation of trade secrets, and other violations.

Expert assumes causation. This stage in the litigation focused on the manufacturer's claim that the printing company's misconduct destroyed its business. The manufacturer offered expert damages testimony that the printing company sought to preclude under *Daubert.*

The manufacturer's theory was that the harm it suffered started four years before its ultimate collapse in 2008/2009, that is, when it signed the contract with the printing company. But for the latter's misconduct, the manufacturer would have followed a different course of business. In his report, the expert made it plain that he did not intend to discuss causation. Rather, the company asked him to assume that certain misrepresentations from the printing company caused the manufacturer's demise and to use certain assumptions for his calculations. For example, the manufacturer claimed that in early 2005 the printing company said it was realistic to expect the sale of 35 to 40 LAVA machines a year, but subsequently it lowered the number to between 30 and 40 for the duration of the parties' four-year relationship. Also, based on the printing company's statements, the manufacturer expected to develop a second generation of LAVA machines and devoted significant resources to the business relationship, which, in turn, caused it to neglect relationships with other partners. The development of the LAVA Gen II machine never materialized. Moreover, the manufacturer did not receive the design support it was expecting from the printing company under the contract.

Based on these considerations, the expert used a destruction of business method to quantify the harm. He explained that this method was appropriate for businesses that had been destroyed, not just injured. Basically, it means calculating the market value of the business on the day of destruction and subtracting any salvage value in the assets. To calculate the business's fair market value as of November 2004, he used an income approach, valuing the company by projecting its expected income stream and discounting it to present value. His report pointed out that he relied on the financial projections the company's management provided. In his deposition, he explained that the projections were prepared in the ordinary course of business in January 2005 and, as he understood it, reflected the company's expectations of developing a new technology that it had not yet fully commercialized.

When asked about the discrepancy between the company's past performance and the projections he relied on, he explained that the company's history was a series of cycles. For most of the decade immediately preceding the projection period, the company was focusing on research and development of new technology, which it expected to sell profitably. "A lot of that negative cash flow was being generated by research and development for future product," he said. In the past, it first had invested in developing new technology that it then was able to sell for a profit, until the technology became obsolete and the company had to pursue new research and development to bring another technology to market. Here the financials preceding the projection period indicated the company was in the "down cycle," but its projections indicated it was "poised to take advantage of all of the research and development efforts that they had undertaken."

He said he tested the projections by speaking with management "about the patents that they had, and about the work that they were doing, and about their expectations prior to using the numbers that were presented in their projection." He also checked the projections against past performance. Even though they did not align with the financial performance "of the last few years," they were consistent with the company's performance levels from a decade ago, the expert said. He explained that, by the time the company retained him, few business records were available, causing him to verify the projections by talking to the company's employees.

In developing the present value of the income, he said he used a "pretty high" discount rate (not stated) and that the zero point would be reached after about 20 years. He concluded that the company's value at the end of 2004 was $6.28 million.

Sudden death vs. gradual decline. Although the printing company acknowledged that the destruction of business method was a recognized method for valuing a company that was destroyed, it objected to its use in this case. It also attacked the expert's use of company projections, rather than "past earnings," and it claimed the expert improperly assumed the company's business would continue "in perpetuity."

The court first addressed the issue of whether the destruction of business method was appropriate in this case. This valuation method is "perhaps most naturally suited" to a case involving the sudden death of an enterprise following a "single crushing loss," the court observed. But it went on to explain that courts have approved use of the method in breach of contract and other commercial cases in which there was a "more gradual business decline." Even though here the time frame between the alleged breach of duty and the collapse of the business was long in comparison with precedent, the court saw no reason why the destruction of the business after "it is induced by misrepresentation to enter into a 'ruinous contract' cannot be gradual." The court was disinclined to set an arbitrary time limit on the use of the destruction of business method. There was evidence that the printing company's misrepresentations and other breaches occurring in 2004 caused the manufacturer to suffer immediate harm that increased as the contract went on. At the same time, the court agreed that the delay raised questions about causation. But since the manufacturer did not offer the expert as an expert on causation and the expert made it clear that he did not express an opinion on this issue, the expert's use of the method did not render his calculation so unreliable that it was inadmissible, the court concluded.

As for the expert's use of projections, rather than past earnings, the objection went more to the quality of the data the expert relied on than to the use of methodology, the court found. He explained why he used the projections and what he did to verify the data. Any questions as to the discrepancies between the company's historical performance and the forecast and other aspects of the expert's analysis were the proper subject of cross-examination.

The court also dismissed the objection that the expert wrongly based his calculation on the assumption that the company would exist "in perpetuity." This argument simply restated the printing company's objection to the use of the destruction of business method as opposed to the lost profits approach, the court found. Also, the expert had explained that "in perpetuity" really translated into "20 years," given the high discount rate he used in his calculation. The court stressed that the manufacturing company had been in business for 20 years prior to the 2004 agreement. Ultimately, it was for the jury to decide whether the expert's 20-year assumption was reasonable. For all of these reasons, the court refused to exclude the testimony under *Daubert.*

Editor's Note: In July 2014, after a day of deliberation, a federal jury awarded the printing company $35.4 million based on its claims against the manufacturer.

Manpower, Inc. v. Ins. Co. of Pa., LLC

Citation: 2013 U.S. App. LEXIS 20959
Date of decision: Oct. 16, 2013
Experts: Eric Sullivan (plaintiff); unknown (defendant)
Judge: Tharp
Country: US
State/Jurisdiction: Federal/Illinois
Court: United States Court of Appeals
Type of case: Damages (incl. Lost Profits)
SIC: 6331 Fire, Marine, and Casualty Insurance (fire, marine, and casualty insurers-direct, except contact lens insurance)

'Undue' Scrutiny of Expert's Data Triggers Erroneous Exclusion

Had the district court "exercised its gatekeeping role under *Daubert* with too much vigor"? This was the question at the heart of a recent appeal at the 7th Circuit arising out of an insurance dispute. The plaintiff sued for damages related to the collapse of its office and offered expert testimony to support its business interruption claim. The district court considered the expert's data selection unsound and excluded the opinion both in a pretrial ruling and a later ruling on the plaintiff's motion for reconsideration, leaving the plaintiff without evidence to establish its claim. As a last resort, the plaintiff asked for review by the Court of Appeals.

The plaintiff was an international recruiting and staffing firm whose Paris subsidiary was unable to conduct business when part of its office building collapsed in 2006. It lost income and incurred expenses from the interruption of its operations. After the plaintiff filed claims for insurance coverage for the various losses, a dispute with the defendant insurer broke out that the parties litigated in federal district court (E.D. Wis.) The court first found that the plaintiff was covered for its business interruption losses (and business personal property) under the defendant's policy and next considered the defendant's *Daubert* motion challenging the opinion of the plaintiff's damages expert.

Problematic growth rate. The expert determined a total loss of about €7.5 million, including a business interruption loss of over €5.1 million. His calculation followed the general procedure set down in the policy—computing lost revenues minus noncontinuous expenses—and the method for estimating the various inputs. For example, for determining net profit, a policy provision required that "due consideration shall be given to the experience of the business before the date of damage or destruction and to the probable experience thereafter had no loss occurred." The expert estimated a growth rate of 7.76% to project total revenues; he derived it by comparing the total revenues from the five-month period that preceded the collapse to total revenues generated in the same five-month period in 2005. Even though he had reviewed economic data from as far back as 2003, he extrapolated the rate from the shorter period based on communication with the subsidiary's managers that credited a change in management and the enactment of new policies for the turnaround of the company by the end of 2005. The expert assumed this growth would continue for 14 months.

No one disputed that the expert was qualified. The district court also found he used an "appropriate and recognized method" to calculate projected revenues. But it said his "analysis [broke] down" when it came to his estimated growth rate, "one of the most important parts of the business-interruption calculation." In essence, he had "uncritically accept[ed] the word of [the subsidiary's] managers." He was not "an expert on business management," said the court, and his conversations with the managers were not a reliable basis for the revenue forecast. He failed to perform an economic analysis of other factors that could have affected growth, such as industry conditions. Had he selected a period that was not so short, the court "might have found his analysis reliable." Despite his access to historical data, which indicated a downward trend in monthly revenues, he treated the company as "essentially a new business." But that meant having to examine other indicators to compensate for the lack of a track record—something he failed to do. His growth rate was based on assumptions, not reliable principles and methods, and as such was unreliable.

The plaintiff asked the district court for reconsideration based on a supplement to the expert's report that provided additional information on how the expert had developed the growth rate. For example, he said he sampled longer and shorter growth periods but concluded rates resulting from the 12-month and 14-month periods were less reliable than the rate yielded from the five-month comparison. He also furnished a table with loss calculations based on different assumed growth rates. The court considered the supplement but adhered to its earlier finding that the expert's "decision to project lost revenues based on a five-month revenue base—and a growth rate of 7.76%" was not reliable. "[C]ompiling a list of possible growth rates and then choosing a rate from this list" based on the expert's judgment and in line with how he usually selected growth rates in the span of his career was not relying on established principles, said the court.

In ruling against the admission of the testimony, the district court effectively nixed the plaintiff's business interruption claim. (Digests of the district court's rulings and the opinions are available at *BVLaw*.)

'Nuanced' data selection. The plaintiff appealed the decisions at the 7th Circuit Court of Appeals. At the start of its review, the appellate court pointed out that "reliability" was the main issue in dispute. Under *Daubert* and its progeny, district courts have great leeway to determine whether expert testimony is reliable. The principal question was: Reliable in regard to what? As the appellate court explained: "Reliability, however, is primarily a question of the validity of the methodology employed by an expert, not the quality of the data used in applying the methodology or the conclusions produced." In other words, the jury, as the trier of fact, not the court, gets to decide whether the data underlying the expert's analysis is sound and whether the expert's conclusions are correct.

In this case, the appellate court noted that the district court rightly found that the expert's methodology was reliable—he followed the methodology the policy prescribed and used growth-rate extrapolation to select the first variable, the company's projected revenue if the collapse had not occurred. The district court's analysis ought to have ceased with these conclusions, said the appeals court, but instead it "drilled to a third level" to evaluate the quality of the data inputs the expert chose for his growth rate extrapolations. In so doing, it "unduly scrutinized" the quality of the data the expert used for his model. It was improper for the district court to suggest that, had the expert chosen a less short period for his calculation, the court "might have found his analysis reliable."

The appeals court also rejected the lower court's suggestion that "future earnings projections are outside the ken of a certified public accountant and require expertise in economics and business management." CPAs regularly perform the steps the expert here undertook when he analyzed information relevant to his growth rate selection. As such, they review financial statements for anomalies and trends, and they rely on management statements, estimates, and forecasts. Therefore, the district court's conclusion that the expert's communication with the subsidiary's managers was not a reliable basis for a revenue forecast was not a solid reason for excluding the opinion.

The 7th Circuit's analysis went further. The court recognized that an expert must consider "sufficient data to employ the methodology" to ensure that the data had some "quantitative or qualitative connection to the methodology employed." A single observation or data point or "a subset of data that was plainly insufficient to support application of the growth projection methodology" would not satisfy Rule 702 of the Federal Rules of Evidence that the opinion be supported by "sufficient facts or data."

But here the district court made it sound as if the expert simply put together a list of possible growth rates and then "picked the one that looked about right to him," when in reality his data selection was "substantially more nuanced and principled than the district court's characterization reflects," the Court of Appeals stated. For example, he calculated growth rates over various periods based on comprehensive data for three years prior for the company's Paris office and all offices in France. He vetted data for anomalies and excluded some of the aberrant data. And he reviewed documents that showed changes in the company's business over the relevant period and discussed them with its current management. This process was not data selection based "on little more than [the expert's] intuition." Whether the expert selected the best data to use was a question for the jury to answer, not the district court. "It does not go toward admissibility," the appellate court pointed out. The district court "set the bar too high," the 7th Circuit concluded, vacating the decision to exclude the expert and reversing the ruling in favor of the defendant on the business interruption loss claim.

Marcus v. Quattrocchi

Citation: 2014 U.S. Dist. LEXIS 19041
Date of decision: Feb. 4, 2014
Experts: Howard Fielstein, Peter von Nessi (plaintiffs); Timothy Barnes (defendants)
Judge: Briccetti
State/Jurisdiction: Federal/New York
Court: United States District Court
Type of case: Breach of Fiduciary Duty
SIC code: 6500 Real Estate

Court Finds 'Market Value Concept' Requires Flexibility

In an estate and trust case featuring a major real estate family, the plaintiff beneficiaries retained two experts to prove damages resulting from the alleged improper depletion of trust assets by way of an investment company in which the defendants had a stake. In their *Daubert* motion, the defendants attacked one of the experts, a highly credentialed business valuator, arguing that he was not qualified to value real estate, the investment company's principal asset. Also, his valuation methodology was unreliable. The court took a more liberal attitude toward admissibility.

The decedent was the head of a leading real estate investment, development, and asset management company. In 1971, her lawyers designed an estate plan that pivoted around a revocable trust that became a flashpoint between the plaintiff beneficiaries and the defendant trustees. The plaintiffs were the decedent's two great-granddaughters; the defendant trustees included granddaughters.

Trustees' broad discretion. The trust had several noteworthy features: (1) it gave the trustees "absolute and uncontrolled discretion" to provide trust income and principal to the decedent, and after her death, to her son; (2) it exempted the trustees from liability for conflicts of interest related to dealings with entities in which they had a monetary interest; and (3) it permitted the decedent's son to "appoint" trust assets to beneficiaries of the trust during his life or by will. After the son's death, the trustees had an obligation to distribute the remaining trust assets in specified proportions to his widows, children, and grandchildren.

The estate plan simultaneously created an investment company that was a partnership between the trust at issue and other family trusts. It provided for the transfer of 90% of the trust's real estate holdings to the company in exchange for a 50.6% controlling ownership interest in the company. The initial capitalization was $1.6 million, to which the trust contributed approximately $800,000. The son was the investment company's general manager and also the sole owner of a third entity that managed all of the family's properties. Two of the trustees were his daughters.

The partnership agreement also provided for redemption of 49% of the trust interest following the decedent's death and redemption of any remaining interest within 10 years. The decedent died in 1972, triggering redemption for $392,000 of the 49% of the $800,000 trust interest. The final redemption did not take place until 1987 for nearly $624,000. Since the defendant granddaughters were beneficiaries of the investment company's remaining partner-trusts, each time the trust redeemed a portion of its interest in the partnership, their interests increased such that they owned all of the real estate assets that the trust originally contributed. The son died in 2005.

The plaintiffs sued the trustees in federal court (S.D.N.Y.) under a number of theories, including breach of trust, common law fraud, fraudulent conveyance, and Rule 10b-5 securities fraud. In essence, they accused the trustees of allowing the investment company to acquire the trust's assets and subsequently redeem them for inadequate consideration. Moreover, they allowed the son to divert trust assets to entities in which he and they had a private financial stake. Also, they concealed the existence of the trust and its substantial assets.

The plaintiffs retained two damages experts to value the assets underlying the investment company and determine the trust deficiency resulting from the trustees' actions during the life of the trust. The defendants offered their own expert. In conjunction with their motion for summary judgment, the defendants also filed a *Daubert* motion to exclude the plaintiffs' experts, reasoning that without damages evidence the plaintiffs had no case.

'Imprecise nature of real estate valuation.' The plaintiffs' first expert was a CPA, who also was a certified fraud examiner, and an accredited senior appraiser in business valuation. To calculate the trust deficiency, he not only considered the investment company's real estate but "all of [its] assets other than the property, plant and equipment" and subsequently subtracted all liabilities to "achieve a 100% control, marketable value of equity." He said he used rent multipliers that the decedent appeared to have generated in 1971 and rent rolls that the defendants provided as evidence of income.

The defendant's expert valued the investment company by determining the market value of its properties based on his estimate of the partnership's net operating income. He said the "typical discount range" for a minority ownership was "anywhere between 25% and 60%." He selected a 36% rate. The trust's minority ownership in the investment company, he said, was "subject to market resistance." (The court's opinion does not provide any figures or additional details.)

1. *Qualification.* The defendants first claimed the plaintiffs' expert lacked the qualifications to appraise real estate, which, they said, was the partnership's principal asset. The plaintiffs retorted that the investment company "was not a piece of real property," but "a business whose assets included stocks and bonds, mortgages receivable, equipment," as well as "accounts receivable"—all in addition to real estate.

The court agreed with the plaintiffs and found the expert was qualified.

2. *Methodology.* Next, the defendants objected to the expert's methodology, particularly what they called his application of "rent multiplier[s] of unknown origin to rental income." Without verification that they reflected the multipliers used in the market, the expert's calculations were unreliable, the defendants argued.

The court was not persuaded. The market value of real estate, it said, "was difficult to establish with precision, particularly when there is no ready market for the property," as likely was the case here. If the defendants wanted to challenge the expert's multipliers, they could do so during cross-examination. The expert's approach—adding up the assets of the partnership and subtracting its liabilities—was not unreliable as a matter of law, "particularly in light of the imprecise nature of real estate valuation," the court added. In fact, it was "hard to see" how his approach differed materially from that of the defendants' expert. For these reasons, the court declined to exclude the testimony.

Complementary valuations. The plaintiffs' second expert, a certified general appraiser, reviewed the income and expense statements for the assets the plaintiffs' first expert valued. Because the defendants did not make the investment company's relevant tax returns available, he was unable to perform a full real estate appraisal. Therefore, he relied on the listed insurance expense for each property to calculate the value of the buildings the company owned but not the land on which they stood. Insurance value, he emphasized, did not include land value and as such did not represent the entire value of the property.

The defendants did not object to the appraiser's qualifications but argued his method undervalued the investment company and thus rendered his valuations "useless" to the jury.

The court saw it differently. Merely because those valuations valued some but not all of the investment company's assets did not make them irrelevant, said the court. To the contrary, his opinion could complement that of the first expert since both opinions concerned the value of real estate assets that the investment company owned in 1987, the year of final redemption. Therefore, the court also admitted the plaintiffs' second expert and denied the defendants' *Daubert* motion and summary judgment motion.

Mercury Companies, Inc. v. FNF Security Acquisition, Inc. (In re Mercury Companies, Inc.)

Citation: 2014 Bank. LEXIS 1230
Date of decision: March 31, 2014
Experts: Neil H. Demchick (plaintiff); Scott P. Peltz (defendant)
Judge: Romero
State/Jurisdiction: Federal/Colorado
Court: U.S. Bankruptcy Court
Type of case: Bankruptcy
SIC code: 6361 Title Insurance

'Reasonably Equivalent Value' Analysis Is Not a Dollars-and-Cents Issue

What does the Bankruptcy Court look for when it assesses "reasonably equivalent value"? A recent decision describes in technical detail the discounted cash flow analyses the parties' experts performed and the limitations of the calculations. The court also explains what factors other than the contract price and appraisals it considers for its conclusion.

Avoidable sale of subsidiaries? The plaintiff was a title agency organization that began in Colorado but expanded into California, Arizona, and several other states in the 1990s. Its downfall began in 2007 when the California housing market cooled. In April 2008, the plaintiff executed a credit agreement as part of a $45 million loan that was secured by most of its and its subsidiaries' assets, including accounts receivable. On July 2008, the lead creditor swept $40 million from the plaintiff's accounts. Based on this event and other considerations, company management decided to stop doing business in 161 locations and close down many subsidiaries. The company had four Colorado-based subsidiaries—three title companies and a software and computer consulting business—for which management anticipated a payroll of nearly $1.6 million due about a week after the sweep.

Since the title company subsidiaries had a 30% share of Colorado's real estate market, management believed they made an attractive acquisition target. But when it offered to sell them immediately to their largest underwriter the intended buyer rejected the offer. Subsequently, management proposed a quick sale of stock in the subsidiaries to the defendant—a major national title insurance company. On Aug. 5, 2008, the parties executed a purchase agreement, which specified a purchase price of $5 million in cash. The defendant immediately wired $1 million of the amount and took control of the Colorado subsidiaries that same day. A day later, it wired an additional $1.48 million toward the purchase price, leaving just over $2.5 million of the purchase price outstanding. Twenty-three days after the sale, the plaintiff filed for Chapter 11 bankruptcy.

Subsequently, the plaintiff sued in Bankruptcy Court (D. Colo.) to recover the alleged value of the Colorado subsidiaries from the defendant, claiming the sale was a fraudulent transfer under Section 548(a)(1) of the Bankruptcy Code. The transaction was avoidable because the plaintiff received less than reasonable equivalent value for the stock in the four subsidiaries and was insolvent on the date of transfer.

Since both parties agreed on the insolvency issue, the court had to rule on reasonably equivalent value.

It considered expert testimony from both parties. The experts' approaches, the court found, were remarkably similar, but their conclusions "vastly different." The plaintiff's expert determined that, on the date of sale, the stock had a positive value of nearly $15 million, whereas the defendant's expert assigned a negative value of about $5 million.

Immediate versus nonimmediate sale. As to the similarities, both experts agreed the three title subsidiaries required a different valuation from the fourth subsidiary because the latter was in a different line of business. Both experts used a going concern value because the entities were operating businesses at the time of sale. And both opted for an income approach. For the title companies, this meant employing the discounted cash flow (DCF) method: projecting their revenues and expenses in the future and discounting them back to a present value as of the date of sale.

Both experts projected a 0.1% revenue growth in 2009 and 6.4% growth in 2010 based on national forecasts and assumed 3.0% growth for 2011 and all subsequent years. But they disagreed about projections for 2008 following the sale. The plaintiff's expert assumed a sale did not have to be immediate. The Colorado subsidiaries could have stayed in business for 30 to 60 days to get to a sale. In contrast, the defendant's expert built his valuation on the immediacy of the sale and the plaintiff's financial distress at the time of sale.

As to specifics, the plaintiff's expert used data from the title companies' income statements covering the period from January 2004 through July 2008. He determined revenue mostly consisted of title revenue and escrow revenue. He also considered the value of "earned credits." The title companies accrued the credits in exchange for holding large amounts of trust funds—the result of their escrow services—in financial institutions. Since they don't own the funds, state law does not allow the financial institutions to pay interest on the funds. Instead, the financial institutions give earned credits, which the title companies use to buy in-kind merchandise and reduce expenses.

The plaintiff's expert explained that the title companies' fair market value was the net present value of the companies during the projection period, plus their terminal value, minus adjustments for dark office liability and adjustments for working capital, minus a discount for lack of marketability because the plaintiff was a closely held company. To determine cash flow, he looked to financial data from January 2008 through July 2008, adjusted for capital expenses and working capital, and added depreciation back to the resulting amount because it was a noncash expense. For future cash flow, he used projections for 2009 through 2012, deducted potential dark office liability, and adjusted for the weighted average cost of capital (WACC), which he obtained from the *Ibbotson Cost of Capital Yearbook*. He determined a cost of capital of 30.28% of debt and based his projections on the current-year median and the five-year average.

The defendant's expert also used Ibbotson, but a different capital structure resulting in 6.38% of debt; moreover, he used the current-year mean figures. In terms of cost of equity, the plaintiff's expert used 22.8% and the defendant's expert 25.5%. Both experts used the Gordon growth model for terminal value.

The plaintiff's expert computed an unadjusted fair market value of over $28.7 million. He then accounted for dark office liability, the working capital shortfall that existed on the sale date and the lack of marketability; he also adjusted for the fact that the sale resulted in a transfer of 100% of the stock to the buyer. These adjustments yielded a value of over $14.6 million, to which he added the value of the fourth Colorado subsidiary—nearly $290,000.

In critiquing the defendant expert's valuation, the plaintiff claimed he excluded "shadow revenue," confusing it with seasonality of the title business, and even after learning about it failed to modify his valuation. Shadow revenue was an accounting tool encouraging title companies to refer business to the plaintiff's non-Colorado subsidiaries. In case of a successful referral, both companies received credit for revenue generated on their income statements and qualified for a commission from the parent company. To prevent "double booking" of revenue, at the end of the year, the shadow revenues were deducted from the title companies' income statements.

The defendant's expert responded that he "made up" for the exclusion. For example, he used management projections existing before the sweep, which tended to be overly optimistic. He agreed that a projected decline in revenues should be in the 30%-to-40% range, rather than the

22% decrease resulting from the projections. He held onto the rate; it and other factors balanced his earlier exclusion of shadow revenue from the projections.

The court called the expert's approach "inappropriate" and said it weakened his conclusion of "negative" value.

The plaintiff also claimed the defendant's expert should not have made a lost business adjustment to account for the effect of the sweep. The court disagreed, finding that fear of lost business was a critical factor in plaintiff management's decision to offer the stock for $5 million and insist on an immediate sale.

Valuations 'excessive' and 'too low.' Neither valuation hit the mark, the court found. It agreed with the plaintiff's expert that a nonimmediate sale would have increased the sales price. But there was no certainty it would have been $10 million higher than the agreed-upon price.

Although it disapproved of the way in which the defendant's expert tried to account for excluding shadow revenue, it approved of his consideration of the immediacy of the sale. But it also found he did not reckon that the defendant was willing to pay $5 million for the four subsidiaries and indeed considered the deal a good one. In sum, one valuation appeared "excessive" and the other "too low."

Ultimately, the court's determination of reasonably equivalent value did not require it to compute a specific dollar value, the court explained. The term "reasonably equivalent value" was not defined in the Bankruptcy Code. But relevant case law provided for a two-step analysis: (1) determine whether the debtor received any value at all; and (2) look to the totality of the circumstances to compare the value of what the debtor received with the value of what it gave. As to the second inquiry, a court could look beyond the contract price and the valuations. And it could factor "indirect" or noneconomic benefits into its determination of the value received, the court added.

In this case, the court found there was no question that the debtor received some value, in the form of the payments from the defendant. As to the circumstances of the sale, the plaintiff's officers held the mistaken belief that they had to sell the subsidiaries immediately. To say the plaintiff lacked the cash to cover the impending payroll was wrong because the plaintiff had access to cash. One day after the sale, the parent company's president stated in court the company had "substantial cash that because of its nature, it did not try to use as working capital." This included $13 million in a nonqualified deferred compensation plan and $4 million in its health and benefits account. According to the court, the more pertinent issue was why experienced business people acted on those mistaken beliefs rather than take steps to obtain accurate information. For one, the company's president panicked. But there also was evidence that he "desired an immediate sale." He contacted the defendant and proposed a discounted $5 million purchase price to enable a quick sale. When the defendant asked for more time to do due diligence, he replied there was no time "for haggling." Management received what it asked for, the court pointed out. It concluded that the sale was conducted for reasonably equivalent value and, therefore, was not avoidable.

Mosaid Technologies Inc. v. LSI Corp.

Citation: 2014 U.S. Dist. LEXIS 25840
Date of decision: Feb. 28, 2014
Experts: Dr. Vince O'Brien (plaintiff); unknown (defendants)
Judge: Andrews
State/Jurisdiction: Federal/Delaware
Court: U.S. District Court
Type of case: Contract
SIC code: 3674 Semiconductors and Related Devices

'Stand-Alone' Lost Profits Claim Sinks, as Does Expert Opinion

A short *Daubert* decision regarding a contract dispute subject to New York law and involving the licensing of patents stands out because it discusses not only problematic expert testimony, but also the use of future lost profits as a measure of damages and the relevance of the hypothetical negotiation framework to the case.

In 2007, the plaintiff acquired several patents from the defendants in a highly competitive bidding process. The defendants transferred the patents under an assignment agreement that included a list of entities that had no license agreement with the defendants specific to the patents. In other words, these entities were prospective licensees for the plaintiff. Lenovo, a Chinese multinational technology company, was on the list.

Subsequently, the plaintiff filed suit (D. Del.), alleging the defendants had made misrepresentations to the plaintiff: Through a series of contracts involving multiple entities, they, in fact, had obtained license agreements with Lenovo. Since Lenovo was no longer a potential licensing target, the plaintiff did not get the benefit of its bargain. Accordingly, the defendants breached the assignment agreement and express warranty. The court found the defendants liable and moved to determine damages. The parties agreed that New York law governed all the contracts in dispute.

Expert does not vet business plan. The plaintiff presented expert testimony on damages. There were two aspects to the calculation: lost profits and the expected return on the plaintiff's investment. As to lost profits, the expert constructed a "but-for-the-breach" world that assumed that, if there had been no misrepresentation, the plaintiff would have made a license deal with Lenovo collecting royalties. The other question was what the plaintiff would have paid for the patents had it known about Lenovo's being licensed. The expert explained that the plaintiff used a 20% cost of capital to evaluate its investment in acquiring the patents from the defendants.

He based several assumptions underlying his opinion on the plaintiff's business plan, "Final Business Case," admitting he did not verify any of them independently. For example, the document claimed that 20% of Lenovo's sold products contained a Wi-Fi-enabling chip from an unlicensed chip supplier and that the plaintiff would have been able to negotiate a license deal with Lenovo "in the fourth quarter of 2010 without litigation." When asked about the percentage of Lenovo sales, the expert allowed that the figure "could be much lower, much higher, or even zero." The same was true for his statement about the 20% cost of capital. He said he did not analyze any of the plaintiff's other investments to confirm that 20% was an accurate or even reasonable figure. He did no more than "to see that's what [the plaintiff] used in the Final Business Case." (The court's opinion does not give any further details on the calculation.)

The defendants attacked the opinion in a pretrial *Daubert* motion, claiming that the plaintiff's expert used unreliable methods and based his calculation on insufficient facts and data. Therefore, it was inadmissible.

In response, the plaintiff defended the business plan and, by extension, the expert testimony. It claimed that the document was "an unbiased assessment"; its authors created it without contemplating litigation. It was "the best evidence to determine [the plaintiff's] state of mind and investment requirements" at the time the parties made the assignment agreement. The plan's assumptions represented the best evidence of what would have occurred if there had been a hypothetical licensing negotiation between the plaintiff and Lenovo. The expert's basis was "factually supported because it stems from [the plaintiff's] Final Business Case."

The court found the plaintiff's arguments and logic unconvincing. Case law featuring similar facts made it clear that an expert's reliance on a company's business plan to estimate damages was improper where the expert did not know the qualifications of the preparer(s) or the assumptions on which the estimates appearing in the plan were based. In order to be able to rely on the plan, the expert had to be able to explain why he relied on the plan's content. Here, there was no evidence that the plaintiff's expert was a member of the team that prepared the Final Business Case. Therefore, he had no personal knowledge of the assumptions in the plan or the qualifications of the persons making the assumptions. Also, he offered no other evidence that the plan's statements were accurate or that he believed them to be reliable.

As to the cost of capital statements, the plaintiff was not able to "fit the 20% cost of capital into any damages theory that makes any sense to the Court." And, while the "hypothetical licensing negotiation" framework was an analytical tool in patent law, it was "irrelevant to breach of contract cases generally and to this breach of contract case in particular."

'Determinable market value.' Finally, the court pointed out that, even if the expert's lost profits theory satisfied the *Daubert* standard, it would not have met the requirements of New York law, which rarely provides for a lost profits award. The applicable 2nd circuit case law requires, among other things, that "the extent of the loss is capable of proof with reasonable certainty." Where an item has a "determinable market value" at the time of the breach, that value is the measure of damages." Here, said the court, the opportunity to license Lenovo had a "determinable market value." How to quantify that value was the "crux of this case and the subject of voluminous pages of expert reports," the court added. In contrast, "the future value of any lost profits is not capable of proof with 'reasonable certainty.'" Future lost profits are part of the market value, it said. "Arguing for lost profits as a stand-alone theory, therefore, is inappropriate," it added.

For all these reasons, the court excluded the proposed expert testimony.

Myhre v. Myhre

Citation: 2013 Minn. App. Unpub. LEXIS 998
Date of decision: Nov. 12, 2013
Experts: Patrick Schmidt (husband & wife jointly); Richard Berning (husband)
Judge: Bjorkman
Country: US
State/Jurisdiction: Minnesota
Court: Court of Appeals
Type of case: Marital Dissolution
SIC: 4813 Telephone Communications, Except Radiotelephone (except resellers)

Experts Propose Equally Sound, but Diverging, Valuations

A recent divorce case featured two business appraisers valuing the husband's telecommunications business, using the same methodology and data, but arriving at an $80,000 difference in value based on their divergent treatment of one of the performance years under review and their choice of capitalization rate. The appellate court found that both witnesses gave "reasoned explanations for their valuations"—but one was more persuasive.

At divorce, the husband and wife stipulated that he should receive his telecommunications business and she her real estate business but disagreed on the value of either business. However, judging from the appellate decision, only the value of the husband's business triggered an appeal.

To establish the value of the husband's company, the parties jointly retained an appraiser to serve as a neutral expert. He prepared a comprehensive report that considered the company's performance between 2007 and 2011 and concluded that it was worth $290,000 as of June 30, 2011. Because the husband considered the value too high, he hired a second expert who prepared a less comprehensive report, applying the same method and using the same data as the initial expert, only to determine that the company was worth $205,000.

At trial, both experts adjusted their valuations upward based on data for the entire year 2011. Consequently, the first expert arrived at a value of $295,000 and the second at a value of $215,000. The difference in their valuations came down to the experts' decisions as to how to deal with the company's unusually strong performance in 2010 and their choice of capitalization rate.

Company's 2010 profitability. Both experts agreed that the company showed a substantially higher income for 2010 than it had in any of the previous years because of the "aggressive marketing measures" the company took to manage the decline and subsequent bankruptcy of one of its significant business partners. But the valuators disagreed over whether to include the year in their respective valuations. The first expert included the year in his computation, deciding that the 2010 result was not an aberration when compared to the company's 2011 profitability. Omitting the result would skew the data, the expert explained. The calculation was more reliable if he accounted for the fluctuation by including 2010 as one of a number of volatile years that he would average together and adjusting the company's capitalization rate accordingly, he believed.

In contrast, the second expert omitted 2010 from his calculation, reasoning that the circumstances that gave rise to the heightened profitability would not recur.

Capitalization rate. Both experts explained that there was a connection between a company's growth and its capitalization: Anticipated growth requires a lower capitalization rate. Both experts started with a 26% capitalization rate, but, in light of the husband's statements that the company's growth was slowing due to drastic industry changes, the second expert decided to increase the rate to 29%.

The first expert declined to make an upward adjustment because he expected the effects of changes in the market in 2010 to normalize; he also believed that the company's profitability in 2011 and the husband's demonstrated good business practices and adaptability augured continued growth, notwithstanding the husband's dire predictions. What's more, a 26% capitalization rate already factored in significant risk and volatility in the industry, he said.

The trial court credited the $295,000 valuation the first expert had prepared.

Husband disavows one expert. The husband challenged the trial court's decision at the Minnesota Court of Appeals, arguing that the first expert wrongly included the year 2010 in his calculation and attributed unsupported growth to the business.

The appellate court disposed of the arguments quickly. At the start it noted that, under the law, a lower court's credibility determination stands unless it is clearly erroneous. Here, the trial court confronted valuations from two experts who gave sound reasons for their choices as to the two factors that were at the heart of the husband's appeal. The lower court had discretion to accept the value the first expert proposed. Therefore, its finding that the company was worth $295,000 was not error.

Myservice Force v. Am. Home Shield

Citation: 2014 U.S. Dist. LEXIS 61207
Date of decision: May 2, 2014
Experts: David Chandler Thomas, Bruce Luehrs (plaintiff); unknown (defendant)
Judge: Padova
State/Jurisdiction: Federal/Pennsylvania
Court: United States District Court
Type of case: Contract
SIC code: 4813 Telephone Communications, Except Radiotelephone (Except Resellers)

Forecast's Assumption Imperils Conjoined Expert Opinions

In this breach of contract action, the admissibility of two expert opinions hinged on a key assumption that informed one expert's revenue projections using the Monte Carlo simulation and that the defendant attacked as invalid. To up the ante, the first expert's revenue figures formed the basis of a second expert's determination of the value of the company. Ultimately, the issue came down to the court's interpretation of a contractual term underlying the suit.

Questionable commitment to contract. The defendant sold warranties that covered larger systems and appliances in the home. It used three types of contractors to perform the work: (1) preferred contractors who had operations agreements with the defendant and a commitment for a certain number of calls per year; (2) network contractors, who had operations agreements, but no call commitments; and (3) direct contractors who had no formal agreements with the defendant. The plaintiff developed a service work order automation and status reporting system that enabled the contractors to report their customer appointments and the date and time of completion of their work orders. In January 2010, the plaintiff and defendant made a two-year agreement that, among other things, mandated that the defendant require preferred and network contractors "to report Appointment Set within 24 hours and SWO Completion within 5 business days," as well as support the plaintiff in its efforts to market its products to the defendant's preferred and network contractors.

The parties' relationship soured when the defendant decided not to pursue steps that would oblige its contractors to use the plaintiff's products. The plaintiff sued in federal court (E.D. Pa.) on a number of theories, but only one claim survived the defendant's summary judgment motions. The defendant said it had complied with the agreement's provision for status reporting requirements by including a requirement in its contracts with preferred and network contractors. The plaintiff asserted that the defendant failed to enforce the requirement it imposed on its contractors and, therefore, breached its duty under the contract of good faith and fair dealing. The court found evidence that the defendant did not track the contractors' compliance and did not impose penalties on its noncompliant contractors prior to June 2010. Accordingly, there was a triable issue as to whether the defendant had willfully failed to diligently enforce the requirements.

The plaintiff retained two damages experts. The first expert determined what the plaintiff's revenues and profits would have been if the defendant had not breached its duty as to the status reporting requirements. The second expert, using the first expert's forecasts, calculated the value the plaintiff would have had at the end of the agreement's second year if the defendant had not breached its duty.

First expert's Monte Carlo simulation. To forecast revenues and profits, the first expert used a Monte Carlo simulation. It was based on the assumption that the defendant had a contractual obligation to make all of its preferred and network contractors comply with the reporting requirements or eliminate those contractors who did not comply. This meant the contractors either would use the defendant's existing services or the plaintiff's products.

He accounted for "potential delays of product rollouts, software defects, and operational failures" in the Monte Carlo simulation by setting up three "business ramp-up scenarios" with different market penetration assumptions. His high estimate model assumed that contractors would have bought products from the plaintiff by the end of the fourth quarter of Year 1 of the agreement. His median estimate model assumed a two-quarter slip in those purchases, and his low estimate model assumed a four-quarter slip in those purchases. He determined that in 2010 the defendant had 1,652 preferred contractors and 3,096 network contractors, totaling 4,748 contractors. In 2011, there were 1,617 preferred contractors and 2,683 network contractors, totaling 4,300 contractors.

The simulation rested on what he called the "market penetration assumptions," which drew on an effort the defendant started in June 2010 to pressure contractors into status reporting compliance. Then, the defendant had selected 191 preferred and network contractors to serve as a focus group for its effort. When the defendant tried to compel them by way of phone calls or reducing their number of service calls, the plaintiff's expert found that between 15 and 29 contractors either bought products from the plaintiff or used the defendant's services. Based on these results, he developed a "range for use in the Monte Carlo simulation that represents the effect [the defendant's] enforcement efforts would have had upon a contractor." Critically, in calculating the range, he excluded the 162 to 176 contractors who did not respond to the defendant's efforts at all. He concluded that a minimum of 28% and a maximum of 53% of contractors would have bought the plaintiff's products to ensure compliance. "[T]his data is representative of the total population of Preferred and Network contractors because it is a statistically significant sample size (191 out of approximately 4,500 Preferred and Network contractors)," he asserted.

In his deposition testimony, he affirmed that he applied the analysis that resulted in the 28%-to-53% figures to the 162 to 176 contractors who in fact did not respond to the defendant's efforts. He assumed, he said, that all 191 contractors in the target group would "eventually" have satisfied the requirements if the defendant had done "what it needed to do to cause them to comply." Importantly, he also believed under the agreement the defendant had to compel all of its roughly 4,500 contractors to comply with the status reporting requirements and, therefore, applied the percentage of contractors from the target group who responded to the entire contractor pool.

The Monte Carlo simulation also included assumptions as to which products the contractors would buy and the corresponding pricing. Further, it assumed that between 64% and 97% of the contractors would use the plaintiff's credit card processing service. And it considered a customer attrition rate of between 3% and 26% based on the expert's review of attrition rates of 13 publicly traded companies whose businesses were similar to that of the plaintiff. The fixed costs the expert used for the simulation related to general, administrative, engineering, and professional services personnel—the variable costs related to maintaining an established data center. Because the defendant's contractor base was a captive market, costs did not include marketing and sales costs.

The first expert concluded that, under his low estimate scenario, Years 1 and 2 together would have resulted in a pretax net income for the plaintiff of over $2.1 million; under the mean estimate scenario, the total would have been nearly $4.2 million; and under the high estimate scenario, it would have been nearly $6.7 million.

The second expert valued the plaintiff at the end of Year 2 using a "Market Multiple" of the first expert's revenue figures. He said his multiples took into account the acquisition values of actual and comparable companies with revenue models similar to that of the plaintiff during the relevant period and the "unique" relationship between the plaintiff and the defendant. He concluded that the plaintiff would have valued between $8.6 million and $27.7 million if the defendant had adhered to its duty of good faith and fair dealing.

Does assumption 'fit' facts? The defendant filed a pretrial motion arguing the opinions were inadmissible under Fed. Rule of Evid. 702 (*Daubert*). The first expert's opinion was based on an assumption that "did not fit" the facts of the case, and his methodology was unreliable. If the court struck the first testimony, it also had to exclude the second expert's opinion because the latter relied on the former's projections.

The biggest problem with the first expert's approach was the assumption that the defendant had a contractual obligation to force its contractors to buy from the plaintiff or cut its ties with them. The agreement imposed no such duty, the defendant said. The erroneous assumption led to the expert's decision to eliminate from his market penetration assumption the 161 to 176 nonresponders, the defendant claimed. In fact, only 4.2% of the target group bought products from the plaintiff during the seven months following June 2010. The expert's conclusion that 28% to 53% of the defendant's preferred or network contractors eventually would have bought the products depended on his improperly eliminating the nonresponders from his calculation.

Also, the defendant claimed the opinion was unreliable because the sample was too small. And there was no proof that the sample group was representative of all the preferred and network contractors. Finally, there was no evidence that the few contractors in the target group who bought the plaintiff's products did so as a result of pressure from the defendant.

At the outset of its analysis, the court explained that "fit" primarily pertained to relevance. Precedent in the circuit required that courts exclude testimony based on assumptions that had no factual foundation in the record. Whether the first expert's assumption fit the case came down to whether the defendant's duty of good faith and fair dealing in terms of the status reporting requirements meant it had to compel 100% of its contractors to comply and terminate the noncompliant ones.

The plaintiff responded that the expert's assumptions aligned with the court's prior decision on the defendant's summary judgment motion. Specifically, the opinion included language that there was evidence that the defendant "willfully rendered imperfect performance ... by failing to mandate 100% timely compliance with status reporting requirements."

The court disagreed. The plaintiff and the expert misinterpreted the agreement, it said. And they took the court's statement out of context. "[O]ur statement does not support [the expert's] assumption that [the defendant] could *only* satisfy its duty of good faith and fair dealing by ensuring that *all* of its Preferred and Network contractors comply with their status reporting obligations *100%* of the time" and by terminating those who did not comply, the court emphasized. Therefore, the expert's market penetration assumptions did not fit the facts of the case and were inadmissible. Moreover, the entire opinion was based on an unreliable methodology and was not helpful to the jury.

Finally, because the plaintiff's second expert prepared a valuation of the plaintiff as of the end of the second year of the contract that used the first expert's unreliable data, the valuation was not sufficiently reliable under Rule 702. In sum, the court struck both expert opinions, leaving the plaintiff with no damages evidence.

Orthoflex, Inc. v. Thermotek, Inc.

Citation: 2013 U.S. Dist. LEXIS 174670
Date of decision: Dec. 10, 2013
Experts: Karl Weisheit (defendant/counterplaintiff); Scott Yates (plaintiffs/counterdefendants)
Judge: Fitzwater
State/Jurisdiction: Federal/Texas
Court: U.S. District Court
Type of case: Damages
SIC code: 3840 - Surgical, Medical, and Dental Instruments and Supplies

Expert Trips Over Fundamental Damage Concepts

Expert opinions come in many shades, and *Daubert* motions have become part of the litigants' arsenal, even though many fail. A recent damages case is noteworthy because it showcases admissible and not so competent testimony. As to the latter, by his own admission, the rebuttal expert did not understand the fundamental concepts informing the rivaling expert's computation and used legal conclusions that the clients' attorneys provided—all of which made it easy for the motion's proponent to discredit him as his clients' mouthpiece.

This multiparty litigation featured companies appearing both as plaintiff and defendant as well as individual defendants and third-party defendants. The original defendant-counterplaintiff designed and developed a medical system to transfer pressure, heat, and cold to various body parts during medical therapy. Its components were a machine and unique wraps that the maker sold to a network of distributors and nondistributors; these, in turn, sold the equipment to hospitals and clinics, which passed them on to patients. The plaintiffs-counterdefendants were medical supply companies. In 2008, their representative, an individual defendant, contacted the maker of the medical system about purchasing some of its products for his various entities. As the relationship developed, he acquired product and sales information. In May 2009, he signed a distributor agreement on behalf of several medical suppliers.

At the same time, he reported problems with the machine and the wraps. The parties litigated over whether these problems were genuine product failures or the representative's ruse to obtain design information from the manufacturer that he subsequently used to develop a competing system, consisting of a similar machine and wraps. Eventually the representative created a business to develop and manufacture wraps and sell them directly to the medical suppliers. In March 2010, he and his affiliated entities sued the original maker for breach of implied warranty, breach of express warranty, and breach of contract. The maker then terminated the distributor agreement effective as of August 2010 and countersued, alleging breach of contract, fraud, and unfair competition.

The manufacturer presented expert testimony from a CPA to support its lost profits claims and the original plaintiffs—the representative and his affiliated entities—offered a rebuttal expert. Both sides attacked the other party's proposed testimony in pretrial *Daubert* motions.

'But for' theory ties damages to party in case. In its counterclaims, the manufacturer argued that "but for" the representative's wrongful conduct the distribution agreement would have remained in effect and the plaintiffs would have continued to buy its wraps. Instead, they bought the competing product from the representative's business. Accordingly, even though the latter entity was no longer a party in the litigation, its sales activity was the basis for the lost profits calculation that the manufacturer's expert performed. For his computation, he also assumed liability as to breach of contract, fraud, and unfair competition and relied on the manufacturer's historical sales patterns, which he assumed would remain constant. His report clearly disclosed the assumptions. Further, he independently tested the data the manufacturer furnished to him.

Given an opportunity to review sales data that the plaintiffs had not produced at the time of his report, he said he was prepared to discuss other methods of calculating lost profits. Specifically, he intended to undertake an estimate of damages based on sales the manufacturer lost as a result of the competitor products' entry into the market.

The plaintiffs objected that, because only one company sold the competitor wraps—the representative's company—and it was not a party in the case, any damages calculation based on its sales activity was not helpful to the trier of fact.

The court disagreed. The issue was relevance. There was no absolute bar to testimony about a nonparty. Here, the manufacturer's "but for" theory tied the damages it suffered to the conduct of the representative, who was a party in the case. Its expert determined lost revenue due to decreased sales volume. Also, a calculation based on the alternative theory that the manufacturer faced increased competition and thus lost profits based on the representative's conduct also linked damages back to a party in the case. Therefore, the testimony was relevant.

As to reliability, the plaintiffs claimed the expert improperly assumed the historical sales pattern would remain in place without accounting for other changes that would have reduced the maker's sales. For example, the latter canceled the distributor agreement, doubled the price of its wraps, and refused to sell additional systems. Moreover, the expert relied solely on representations from the manufacturer.

In a footnote, they cited an antitrust case to contend his analysis was inadmissible because he failed to examine whether the maker had the manufacturing capacity to satisfy increased demand; without this analysis, he could not opine reliably on "hypothetical lost sales."

All of the plaintiffs' objections lacked force with the court. It found that the historical sales pattern argument related to the manufacturer's theory of liability. "But for" the representative's misconduct, the manufacturer would not have done any of the other things that the plaintiffs claimed could have brought down sales. "Experts are permitted to assume the fact of liability and opine about the extent of damages," the court pointed out. Further, the plaintiffs would have a chance to cross-examine the expert at trial as to other variables that might have caused a decrease in sales. Also, the expert's report clearly stated the assumptions he used for his calculation. And the record showed he independently reviewed the data that the company had given to him. He based his computation on "conventional principles of financial analysis," just as he was qualified to do as a CPA, the court said.

Moreover, manufacturing capacity was not the issue here since he did not assume increased sales or demand but based his lost profits calculation on the assumption that sales and profits would have continued at the rate they were immediately preceding the events at the heart of the lawsuit. In sum, the testimony was relevant and reliable, and, therefore, admissible.

Unsupported 'reliable business principles.' Although not a CPA, the plaintiffs' rebuttal expert had a graduate degree in business administration and 20 years of management and consulting experience.

In his deposition, he admitted he did not "understand what unjust enrichment is" or "what disgorgement is." He said he did not know what the proper measurement of damages for unfair competition was. When asked whether lost profits were a correct measurement, he replied: "I do understand that lost profits are a piece of the puzzle for such claims."

He said he would prefer to focus on the competing expert's actual report and his calculations. "Could you refer to something of the way [the rivaling expert] calculated and have me comment on those specifics," he asked the deposing attorney. He admitted he did not interview the representative whose conduct was at the root of the counterclaims or any of the accountants, and he repeated in his report legal conclusions that the plaintiffs' counsel made, including the claim that the competing expert improperly considered the sales activity of a company that was not a party to the case. Making those determinations was "inappropriate and unfounded," the rebuttal report stated. At his deposition, he admitted those statements were based on his conversations with the plaintiffs' counsel. But he also repeatedly said that he based his opinions and assumptions on "reliable business principles."

The manufacturer contended the rebuttal expert was unqualified to render an opinion on any level. On the most general level, he lacked the necessary educational background to discuss unfair competition damages since he was not a CPA and did not have the professional background, considering his experience was in bankruptcy consulting. Further, he had never served as an expert witness. More specifically, even if he were qualified to opine on unfair competition damages generally, he lacked the knowledge he needed to assess this case. He did not understand concepts central to the testimony he critiqued. He did not interview the representative or the entities that the maker accused of wrongdoing; also, he only reviewed documents that the plaintiffs' counsel selected, and he did not perform his own investigation into the facts and data to develop accurate conclusions about damages. Finally, even if he were capable of testifying about this case, he failed to support his conclusions with an accepted and identifiable methodology. The plaintiffs used him as an expert witness to present their theory of the case, the manufacturer argued.

The court disagreed about the rebuttal expert's general qualifications. His analysis merely required that he apply accounting principles to the data the parties provided, which he was qualified to do based on his graduate degree and work experience.

But in other respects the testimony was fatally flawed. Neither he nor the plaintiffs explained the "reliable business principles" underlying his testimony. Without specifying what methodology he used to form his opinion, his testimony was subjective belief or unsupported speculation. Also, "an expert cannot forgo his own independent analysis and rely exclusively on what an intended party tells him." Here, the plaintiffs failed to show that they merely called the expert to synthesize their arguments and present them under the cloak of expert opinion. For all these reasons, the court struck the rebuttal expert testimony.

Packgen v. Berry Plastics Corp.

Citation: 2014 U.S. Dist. LEXIS 127708
Date of decision: Sept. 12, 2014
Experts: Mark G. Filler (plaintiff); Nancy Fannon (defendants)
Judge: Woodcock, Jr.
State/Jurisdiction: Federal/Maine
Court: United States District Court
Type of case: Contract
SIC code: 3089 Plastics Products N.E.C.

Court Emphasizes Benefit of Hindsight in Evaluating Loss Period

How qualified is a business valuation expert under *Daubert* to testify to damages where he only has a fundamental understanding of statistics but his lost profits calculation relies on the use of a statistical method? Also, what, if any, role should hindsight play in assessing the proposed, lengthy loss period? These were questions at the forefront of a contract dispute playing out in federal district court (D. Me.).

Plaintiff sues third-party supplier. The plaintiff manufactured specialty containers for transporting and storing catalyst, a hazardous chemical agent used in refining crude oil into petroleum products. In 2007, it worked with a long-time customer, a catalyst manufacturer, to redesign the containers by using laminated fabric to meet the customer's specialized requirements. It contracted with the defendants—the original producer and its successor company—to supply the laminated fabric. The plaintiff alleged that six months later the catalyst manufacturer cancelled its pending container orders because the receptacles kept rupturing and thus created an unsafe situation during transport to destinations around the world. According to the plaintiff, the defendants had supplied laminated fabric of inferior quality making the containers unsuitable for the customer's purposes. The product failure, the plaintiff contended, "changed everything." The customer had not bought from the plaintiff since and said it would not do so in the future.

Moreover, the plaintiff claimed that prior to the incidents it had actively marketed its new containers to 37 refineries, which, in turn, had informed its sales manager that they would be placing orders within a year. Because of the product failure, the plaintiff lost not only the contract with the long-standing customer, but also deals with the 37 refineries. The plaintiff sued for lost profits under a number of legal theories, including breach of contract and breaches of express and implied warranty.

At issue in the instant case was the defendants' *Daubert* motion to exclude the damages testimony of the plaintiff's expert.

Two damages models. The plaintiff's expert worked as a CPA for over four decades and was certified as a valuation analyst and business appraiser. He stated that in college he had taken an introductory course in statistics and since then participated in annual continuing education courses featuring statistics. Also, in performing valuations, he used statistical tools regularly, he said. He had given presentations on proving lost profits damages with statistical analysis, including at the National Association of Certified Valuation Analyst's "Litigation Boot Camp."

He defined lost profits as "sales not made minus costs avoided." He reviewed the plaintiff's financial data including both CPA-reviewed and internal financial statements, sales history, and corporate tax returns, he said. He also visited the plaintiff's plant, questioned the plaintiff's bookkeeper, and interviewed the company president on issues of manufacturing capacity, the market for catalyst containers, the factors that could affect sales, and the impact of the product failure. Moreover, he consulted a database of purchase and sale transactions in the industry for companies similar to the plaintiff. He considered the "appropriateness" of each of the "four accepted methodologies for computing lost profits" and concluded the sales projection method was best suited to calculate the plaintiff's damages. This method, he explained, projects sales that would have occurred but for a defendant's alleged wrongdoing. He performed separate analyses for lost sales for the catalyst manufacturer and for the 37 refineries.

The damages model related to the catalyst manufacturer was based on actual sales data, rather than internal projections, he stated. In essence, he projected sales that "would have occurred but for the product failure by using the number of units sold and unit prices from the six-month sales history of the customized [containers]." He next analyzed costs and deducted them from gross revenues to arrive at net profits and also applied an appropriate discount rate (not stated). He explained that this particular model "shows the annual net present value of [the plaintiff's] lost profits for each of the ten years following the product failure."

He noted that he took into account the plaintiff's six-year relationship with this "steady and sizable customer" and the fact that the plaintiff worked closely with the customer to redesign its containers in 2007 so as to ensure it made a product that precisely fit the customer's needs. The collaboration showed the customer's commitment to buying the redesigned containers, he concluded. What's more, the customer actually bought "large numbers" of them—an average of 1,269 per month—for six months and had ordered 1,379 more for the seventh month. The damages model was conservative in that it did not allow for any increases in unit sales or unit prices, he said.

The lost profits calculation related to the 37 refineries relied on a "probabilistic model," he explained, in order to account for future contingencies, such as changes in technology or competition. These were necessary considerations because the plaintiff did not have a lengthy track record selling the new containers to the refineries. He said he "used a simulation software program to run 5,000 trials with a broad range of potential outcomes" given the possibility of contingencies. He explained that he translated the contingencies into estimates of "best case, most likely case, and worst case scenarios for unit sales, unit prices, and costs." He admitted that he used a coefficient from a linear regression that was not statistically significant to allocate overhead costs. Even though he recognized that the test was not statistically significant, he said, he found it "helpful and an improvement over the simple average" for purposes of allocating overhead between fixed and variable expenses. At the same time, he said his calculation would not have changed if he had used the simple arithmetic mean to allocate costs.

All of the refineries included in the model had indicated to the plaintiff that they would be placing orders. He also considered the "substantial economic advantages" customers would reap from using the plaintiff's containers, the plaintiff's business reputation, and its actual sales during the past six years. Hindsight confirmed the "validity of a ten-year loss period," he noted. By his account, "it would take five years for the negative effects of the product failure to dissipate and then five years for refinery sales to recover to the level they would have reached if the product failure had not occurred." The model, he said, showed the annual net present value of lost profits for each year of the 10-year period for the refineries. He assumed the plaintiff had a one-in-10 chance of selling the new containers to the refineries within one year notwithstanding the plaintiff's expectations of a higher-than-10% success rate. He did not conduct a market survey of the refineries to determine the likelihood that any particular refinery would buy the plaintiff's special containers.

The defendants challenged the testimony on a number of grounds, which the court considered in turn.

Not a statistics expert. For one, the defendants argued the testimony was inadmissible because the expert developed models that "embedded statistical calculations," even though, by his own admission, he was not an expert in statistics. Specifically, he used a linear regression model to allocate overhead costs for the long-time customer and the refineries and relied on a coefficient that was not statistically significant. According to the defendants' expert, this approach "violates every statistical principle about why you're doing the test in the first place."

Moreover, for the damages model related to the refineries, he used XLSim, a computer simulation program that incorporates statistical analysis. The defendants characterized this approach as a way for the expert to let a computer program make calculations for which he was unqualified and to circumvent questions as to his qualification. Given his lack of expertise in statistics, it was impossible for opposing counsel to conduct a meaningful cross-examination about the program, the statistical validity of his model, or the interpretation of the results. Testimony from the defendants' own expert made it clear that a qualified statistician would not have used the computer simulation for that exercise; considering the selection of data and parameters was so integral to the outcome, a person lacking expertise in statistics was unable to make reliable choices.

The plaintiff objected that linear regression was a simple statistical tool that a college student could learn in the type of introductory course the plaintiff's expert had taken many years ago. It likened the defendants' argument to the claim that "a damages expert cannot use algebra equations unless he has a Ph.D. in mathematics." The expert had extensive experience with statistical tools, it said. In any event, the statistical analysis he performed for his calculations in the instant case was limited. The plaintiff contended that simulation programs were for users lacking expertise in statistics; however, it also said that its expert qualified as an expert even if statistical knowledge were required and that he would be able to explain the model. Finally, it described his lost profits calculation as a "straightforward mathematical calculation requiring no statistical expertise."

The court found the expert was qualified to use statistical analysis in his lost profits models and by extension to use and speak to the simulation program. This finding, it noted, did not answer the issue as to "whether financial experts must always be qualified in statistics to issue opinions that employ simulation."

Loss period a 'guess'? The defendants primarily focused their attack on the damages model for the catalyst manufacturer on the expert's use of a 10-year loss period. It had no factual support, they claimed. The only data underlying it were the plaintiff's six-month sales history. Further, there was evidence that the customer's purchase history was "volatile." After increasing between 2003 and 2005, purchases decreased by almost 50% in 2006. This meant the 10-year period was a "guess" because the customer could stop buying at any time. Finally, basing a 10-year projection on a six-month sales history ran counter to state law requiring that a lost profits award be based on "credible evidence."

The court rejected the arguments. The expert based the loss period on a "detailed platform of factual information" about the company's finances, its sales history, and its current business relationship with the catalyst manufacturer, the court found. He considered that, at the time of the incidents, there was only one other supplier for catalyst containers from whom the customer could have bought; market conditions remained unchanged in the years following the incident. Also, the plaintiff was well positioned in the market. The court emphasized the benefit of hindsight. Considering the few changes in the competitive environment in the six years since the incidents, it said, the expert's "loss period incorporates the systemic uncertainty of only four years' worth of market conditions." In other words, history has shown that from 2008 to the present, the plaintiff "continue[d] to successfully operate its business." Therefore, in 2014, the 10-year forecast had fewer unknowns than it would have if the expert had to look 10 years into the future starting now, the court pointed out. Also, the model was conservative in that it did not provide for increases in revenue over time despite six months of robust sales to the customer and similar orders in place for a seventh month until the product failure.

The court allowed that the expert made assumptions based on the facts and that the defendants gave "sound reasons to doubt the expert's assumptions." However, the place to test the assumptions was at trial. Moreover, the court noted that the defendants cited case law regarding the required threshold of evidence that applied to trial and post-trial motions but not to *Daubert* motions. In conclusion, the court found the loss period was based on sufficient facts and data for *Daubert* purposes.

One-in-10 success rate assumption. As to the loss calculation for the 37 refineries, the defendants particularly attacked the expert's assumption that the plaintiff had a one-in-10 chance of selling to the refineries. This, too, was "a guess" and not supported by "objective facts and data," they claimed. Moreover, he failed to perform a market survey or use a similar method to obtain "empirical data."

The court saw it differently. It stressed that the plaintiff did not create the list of 37 refineries for litigation but used a list that existed before the product failure. It was the result of efforts by the plaintiff's sales team to market the new containers to refineries that would "enjoy substantial cost savings" from using the new product. The listed refineries had indicated that they would place orders during the next catalyst cycle, that is, within a year. In terms of the strength of their commitment, the expert specifically considered data indicating a 25%-to-50% savings in catalyst moving costs and testimony from an industry expert that demand might increase 3% to 5% during the relevant period. The damages expert did not have much data to work with, the court noted. He had to assess a hypothetical situation—one that featured a market with only two suppliers. He did the best he could; any questions about the assumptions he made went to weight and credibility, not admissibility, the court decided.

It also dismissed the defendants' critique regarding the missing market survey. The list of 37 refineries served the same purpose, it found. A survey was not necessarily better-quality evidence since it would have to ask a hypothetical question concerning a product from a supplier whose reputation the product failure might have "severely tarnished." For the court to rule in favor of the survey would mean it improperly evaluated the persuasive quality of the data the expert used. The defendants had to "sort out" their quarrel with the expert's assumptions at trial, the court found.

Based on largely the same facts that informed the expert's 10%-success-rate assumption, the court also found his assumption of a 10-year loss period for the refineries admissible. The expert could testify at trial, the court concluded.

Personalized Media Communications, LLC v. Zynga, Inc.

Citation: 2013 U.S. Dist. LEXIS 160247
Date of decision: Nov. 8, 2013
Experts: Dr. Stephen L. Becker (plaintiff); unknown (defendant)
Judge: Payne
State/Jurisdiction: Federal/Texas
Court: U.S. District Court
Type of case: Intellectual Property
SIC code: 7371 Computer Programming Services

Plaintiff's Infringement Theory Constrains Apportionment

Several 2013 court decisions made it clear that, in a patent infringement case, determining the smallest salable unit does not necessarily mean the end of the plaintiff expert's damages analysis. An accurate valuation of the contribution a protected feature makes to the accused technology may require a finer strainer. Not surprisingly, inadequate apportionment is an argument defendants routinely make in trying to exclude competing expert testimony. It does not always hit the mark, as a recent *Daubert* case shows.

The plaintiff developed, owned, and licensed patents that enhance media delivery and content. Its inventions worked on various media platforms, including cable and satellite TV and the Internet. The defendant was a social game developer whose games worked on mobile apps and on the Internet, as well as via social networking sites. The plaintiff sued in federal district court (E.D. Tex.), claiming that the defendants' games violated its patents in suit, which enabled "personalized" programming by consumers.

Patented technology is the game. The plaintiff's expert based his damages calculation on the assumption that the patented technology represented "foundational aspects of [the defendant's] games, without which the game itself could not operate." (The opinion does not detail the analysis.)

In its pretrial *Daubert* motion, the defendant sought exclusion of the testimony based on a violation of the entire market value rule (EMVR) under the Federal Circuit's 2011 *Uniloc* and 2009 *Lucent v. Gateway* decisions. Further, it said, the expert's use of the smallest salable unit to establish the reasonable royalty base was not enough; case law required him to perform a more nuanced apportionment.

The court swiftly dealt with the arguments.

1. *EMVR.* Considering that the plaintiff's theory of infringement held that each game as a whole violated the patents in suit and its expert considered the plaintiff's technology essential to the operation of the games, this case was unlike the Federal Circuit cases in which the accused component represented only a small portion of a much larger piece of software. Here, the accused technology was the entire software. Therefore, EMVR did not apply, said the court.

2. *Smallest salable unit.* The court acknowledged that recent decisions held that simply because an expert used the smallest salable unit for his calculation of the reasonable royalty base did not make his analysis reliable. See, e.g., *AVM Techs. v. Intel Corp.*, 2013 U.S. Dist. LEXIS 1165 (2013), and *Dynetix Design Solutions, Inc. v. Synopsys, Inc.*, 2013 U.S. Dist. LEXIS 120403 (2013). But, the court continued, it was unclear how the expert in this case could and should have divided the defendant's games and revenue in light of the plaintiff's claim that each entire game infringed. The defendant failed to explain what "further subdivision might be made." What's more, it was not certain that the expert in fact used a smallest salable unit that was "greater than the patent feature."

For all of these reasons, the court found the testimony admissible.

Editor's note: Following trial, shortly after the ruling, a jury cleared the defendant of all infringement claims.

All of the cases appearing in the text are available at *BVLaw*.

PharmAthene, Inc. v. SIGA Technologies, Inc.

Citation: 2014 Del. Ch. LEXIS 142
Date of decision: Aug. 8, 2014
Experts: Jeffrey L. Baliban (plaintiff); Dr. Keith Ugone (defendant)
Judge: Parsons
State/Jurisdiction: Delaware
Court: Delaware Court of Chancery
Type of case: Damages
SIC code: 2384 Pharmaceutical Preparations

Chancery's Reversal on Damages Opinion Bodes Well for Plaintiff

After a failed relationship, two pharmaceutical companies involved in developing an antiviral drug embarked on a court fight that is now in its eighth year, with no end in sight. The stakes are high, with the plaintiff seeking expectation damages of over $1 billion. Following the parties' appeal to the Delaware Supreme Court, the case returned to the Delaware Court of Chancery for a re-evaluation of damages testimony the plaintiff had offered earlier at trial. Reversing itself, the Chancery found that the plaintiff's expert's damages model met the legal "reasonable certainty" requirement but required adjustments. Post-trial developments surrounding the drug bolstered its change in attitude, the court noted.

Backstory. The plaintiff and the defendant performed biodefense research and development. The defendant had acquired a promising drug to treat smallpox, ST-246, but was running out of money. By late 2005, it needed about $16 million to complete the development process. Lacking the institutional experience to take a drug to market, the defendant pursued a business relationship with the plaintiff. Whereas the plaintiff wanted a merger between the two companies, the defendant insisted on outlining a license agreement, which included a term sheet (LATS) that addressed key issues such as patents covered, licenses, license fees, and royalties. The parties never signed the LATS, and a draft merger term sheet provided that the parties would negotiate the terms of a definitive license agreement in accordance with the terms appearing in the LATS.

By late 2005, the defendant valued ST-246 conservatively at approximately $1 billion. As the parties were preparing for a merger, the defendant achieved important milestones in the development of the drug and received millions of dollars in funding from the government. Subsequently, the sale of stock and the stock price soared. The defendant experienced "seller's remorse" and decided to break off merger plans with the plaintiff. Ultimately, it also walked away from discussions with the plaintiff about a license agreement. Around the time of the breach, the defendant internally valued the drug at between $3 billion and $5 billion.

Lawsuit history. In December 2006, the plaintiff sued in the Delaware Court of Chancery, arguing in essence that the LATS was a binding agreement, which the defendant had breached. The Chancery disagreed but found the defendant had violated its explicit contractual obligation to negotiate in good faith a license agreement "with economic terms substantially similar to those outlined in the LATS." As a remedy, the Chancery awarded the plaintiff an "equitable payment stream or equitable lien" based on the defendant's future profits from the successful commercialization of the drug. At that stage, the Chancery found that lump-sum expectation damages were too speculative and, therefore, inappropriate.

Both sides appealed the ruling to the Delaware Supreme Court, which in turn affirmed the Chancery's bad-faith finding but remanded for a damages award based on contract liability only. The Chancery read the high court's opinion as an invitation to reconsider its prior rejection of a lump-sum award. Any meaningful review, the Chancery said, required a re-examination of the original expert testimony on damages. And a re-evaluation of the testimony required the court at least to take notice of the $460 million contract the defendant was able to procure with the government's Biomedical Advanced Research Development Authority (BARDA) following the court's original holding. According to the Chancery, this fact greatly reduced its earlier concern that the drug might never generate a profit.

Four key assumptions. To support its claim for expectation damages, at trial the plaintiff retained an expert with decades of experience in forensic accounting and economic valuation. On remand, the court found his testimony credible and helpful. The defendant offered rebuttal expert testimony only. In the court's view, this expert was far less credible because all he did was try to discredit the opposing expert's analysis without providing his own, alternative calculation. "This Court has been critical of such an approach in the past."

The plaintiff's expert offered calculations based on six scenarios, but the court found only one relevant. This scenario contemplated damages according to the terms of the LATS based on facts available to the parties on the date of breach, December 2006.

In early 2006, while the parties were still discussing a potential merger, they used a financial model (PHTN model) that served as the starting point for the plaintiff's expert's calculation. The model projected the quantity and price of ST-246 sales to the U.S. government and the rest of the world (ROW) over a 10-year period, from 2008 to 2017. The expert concluded that, during that time, the plaintiff would have sold in total about 91.9 million courses (i.e., treatments) at approximately $100 per course. He subtracted the plaintiff's projected costs and used a "probability of success" factor of 84% to risk adjust the plaintiff's earnings to account for the possibility that the plaintiff would not succeed in commercializing the drug. He applied a 23.1% discount rate to the risk-adjusted earnings and arrived at a net present value of lost profits resulting from the defendant's depriving the plaintiff of the opportunity to develop and sell the drug in accordance with the LATS. The expert concluded that the plaintiff's expectation damages were $1.07 billion.

In assessing the calculation, the court focused on four underlying assumptions:

1. *Product's commercial viability as of December 2006.* The defendant claimed that, around the date of the breach, it was wholly uncertain as to whether the drug would ever be sold commercially, not to mention successfully. Since this was a pharmaceutical drug, it required approval from the Food and Drug Administration (FDA) before it could be sold to the public. No one in 2006 could know whether it would receive approval; in fact, eight years later, it was still unclear when the FDA would approve it. Also, the expert's model incorporated a probability of success figure as to FDA approval that had no reasonable basis given the inherently uncertain process and made the entire calculation speculative.

The plaintiff countered that the defendant overemphasized the importance of FDA approval in terms of the drug's prospect for commercialization. At the time of breach, both parties could be confident that the U.S. government would be the most likely and most important buyer of the drug because it wanted to augment its arsenal against bioterrorist attacks. Also, both parties understood that the government's criteria for buying drugs for the Strategic National Stockpile (SNS) were less stringent than the FDA's; drugs qualified for acquisition into the stockpile even without FDA approval. The SNS was the target market for ST-246.

The plaintiff's arguments had traction with the court. It pointed to other evidence that supported a finding that at the time of breach the parties had a reasonable expectancy of commercializing the drug in the near future. For example, even though the government's BARDA did not exist then, both parties knew its establishment was imminent. The court also pointed out that the defendant's criticism as to the 84% probability rate missed the mark. The damages model was premised on the U.S. government's acquiring the drug for SNS rather than the likelihood of FDA approval. Considering that at the time of breach the drug had reached important milestones and qualified for government funding, the plaintiff had a reasonable expectancy that the government would purchase it.

The court looked further. It pointed out that BARDA subsequently did in fact agree to buy at least 1.7 million courses for the stockpile even though the drug had not yet obtained FDA approval.

2. *Assumed date of sale to the government.* Another issue of contention was the plaintiff's expert's assumption that sales to the government would begin in 2008.

The defendant contested the 2008 date claiming the parties could not know in 2006 when sales would begin. What's more, it took until the first quarter of 2013 to deliver the first courses of the drug. The plaintiff defended the expert's use of the date, saying it was the date the parties themselves had used as a start date during their negotiations over the license agreement. Also, any delay was due to the defendant's inexperience and inability to develop the drug efficiently. But for the breach, the plaintiff would have controlled the drug's development and produced it more expeditiously.

The court found the 2008 date had no support in the record. At the time of the breach, it remained unclear how long BARDA—once established—would take to implement the standards for SNS acquisition, solicit proposals from drug makers, and select the drugs it wanted for the stockpile. The best facts available suggested that, at the time of breach, the plaintiff had a reasonable expectancy that the government would begin buying the drug within four years, by 2010, at the latest, the court said. Therefore, the expert's damages model should use 2010 as the starting date for sales.

3. *Assumed $100-per-course price.* The court found the plaintiff's expert independently tested the $100-per-course price the parties had assumed during their license negotiations. He showed that the figure aligned with prior government purchases of pharmaceutical countermeasures. He also properly assumed a 3% annual increase after the first sales of ST-246 to account for inflation. Finally, the court pointed out that the 2011 BARDA contract to buy the drug required the government to pay considerably more: The defendant was eligible to receive at least $180 per course. Therefore, no price adjustment was necessary.

4. *Number of courses sold to government.* The plaintiff's expert assumed that between 2008 and 2012 the plaintiff would have sold over 29.8 million courses of the drug. This figure included nearly 14.7 million sales to the government for the stockpile, nearly 250,500 courses sold to the defense department for the military, and nearly 14.7 million sales to the rest of the world. Also, he assumed that the drug had a limited shelf life and that the three purchasing entities would replace their orders every five years.

- In terms of stockpile sales, the expert's figure represented a nearly 4.5 million increase over the procurement projection the parties' original financial model provided. The parties' model assumed that the size of the stockpile was roughly equal to the size of the U.S. population. It multiplied the stockpile figure by the percentage of the U.S. population that was contraindicated for vaccination, assuming a 5% rate. The expert found the model significantly understated the size of the stockpile and the contraindication figures. He used the stockpile-population relationship to update the size by referring to the U.S. Census figure that immediately preceded the December 2006 date—295.5 million. He found the contraindication figure actually was in the 20%-to-30% range but decided to be conservative and apply the original 5% rate.

  The court found both steps justified. The contraindication rate was one both sides incorporated into the projections that were the basis of their negotiations, it found. The court also approved of the conservative contraindication rate, noting it did much to offset any alleged overstatement of damages.

- In terms of the Defense Department sales, the court disapproved of the expert's use of a 10% contraindication rate. The expert himself acknowledged he did not know why the original model used different contraindication rates for the stockpile and the Defense Department purchases.

  Consequently, the court ordered a recalculation of the sales to the Defense Department.

- In terms of ROW sales, the Chancery rejected the expert's assumption that sales to the rest of the world would equal stockpile sales. This assumption would have been proper if the plaintiff had proven it had a reasonable expectancy of foreign ST-246 sales, but it did not, the court found. While plans by the U.S. government to augment its preparedness in case of a bioterrorism attack were known to exist at the time of the breach, the plans of foreign governments were entirely unclear. Moreover, even assuming other countries had similar plans, it was unclear what criteria they would use for purchasing drugs for their stockpiles, the court said.

  Consequently, the court refused to award lost profits on foreign sales.

- As for the assumed replacement purchases, the court agreed with the defendant's rebuttal expert who claimed that at the time of breach the U.S. government's long-term plans as to what drugs to buy and how much to spend on countermeasures were too uncertain. Moreover, the more time that passed since the breach, the likelier it was that a viable competing product would enter the market and affect sales of ST-246.

  According to the court, in December 2006, the plaintiff could reasonably expect to make a single sale of over 14.9 million courses—to the U.S. government (stockpile and the Defense Department), which would be delivered in equal installments over five years.

In sum, the Chancery found the plaintiff had established its right to a lump sum for lost profits and ordered the plaintiff's damages expert to modify his calculation based on its ruling.

Piche v. Braaten

Citation: 2014 Minn. App. Unpub. LEXIS 92
Date of decision: Feb. 3, 2014
Experts: Unknown (appellants); Unknown (respondent)
Judge: Kirk
State/Jurisdiction: Minnesota
Court: Court of Appeals
Type of case: Judicial Dissolution
SIC code: 7363 PEO (Professional Employer Organizations)

May Court Disregard Shareholder Agreement in Judicial Buyout?

In a shareholder dispute, the district court ordered the majority owners to buy out the minority owner for a price and in a manner that deviated from the parties' stock purchase agreement and also from the expert testimony at trial. The majority stockholders appealed the buyout order and the court's valuation.

In 2006, 10 years after joining one of the eight companies that made up a closely held corporation, an employee became a shareholder when he signed a stock purchase agreement. It did not specifically discuss the transfer of shares in the event of a court-ordered buyout, but it contained a clause discussing what would happen if there were a "triggering event." The term included death, divorce, and bankruptcy of a shareholder. The three majority shareholders would pay the minority stockholder $8,333 per month until they had repaid the full purchase price of $1.5 million. Under the agreement, the shareholders also were to revise the purchase price annually. By the time an irremediable dispute between the majority and minority shareholders broke out, resulting from the minority shareholder's problematic workplace conduct, he owned a 22% share in the corporation. In 2010, the majority owners terminated his employment and subsequently froze him out as a shareholder.

The minority owner sued, claiming he was wrongfully terminated as an employee and the majority shareholders acted in an "unfairly prejudicial" manner toward him as an owner of the company. The majority shareholders countersued, arguing that he breached the noncompete provision of his employment contract and his fiduciary duties to them as a shareholder.

No comparables. During trial, it became clear that the parties had never revalued the minority owner's shares. Therefore, both sides offered expert testimony as to the stock's fair value as of Dec. 31, 2010. Both experts used a market approach but were unable to find comparables—companies within the same industry or with similar revenue streams. The minority owner's expert said his interest was worth approximately $2.2 million, whereas the majority owners' expert valued it at $1.3 million. (The opinion does not provide details on the calculations.)

One of the majority owners testified that the $8,333-per-month payment stated in the contract was based on an agreement among the shareholders to make a lower monthly payment to ensure the financial solvency of the corporation in case there was a stock sale.

The district court found that there was no wrongful termination but that the majority shareholders acted improperly toward the minority owner as a shareholder. It concluded that relations among the parties were irreparable and ordered a buyout. It dismissed the agreement's price and the experts' valuations as "unreasonable." The terms of the agreement did not apply, the district court said, because it did not contemplate a judicial buyout as a triggering event. The court ordered the majority owners to pay the minority owner a lump sum of $1.6 million, instead of making monthly payments, finding that their companies had a net value of more than $7 million and likely could obtain financing to ensure the corporation continued to be solvent.

Valid solvency concern. The majority shareholders appealed, contesting the district court's buyout order and its valuation. The court should have abided by the terms and price of the stock purchase agreement, they contended.

The appellate court affirmed the buyout "given the acrimonious history among the parties." Had the status quo continued, there would have been endless litigation, it said. It also agreed with the district court's $1.6 million valuation. But it found the district court erred when it disregarded the agreement's providing for monthly payments since this provision reflected the shareholders' concerns and reasonable expectations. Therefore, the Court of Appeals ordered the majority shareholders to make monthly payments of $9,005—$672 more than the agreement had stated to cover the valuation increase—in accordance with the agreement's 15-year formula.

Potok v. Rebh

Citation: 2014 Phila. Ct. Com. Pl. LEXIS 318
Date of decision: Sept. 16, 2014
Experts: Brett Margolin (plaintiff); Scott Salpeter and Christopher Mansueto, Ladenburg Thalmann & Co., Inc. (defendants)
Judge: Snite, Jr.
State/Jurisdiction: Pennsylvania
Court: Philadelphia Court of Common Pleas, Trial Division
Type of case: Dissenting Shareholder
SIC code: 7319 Advertising NEC

Multimillion-Dollar Personal Goodwill Allocation Leaves Court Stunned

A recent state court ruling in a dissenting shareholder case drills down to the economic and legal theories underpinning personal goodwill. The CEO of a company was asked to allocate the proceeds of a buyout that was linked to a settlement of a protracted lawsuit to a limited number of categories. He designated over $10 million as personal goodwill for himself and three other officers although all four individuals had received separate compensation for signing consulting and noncompete agreements. The main issue was whether the personal goodwill allocation was justifiable or self-dealing by the defendants, as the plaintiff claimed.

Cutthroat competitor. In the early 1990s, the plaintiff came up with the idea of floor advertising in supermarkets and began to develop the concept. He soon realized he needed help and additional financing to succeed. Eventually, the four individual defendants joined the company as officers. Two of the defendants were instrumental in securing a $5 million investment. In exchange for funding, the investors required the officers to sign employment contracts with the company. The employment contracts contained noncompete provisions. The company acted as a link between retailers and consumer packaged goods manufacturers (CPGs): Retailers paid the company nothing, but received revenue by making floor and shelf space available; CPGs, on the other hand, entered into business with the company because there was no competition and the company's new personnel, the individual defendants, had contacts. A key ingredient to getting contracts with CPGs was for the floor advertiser to have contracts with anchor chains, large retail chains. The CPGs saw less value in having access to a retailer network of many stores.

In 2000, a competitor emerged in the form of a company that already provided other in-store services and decided to expand into floor advertising. The new company (Newco) used whatever means necessary to lure customers away from the subject company, even if it meant paying above-market prices to anchor chains. The tactics worked; the subject lost important anchor chain retailers and access to CPGs. In 2004, it sued Newco over the legality of its methods. The five-year court fight became the catalyst for the transaction that gave rise to the case at issue. Also, in 2004, the defendants became majority shareholders of the subject company and the plaintiff was relegated to a minor role. Two years later, the company terminated his employment and ejected him from the board of directors. His ouster prompted a separate lawsuit.

Around that time, the company approached a third party that was engaged in yet another aspect of in-store advertising, proposing a buyout or a joint venture. The prospective buyer also had a retail store network. However, it rejected the subject's overtures, stating that it did not want to get into the floor advertising.

In 2009, the litigation with Newco went to trial. The initial week did not augur well for the subject company. At some point, Newco and the individual defendants entered into rapid-fire settlement discussions that concluded with Newco's settlement offer.

Price first, valuation second. Newco insisted on buying only the subject's assets, not its stock, and it wanted to eliminate the risk of future competition from the subject company or the individual defendants. In return, it offered $29.5 million on a "take-it-or-leave-it" basis. This amount was not based on any prior valuation of the subject's assets. The transaction came with several conditions:

- Newco did not allow for the allocation of any of the $29.5 million toward the settlement so as not to admit liability for any of the claims in the lawsuit;
- It required the subject company to execute a noncompete agreement;
- It required the four individual defendants to execute noncompete agreements;
- It required the four defendants to enter into one-year consulting agreements at $1,000 per month for each of the individuals; and

- It required that the transaction amount be allocated to one of four categories: (1) retailer contracts; (2) inventory; (3) noncompete agreements; and (4) consulting agreements.

Newco never requested to buy any goodwill.

The subject's CEO performed a preliminary allocation, which was subject to a "true up" by a recognized valuation firm. The only fixed value was the $48,000 covering the defendants' consulting agreements. The CEO's valuation looked like this:

- $13 million to cover the value of the company's assets and inventory;
- Over $4.45 million to cover the defendants' noncompete agreements;
- $48,000 to cover the consulting agreements; and
- $12 million to cover the four officers' "personal goodwill."

To value the retailer contracts, the CEO assumed that revenue from advertisers paying for his floor space was approximately $4 million and that the space could generate about three times the revenue when utilized by an able competitor. He also concluded that his space would generate perhaps seven times the subject's revenue under the control of Newco because the latter already had a connection with CPGs and major anchor chains under exclusive contracts.

Further, the CEO remembered from his law school days a tax case that permitted corporate executives to receive cash for their personal goodwill—specifically, *Martin Ice Cream Co. v. Commissioner*, 110 T.C. 18 (1998) (available at *BVLaw*). Based on the case, he allocated about 40% of the $29.5 million transaction price to the defendants' combined personal goodwill. Newco accepted the allocation.

The true up did not occur until some eight months later. The CEO chose the appraiser, and Newco approved the selection. The CEO served as the point person for responding to questions. The appraiser's valuation allocated:

- $9.3 million to the retailer contracts;
- $275,000 to the company's inventory;
- $48,000 to the defendants' consulting agreement;
- Over $3 million to cover the noncompetes; and
- Over $16.7 million to cover the defendants' personal goodwill.

'Solving back.' At trial, the firm's valuation analyst explained that he was not allowed to create any new categories. He said he applied the usual valuation methods to obtain a fair market value of the categories but conceded he was "solving back" to the purchase price. He said he was told that the subject generated about $5 million in revenue from all its business (down from $70 million in 2004) but operated at a loss. He initially questioned the overall purchase price.

The analyst ultimately accepted the CEO's three times revenue approach based on another competitor's synergies and used a discounted cash flow analysis to calculate the $9.3 million value for the retailer contracts. For the noncompetes, he assumed that, on the day Newco received the retailer contracts, the subject and the individual defendants would have no floor space and as such no way to generate revenue. But as the retailer contracts expired, the company and defendants would be able to compete again, assuming no noncompetes. The revenue they could generate would theoretically be lost to Newco. This revenue, the valuator explained, could establish a cash flow that, discounted to present value, resulted in the $3 million fair market value of the noncompetes. Finally, the appraiser's report explained that it also used an income approach to determine the fair market value for the defendants' personal goodwill. It said:

> [W]e determined the cash flows that would be lost without the Personal Goodwill and without the Non-Compete Agreements in place in effect deriving combined cash flows for the Non-Compete Agreements and the personal Goodwill.

The CEO, on behalf of the subject, retained the proceeds to reinvest in other ventures and never made a distribution to the stockholders. Ultimately, Newco sued the company for the entire amount it paid for the transaction. The plaintiff sued on behalf of the minority shareholders, alleging breach of fiduciary duty.

The issue boiled down to whether the transaction was fair to the minority shareholders. At trial, the plaintiff's expert maintained that at the time of the transaction the company had little, if any, value. Since it had no anchor store, no CPGs would do business with the company. In fact, the smaller retailer contracts to which it was able to hold onto actually caused negative cash flow. Consequently, the noncompete agreements from the four defendants were worthless and the money allocated to the noncompetes, the consulting agreements, and the personal goodwill should go to the company. The entire $29.5 million purchase price was in effect payment for settling the lawsuit and belonged to the company.

Valuation gets 'short shrift.' The court agreed with the plaintiff that the restrictions operating on the appraisal firm made a meaningful valuation impossible. This was not an arm's-length transaction in an open and unrestricted market. According to the court, "it was done rapidly and with short shrift to traditional economic evaluations." Without the settlement, Newco had to offer anchor chains above-market incentives to secure them as customers and prevent the subject from producing revenue from CPGs. Following the settlement, Newco could take possession of the company's retailer contracts and return to fair market pricing and save tens of millions of dollars. At the same time, the transaction had value to the subject company, which was facing the possibility of no equity whatsoever. Accepting Newco's $29.5 million offer was reasonable.

Moreover, the court found that in light of the potential the company had to synergistic buyers—Newco and the third party with whom the subject had discussed a buyout or joint venture earlier—it was reasonable for Newco to pay $13 million for the retailer contracts. This amount should go to the company, the court determined.

Further, the court said, it was reasonable for the defendants to be compensated for their consulting agreements. These agreements are "a method to 'buy' the personal goodwill of individuals who might be instrumental in the execution of the transaction." Since Newco required the agreements and specified a price, $48,000 in total, they were the property of the defendants, the court determined.

The court also disagreed with the plaintiff's expert over the $4.45 million related to the noncompetes. The defendants were instrumental in obtaining $5 million funding for the company and in growing the company initially. They developed a reputation in the industry as capable businessmen. They made the company competitive, even though its situation looked bleak at the time of trial. For Newco to eliminate all competition, a noncompete from the company was insufficient. It required the individual noncompetes.

The court discredited the company appraiser's rationale for the individual noncompetes. That analysis failed to consider that there was a noncompete for the company that rendered the defendants unable to compete as long as they were officers of the company. If they decided to leave the company, they had to find new employment or strike out on their own. Their leaving would damage the company's ability to produce and as such their equity in the company, the court observed. Ultimately, the court accepted the $4.45 million value the CEO had assigned to the contracts.

Unlike *Martin Ice Cream*. The court flat out rejected the 40% allocation to personal goodwill. Considering the dire financial situation in which the company found itself at the time of the transaction, it would take a lot to convince a fact finder that it is appropriate for the CEO of the company to award himself and the other officers $12 million because "they worked so hard and deserved it," the court said. The personal goodwill agreements were "stunning in that it is not clear that anything is being sold." What's more, said the court, "it does not appear to set a time limit." Under case law, "it is unreasonable to assume that personal goodwill, if it can be purchased, can be purchased forever." The court dismissed the appraiser's attempt at valuing the personal goodwill, noting that the appraiser was forced to create a figure and also forced to create a valuation methodology. The appraiser had never previously valued personal goodwill, it observed. It rejected the idea that personal goodwill could serve as a "plug" figure.

The court agreed with the plaintiff's expert that there are two ways to convert personal goodwill into economic value: (1) the employment contract or consulting agreement; and (2) the noncompete agreement. Here, the noncompete, purchase, and consulting agreements ensured Newco achieved its aims. Beyond that, there was no other transfer of personal goodwill. The court called the idea that there was personal goodwill resulting from the combined efforts of the individual defendants an "extremely risky proposition." Without explicitly saying so, the court also seemed to acknowledge that there was "pure goodwill" that is not salable. Even if one recognized that the defendants had unique abilities, skills, or experience or other personal characteristics or qualifications, these attributes did not "exist in such form that they could be subject to transfer," the court observed.

Finally, the court went to great length to distinguish *Martin Ice Cream* from the case in front of it. For one, unlike the sole shareholder in *Martin Ice Cream,* the defendants did not develop all of the crucial relationships with the company's clients and therefore "could not, and did not, develop the same degree of personal goodwill with retail customers." By the CEO's admission, the company had a sales team to recruit and maintain clients. Unlike the *Martin Ice Cream* shareholder, three out of four defendants did not bring business relationships with them to the company that would have provided it with substantial revenue streams. Three out of four also lacked relevant industry experience. Importantly, unlike the sole shareholder in *Martin Ice Cream*, the defendants had entered into employment contracts with the company, at least for the critical initial period. The court found their argument that they subsequently terminated the agreements—a disputed issue—not credible.

Most critically, the court was convinced that Newco never wanted to buy any goodwill from either the company or the individual defendants. The CEO admitted as much when he testified that he was not sure whether Newco was even "familiar with the concept" of personal goodwill. Newco also never used the defendants' consulting services. It did not need the defendants to succeed with the retailer contracts it obtained from the company. "The law does not support an individual forever selling his personal goodwill to a competitor where the competitor is 'buying out' the individual and is not rewarding the individual for past or future services," the court said.

The defendants were unjustly enriched by the $12 million allocation for personal goodwill, the court concluded, and ordered them to pay their share of the amount to the company.

Prevost v. Prevost

Citation: 2014 Minn. App. Unpub. LEXIS 288
Date of decision: April 7, 2014
Experts: Leonard Waschko (wife); Richard C. Berning (husband)
Judge: Hudson
State/Jurisdiction: Minnesota
Court: Court of Appeals
Type of case: Marital Dissolution
SIC code: 1522 General Contractors-Residential Buildings, other than Single-Family

Court Affirms 'Market Valuation Assessment' of Family Businesses

A recent appeals court decision tackles the issue of how to value a closely held business for marital property purposes where state law on the one hand has leaned heavily on the eight factors set forth in IRS Revenue Ruling 59-60 and on the other hand has cautioned against their rigid application and a too-narrow approach. The case serves as a reminder for valuators to familiarize themselves with the applicable case law.

During the marriage, the husband started two companies: He was the sole owner of a construction company he had formed in 1984, and he owned 51% of a maintenance company, with his brother owning the remainder. The parties agreed that the husband should get the entire interest of both companies but argued over their values. At trial, they presented expert testimony.

The wife's expert undertook a "market valuation assessment" for both companies using four different approaches to determine the price at which the companies would sell to a willing buyer: a percentage of average annual sales, a percentage of gross sales of the most recent full year, a percentage of gross profits, and a multiple of the average annualized seller's discretionary earnings (SDE). The use of the SDE allowed buyers to estimate the "true" cash flow necessary to pay themselves, make payment on interest and principal on any debt financing, and retain earnings in case of contingencies, the expert explained. He reviewed the businesses' internal tax returns from 2010 and 2011 and their internal profit and loss statements for 2010 to 2012. Moreover, he considered the effect of the 2008 economic downturn on the construction industry as well as signs of an upward trend between 2010 and 2012 and looked at sales of other comparable businesses. He also used industry rules to measure the sales value of contracting services.

He pointed out that some of the assets of the business had more value than the corporate books showed; for example, the construction company's balance sheet indicated more than $223,000 in fixed assets, reduced by a little over $189,000 in depreciation. He concluded that the construction company probably would sell for $288,000 and the husband's interest in the maintenance company was worth $11,000.

The husband's expert applied various valuation methods for both entities. As to the construction company, under the cost approach, looking at the value of its assets, he found it had a negative book value of about $82,700. After adjustments, he concluded it was worth approximately $4,200. For the income approach, he used the "capitalization of earnings method" to estimate the earnings capacity of the company. He found there was no record of compensation for the husband and modified the earnings to reflect an "appropriate market officer compensation," which he set at about $120,300 per year. Subtracting that amount from the company earnings yielded a negative income. He concluded there were no earnings to capitalize. Even though the company existed since 1984, the expert said he was unable to use the market approach because the business was a startup.

For the maintenance company, the asset approach generated a negative value. Further, the expert concluded that deducting market wages for the husband under the income approach also yielded a negative value. And, since the company only existed since 2010, he said he was unable to do a market valuation.

Improving market, but negative value? The trial court credited the valuations of the wife's expert but lowered the value of the maintenance company by half—$5,500—to reflect the difficulty in selling a company with divided ownership. It said the valuations the husband's expert proposed were not persuasive. How could a business be worth only $4,200 in 2012 "when the market is improving and there are no demonstrated, significant changes to the business," the court asked. Both businesses showed rising ordinary business income between 2010 and 2012. Also, since the construction business was not a startup company, there was no reason not to do a valuation under the market approach.

In a motion for a new trial, the husband contended the wife's expert "put together a marketing proposal" instead of a valuation. He did not "follow established methods." The trial court disagreed and denied the motion.

The husband then appealed to the Minnesota Court of Appeals, claiming the wife's expert did not know the applicable law—specifically, IRS Revenue Ruling 59-60 and the case that applied it. Therefore, his valuations were unreliable and the trial court erred in adopting them.

No one approach fits all. At the outset of its analysis, the appeals court emphasized that state courts have employed a number of different approaches to value closely held corporations for marital property purposes. In an influential case, the state Supreme Court said: "Although Revenue Ruling 59-60 sets out the procedure used by the Internal Revenue Service for estate and gift tax valuation, we regard the eight fundamental factors therein identified as equally appropriate for use and analysis in determining the value of a closely held corporation as marital property for purposes of equitable distribution." *Nardini v. Nardini, 987 Minn. LEXIS 841* (1987) (available at *BVLaw*).

The eight factors are: (1) the nature of the business and the history of the enterprise from its inception; (2) the economic outlook in general and the condition and outlook of the specific industry in particular; (3) the book value of the stock and the financial condition of the business; (4) the earning capacity of the company; (5) its dividend-paying capacity; (6) enterprise goodwill or other intangible value; (7) sales of the stock and the size of the block of the stock to be valued; and (8) the market price of stocks of corporations engaged in the same or a similar line of business having their stocks traded in a free and open market.

But the *Nardini* court pointed out that a proper valuation not only was a matter of applying the relevant facts, but also required the use of common sense and sound judgment in weighing the facts and "determining their aggregate significance." And it noted that the value of a family business "cannot be less than a sum equal to the net proceeds which could be realized from the forced sale of the tangible [and intangible] assets … after payment of all liabilities."

Besides *Nardini*, the appeals court here looked to a treatise on valuing closely held corporations in the divorce context, which proposed four methods: book value, capitalization of earnings method, dividend paying, and liquidation value to compute the entity's fair market value. But the authors caution that state courts have discredited book value because it is subject to manipulation and inaccuracies. See 14 Martin L. Swaden and Linda A. Olup, *Minnesota Practice* § 9:7 (3rd ed. 2008).

In this case, the appeals court found that the four-prong approach the wife's expert took, his considering the economy and the conditions particular to the industry, and his comparing the husband's business to others that sold as reported in national databases represented steps in line with the IRS revenue ruling and *Nardini*, even if the expert did not refer to those authorities in his report. Further, the expert addressed certain inaccuracies related to book value. As for the district court, it gave reasons for rejecting the valuations of the husband's expert. And, by discounting the value of the maintenance business to reflect divided ownership, the trial court showed it did not blindly accept the valuation of the wife's expert. In sum, even though the methods the wife's expert used were not the only ones with which to value the entities under state law, they provided sufficient support for the trial court's value conclusions. Therefore, the appeals court affirmed the findings.

Rembrandt Social Media, LP v. Facebook, Inc.

Citation: 2013 U.S. Dist. LEXIS 171127
Date of decision: Dec. 3, 2013
Experts: James E. Malackowski (plaintiff); unknown (defendant)
Judge: Ellis
Country: US
State/Jurisdiction: Federal/Virginia
Court: United States District Court
Type of case: Intellectual Property
SIC: 7379 Computer Related Services, NEC (except computer systems consultants and disk conversion services)

Inexact Apportionment Invalidates Expert's Royalty Calculation

In a patent dispute, the plaintiff alleged that two of Facebook's features infringed its patents and presented expert testimony as to reasonable royalty damages. Facebook attacked both the royalty base and royalty rate determinations under *Daubert,* alleging a host of improprieties, including violations of the entire market value rule (EMVR) and flawed apportionment. One attack "misse[d] the mark," the court found, but the other was "fatal."

The plaintiff was a nonproducing limited partnership that had acquired two of the patents in suit by way of assignment. In its suit (E.D. Va.), it claimed that Facebook, the globally recognized social networking service, infringed the patents when it introduced two new features to its website: BigPipe and Audience Symbol. The plaintiff admitted that no violation occurred without those two features. It sought damages covering the period from February 2009 to February 2013.

Two levels of apportionment. The damages claim rested entirely on testimony from a notable expert, who calculated a reasonable royalty based on a hypothetical negotiation between the parties and the *Georgia-Pacific* framework. He performed three steps.

(1) Royalty base. For the base, he first considered Facebook's entire revenue stream during the alleged infringement period. Next, he decided to exclude 50% of that figure because it represented the amount of revenue attributable to the use of Facebook's noninfringing mobile applications. Then he considered three customer and advertiser surveys that asked survey participants to rank a number of Facebook features in order of importance to the user. Importantly, four of the tested features could be used independently, without BigPipe and Audience Symbol, and thus without infringing. Also, the surveys did not test the importance the BigPipe and Audience Symbol features themselves assumed for the survey takers.

For his second apportionment, the expert first assumed that the weighted importance of any given feature corresponded exactly to the percentage of advertising revenue Facebook received from it and then excluded revenue attributable to features that did not cause infringement. However, he did not try to calculate how much revenue actually was attributable to BigPipe and Audience Symbol, the features responsible for the alleged infringement. The court's opinion redacted the final claimed royalty base amount but stated that, by the expert's estimation, it was 65.19% of Facebook's total revenue stream.

(2) Royalty rate. For the rate, the expert first considered prior license agreements involving similar technology. These contracts did not involve the plaintiff, but the original patent holder and two other companies, and they licensed rights not to the patents in suit but to a complete and operational product and related services. Based on these licenses, the expert determined a "lower bound" of 2.3%; this was the minimum that the patent holder would accept in a hypothetical negotiation, he stated. Based on revenue he thought stemmed from the infringing features, he set an "upper bound" of 21.99%; this, he believed, was the maximum amount Facebook would pay for use of the patents. Next, he applied the 15 *Georgia-Pacific* factors to the bounds to arrive at a final royalty rate of 5% to 6%.

Finally he multiplied the royalty rate by the royalty base to arrive at his total royalty, a figure the court opinion redacted.

Problematic use of surveys. Trying to exclude the testimony, Facebook challenged both the expert's royalty base and royalty rate calculations on multiple grounds. The court considered the arguments in turn.

(1) EMVR violation. Facebook claimed use of Facebook's entire revenue stream as a starting point for the royalty base violated the EMVR.

That attack "misses the mark," the court said, because the expert did not use the entire value for the royalty base. Rather, he began his calculation of the base with the entire revenue but then performed two separate apportionments. The EMVR did not come into play.

(2) Flawed apportionment. Facebook argued that, in calculating the royalty base and royalty rate, the expert failed to apportion revenue to the two features that caused the alleged infringement, that is, BigPipe and Audience Symbol.

This argument was lethal to the plaintiff's claim, the court found. Because the accused technologies represented only a small improvement to an existing technology, the plaintiff only had a right to a royalty based on the "incremental value provided by that improvement" (citing *Lucent v. Gateway*, 580 F.3d 1301 (2009)) (available at *BVLaw*). Here, the expert's apportionment did not properly represent the amount Facebook would have been willing to pay to license the patents in suit. Allowing the expert to use as the royalty base the entire value of four features that could function without infringing, on Facebook's mobile platform, while not using the value of the allegedly infringing features, BigPipe and Audience Symbol, "would be a mistake of the same kind as allowing [the expert] to use the entire value of Facebook," the court said. For this reason alone, the testimony was inadmissible.

But, the court continued, the improper apportionment based on the four features also affected the expert's royalty rate calculation. To calculate the upper limit of the rate (21.99%), he also took into account the three market surveys that listed the four features while not ranking BigPipe and

Audience Symbol. Because he failed to use only the portion of the revenue stream attributable to the infringing features, his entire damages analysis was unreliable, the court concluded.

(3) Improper use of surveys. Facebook further contended that the way the expert used the customer surveys to calculate the royalty base was unsound. He simply assumed that a certain rating of a feature directly translated into the percentage in advertising revenue the feature generated for Facebook. The court agreed. The record showed that the surveys only tried to determine what features most drive Facebook's usage but did not claim there was a direct link between usage data and revenue, the court pointed out. The expert should have analyzed the correlation between usage and revenue but failed to do so. Therefore, his methodology was unreliable.

In sum, because the expert overcompensated the plaintiff for the alleged violation, the opinion was inadmissible, leaving the plaintiff with no support for its damages claim.

In re Residential Capital, LLC

Citation: 2013 Bankr. LEXIS 4844
Date of decision: Nov. 15, 2013
State/Jurisdiction: Federal/New York
Court: United States Bankruptcy Court
Type of case: Bankruptcy
Experts: Marc D. Puntus (debtors); Michael Fazio, Jeffrey M. Levine, John A. Taylor, and P. Eric Siegert (Houlihan Lokey Capital, Inc.)(defendants)
Judge: Glenn
SIC: 6162 Mortgage Bankers and Loan Correspondents (mortgage bankers and originators)

Creditors' Valuation Spoils Diminution in Value Claim

A recent ruling in the multifaceted Chapter 11 bankruptcy litigation of Residential Capital (ResCap), a large residential mortgage loan company, and its affiliated debtors contains a noteworthy analysis of the alleged diminution in value of the collateral of junior secured noteholders (JSNs). This valuation issue arose in the context of the JSNs' adequate protection claim—one of the many claims they presented in their opposition to the debtors' proposed reorganization plan.

Background. ResCap was a leading originator of residential mortgage loans and, together with nondebtor affiliates, the fifth largest servicer of residential mortgage loans in the country. In May 2012, ResCap and its affiliated debtors petitioned for Chapter 11 bankruptcy. The defendants in this case were entities holding or managing entities that hold junior secured notes. In connection with the bankruptcy, ResCap proposed a reorganization plan. A few days later, the U.S. trustee appointed the Official Committee of Unsecured Creditors, which began investigating what it alleged were security interests the defendants improperly claimed. Subsequently, the defendants filed a series of counterclaims related to the junior secured notes ResCap had issued in 2008 and the collateral securing those notes.

To keep their business operating as debtors in possession, the debtors sought to obtain post-petition financing and authorization to use the cash collateral encumbered by existing debt facilities. In essence, the funding would allow them to continue to issue loans and offer loan modifications to thousands of borrowers; service mortgages and make advances associated with such servicing obligations; comply with the Federal Reserve and FDIC consent order; comply with agreements they had made with government-sponsored entities (GSEs) as to the care they needed to apply in servicing their loans; and retain hundreds of employees to protect against an increase in delinquencies, which could diminish the value and jeopardize the sale of the debtors' mortgage servicing rights (MSRs) and other assets. The debtors and the JSNs negotiated a cash collateral order that established the JSNs' right to adequate protection for the use of their collateral. As of the petition date, the JSNs' secured claims against ResCap and certain affiliated debtors had a face value of $2.2 billion, including $2.1 billion in unpaid principal and $101 million in unpaid prepetition interest.

In the "Phase I" trial in front of the Bankruptcy Court (S.D.N.Y.), the JSNs argued, among other things, that they had a right to recover an adequate protection claim of $515 million based on the diminution in aggregate value of their prepetition collateral as used during the case pursuant to a number of consensual orders.

Both sides agreed that the amount of the adequate protection claim was the difference in the value of collateral between the effective date and the petition date. Moreover, they agreed that $1.88 billion was a baseline value at the effective date. They disagreed over the value of the collateral on the petition date and retained valuation experts to support their arguments.

They also disagreed over how to value the collateral: The JSNs claimed case law required use of the fair market value of the collateral in the hands of the debtors. In contrast, the debtors contended the foreclosure value of the collateral in the hands of the secured creditor was the appropriate measure.

JSNs offer 'global summary' of various valuations. The JSNs had the burden of proving the diminution in value. They presented opinions from four experts who valued different assets. To determine the fair market value of each asset that was part of the collateral, where applicable, the experts considered the prices the debtors' various assets commanded in a post-petition auction process, adjusting for cash flows and loan balances back to the petition date. They also performed a "bottoms-up" fair market valuation as of the petition date. One of the experts presented a single "global summary" of the opinions arriving at a net fair market value of $2.79 billion. He calculated this value by summing: (1) the valuations of the debtors' cash, various assets, unsold servicing advances, loans, equity interests, hedge contracts, and certain other contracts; (2) the valuation of the debtors' sold servicing advances; and (3) his own valuation of the various intangible assets based on his analysis of the other valuations. This approach yielded a value of $4.450 billion, from which he subtracted various liabilities to conclude that the collateral was worth $2.79 billion on the petition date.

Debtors' expert devises methodology. The debtors' expert served for two years as their lead investment banker and in this capacity was involved in their decision to market their assets and in arranging a prepetition marketing process and post-petition sale process. He used two initial bids that did not materialize (stalking horse agreements) to determine a $1.74 billion benchmark value. This benchmark, he said, did not represent his opinion of the value of the collateral for purposes of adequate protection because the purchase prices the stalking horse deals proposed were contingent on the continued operation of the debtors' business in Chapter 11. To estimate the value of the JSNs' collateral as of the petition date in the hands of the creditors' agents upon foreclosure, he made downward adjustments to his benchmark valuation based on two alternative scenarios: "Alternative A" assumed the collateral would be monetized by the collateral agents over a three-to-four-month period ($1.47 billion), while "Alternative B" assumed a five-to-six-month period ($1.59 billion). Other factors required further reductions, he believed, and lowered the "Alternative A" valuation to $1.05 billion and the "Alternative B" valuation to $1.13 billion.

Valuations leave court 'unimpressed.' The court found neither side's valuation was convincing. At the outset of its analysis, it agreed with the defendants that, for the purpose of a finding on whether the secured creditor was adequately protected, "the going concern/fair market value" in the hands of the debtors was the correct measure. The parties in this case did not on the petition date contemplate that the creditors might conduct a foreclosure sale, said the court. Rather, the JSNs agreed to the cash collateral order to enable the sale of assets as a going concern.

But this ruling in favor the defendants did not mean they were able to prove a diminution in the value of their collateral, the Bankruptcy Court continued. Their valuation was defective for various reasons:

(1) The valuation incorrectly assumed the debtors could have sold the JSN collateral on the petition date free and clear of certain obstacles. However, at trial, one of the experts admitted that the sale of mortgage servicing rights would have required consent from the residential mortgage backed securities (RMBS) trustees and the GSEs. At the same time, that expert's valuation did not account for costs related to obtaining consent. These costs, said the court, were considerable. They included payments of hundreds of millions of dollars to the GSEs to "cure alleged liabilities" prior to obtaining their consent to a sale. Moreover, the debtors agreed to settle billions of dollars of potential RMBS liability to obtain the RMBS trustees' consent to a sale.

(2) Even assuming the debtors could have sold their assets on the petition date, the defendant experts' valuation was not credible. Instead of considering sales other distressed companies "on the brink of bankruptcy" made, they only considered a solvent company that was able to obtain fair market value for its assets. In this case, however, most of the assets could not simply be handed to a buyer who could instantly benefit from full value "as if the assets were commodity products." According to the court, the experts "ignored the reality" of the dire situation in which the debtors were just prior to the bankruptcy. "ResCap was an insolvent company, over-burdened with debt, owning assets that had to be 'fixed' before they could be sold, and facing a real possibility of being shut down."

The Bankruptcy Court added it was "equally unimpressed" with the valuation the debtors' expert had proposed. He performed subjective valuations of risks related to the collateral. At trial, he admitted that he had never seen a valuation analysis relying on a similar methodology before. "Nor is it likely that [the expert's] valuation methodology could be used in other contexts," noted the court. But even if his methodology was unreliable, "the numbers he reached may well be closer to the actual value of the JSN collateral on the petition date," the Bankruptcy Court stated.

The court was "mindful" of the JSN money the debtors had spent during the case, but, it said, this spending did not mean they incurred a diminution in the aggregate value of their collateral. There was no right to an adequate protection claim on a dollar-for-dollar basis for cash collateral used during the case. Considering the value of the collateral on the petition date was significantly impaired because of existing defaults that prevented the debtors from disposing of most of the collateral, the court did not believe the value then was higher than the value on the effective date. By way of settlements and consents, the debtors were able to sell most of their assets on very favorable terms. "The JSNs and all estate creditors will benefit from this accomplishment," the court concluded. For all these reasons, it denied the request for adequate protection.

Editor's Note. The court noted that a "Phase II" trial and a contested confirmation hearing likely would get underway at the end of 2013 based on the JSNs' strategy to "contest everything and concede nothing," resulting in "protracted proceedings that have burdened the estate and reduced funds available to satisfy creditor claims."

Estate of Richmond

Citation: 2014 Tax Ct. Memo LEXIS 26
Date of decision: Feb. 11, 2014
Experts: Peter Winnington (petitioner, Form 706), Robert Schweihs (petitioner, trial), John A. Thomson (respondent/IRS, trial)
Judge: Gustafson
State/Jurisdiction: Federal
Court: United States Tax Court
Type of case: Estate and Gift Taxation
SIC code: 6720 Investment Offices

Tax Ct. How-to of Valuing Holding Company, Avoiding Accuracy Penalty

Capitalization-of-dividends approach or net-asset-value approach? In what looks to be one of the most important valuation decisions in 2014, the Tax Court recently explored which methodology produced the most reliable value of a decedent's interest in a holding company whose underlying assets were marketable securities. A secondary issue—but one that resonates with valuation professionals—was what type of appraisal may excuse an undervaluation and exempt the taxpayer from any accuracy-related penalty.

Background. At the time of her death in December 2005, the decedent owned a 23.44% interest in a family-owned investment holding company (C corp.) most of whose assets were publicly traded securities. She was the second-largest shareholder but never in a position to unilaterally change or control the company's management or investment philosophy. The total assets then were worth nearly $52.16 million, of which $45 million—or 87.5% of the portfolio's value—was unrealized appreciation.

The company's philosophy was to maximize dividend income for the family shareholders while minimizing taxes and preserving capital. Historically, it turned over stock at a slow, 70-year, pace, notwithstanding financial advice to sell substantial amounts of the securities for the purpose of diversifying. The built-in capital gain tax (BICG tax) to the unrealized appreciation was over $18.1 million.

The executors retained an accounting firm to value the company stock for purposes of reporting estate tax. Based on an unsigned draft valuation, the estate declared that the decedent's interest was $3.15 million on the federal estate tax return, Form 706. In sharp contrast, an auditor for the Internal Revenue Service (IRS) determined that the interest was worth over $9.2 million. This assessment triggered a deficiency notice and a 40% gross valuation misstatement penalty of over $1.14 million. In response, the estate petitioned the Tax Court for review of two issues: (1) what was the FMV of the decedent's interest; and (2) whether there was an underpayment subject to an accuracy-related penalty.

At trial both parties offered valuation expert testimony.

Experts. Three experts played a role in the outcome of the case: the two trial experts and the author of the draft report that gave rise to the initial $3.15 million valuation. The court noted that the IRS deficiency notice did not give any details as to the auditor's valuation methodology.

1. *Draft report author.* The accountant who did the initial valuation was a CPA and a certified financial planner, a member of the American Institute of Certified Public Accountants (AICPA), the Delaware Society of CPAs (DSCPA), and the Wilmington Group. Although he had written somewhere between 10 and 20 valuation reports and testified in court, he was not a certified appraiser.

To generate the draft, he used the capitalization-of-dividends method and relied on information the estate provided regarding stock transactions in the 1990s, valuations for prior estates that included the company's stock, and company information on file with his firm: audit reports, corporate tax returns, company investment reports, and other indicators of the company's particular investment philosophy. After submitting an unsigned draft to the estate's executors and tax return preparer, neither consulted with him further or asked him to finalize his valuation before using his $3.15 million value in the IRS filing.

2. *IRS expert.* The Service retained an expert in business valuation. He used the discounted net asset valuation (NAV) approach. Broadly speaking, he began with the stipulated net asset value of $52.1 million to calculate that the decedent's interest was worth $12.2 million. He then applied a 6% discount for lack of control (DLOC) and a 36% "marketability" discount that included a 15% discount for the BICG tax. He concluded that the decedent's interest was worth approximately $7.3 million—about 20% less than the value in the deficiency notice.

3. *Estate's expert.* The estate's expert was a certified business appraiser and valuation analyst. He also relied primarily on the capitalization-of-dividends method. Based on historical data, he assumed an annual 5% increase in dividend payments, which would continue indefinitely. He found the market rate of return for a company with a similar profile was about 10.25%, resulting in a capitalization rate of 5.25%. Dividing the decedent's expected dividend return for the following year by the cap rate, he arrived at a present value of about $5 million for future dividends.

The estate asked the court to adopt his calculation, not the value it had reported based on the draft valuation report. Accordingly, the estate agreed to a value that was 60% more than the initial figure. Considering the new valuations, the difference in value between the parties shrank from over $6 million at the deficiency notice stage to not quite $2.3 million at trial.

In the alternative, the estate's expert also provided a valuation based on the NAV method; it essentially critiqued and modified elements of the IRS expert's valuation. For example, the estate expert applied a 100% BICG discount, reducing the total $52.2 million NAV by over $18.1 million. To the resulting total, he applied an 8% DLOC and a 35.6% discount for lack of marketability (DLOM). This calculation produced a $4.7 million value for the decedent's interest.

Valuation method. In deciding the "big" issue first—what's the appropriate valuation method—the court noted that dividend capitalization was one legitimate way to value a business and "may be entirely appropriate where a company's assets are difficult to value." But, the Tax Court continued, this approach was based entirely on projecting, or estimating, a future income stream (and discounting it to present value). The court recognized that in this case the company had a history of predictable dividend payments and in fact made predictability a stated investment goal; further, during the past 35 years it showed a steady 5% annual increase. These facts buttressed the estate expert's projections as to the company's future payouts. But, said the court, "even small variations in those estimates can have substantial effects on the value determined."

By relying on the capitalization-of-dividends approach, the estate's expert "ignored the most concrete and reliable data of value ... the actual market prices of the publicly traded securities" in the company's portfolio, the Tax Court noted. In contrast, the NAV approach, in this case, starts out on "firm ground," with stock values one can simply look up. What's more, a potential investor would have known that the company held assets whose value was easily attainable and would take those values as a starting point.

The court distinguished cases the estate cited in support of its approach, finding they either featured a company that held stock in a closely held operating company or the company was itself an operating business. Consequently, it was difficult to value their assets.

Once the court settled on the NAV approach, it addressed some of the "difficulties and uncertainties" going along with it, that is, determining the applicable discount rates.

BICG tax. No interested investor in the company would have been indifferent to the eventual $18.1 million tax liability, said the Tax Court. The market would have demanded a discount, and a fair market valuation had to reflect it. At the same time, the court dismissed the estate's contention that the BICG reduction should be dollar for dollar, based on 5th and 11th Circuit law. For one, said the court, these decisions are not controlling here; if there were an appeal in this case, it would be in front of the 3rd Circuit since the executors resided in Pennsylvania and New Jersey. Also, the Tax Court, itself, has considered this treatment "plainly wrong in a case like the present one," the court reminded the parties.

The key question is what price a willing buyer and a willing seller would agree to. According to the court, no reasonable investor would equate a company burdened by an $18.1 million BICG tax with one burdened by an $18.1 million note payable due tomorrow, which was what the estate's approach suggested. "[A] prospective BICG tax liability is not the same as a debt that really does immediately reduce the value of a company dollar for dollar." The court also found the methodology behind the IRS expert's 15% rate "problematic" but thought his $7.8 million bottom line "reasonable." In essence, the expert assumed that a buyer would be indifferent to the effects of the BICG tax to the extent attributable to unrealized appreciation up to 50% of the company's NAV but would require a dollar-for-dollar discount for the portion above 50%. He presented no data supporting this theory, the court found.

The "most reasonable discount is the present value of the cost of paying off that liability in the future," said the court, referencing *Estate of Jensen,* T.C. Memo. 2010-182 (available at *BVLaw*). Assuming a 20-year or 30-year holding period, which the court said a potential investor would expect despite the 70-year historic rate, the court arrived at a range between $5.5 million and $9.6 million. Since the IRS expert's $7.8 million figure fell "comfortably" within it, the court found it reasonably captured the BICG reduction.

In a footnote, the Tax Court also called the IRS expert's decision to incorporate the BICG discount as part of the DLOM discount "not especially helpful." The BICG tax liability should be determined at the entity level, considering it is the liability of the company and affects its net asset value. Subsequently, the other discounts are applied sequentially, the court explained.

DLOC. Both the IRS expert and the estate's expert used the same data set—the NAV values and trading prices of 59 closed-end funds for the first full week of December 2005. The IRS expert used the mean, which he then adjusted downward based on his observation that, even though the decedent did not control the company, she held a "large and influential block" of company stock. The court called this reduction "visceral" and unjustified.

It also dismissed the estate expert's use of the median because it reflected his mistaken assumption (corrected by the time of trial) that a director of the company had to be a family member. There was no such restriction, the court said. The court itself removed three outlier results that it said skewed the mean; this adjustment yielded a 7.75% DLOC.

DLOM. Based on the IRS expert's review of seven studies of restricted stock that indicated DLOMs from 26.4% to 35.6%, the court adopted the average rate: 32.1%. It questioned the IRS expert's rationale for starting with the lowest point, 26.4%, and it found that, even though he gave reasons for making downward adjustments, he gave no basis for the "quantum of the adjustment attributable to each [of the reasons]."

The estate's expert did not perform his own DLOM analysis but instead accepted the rivaling expert's approach and data and simply chose the very top of the range. His contention that the entities in the studies had stock that relatively soon would be freely marketable had no power with the court.

Accuracy-related penalty. The court clarified that the applicable rate of penalty in this case was 20% of "any portion of underpayment of tax required to be shown on a return," not 40% as the IRS initially claimed. Here, there was a "substantial" valuation understatement because the estate tax amount reported on the return was less than 65% of the proper value. To escape the penalty, the estate had the burden of showing it acted "reasonably" and "in good faith" with regard to the valuation of the subject stock and the decedent's interest. The relevant inquiry focused on the initial appraisal, specifically the methodology the first appraiser used, the appraised value, the circumstances under which it was attained, and the appraiser's relationship to the taxpayer.

In this case, the Tax Court said, the estate did not act reasonably and the penalty applied. The estate based its reporting on an unsigned draft report from an accountant who was not a certified appraiser, even though he had some appraisal experience. The estate's claim that the fact that four different appraisers generated four substantially different values shows just how difficult it was to value the decedent's interest did not sway the court. If anything, the Tax Court said, this scenario "further supports the importance of hiring a qualified appraiser."

Robocast, Inc. v. Microsoft Corp. (I)

Citation: 2014 U.S. Dist. LEXIS 5836
Date of decision: Jan. 16, 2014
Experts: Creighton Hoffman (plaintiff); Christopher Martinez (defendant)
Judge: Andrews
State/Jurisdiction: Federal/Delaware
Court: U.S. District Court
Type of case: Intellectual Property
SIC code: 7371 Computer Programming Services

May Expert Use Valuation With Unknown Discounts for Royalty Analysis?

The plaintiff's *Daubert* challenge in this intellectual property case is noteworthy because the plaintiff sought to enlarge the concept of comparability when arguing that Microsoft's damages expert produced an unreliable calculation. It also attacked the expert for using the plaintiff's own valuation of the patent in suit even though he did not know the embedded discounts accounting for uncertainty.

The plaintiff, Robocast, owned a patent related to automated Web-browsing tools that caused customers to spend more time on a client's site and increased advertising revenues. In its suit in federal court (D. Del.), it claimed that, after it had engaged in talks with Microsoft, the defendant, starting in 2000, it gave confidential information about its proprietary technology anticipating a buyout.

But the acquisition did not happen. Instead, Microsoft appropriated the technology to secure its own patents covering the infringing technology and develop products with video playlists, such as Bing.com, and changing tiles, such as Windows 8 Xbox Music Software and Xbox 360 "Video" and "Home" channels. In all, Robocast identified five to 11 "litigation targets" whose products allegedly infringed the patent at issue.

In a pretrial *Daubert* motion, the plaintiff tried to exclude testimony from Microsoft's damages expert, arguing that his methodology was unreliable. (Because many of the parties' motions are under seal, the court's opinion provides few details of the expert's testimony.) At issue were two aspects of his calculation:

1. Comparability. Using the *Georgia-Pacific* framework, Microsoft's expert relied on the plaintiff's earlier sale of patent rights (the "Tarabella sale") involving similar technology to determine the value of a license agreement for the patented technology that the parties would have negotiated. As for the Tarabella sale, he said he knew the outcome of the sale, but not the facts surrounding the sale.

The plaintiff claimed that, even assuming that the technology underlying the Tarabella sale was similar to the technology in suit, the expert's calculation was not reliable because he did not know whether the earlier transaction was "economically comparable." Microsoft argued that questions of comparability between the proposed license and an earlier license or sale of patent rights went to weight, not admissibility, and, therefore, were a matter for cross-examination.

The court agreed with Microsoft. The plaintiff's argument that, "in addition to technological comparability, there must be economic comparability of the value of the technology" was "circular," the court said. The requirement of technological comparability rests on the assumption that similar technologies have a similar value, the court explained. What the parties to the Tarabella sale expected in terms of economic value was unknown, but "what actually happened as a result of the technology at issue can be evaluated and taken into account as a *Georgia Pacific* factor," the court continued.

It cautioned the plaintiff about "conflat[ing]" economic comparability with the economic value of the patent. Economic comparability concerns the specifics of the transaction that influence the price a party would be willing to pay and include exclusivity and geographic scope.

Here, the court found that the prior transaction "actually overstates" the value that Microsoft would attach to a licensing agreement for comparable technology because it was an outright sale of patent rights, not just a licensing agreement. Nevertheless, the value could serve as a "data point" in a hypothetical negotiation between the parties over the rights to a technologically similar patent.

2. 'Straightforward' lump-sum calculation. Microsoft's expert based his calculation on a valuation that the plaintiff itself had done at or near the time of the hypothetical negotiation regarding the patent in suit. As the latter was the plaintiff's only asset, his analysis was "fairly straightforward." Since Microsoft accounted for 3% to 6% of the market using the technology, its infringement was 3% to 6% of the value to the plaintiff. He also considered the five to 11 defendants the plaintiff was targeting and assumed each of them was liable for the same amount of damages. This meant that

Microsoft's damages were at most one-fifth of the plaintiff's value. He admitted he did not know what discounts the self-valuation included to account for issues such as validity, infringement, or the time value of any income streams. He said that he worked based on the required assumptions of validity and infringement. In fact, his determination was "likely on the high end of the reasonable royalty range" because he believed that statements surrounding the plaintiff's valuation indicated a belief that the patent was valid and infringed. He arrived at an "absolute maximum" royalty of $4.2 million.

The plaintiff claimed that the expert could not rely on its self-valuation because he lacked knowledge of the discount rates that figured into the plaintiff's calculation. But, since he used it, his computation was unreliable.

This argument also had no traction with the court. "Lump sum licenses are frequently made in the absence of certainty regarding infringement and validity" but still may inform reasonable royalty calculations, the court said. "Of course, it may also be proper to adjust the reasonable royalty upwards due to this uncertainty." The court assured the plaintiff that it would have an opportunity to explore the discount issue on cross-examination.

For all of these reasons, the district court admitted the testimony.

Robocast, Inc. v. Microsoft Corp. (II)

Citation: 2014 U.S. Dist. LEXIS 10745
Date of decision: Jan. 29, 2014
Experts: Creighton Hoffman (plaintiff); Christopher Martinez (defendant)
Judge: Andrews
State/Jurisdiction: Federal/Delaware
Court: United States District Court
Type of case: Intellectual Property
SIC code: 7371 Computer Programming Services

Nash Bargaining Solution a 'Non-Starter' for Royalty Analysis

After rejecting the plaintiff's *Daubert* challenge in an earlier ruling, the federal district court next turned to defendant Microsoft's attack on the plaintiff's damages expert, specifically its claim that his reasonable royalty calculation was the result of the Nash bargaining solution—an impermissible rule of thumb that did not tie the royalty rate to the particulars of a case.

Robocast, the plaintiff, owned a patent related to automated Web-browsing tools and in its infringement suit claimed that Microsoft appropriated its technology to secure its own patents covering the infringing technology and develop products with video playlists, such as Bing.com, and changing tiles, such as Windows 8 Xbox Music Software and Xbox 360 "Video" and "Home" channels. All together, Robocast identified between five to 11 "litigation targets" whose products allegedly violated the patent at issue.

Equal profit split. In his damages analysis, the plaintiff's expert discussed the various *Georgia-Pacific* factors and concluded that the parties would have negotiated reasonable royalties for the use of the patent in suit and that a hypothetical negotiation would have produced a running royalty that "would effectively result in an equal sharing of the incremental revenue and profit from the use of the patented technology." He gave four reasons for the 50-50 split, which he believed was generous to Microsoft: (1) the patented technology provided new revenue-generating opportunities; (2) Web pages including the infringing video ads may include nonvideo Web ads; (3) Microsoft earned substantial revenues and profits from the infringing products and services; and (4) the patent had another 12 years remaining and awaiting its expiration was not a viable business alternative for Microsoft. The expert's report did not refer to the Nash bargaining solution (NBS).

He acknowledged that he considered licenses Microsoft had made for technology that was not comparable to the one in dispute for his lump-sum analysis. He concluded a $5 million payment for non-revenue-generating instrumentalities was appropriate.

In its *Daubert* motion, Microsoft raised three objections to the testimony: (1) the reasonable royalty analysis relied on the Nash bargaining solution; (2) it violated the entire market value rule (EMVR); and (3) the $5 million lump-sum analysis was not based on a sound methodology.

The plaintiff countered that the expert did not apply the NBS, and, even if he did, it was sufficiently tied to the facts of the case. Also, he relied on Microsoft's history of lump-sum payments to arrive at his $5 million proposed payment.

1. Nash bargaining solution. The court considered Microsoft's first objection to be the most critical one. It noted that earlier decisions described NBS as an equal division of surplus profits resulting from cooperation between the parties. Here, there could be no doubt that the 50-50 profit split the expert advanced was premised on this model even if he did not mention it by name. The real issue, said the court, was whether the proposed division of profits had the requisite basis in the facts.

The court found that all of the criticism the Federal Circuit directed at the 25% rule of thumb applied equally to NBS. Both represented theoretical constructs that: (1) fail to consider the unique relationship between the patent and the infringing product; (2) fail to consider the unique relationship between the parties; and (3) do not fit into the applicable framework of a hypothetical negotiation that is specific to the parties and the technology in dispute. NBS, said the court, relied on generalized assumptions, including the assumption that both parties had equal bargaining power. In the court's view, the discredited 25% rule of thumb, which at least allocated 75% of the profits to the licensee and rested on empirical studies, was "arguably more realistic than the equal bargaining power assumption."

Here, the expert failed to discuss the parties' relative bargaining power. Although he gave four facts specific to the case, three of them provided no basis to support a 50-50 split, said the court. Only the fourth factor regarding the remaining term of the patent arguably related to bargaining power in that it affected the business alternatives available to Microsoft. But the expert provided no rationale for concluding that Microsoft could not afford to wait for the patent's expiration.

According to the court, when the Federal Circuit requires an analysis "related to the facts of the case," it means the kind of facts that are critical to a reasonable royalty determination. In this case, they would include Microsoft's history of licensing similar technology for a 50-50 split of the profits or the plaintiff's history of licensing the patent in suit for half of the profits. The plaintiff's expert did not consider these facts.

In a world where damages must be tied to the facts of the case, said the court, methods such as NBS and the 25% rule of thumb are "non-starters." Because NBS is what the plaintiff's expert applied, the court excluded his reasonable royalty testimony.

2. *EMVR.* Since it excluded the analysis, the court declined to decide whether the proposed royalty violated the entire market value rule.

3. *History of licensing.* The court said there was confusion as to whether the plaintiff's expert actually relied on licenses for noncomparable technology. Assuming he considered such licenses at all, he was only allowed to infer from them that Microsoft was willing to license technology, said the court. He was not able to rely on them for his calculation of a lump-sum payment for the technology in dispute. But since there was no other basis for the lump-sum royalty, the court decided the expert could not testify to it.

For all of these reasons, the court granted Microsoft's *Daubert* motion.

Note: A digest of the court's earlier *Daubert* ruling in *Robocast, Inc. v. Microsoft Corp.*, 2014 U.S. Dist. LEXIS 5837 (Jan. 16, 2014), appears in the April edition of *Business Valuation Update* and at *BVLaw.*

Roll-Rite, LLC v. Shur-Co, LLC

Citation: 2014 U.S. Dist. LEXIS 73026
Date of decision: May 29, 2014
Experts: John Bone (plaintiff); unknown (defendant)
Judge: Ludington
State/Jurisdiction: Federal/Michigan
Court: U.S. District Court
Type of case: Damages
SIC code: 3621 Motors and Generators

Expert's Per-Unit Lost Profits Calculation Satisfies Daubert

A recent *Daubert* case offers an excellent review of what it means to establish lost profits by using the four-factor *Panduit* test. In assessing the expert's damages calculation, the court explained how

Panduit combines with the burden to reconstruct the hypothetical market and "but for" causation in a lost profits analysis; it also explained other legal principles an expert must consider in analyzing the four factors.

The plaintiff owned a patent for the use of a spur gear motor in an electric tarp spool system. That system is featured in open-top vehicles, including dump trucks. In 2006, the company began selling two types of motors to the defendant, which, in turn, built the devices into its Series 3500 tarp systems and sold them to its customers—many of them in the agricultural market. When the defendant kept experiencing problems with the plaintiff's motors, it hired a company to design and build a similar motor that it then used with its new Series 4500 tarp systems. The defendant began selling the 4500 Series in late 2011 and subsequently applied for a patent for the newly designed gear motor. Meanwhile, the plaintiff lost the defendant's business and, in March 2012, sued in federal court (D. Mich.), claiming patent infringement and demanding lost profits.

Incremental profit determination. To establish damages, the plaintiff retained an expert, who was a CPA and certified in financial forensics. He used the four-factor *Panduit* test to reconstruct the market as it would have developed absent the defendant's infringing product and to show how much the patent holder would have made in profit. The crux of the plaintiff's argument was that the infringing product was the defendant's 4500 Series system. Absent its introduction into the market, customers would have bought the 3500 Series that used the plaintiff's gear motors.

On the date the expert's report was due, he did not have complete information about the defendant's sales of the 4500 series; therefore, he was unable to say how many gear motors the plaintiff hypothetically would have sold. Instead, he calculated lost profits on a per-unit basis based on the data he had received and reserved the right to update his analysis upon receipt of additional data.

He found that in 2012 lost profits per unit for one type of motor were $167 and for the other type were $164. In 2013, lost profits were $153 and $150, respectively. He explained that the numbers were the result of determining the incremental profit the plaintiff would have earned during the damages period. "Incremental profit is the difference between the lost revenue and the additional costs that Roll-Rite would have incurred in order to generate those sales (i.e., incremental costs)." The expert's calculations took into account material costs, labor costs, variable overhead costs, warranty material costs, freight costs, working capital costs, and utility costs.

The defendant tried to exclude the testimony under *Daubert*. The expert's opinion was "incomplete, calculated to mislead the jury and based on unreliable methodology," the defendant argued. The expert failed to reconstruct the market accurately; specifically, he did not analyze the effect the 4500 Series had on the hypothetical market. Also, the defendant said, the expert failed to satisfy Factors 1 and 4 of the *Panduit* test, which serve to show the infringement caused the lost profits.

***Panduit* to reconstruct the market.** The court took a different view. At the start of its discussion, it explained that the *Panduit* test was a widely used and approved method for establishing causation and reconstructing the market. It also pointed out that the defendant incorrectly separated the question of whether the expert reconstructed the market from the question of whether he failed to establish the test's four factors. The two issues go together, the court noted.

It then considered the expert's testimony against the applicable four factors.

Factor 1. Did the patent holder establish demand for the patented product?

The expert maintained that the plaintiff's past success in selling its two types of motor to the defendant and the defendant's competitors proved there was demand for the product. Moreover, the defendant's CEO earlier had confirmed that the electric tarp system market was strong: "I think we're all rising with the tide. I think the demand is greater and that everyone's business should be benefitting from it."

The defendant objected that the expert failed to show demand because he did not do any analysis of the customers who ultimately bought the 4500 Series products. Without knowing why they bought them, the expert was unable to say that the plaintiff would have captured 100% of the 4500 Series' sales. Specifically, the tarp systems in the 4500 Series included many components other than the gear motor and anyone of them may have prompted the customer to buy the 4500 Series rather than the 3500 Series, the defendant added.

The court clarified that *Panduit* does not require investigating a consumer's reason for buying a product featuring the patented functionality (citing *Versata Software, Inc. v. SAP America, Inc.*, 2013 U.S. App. LEXIS 8838) (available at *BVLaw*). The first factor merely asks whether demand exists for a product that is covered by the patent in suit or that directly competes with the infringing device, the court went on to say. For the purpose of admissibility, it was irrelevant that in this case there may have been other drivers of demand, the court added. Therefore, the plaintiff, through the expert's report, satisfied the first factor.

Factor 2. Was there an absence of noninfringing alternatives?

The expert explained the plaintiff had a right to 100% of the defendant's 4500 Series' sales because there were no noninfringing alternatives. He found that only three types of systems were making up the entire tarp system market. One of the systems used the plaintiff's patented gear motor. The other two systems were "less efficient and did not provide sufficient torque" and, therefore, were no substitutes for the third system. Other than the plaintiff's motor, he said, "there were no spur gear direct drive actuator assemblies in the marketplace at the time of the first infringement." He also believed none were "currently on the market." Consumers would have bought the 3500 Series instead of the infringing 4500 Series, he said. He concluded that the hypothetical sales of the 3500 Series would be equal to the actual sales of the 4500 Series and the plaintiff was entitled to the profits stemming from the gear motors featured in the 3500 Series.

The defendant did not suggest there were no noninfringing alternatives, but it argued instead that the expert should have considered the advantages its 4500 Series offered to consumers over the 3500 Series that featured the patented gear motors. The defendant claimed that, owing to the failure rate it experienced with the plaintiff's gear motors, it "had no choice but to abandon further use of the [plaintiff's] gear motors and to go to the market with a new tarp system." And, because the 4500 Series was superior to the 3500 Series, it sold better than the 3500 Series would have done during the relevant period. Ignoring these factors, the expert failed to reconstruct the market, the defendant contended.

The court disagreed. For one, it said, the defendant's claim that it "had no choice" but to design the 4500 Series bolstered the expert's conclusion that there were no suitable noninfringing substitutes for the plaintiff's gear motors. In fact, the defendant's argument suggested that it would have chosen to leave the market completely rather than continue to buy the plaintiff's motors. Consequently, the court refused to exclude the expert's testimony regarding noninfringing alternatives.

Factor 3. Did the patent holder have the manufacturing and marketing capacity to exploit demand?

The expert explained that, because the defendant did not manufacture other gear motors, it would have to buy them from the plaintiff had it not developed the infringing 4500 Series. The plaintiff had a production and manufacturing strategy that ensured it would have met the defendant's demand.

The court found the testimony met Factor 3.

Factor 4. What was the amount of profit the patent holder would have made?

The defendant contended the expert's profit calculation was unreliable because he failed to explain why the plaintiff had a right to 100% of the defendant's infringing sales.

The court dismissed the argument, saying it simply repeated the defendant's earlier objection. It found the expert explained that the plaintiff sold 100% of the spur gear motors and that there were no noninfringing substitutes available. Therefore, he concluded that, but for the infringement, the plaintiff's hypothetical sales would be equal to the 4500 Series' actual sales.

Incomplete report. Finally, the defendant claimed the expert's testimony was inadmissible because the expert did not provide the number of gear motors the plaintiff would have sold but for the alleged infringement. Instead, he calculated lost profits on a per-unit basis without establishing the actual damages amount.

The court also rejected this argument. The patent owner's burden to prove damages is not absolute, the court noted, citing case law. The plaintiff need only provide a "reasonable approximation." Here, the plaintiff's expert explained why he used a per-unit basis and how he intended to calculate total damages once he obtained additional sales data from the defendant: multiply the per-unit gear motor profit by the number of motors the defendant bought from its manufacturer. This methodology, the court found, would result in the requisite reasonable approximation of the plaintiff's lost profits.

The expert's use of *Panduit* and his method of calculating lost profits were sufficiently reliable to admit the testimony under *Daubert*, the court concluded.

St. Alphonsus Diversified Care, Inc. v. MRI Associates, LLP

Citation: 2014 Ida. LEXIS 200
Date of decision: Aug. 4, 2014
Experts: Bruce Budge, Charles Wilhoite (defendant/counterclaimant)
Judge: Eismann
State/Jurisdiction: Idaho
Court: Supreme Court of Idaho
Type of case: Contract
SIC code: 8071 Medical Laboratories

Usurped Opportunity Case Justifies Use of Defendant's Profits

A recent lost profits case that revolved around a hospital's breach of a partnership agreement's noncompete clause raises issues about the right measure of damages and illustrates how an expert's testimony succeeds in fending off various forms of attack from the opposing party.

In 1985, a hospital entered into a partnership, MRI Associates (MRIA), whose primary purpose was to buy and operate diagnostic and therapeutic equipment, starting with an MRI scanner. Subsequently, MRI Associates formed two limited partnerships. One, MRI Center, was located on the hospital's campus; the other, MRI Mobile, owned and operated mobile MRI scanners. In 1998, a group of radiologists that had interpreted the scans done at MRI Center formed a competing company, IMI, with an outpatient facility some three miles away from MRI Center. Around the same time, the hospital secretly began to negotiate with IMI against MRI Associates. In 2000, MRI Associates wanted to open another facility about seven miles away from MRI Center, but the hospital, as a partner in the company, opposed the plan. In 2001, the hospital became a member of IMI. There was evidence that it financially assisted IMI in violation of its contract with MRI Associates. In 2002, the hospital supported IMI's opening a second facility at the very location where MRI Center had wanted to set up another business.

In 2004, the hospital informed MRI Associates that it wanted to dissociate from the partnership effective April 2004. Based on the partnership agreement, it could not compete with MRI Associates for a year. The hospital subsequently sued MRI Associates to recover the value of its partnership interest, and MRI Associates countersued. A jury found against the hospital and awarded MRI Associates $36.3 million. This judgment was nullified on appeal, and a new trial took place in which MRI Associates added MRI Center and MRI Mobile as complainants. The three MRI entities claimed breach of contract, intentional interference with a prospective economic advantage, breach of fiduciary duty, and civil conspiracy.

At trial, the MRI entities offered damages testimony from two experts. The main expert was an accountant who had nearly four decades of experience and who had worked for Arthur Andersen and KPMG. He calculated lost profits from 2001 through 2010, assuming causation. The second expert used the first expert's computations to project future lost profits to 2015.

'Massive migration of referrals.' The first expert determined the profit MRI Center lost by estimating the number of scans it lost to its competitor, IMI, during the period when the hospital was prohibited from competing with MRI Center. He identified all of the doctors who referred patients to MRI Center prior to IMI's opening its facility and assumed the referrals would have kept up. He also identified the new physicians in the area whose sole affiliation was with the hospital and assumed they would refer patients to the facility on the hospital campus, i.e., MRI Center. Referrals from the two groups made up 42% of the MRI scans performed at IMI's original facility, he concluded. His estimate of lost scans did not include scans ordered by physicians who could admit patients to the hospital and to another major hospital in the area. Moreover, he excluded scans that were referred to other facilities by physicians who previously had referred patients to MRI Center.

His lost profits calculation for MRI Mobile was based on the profits IMI's second facility made. He approached this calculation as a business opportunity for MRI Associates that the hospital had usurped. Had the hospital supported MRI Associates when it expressed a desire to open a new facility, in 2000, the latter would have been in the same competitive market as IMI was when it opened its second facility. Further, he assumed that the costs for opening a second facility to MRI Associates were the same as the costs to IMI. He also calculated the annual profit margin for MRI Center and IMI's second facility and found that the former had a higher profit margin than the latter. For the lost profits calculation, however, he relied on IMI's financial information.

At trial, the expert also produced a chart showing both the number of scans MRI Center performed each year from 1998 through 2006 and the number of scans IMI performed for much of that time. The chart demonstrated that there was a drop in scans for MRI Center when the hospital partnered with IMI in 2001 and an even more pronounced decrease in the number of scans when the hospital and IMI opened a second facility. At the same time, the number of scans done at IMI increased steadily. The aggregate data supported the conclusion that there was "a massive migration of referrals from MRIA to IMI," the expert said. He added that he also tried to identify the specific customers MRI Associates lost.

At trial, he was asked repeatedly about changes to his calculation if the hospital were not liable for prior bad acts and competed rightfully after April 2005. He allowed that under that hypothetical the MRI entities would have suffered substantially less damage after that date than claimed and no damage after about 2010. Assuming there were no unlawful diversions, only lawful competition, he said, would require a reduction in his calculation by about $14.4 million. But he emphasized that this reduction only applied if there were no bad acts prior to April 2005.

The jury found the hospital liable for breach of the noncompete and awarded the MRI entities a total of over $52 million. It also awarded the hospital $4.8 million for its partnership interest. The hospital challenged the verdict in a post-trial motion claiming the MRI entities failed to prove that post-April 2005 lost profits were the result of prior bad acts. The trial court denied the motion, finding that the entire theory of the MRI entities was that the hospital's wrongdoing destroyed their business. If the jury found prior bad acts that made MRI Associates no longer competitive, the jury could infer that the number of scans shown to have gone to IMI would have gone to the MRI entities.

Misstating expert's testimony. Both sides appealed to the state's highest court. On appeal, the hospital did not contest the jury's liability findings but claimed there was insufficient evidence to prove lost profits. It specifically targeted MRI Associates' principal damages expert. First, it argued that his methodology was flawed because he failed to allow that other factors, besides the hospital's conduct, could have caused all or part of the claimed business migration from MRI Center to IMI, and, the hospital said, the calculation of the lost scans "was nothing much more than a rough guess."

The appellate court disagreed. This was a market exclusion case in which the expert's chart of MRI scans represented the kind of proof case law required. Moreover, the expert tried to show the loss of specific business.

Further, the hospital contended that the expert's basing damages to MRI Mobile on IMI's financial data was inappropriate. Under controlling case law, the measure of damages for breaching a non-compete clause is the amount the plaintiff lost due to the breach, not the amount the defendant made in profits, the hospital stated.

The court saw it differently. This was not an instance in which the breach of the noncompete clause created competition between two existing businesses. Instead, here, the hospital, in violation of its partnership agreement with MRIA, deprived MRIA of the opportunity to open a facility away from the hospital campus while actively supporting its competitor IMI in doing just this. In this situation, the court said, "The measure of lost profits would be the net profits of [IMI's] facility." It would not make sense to hypothesize about the net profits a hypothetical MRI entity could have made and against which IMI's facility hypothetically could have competed, the court explained.

Finally, the hospital in various ways tried to argue that the expert conceded that, if one assumed lawful competition after 2005, damages would decrease by about $14.4 million.

The appeals court called that statement "incorrect." The expert only said that, hypothetically speaking, if there had been no wrongdoing before April 2005 that caused damages after that date, he would exclude that amount from the damages. Since the jury had found prior wrongdoing—a finding that the hospital did not challenge—the expert's damages model required no change. For all of these reasons, the state high court affirmed the $52 million lost profits award.

SHC Half Moon Bay, LLC v. City of San Mateo

Citation: 2014 Cal. App. LEXIS 446
Date of decision: May 22, 2014
Experts: James A. Gavin, Duff & Phelps (plaintiff/appellant); Thomas E. Callahan, First Service PKF Hospitality (defendant/respondent)
Judge: Jones
State/Jurisdiction: California
Court: Court of Appeal
Type of case: State Taxation
SIC code: 7011 Hotels and Motels

Taxpayer Scores Partial Success in Cal. Hotel Property Tax Suit

Under California law, how do you assess a hotel for property tax? This was the overriding question the California Court of Appeal recently confronted in a taxpayer refund suit that alleged the county assessor's version of the income approach violated the law because it failed to identify, value, and exclude certain intangible assets, including goodwill, from the valuation.

In 2004, the taxpayer, a limited liability company, bought the luxury Ritz-Carlton Half Moon Bay Hotel in San Mateo County, Calif., for $124.35 million. The purchase price included real and personal property (furniture, fixture, and equipment) as well as intangible assets and rights. The buyer had a long-term management agreement with the Ritz-Carlton Hotel Co. At the time, the county assessor valued the hotel under the California Constitution at its purchase price and deducted the value of personal property. Because the total value was within 5% of the purchase price, he enrolled the hotel at that price.

Specifically, the assessor used the sales, cost, and income approaches but decided the "income capitalization approach" resulted in "the most persuasive and supportable conclusions when valuing a lodging facility." This approach was known as the "Rushmore method," which she explained represented a model for hotel valuation in the industry. "Basically, the net operating income from a stabilized year is calculated by removing the income attributable to ... the business/going concern. What is left is the income attributable to the land and improvements. This is then capitalized into an estimate of value."

The assessor calculated a stabilized income stream for the hotel and then estimated the hotel's stabilized occupancy rate of 71% with net revenue per room of $330 at 3%. She reduced projected income for fixed expenses such as insurance, subtracted $1.6 million in management and franchise fees, and deducted for reserves and taxes, concluding the hotel's net operating income was 18%. Using a 6.5% capitalization rate, she calculated a fair market value of $129.7 million. She then deducted $7.34 million in personal property and determined the value of the hotel was $122.3 million. "Since the appraised value is within 5% of the indicated sale price of $124,350,000, the purchase price assumption ... validates the base year enrollment," she stated.

California tax principles. The California Constitution requires assessors to tax all property at fair market value. Under the state's tax code and case law, intangible property is "exempt from taxation." Therefore, the value of intangible assets and rights "shall not enhance or be reflected in the value of taxable property." At the same time, the regulations say that "[t]axable property may be assessed and valued by assuming the presence of intangible assets or rights necessary to put the taxable property to beneficial or productive use." According to the state's high court, "assessors cannot tax *the value* of intangible assets directly ... but that principle does not prevent assessors from assuming the presence of intangible assets when valuing *taxable property*."

In an important decision, the state's high court clarified that intangible assets such as the goodwill of a business, customer base, and favorable franchise terms or operating contracts all contribute directly to the going concern value of a business and their quantifiable fair market value must be deducted from an income stream analysis prior to taxation.

To add another layer of complexity, in 1995 the state's Board of Equalization adopted the Assessor's Handbook to provide guidance for assessors on "the taxability of intangible property," a perennial point of contention between assessors and taxpayers. The handbook says that "[t]he value of intangible assets and rights cannot be removed by merely deducting the related expenses from the income stream to be capitalized. Allowing a deduction for the associated expense does not allow for a return on the capital expenditure." By way of example, "the deduction of a management fee from the income stream of a hotel does not properly recognize or remove the value attributable to the business enterprise that operates the hotel." Pursuant to case law, the handbook does not have the force of law, but it is a valuable guide particularly when it comes to interpreting valuation questions.

Cost vs. income approach. In this case, the hotel owner first challenged the valuation at the Assessment Appeals Board (board), contending the assessment included $16.85 million in nontaxable intangible assets and citing to the handbook.

The hotel's expert presented a report that allocated "relevant tangible and intangible assets of the [property]" according to Statement No. 141 of the Financial Accounting Standards Board (FASB 141), "Business Combinations." The analysis was "to provide an allocation of value for financial reporting purposes." The expert used the cost method and found the tangible assets valued $99.5 million, including land worth $20.1 million and building and site improvements worth $79.4 million. He determined that tangible assets made up $107.5 million of the purchase price. He allocated the remaining $16.85 million to intangible assets, including:

- The hotel's assembled workforce—$1 million;
- The hotel's leasehold interest in employee parking—$200,000;
- The hotel's agreement with the golf course operator—$1.5 million; and
- Goodwill—$14.15 million.

At the board hearing, he explained that the goodwill was residual, "taking the purchase price and working your way through all the different elements and all the different ... tangibles and intangibles to get down to what is left over." He conceded that people in the industry "trading hotels" use the income method to establish value but urged the board to follow the handbook's recommendation, which is to identify the various intangible assets and rights, value them, and deduct them from the business enterprise as a going concern to arrive at the taxable value of the property.

The county defended the income approach and claimed the assessor's deduction of the management and franchise fees ensured exclusion of nontaxable intangible assets. "If you follow the income approach, the goodwill is accounted for within the management fee." The hotel's expert used a "controversial methodology that is not generally followed in the appraisal industry or by the Assessor's Offices for valuing hotel real property." The county added that FASB 141 was used for financial reporting but not "for deciding the real property value."

In his report, the county's expert pointed out that the "intangible or business value associated with a hotel is typically removed from the value of the hotel's real property through deduction of a market rate management and (if appropriate) franchise fee. The resulting income stream after this deduction is typically viewed by the investment community as a return on … the hotel's real and tangible personal property." According to him, "the majority of the property's business value has been removed through the deduction of the management fee payable to the Ritz-Carlton Hotel Company." He acknowledged that, "[i]n addition to the deduction of market rate management and franchise fee, the capitalized value of pre-opening expenses (e.g. the cost of assembling and training a work force, pre-opening marketing, etc.) necessary to open the business is also often deducted as an intangible value of the hotel."

At the hearing, he repeated that the industry's view was that deducting a market rate management franchise fee from the income stream "strips out the majority—not all, but the majority of the intangible value of the property." But he also said that "other components … should be deducted," such as "a capitalized value for developing the workplace in force, pre-opening expenses and working capital." "For a property of this caliber, that would probably be about $6,000 per guest room," he specified. The question, he said, was whether the majority of the business value was deducted by way of the management and franchise fees. "It's either a hundred percent or it's like ninety percent," he concluded. He allowed for taking off an additional million dollars for labor in place. "But it's relatively small dollars when we're talking about a hotel of this caliber." Yet, he admitted that assets such as the hotel's workforce, its leasehold interest in the employee parking lot, and its agreement with the golf course operator were worth $2.7 million.

He voiced disagreement with the handbook and concluded that using the cost method was "absolutely always wrong for luxury properties."

The board sided with the county for several reasons. For one, there was a presumption that the assessor's valuation was correct. Also, the income method was "appropriate and permissible" to value the property. But even if the board were to reject it and adopt the cost approach, the evidence "supported higher construction costs than those set forth in the ... FASB 141 report." Although the FASB 141 allocation may be appropriate for financial reporting purposes, it did not "provide an accurate 'appraisal' for property tax purposes." Moreover, because the management and/or franchise fees largely covered goodwill, its value should be zero ($0), as opposed to $14.15 million the hotel owner's expert proposed. Last, but not least, the board said the handbook was not binding on county assessors.

Authorized method, comprehensive analysis. Following the board's decision, the hotel owner filed a complaint in state court, arguing the assessment was incorrect and asking the court for a refund of the taxes paid and an order to the board to re-determine the value of the property.

Following a bench trial, the court affirmed the board's findings. The evidence showed that the assessor used three methods authorized by statute to determine the property's fair market value, the court said. His analysis was comprehensive; for example, it included details of the parcels at issue, comparable sales of luxury hotels nationwide, Marshall & Swift cost estimates, a discounted cash flow analysis and historical costs, and background information on valuing hotels as income producing properties. "There is nothing in the record to indicate the assessment is contrary to law." Finally, the court agreed that the handbook was "not mandatory" but represented "a set of recommendations for how to value property."

The hotel owner then appealed the decisions at the California Court of Appeal. Its principal argument was that the income approach the assessor used violated California law because it failed to identify, value, and exclude the value of intangible assets from the calculation.

Ignoring credible contradictory evidence. At the start of its analysis, the appeals court decided the appeal presented a legal, rather than a factual, issue. Therefore, the case was subject to independent review. At issue was the validity of the methodology the assessor chose, not whether she misunderstood or distorted the available data.

The county's approach was problematic, the appeals court said. The assessor and board ignored credible evidence from the hotel's expert that there were certain intangible assets whose value was improperly subsumed in the assessment. The county's expert conceded more than once that the valuation did not remove all intangible assets and rights. He said that the management and franchise fees covered only a majority of the business value, and he admitted that it was appropriate to deduct "other components," including "labor in place." The assessor's method was legally wrong because it "failed to attribute a portion of [the hotel's] income stream to the enterprise activity that was directly attributable to the value of intangible assets and deduct that value prior to assessment."

The assessor did not explain how the management and franchise fee deduction encapsulated the majority of intangible property. Relying on the deduction and refusing to identify and value certain intangible assets was "akin to paying lip service to the concept of exempting intangible assets from taxation," the appeals court pointed out.

However, the court did not side with the hotel owner on the issue of goodwill. Whether the value of goodwill was $14.5 million using the residual approach the hotel's expert had used or whether the assessor had accounted for it in the management and franchise fees was a question of fact for the board to decide. The hotel did not prove that there was insufficient evidence to support the board's resolution in favor of the assessor. At the same time, the appeals court seemed to leave the door open for a future challenge. "There may be situations where the taxpayer can establish the deduction of a management and franchise fee from the hotel's income stream does not capture the intangible asset of goodwill," it said.

In conclusion, the state Court of Appeal reversed the trial court's decision and ordered it to remand the matter to the board for the purpose of recalculating the value of the property, using the income method, but excluding from the income stream prior to taxation the value of: (1) the hotel's workforce; (2) the hotel's leasehold interest in the employee parking lot; and (3) the hotel's agreement with the golf course operator.

Sloan Valve Company v. Zurn Industries, Inc.

Citation: 2014 U.S. Dist. LEXIS 39678
Date of decision: March 26, 2014
Experts: Richard Bero (plaintiff)
Judge: St. Eve
State/Jurisdiction: Federal/Illinois
Court: U.S. District Court
Type of case: Intellectual Property
SIC code: 3432 Plumbing Fixture Fittings & Trim

Abandoning 'Classic Way' to Royalty Analysis, Expert Gets Lost

In a patent infringement case about a flush mechanism in toilets, the defendant attacked the plaintiff expert's reasonable royalty analysis in a *Daubert* motion. In ruling on admissibility, the court gave a comprehensive review of the applicable legal principles and explained why the calculation failed not only on specific elements, but also on the overall methodology.

Both the plaintiff and the defendant are leading providers of plumbing products and major players in the flush valve industry. In 2010, the plaintiff filed suit against the defendant (two related entities) claiming infringement of its patent for "manual dual-flush flushometer valves." The invention allows users to select one of two flush volumes depending on which way they turn the handle. The plaintiff first applied for its patent in 2006.

It retained a CPA and experienced valuation analyst to calculate a reasonable royalty and determine price erosion damages. The expert based the reasonable royalty analysis on a hypothetical negotiation between the parties, applying the *Georgia-Pacific* factors. He acknowledged that a reasonable royalty had two parts: a royalty base multiplied by a royalty rate. In this case, he found, the entire market value rule (EMVR) applied because customers chose the protected manual dual-flush valves or replacement handles over manual single-flush valves, more expensive automatic flush valves, lower volume flush valves without the dual-flush capacity, and larger volume flash products. In other words, the plaintiff's patented technology drove the market for the dual-flush valves as well as the replacement handles.

Royalty base and rate take different form. But then the expert deviated from the customary way to determine the royalty base. He claimed the total revenue from the sale of the infringing products did not represent the full value of the patented technology because it did not factor in the value of sales of collateral goods and the plaintiff's pricing considerations. Consequently, he decided to use the number of infringing products that the defendant sold as the royalty base, instead of the total revenue. For the royalty rate, instead of applying a percentage of the revenue owed to the patent holder, he used a dollar figure. He arrived at the amount by applying the *Georgia-Pacific* factors "quantitatively and qualitatively." He explained that the quantitative analysis was based on "the income valuation approach," which "considers the amount of profit that is attributable to the invention and/or the increased profits derived from the invention." He was mainly concerned that the plaintiff "would be directly licensing away its profits on its Patented Products and collateral sales as well as subjecting itself to ongoing pricing pressure on its Patented Products from [the defendant] that otherwise would not exist."

He determined that, in the hypothetical negotiation, the plaintiff would seek a minimum of $141 per accused product unit. The price included profits related to: (1) the sale of the patented manual dual-flush valve packages and handles ($35); (2) the sale of collateral products, such as replacement diaphragm kits, urinal valves, and faucets ($35); and (3) "the price effect" ($71). The term "price effect" referred to additional profits that the plaintiff would have made by raising prices if the defendant had not entered the market. "The pricing effect is based on [the plaintiff's] initial and subsequent pricing being lower than its intended pricing." The expert initially said that testimony from company executives showed the plaintiff could have sold the patented products at the higher prices without losing volume. After the court excluded the executives' testimony, the expert, at the *Daubert* hearing, gave a different rationale: The products were salable at the higher price because there were no acceptable alternatives for the dual-flush valve; the water savings to customers would be substantially higher than the intended premium; and a newsletter, which he had cited in a footnote in his report, suggested that, when Purdue University installed the valves in two of its bathrooms, they paid for themselves within a year.

He used *Georgia-Pacific* Factor 6, which considers how the patented product may promote the sales of other products the patent holder has, to explain why he included profit from the sale of collateral goods. He said *Georgia-Pacific* Factor 5, which considers the relationship between the patent holder and the licensee, justified including the "price effect" item.

At the same time, he reasoned that going into the negotiation the defendant would at most be willing to pay $60 per unit—the profit it would expect to make if it did not enter into a licensing agreement. The difference in the parties' figures was a "negotiation gap." He decided that $100 as the midpoint between the two was the "quantitative" starting point for the negotiation, to which the "qualitative" *Georgia-Pacific* factors applied. Ultimately, he concluded that $106 per unit was the most reasonable royalty rate. When he multiplied it by the number of infringing products, he arrived at a royalty of $7.8 million from 2006 through 2013.

In his initial report, the expert also calculated $4.3 million in price erosion damages "over and above the amount of the pricing effect" that figured into the royalty rate. He subsequently lowered the amount to $2.1 million, only to raise again it to $2.3 million. At the *Daubert* hearing, he said the amount was only $1.2 million after accounting for competition from lower-volume flush valves on new construction projects. Accordingly, the plaintiff's total claim for damages was $9 million.

Overinclusive royalty base. In its motion to strike the testimony, the defendant identified numerous flaws in the expert's analysis and methodology, which the court considered in turn. As a general matter, the defendant contended that the expert failed to restrict his royalty rate to the value the patented technology contributed to the accused products. He did not apportion the profits on the accused products between the patented and unpatented features.

The expert acknowledged that in his calculation the patented products encompassed the valves, "packages" (toilet valves, bowls, and related accessories), and handles.

1. *Valves.* The plaintiff argued that the patented invention was the entire flush valve and the manual dual-flush valve was the "smallest salable patent-practicing unit."

The defendant did not contest that claim. But it said that the calculation violated the EMVR: Consumers bought the manual dual-flush valves for many reasons that had nothing to do with the valve's dual-flush capacity. Consumers cared about price, brand, loyalty to a manufacturer, and the fact that the valves came with an antimicrobial handle. Also, since the patented invention was merely "an improvement" over the existing manual single-flush value, the expert had to limit his royalty rate to the portion of profit that was attributable to the value of the improvement.

The plaintiff countered that the patented technology formed the basis for consumer demand. The dual-flush valve succeeded because of its water-saving technology. Consumers were willing to pay a premium for it because they wanted the benefits of the patented technology. The antimicrobial handle was not an essential or primary feature and optional on the plaintiff's products.

The court agreed with the plaintiff. As to the valves, the expert used the smallest salable unit. Further, the plaintiff showed that, when it came to the valves, the patented technology drove consumer demand.

2. *Packages and handles.* The connection between the patented device and packages and handles was more attenuated, and the plaintiff strained to justify damages for the full value of these products. It claimed that "only a small portion" of the plaintiff's and the defendant's sales of dual-flush valves (1% and 16%) stemmed from the sale of packages.

Also, the expert did not base his damages calculation on the revenues from the sale of packages but on the number of packages sold, and he attributed a lower profit to the sale of packages than to the sale of dual-flush valves alone. Therefore, he did not have to apportion.

Contradicting its own expert, the plaintiff originally argued the EMVR did not apply. But, to include the full value of the packages and handles, it subsequently said that, if the rule did apply, there was "ample evidence" to support a jury finding that the protected dual-flush technology was the basis for consumer demand for the valves and handles the defendant sold. But in analyzing consumer demand it only discussed the dual-flush valves, not packages and handles.

The court found none of the plaintiff's arguments persuasive. How few sales of dual-flush valves were made as part of packages did not matter in terms of the legal requirement to prove that the patented product drove consumer demand if the plaintiff claimed the full value of the packages. Also, the plaintiff conceded that the dual-flush valve was the patented invention. The invention did not include toilet bowls, handles, or other accessories. The plaintiff also could not claim that the EMVR applied because the protected valves constituted a functional unit with the bowls or handles. They did not. Therefore, the expert had to apportion the value of the valves sold as part of the packages and handles.

3. *Collateral products.* The defendant claimed that the expert could not justify adding the entire amount of lost sales for collateral goods based on one *Georgia-Pacific* factor. This was an improper application of the framework. Case law discussing *Georgia-Pacific* requires that experts apply the factors qualitatively, by determining whether a factor weighs in favor of or against increasing the contemplated royalty. It does not support a quantitative application—using a factor to add a separate figure to the royalty base.

The court agreed with the defendant, noting that under Federal Circuit law the proper application of the *Georgia-Pacific* methodology is to explain "the effect each factor would have on a negotiated royalty." It does not allow for including sales of nonpatented items in the royalty base but allows for using a factor to demonstrate that the sales were relevant to determining the royalty. In this case, the court said, the royalty base was "overinclusive." The court also pointed out that the expert had calculated a value of $35 per unit for collateral goods, "an amount that equals the value of his calculation for the sale of the patented product." This he could not do.

4. *'Price effect.'* The court rebuffed the arguments to support the "price effect" item. Following the exclusion of the executive testimony, the expert recognized he lacked a proper foundation on which to base his claim that the plaintiff would have made every sale the defendant made even at the intended higher price. The expert's explanations did not appear in his two reports, and he failed to undertake any economic or market studies on the effect of water savings on consumer price sensitivity. Also, he created that item by misapplying another *Georgia-Pacific* factor—applying it quantitatively rather than qualitatively. Importantly, the court found the "price effect" figure made up half of the royalty price and was twice as large as the value he attributed to the patented product. The court called it an attempt "to cover what appears to be lost profits," when the expert acknowledged that the plaintiff had no right to lost profits. Therefore, the court struck the "price effect" element from the royalty analysis.

Arbitrary starting point. The defendant described the expert's $100 starting point as "splitting the difference between the two parties' assumed positions." It lacked any economic analysis and, therefore, was arbitrary and unreliable.

The plaintiff characterized the expert's calculation of the plaintiff's entry rate of $141 as a "quantitative analysis," based on which the expert "qualitatively determined that the fair starting point of a hypothetical negotiation was the midpoint of $100."

The court agreed with the defendant. No matter how the plaintiff and the expert explained the $100, they failed to show why it was a fair, reasonable, or economically sound starting point. Accordingly, this element of the calculation also fell down.

Problematic methodology. But the court not only found certain elements underpinning the royalty analysis problematic; it also found that the methodology overall was unreliable. The expert failed to adhere to the "classic way to determine" the reasonable royalty amount: multiplying the royalty base, which represents the revenue generated by the infringement, by the royalty rate, which represents the percentage of revenue owed to the patentee. He cited no authority to support his use of the number of units and dollar amount per unit for the base and rate, respectively. He also included elements that represented lost profits, even though he acknowledged this form of damages was not available to the plaintiff. The methodology bore no resemblance to a reasonable royalty analysis, the court held. "What [the expert] effectively did is create an expansive royalty base without applying a royalty rate to that base." Accordingly, the analysis as a whole was unreliable.

Convoluted price erosion claim. The defendant also challenged the expert's price erosion calculation. Federal Circuit law required him to conduct a scientific analysis of price elasticity, it claimed.

The court said the defendant overstated the plaintiff's burden. Federal Circuit law only required a "credible economic analysis" or "sound economic proof" to bolster the damages. But the court found other reasons for excluding the price erosion analysis. For one, it rested on the inadmissible testimony of the plaintiff's executives that in a two-supplier market with no noninfringing alternatives, customers would have paid the contemplated higher price for the patented device. Also, at some point, the expert admitted that the manual dual flush valves were not a necessity and there would have been a price point at which customers would have balked. Finally, the expert gave conflicting opinions on noninfringing alternatives. First, he said there were none, but at the *Daubert* hearing he explained his lowering of the damages by pointing to competition. He conceded, he said, because of the court's ruling on the executives' testimony. There were simply too many problems with the analysis to find it admissible, the court concluded.

Sparks v. Sparks

Citation: 2013 Mo. App. LEXIS 1421
Date of decision: Nov. 26, 2013
Experts: David Davenport (business valuation, wife); Kenneth Ehlen (business valuation, husband)
Judge: Mitchell
State/Jurisdiction: Missouri
Court: Court of Appeals
Type of case: Marital Dissolution
SIC code: 0742 Veterinary Service for Animal Specialties

Dated Valuation Not Per Se Unreliable Indicator of FMV

As the husband pursued a divorce, he thought it necessary to sell part of his animal hospital to comply with any upcoming equalization payment order and procured a valuation. The trial court stayed the sale during the litigation but credited the valuation even though it predated trial by 26 months. The wife appealed, claiming the trial court's reliance on an outdated valuation was error as a matter of law.

Wife short-circuits hospital's sale. The husband was a doctor of veterinary medicine (DVM) and owned a small animal hospital. In the spring of 2010, the husband and wife separated. At that time, the husband contemplated selling a 49% interest in his practice to his associate for two reasons: (1) he considered the associate a "stellar veterinarian" against whom he did not want to have to compete in the future; and (2) he believed he would need to liquidate the business to pay for the wife's share of the practice's value following the finalization of divorce. Consequently, the same year, the husband hired a valuator—a former DVM who, upon retirement, became an expert appraiser of veterinary practices. The husband-seller and associate-buyer also prepared a stock-purchase agreement, which was dated March 2011, the date on which they hoped to finalize the sale. Under it, the associate would receive a monthly bonus that equaled the monthly payments he would pay to the husband to purchase his share in the business.

But, as the divorce proceeded through court, the wife obtained a temporary stay of the sale. At trial, in October 2012, the husband testified that the sale was still on; in fact, the prospective buyer was "chomping at the bit."

To determine the hospital's FMV, the husband's expert spoke with the husband, reviewed three years of the business's tax returns and other relevant financial statements, and visited the practice in August 2010. His contemporaneous report set the practice's gross earning value at $1.3 million and concluded that after subtracting long-term liabilities the FMV was slightly less than $1.07 million. At trial, the expert noted that the calculation did not factor in accounts receivable or accounts payable because there was no actual sale yet; he recognized that accounts payable could lower the value of the business's assets. He also acknowledged that by then the valuation was "somewhat dated" and should be updated "to effectuate an actual sale." But he believed the practice was a "very good business," and he did not expect there to be a "dramatic upward or downward change" to the valuation.

Shortly before trial, the wife retained an expert whose qualifications tracked those of the husband's expert and whose purpose it was to critique the latter's appraisal. He reviewed various financial documents, including the competing expert's report. At trial, he agreed with the $1.3 million gross earning value but said decreased existing long-term liabilities and new long-term liabilities (which he did not identify) increased the FMV to $1.2 million.

The husband offered a CPA to serve as rebuttal witness. This expert neither interviewed the husband nor prepared his own valuation of the clinic. At trial, he said that the 2010 valuation stated a "reasonable, if not high" FMV.

In a similar vein, the parties offered expert testimony from two CPAs as to the husband's projected income. The husband's expert had prepared the couple's personal as well as the business's tax returns since 2003. For his calculation, the expert took into account the proposed sale of the 49% interest in the business. He noted that, under the sales agreement, over 10 years, the associate would pay the husband approximately $523,000, or 49% of the $1.07 million valuation. This arrangement benefited the husband because "in this type of business it is better to have more than one owner." Also, the prospective buyer was investing "sweat equity and future cash," and the husband was investing in the "preservation of the future of his business." He said the husband's income should be "normalized." Accounting for other adjustments, the expert projected the husband's income for 2012 was almost $160,000.

The wife's income expert entered the case only two days before he testified. He did not speak with the husband, did not visit the business, and did not know what expense obligations the LLC had. To prepare for his testimony, he reviewed the husband's 2011 tax return and relied on one exhibit that showed calculations he admitted he had not prepared himself, nor did he know who had prepared them. He concluded the projected income was $266,000.

Finally the husband offered a rebuttal expert, also a CPA, who cautioned about double counting. It would be "inappropriate to impute [to the husband] any income ... above a normalized compensation" without an adjustment to the value of the hospital, he said. The higher the husband's normalized income, the lower the hospital's value because all the profit that went into the FMV calculation of the hospital would go toward the husband's income. Based on the hospital valuation from the husband's expert, he believed the normalized annual income would be between $100,000 and $125,000. He admitted that he had not done research on veterinary doctors' salaries but thought $100,000 was not "unreasonable."

Inadequate expert disclosure. The trial court adopted the $1.07 million FMV that the husband's business valuation expert proposed. It found the wife's expert not credible, noting that he had only "limited time within which to complete an analysis and develop an opinion regarding the valuation of [the hospital]." Moreover, he failed to submit the requisite reports or curriculum vitae to support his testimony to the court. His opinion "was essentially a different interpretation of the valuation report provided by [the husband's expert]," the court concluded.

As to the amount of income, the trial court found the husband's CPA expert credible, emphasizing his long working relationship with the husband and wife. It pointed out that the wife's expert arrived shortly before trial and not only did not make the calculations appearing in an exhibit he claimed supported his testimony, but also failed to explain who made them or on what information they were based. Therefore, the exhibit was inadmissible hearsay. His testimony was not credible, the court held. It noted the rebuttal expert's statements in support of a "normalized" income but did not adopt his conclusion as to the amount.

No 'artificial cut-off date' for valuation. The wife challenged numerous aspects of the trial court's dissolution decree at the state Court of Appeals, including rulings on expert witnesses. But the valuation of the hospital was at the heart of her appeal.

1. *Expert witness objection.* The wife claimed that the trial court mistakenly "disallowed" the testimony of her income expert based on hearsay. She requested a remand on whether the testimony was admissible and, if it was, a directive to the trial court to reconsider the evidence.

The argument had no traction in the appellate court, which noted that the trial court merely excluded the exhibit the expert relied on for determining the husband's income. It did so because he did not make the calculations it contained and did not know who did. The trial court admitted the expert's testimony but simply found it not credible. Appellate courts give great deference to a trial court's credibility determination.

2. *Hospital valuation.* The wife contended that the trial court "misapplied the law" when it adopted the $1.07 million value the husband's expert proposed in a valuation that he performed more than two years prior to trial. Under the law, a valuation must take place at the time of trial.

The appeals court found that case law allowed for a more flexible attitude. Even though the date of valuation is the date of trial, "this does not mean that there is an artificial cut-off date beyond which a previously prepared valuation of the property becomes legally stale." How much weight a trial court should give to a valuation is a determination of the facts and circumstances of the case. In this instance, the issue was whether, in light of the facts, the husband's expert "provided a sufficient evidentiary basis" for valuing the hospital at $1.07 million, said the appellate court.

To determine the worth of a business, the court generally seeks to find the price a hypothetical willing buyer would offer a willing seller. Here, the value that the expert calculated actually served as the agreed-upon sale price, when, in 2011, the husband's associate agreed to buy 49% of the practice for $523,000. "Thus, speculation on the issue of valuation was not required," the court pointed out. And, even though the sales agreement was not final and the sale not complete by the time of trial (because of the stay), the record showed that the prospective buyer was still "ready and willing" to go forward. Also, since the business was a small veterinary practice and the husband had to sell part of it to finance the divorce, he "logically negotiated" a sale to his associate. The valuation underlying the negotiation was substantial evidence of the business's FMV regardless of the delay.

Generally a delay only affects the evidentiary value of the suggested FMV when the value of the asset is "volatile in nature," the court continued. Here, no such volatility existed; the husband's expert said he did not expect a dramatic upward or downward shift in the August 2010 value.

According to the appeals court, the wife's real complaint was that the trial court did not credit her expert. However, the trial court had no reason to do so in this case. It confronted a dated valuation "that was nevertheless supported by evidence of a ready and willing buyer" and the opinion of an opposing expert who came into the litigation shortly before trial and, "rather than perform his own valuation, merely critiqued the other expert's work." Under these circumstances, it did not abuse its discretion in relying on the 2010 valuation.

The appeals court declined the wife's request to ignore the findings of the trial court and undertake its own valuation based on the numbers on record so as to update the 2010 valuation.

Stadtmueller v. Fitzgerald (In re Epic Cycle Interactive, Inc.)

Citation: 2014 Bank. LEXIS 2622
Date of decision: June 6, 2014
Experts: Alan Myers (trustee); Michael Corson (defendants)
Judge: Latham
State/Jurisdiction: Federal/California
Court: U.S. Bankruptcy Court
Type of case: Bankruptcy
SIC code: 7373 Computer Integrated Systems Design

'Blurred' Solvency Analysis Diminishes Expert's Credibility

A recent Chapter 7 bankruptcy case involving the quintessential startup provides valuable insight into what makes one expert's analytical approach to ascertaining the debtor's going concern value more reliable than the opposing expert's and shows how the court determined solvency.

This Chapter 7 bankruptcy case centered on a loan between the defendants, the founder of a company that embodied "every sense of the term 'start-up,'" according to the Bankruptcy Court, and the founder's mother. The company developed and marketed website design software. The initial funds in 1998 came from close family and friends, but in subsequent years the company also obtained funding from venture capital (VC) firms. By 2005, it pursued expansion, culminating in the acquisition of an advertising distribution network company. It also secured large contracts with CBS and newspapers belonging to the Tribune group. The debtor required additional financing to ensure its ability to perform on the contracts. At the end of 2007, VC firms provided bridge financing in exchange for which they received so-called bridge notes that bore 10% annual interest, payable on demand or at a specific date, and that automatically converted to equity shares if a qualifying financing transaction occurred. At this point, the relationship between the debtor's management and the VC firms was hostile. In need of an additional $100,000, the founder turned to his mother; she agreed to make a loan that had a 60-day maturity rate, after which she could either ask for repayment or convert the note to equity. The note had a pari passu provision to ensure equal treatment with the bridge notes. Upon maturity, the mother demanded repayment, which prompted the debtor to wire the funds on Feb. 22, 2008, at full face value, plus interest.

In January 2008, the VC funds filed suit against the founder and the company, alleging breach of contract and fiduciary duty. Settlement efforts on the debtor's part went nowhere. On Feb. 28, 2008, the VC firms formally demanded repayment of the outstanding bridge note, and, in April 2008, they obtained an order of attachment on the debtor's assets. On April 22, 2008, the debtor filed for Chapter 11 bankruptcy (S.D. Cal.), which the court later converted to Chapter 7 bankruptcy. The debtor ended up repaying only the note owed to his mother.

The trustee sued under the Bankruptcy Code's Section 547 to avoid and recover the alleged preferential transfer. To succeed on his claim, the trustee had to show that the debtor was insolvent on the date of transfer. Solvency was the only critical element in dispute, and both sides offered expert testimony to support their positions.

Trustee's expert uses narrow time frame. The starting point for the experts' analyses was the court's pretrial finding that the company had to be valued as a going concern for three reasons: (1) by late 2007, it had entered into lucrative contracts that were not in default; (2) it was generating substantial gross revenues; and (3) for more than a year after filing for bankruptcy, it operated as a debtor-in-possession.

The trustee's expert was a CPA, who, since 1989, focused on handling bankruptcy matters. For his analysis, he moved asset by asset to determine the fair market price for each asset category. Specifically, he used the book value of each asset, as it appeared on the balance sheets, and made a series of adjustments (discussed below). He clarified that his definition of the fair market price assumed that the assets "had been sold as a unit in a prudent manner and within a reasonable time."

He said two dates established the most accurate time bracket for his analysis and conclusion as to the debtor's financial condition on Feb. 22, 2008. They were Feb. 21, 2008, the date before the wire transfer, and Feb. 29, 2008, the day after the demand for repayment of the bridge note. The expert reviewed the company's 2007, 2008, and 2009 corporate income tax returns and compared them to the company's balance sheets for Jan. 31, 2008, Feb. 21, 2008, Feb. 29, 2008, April 22, 2008, and June 30, 2008. But for a one-dollar difference, the numbers matched. He also analyzed the debtor's bank statements for the first three months of 2008.

Under his analysis, the debtor's assets on February 21 amounted to $1.35 million and its liabilities to over $1.82 million. Therefore, the debtor was insolvent by over $477,000. On February 29, its assets were worth nearly $809,000 and its liabilities totaled over $1.4 million. Its insolvency had increased to over $600,000, he found. Consequently, he said, the debtor was insolvent when it repaid the $100,000 loan.

Auctioneer assigns liquidation value. The defendants' solvency expert also was a CPA, with 40 years of experience, including 10 years performing as corporate controller and CFO. He used a wider bracket for his analysis: Jan. 1, 2008, and April 22, 2008. He interviewed the company's founder and reviewed the debtor's disclosure statements, tax returns, and operating reports. He placed great weight on the debtor's Dec. 31, 2007, balance sheet because, he said, a CPA had prepared it and the debtor had included it in its 2008 tax return, under penalty of perjury. But the expert acknowledged that the internal accounting in this case closely matched the tax return statements. He asserted the opposing expert's report was not a true going concern valuation but a liquidation analysis.

The defendants' expert found that the company's 2008 tax return showed assets of over $2.5 million as of Jan. 1, 2008, and total liabilities of over $1.86 million. Therefore, on that date, the company was solvent by over $646,000. The expert did not adjust the figures for this date.

For April 22, 2008, the expert used the bankruptcy schedules, rather than the internally produced balance sheet, because the schedules were filed under penalty of perjury. He made a number of adjustments (discussed below) and arrived at nearly $1.17 million in assets. He also adjusted the liabilities to arrive at a total of nearly $890,000. By his calculation, the debtor was solvent on that day. Since the debtor was solvent at both data points, it necessarily was solvent on the transaction date, the defendants' expert concluded.

The defendants also retained a certified auctioneer who assigned a liquidation value to the debtor's fixed assets comprising a "piecemeal auction valuation" of the assets on Dec. 9, 2008. If the system had been sold as an operational data center, it likely would have brought in $148,000, the auctioneer said. He added that in 2008 there were many sales of older computer equipment and it was a buyer's market.

Court uses asset-by-asset approach. The court found all the expert witnesses "generally credible" but on balance thought the defendants' expert's analysis provided the more reliable going concern value. The trustee's expert "blur[red] the line between going concern and liquidation value such that the court cannot fully credit his testimony without contravening applicable case authority," it said. But the court adopted the trustee expert's time frame. His "bracketing methodology more precisely captures the data necessary to determine the Debtor's solvency on the transfer date."

The "most expeditious" way to assess solvency, the court said, was to move asset by asset. It did so by relying on the debtor's balance sheets and "applying both experts' logic where appropriate." In terms of adjustments, the disagreements focused on the following:

(1) *Accounts receivable.* The trustee's expert reduced the amount by 18% to account for doubtful accounts, but he did not consider the debtor's actual performance when it came to collecting its receivables. In contrast, the defendants' expert used a 15% discount based on the debtor's past history of cash collections.

The court adopted the 15% discount.

(2) *Security deposit.* The debtor had a $72,800—book value—cash security deposit related to obligations to its landlord. The trustee's expert assigned zero value to it for both Feb. 21, 2008, and Feb. 29, 2008. He noted the account had dwindled to $800 by the time the debtor filed for bankruptcy and thought it unlikely that the debtor would have been able to convert this asset to cash on Feb. 22, 2008.

The defendants challenged that assumption, and the court found it was an unpersuasive ex post analysis. The point was to rely on information available on the transfer date. Since the trustee did not propose a "principled way to discount this asset, other than at zero or full book value," it adopted the $72,800 figure for both dates.

(3) *Letter of credit.* Among the assets on the balance sheet was an item called "letter of credit" for $161,200. It pertained to the debtor's licensing rights to a computer game for which it paid royalties to the license holder. If the debtor missed a payment, the licensor had the right to draw on the deposit account. If the debtor performed, it had the right to the full funds.

The trustee's expert understood that, between June 2009 and April 2010, the debtor was able to recover $150,000 of the letter of credit. Based on this knowledge, he adjusted his valuation to $125,000 as of February 2008. As for information available on the transaction date, he believed the debtor would have been unable to convert the asset to cash on February 21 or February 29 and discounted its value to zero.

At trial, he took a different tack, valuing it as a type of accounts receivable, applying factor rates at 1%, 2%, and 3%. The result was values of $100,000, $45,000, and a negative number. But he then returned to his claim that this item had zero value on the two relevant dates. He also thought it highly unlikely that a buyer would purchase the note considering the entity performing on it was not financially sound and there was a three-year window of performance on it.

The defendants' expert thought it should be given book value, in line with valuing the debtor as a going concern.

The court pointed out that a hypothetical buyer would assess the likelihood of the debtor's performing on the contract. Neither its performance nor its failure to perform was a certainty. Since the trustee failed to offer a way to discount the value, the court adopted the $161,200 book value.

(4) *Prepaid expenses.* The balance sheet included over $33,600 in prepaid utility deposits, which the trustee's expert valued at zero, saying this asset was spent money that the debtor could not convert to cash.

The court found a zero valuation unpersuasive. There was a possibility that the debtor might assign the lease interest and preserve some value in the accounts. Lacking evidence of how to discount the amount, the court accepted book value.

(5) *Fixed assets.* The fixed assets consisted primarily of computer equipment, whose book value was over $418,400. The trustee's expert discounted it to $101,300 based on an admittedly novel formula whose underlying logic was far from persuasive, the court said. The court also disregarded the net book value the defendants' solvency expert proposed.

Instead, the court relied on the auctioneer's liquidation valuation. It found the assets were worth slightly over $248,900 on Feb. 21, 2008, and Feb. 29, 2008. This figure, it said, equaled the sum of the $74,100 and $64,200 liquidation figures from the auctioneer's report, multiplied by two to represent the computers' "fully operational" value and deducting a 10% sales commission. Even though the auctioneer's valuation related to December 2008, his analysis was more reliable than the defendants' expert's valuation.

(6) *Acquired company.* The book value of the advertising distribution company that the debtor bought in 2005 was $50,000. The trustee's expert assigned zero value, reasoning that the debtor did not sell it even though it was experiencing losses. Also, it appeared as an investment on the tax return balance sheet. Had there been a market for it, the debtor would have sold it, the expert concluded.

At trial, the founder testified that the acquired entity actually generated considerable gross revenues and that the debtor had received multiple offers to purchase it for about $1 million. It was the VC firms that prevented a sale by way of their seats on the board of directors. The trustee's expert said that, if he had known this information, he would have explored the investment. But he did not explain how any additional information might have affected his valuation.

The defendants' expert said he would have tried to determine whether the offers represented a bona fide arm's-length deal and whether the potential buyers were able to perform. If so, he would have valued the asset at the offer amount. Without this analysis, he settled on the $50,000 book value, which the court adopted.

(7) *Goodwill and intangible assets.* The debtor's balance sheet amortized goodwill of approximately $110,000 on the relevant dates. The trustee's expert discounted it to zero saying the debtor would have been unable to sell it. He noted that, by 2007, the debtor showed a retained earnings deficit of $4.8 million and concluded its assets would not have generated a premium.

The defendants' expert relied on a liquidation report an accounting and auditing firm had prepared and proposed a $100,000 intangible asset value. He said that offers to buy the advertising distribution company at a significant premium and the debtor's long-term revenue contracts supported that figure.

The court agreed with the trustee's expert that the debtor's goodwill balance sheet entry should be excluded. "The appearance of goodwill on [the debtor's] balance sheet more than likely represented a specific asset purchase, rather than the intangible value attributable to [it] as an enterprise," it noted. It was unlikely that the debtor could generate any value from the historic cost to satisfy creditors' claims.

But the court agreed with the defendants' expert that a prospective buyer of the debtor as a going concern would place an economic value on the contracts the company had secured and on its ability to perform. Therefore, the court accepted the defendants' expert's $100,000 intangible asset figure.

(8) *Liabilities.* The experts' disagreement centered on the treatment of the VC firms' bridge notes: whether the court should discount for the possibility that they would convert to equity and what the appropriate discount rate would be.

The trustee's expert credited the liabilities at face value. The defendants' expert was under the mistaken impression that the parties had agreed to write down the loan balance by $250,000.

The court pointed out that neither expert performed a contingency analysis for the court. But the hostility between the VC firms and the debtors and other facts suggested that a conversion was a "virtual uncertainty" as of the transfer date. Therefore, the court found it was appropriate to assign face value to all liabilities on the relevant dates.

Court calculates daily rate of losses. The court concluded that, on Feb. 21, 2008, the debtor's assets exceeded liabilities by nearly $99,300. On Feb. 29, 2008, its liabilities exceeded assets by nearly $11,200. The net loss for 2008 as of February 21 was nearly $341,460; as of February 29, it was nearly $450,540. This meant there was a deficit of nearly $109,080 in eight days. By extension, the court found the company lost $13,635 a day, which led it to conclude that on February 22 the debtor's assets still exceeded its liabilities by over $85,600. Accordingly, the court found the debtor was solvent and the trustee was unable to avoid the transfer.

Starling v. Starling

Citation: 2013 Va. App. LEXIS 248
Date of decision: Sept. 10, 2013
Experts: Joseph Simmons (wife); William David Miller (husband)
Judge: Hurley, Jr.
State/Jurisdiction: Virginia
Court: Court of Appeals
Type of case: Marital Dissolution
SIC: 3621 Motors and Generators

Hard Asset Value Best Captures Worth of Family Business

Because the trial court found neither spouse's expert offered a convincing valuation for a family business, it opted to adopt the liquidation value the company's CPA proposed. On appeal, the husband contested both the trial court's classification of the business as hybrid property as well as its valuation.

Who generated increase in value? In 1981, one year before he married, the husband and his father started a business providing motors and pumps for industrial and mining use. The husband was actively involved in running, managing, and staffing the business during the marriage. At the divorce trial, the couple's daughter testified that the husband "spent long hours at the company." His sister said, "[The husband] runs the company," acting as "the supervisor and a worker." One of the husband's own experts stated the husband's father worked on average only 20 hours per week, and one of the wife's experts noted that the father was "mostly retired or not rendering any substantial service."

Both spouses retained business appraisers to calculate the value of the business, and the trial court also heard from the company's CPA.

The husband's expert valued the business at $224,000. The wife's attorney asked him about intrinsic value—the applicable standard of value in the state (Virginia)—and challenged his valuation claiming the business grossed $2.1 million and had $700,000 in assets. The expert countered that it also had over $266,000 in liabilities.

The wife's expert said that in 1981 the company showed $12,000 in gross business, which by 2009 had risen to $1.8 million. He valued the company at $1.1 million. He suggested that in a case such as this, where "there's no ready market as would be the case with a publicly traded stock, the intrinsic value is essentially the same thing as fair market value."

On the other hand, the company's CPA said that as of 2009 the company was worth $400,000 based on the company's liquidation value. This included "the cash, the receivables, the equipment at its appraised value less the cost of disposing of it, the inventory that was appraised, less the cost of disposing of it, less the accounts payable at the end of May 31st, 2009."

The trial court made two determinations regarding the business related to its classification and its valuation.

1. *Classification.* The business was a hybrid, including both separate and marital property, the court found. Specifically, whatever value the company had before the marriage belonged to the husband as separate property, but any increase in value during the marriage was marital property. The testimony of the wife's expert showed that the company's value grew substantially during the marriage. Moreover, testimony from other witnesses proved that the increase was largely due to the husband's efforts, rather than his father's. Therefore, the community had a right to the increase in value.

2. *Valuation.* Next, the trial court found that the spouses' experts failed to provide "convincing valuations." The figure the husband's expert set down was "far less than the value of [the company's] hard assets if they were to be liquidated." In contrast, the wife's expert proposed a value that was "anomalously high because it does not seem to give due credit for the risks this company faces and will continue to face."

Instead, the trial court used the 1982 and 2009 values of the hard assets, which the witnesses (the wife's expert and the CPA) put at $30,609 and $400,000, respectively. The value of the hard assets was a little over $369,000, the court determined. Accordingly, the marital share was approximately $184,600, and the wife's half was worth over $92,300.

No 'convincing' expert valuations. The husband appealed to the Virginia Court of Appeals, attacking both the trial court's classification and its valuation. The appellate court dealt with the arguments quickly.

As to the classification, the husband claimed that the entire business was separate property because any increase in value stemmed from his father's efforts. He, the husband, "did nothing more than the rest of his crew."

The appeals court disagreed. There was sufficient evidence for the lower court's finding that the husband's efforts were significant and instrumental in the increase in value, it said.

As to the valuation, the reviewing court found that, even if expert testimony was the preferable method for valuing marital property, the trial court was not required to "accept as conclusive the opinion of an expert." Because neither expert testimony was persuasive, it properly relied on other information the parties presented to determine the company's value. Accordingly, the Court of Appeals declined to upend the trial court's decision.

Surgem, LLC v. Seitz

Citation: 2013 N.J. Super. Unpub. LEXIS 2491
Date of decision: Oct. 16, 2013
Experts: Michael Lehner (plaintiffs); Timothy Blackmer (defendant)
Judge: Lihotz
State/Jurisdiction: New Jersey
Court: Superior Court, Appellate Division
Type of case: Judicial Dissolution
SIC code: 8011 Offices and Clinics of Medical Doctors

Expert's Calculation Report Fails to Yield 'Actual Fair Valuation'

A calculation report is not a valuation, as a recent appellate decision drives home. A litigant trying to pass it off as evidence risks being left without the expert testimony necessary to controvert the opposing side's value determination.

The plaintiff, "an accomplished board certified urological surgeon and astute businessman," founded a company that provided development and management services to ambulatory surgical centers. He hired the defendant, whom he believed to be an equally business-savvy entrepreneur with considerable experience in medical management, as the company's president. Several oral and written agreements between the parties provided for the plaintiff's granting the defendant 300,000 membership units in the company, which amounted to a 10% interest, in exchange for the company's right to buy back the shares if it terminated the defendant for cause or he resigned from the company.

To settle a dispute with "disgruntled financiers," the defendant, with permission from the plaintiff, sold 30,000 shares to two investors for $10 per share. At some point, the defendant also proposed a buy-sell agreement that mentioned a $10-per-share price, but the plaintiff never accepted it or signed on to it.

After a few years, the relationship between the plaintiff and defendant went south and the former terminated the defendant for cause. Subsequently, the plaintiff and the company sued to establish the fair value of the company's stock both to determine the value of the defendant's interest and to exercise their right to repurchase the stock. The defendant counterclaimed to enforce his right as 10% shareholder of the company.

Inconsequential buy-sell agreement. At a bench trial, both sides presented appraisal experts. The defendant's expert testified that he had only been hired to prepare a "calculation of value," not a full appraisal. He said that the defendant had not furnished the numerous materials necessary to perform a valuation and that "more work should have been done" for a fair valuation of the company at the date of termination. He mentioned that the defendant's proposed buy-sell agreement would be "part of the consideration" if he were to value the defendant's shares alone but not if he were to determine the company's worth on the termination date.

According to the plaintiff's expert, the $10-per-share price was an "arbitrary amount" that was based on unreliable projections. He concluded that the company's fair value was $4.2 million and the fair value of the defendant's interest in the company was $368,700. (The opinion does not discuss the methodology and analysis the expert used to reach his conclusion or details about the defendant expert's "calculation of value.")

The trial court rejected the buy-sell agreement as support for the defendant's $10-per-unit claim. What's more, it declined to accept the opinion of the defendant's expert since he did not determine the fair value of the company or of the defendant's interest. The "calculation of value" represented nothing more than an agreement between the appraiser and the client, the defendant, "as to the manner in which the appraiser's work is to be done." By the defendant expert's own account, his calculation of value fell far short of the work required to prepare a report that contained an "actual fair valuation of [the company]," the court concluded.

The trial court's ruling meant the testimony of the plaintiff's expert was uncontested; the court adopted his analysis and calculations and concluded the fair value of an 8.74% interest in the company was $368,700.

The defendant appealed the trial court's valuation of his interest, claiming a right to $10 per unit as supported by his expert's testimony, the buy-sell agreement, and the prior stock sale for that price.

The appellate court disagreed. The trial court properly disregarded the agreement and provided sound reasons for rejecting the defendant expert's calculation of value. Further, his expert never had contended that the operating documents "dictated" the defendant had a right to $10per share. There was no challenge to the plaintiff expert's valuation. He applied the correct standard and provided evidence on which the trial court relied for its conclusion. Accordingly, there was no need for a new trial on the value of the defendant's interest in the company, the appellate court held.

Estate of Tanenblatt v. Commissioner

Citation: 2013 Tax Ct. Memo LEXIS 273
Date of decision: Nov. 18, 2013
Experts: Management Planning, Inc., Jacques O. Tuchler & Associates, Dr. Laura J. Tindall (petitioner); John A. Thomson (respondent)
Judge: Halpern
Country: US
State/Jurisdiction: Federal Circuit
Court: United States Tax Court
Type of case: Federal Taxation
SIC: 6519 Lessors of Real Property, NEC

Tax Court Foils 'End Run' Around Expert Rules

In challenging the Internal Revenue Service's deficiency notice related to estate taxes for the decedent's interest in a limited liability company, the taxpayer pulled out all the stops. He disavowed the initial appraisal that was the basis for his estate tax filing, claiming it overvalued the interest, and sought to compel the agency to stipulate an alternative, lower, valuation without making the appraiser available for expert testimony at trial. In addition, he attacked the government expert's methodology and discounts. None of the arguments gained traction with the Tax Court.

The decedent had a 16.67% interest in a New York limited liability company (LLC) whose principal asset was a 10-story commercial building with office and retail space in Manhattan. On the valuation date, it was fully leased.

The LLC was subject to an operating agreement whose provisions specified that membership was available to members of three family groups and transfer of membership interests to outsiders was subject to restrictions. Members participated in the management and control of the LLC, whereas a nonfamily member transferee could receive distributions and allocations of profits and losses but had no right to weigh in on management and control. To become a member, a transferee had to secure unanimous consent from other members. At the time the decedent transferred her interest in the LLC to a trust, she was a member in the LLC, but, on the date of death, the trust was the member.

Various valuation methods in play. For estate tax purposes, the petitioner obtained a valuation of the decedent's interest in the LLC that was based in part on an appraisal for the LLC's main asset, i.e., the building.

The building appraisal firm used a sales comparison approach, which yielded a value of $22.8 million. It also used an income approach based on the discounted cash flow (DCF) method. The appraiser projected building income for six years, capitalized the sixth year's income to compute a terminal value, and discounted the income stream to present value, which was almost $20 million. Disregarding the first approach, the building appraiser concluded the asset was worth nearly $20 million based on the income approach.

The LLC valuation firm added the company's cash and other current assets to the $20 million amount, subtracted liabilities, and arrived at a net asset value on the date of death of some $20.6 million. It then sequentially applied a 20% discount for lack of control (DLOC) and a 35% discount for lack of marketability (DLOM) to conclude that the fair market value of the interest at issue was $1.78 million.

The Internal Revenue Service (IRS) determined the taxpayer had undervalued the interest and issued a deficiency notice. Its expert regarded the LLC primarily as a real estate holding company and, therefore, relied exclusively on the discounted net asset value approach. He determined the interest was worth $2.3 million, accepting the petitioner's proposed $20.6 million net asset value based on the LLC's relevant tax return and the building appraisal but reducing the discounts to a 10% DLOC and a 26% DLOM (elsewhere the opinion states a 20% DLOC).

The petitioner challenged the IRS's determination and asked the Tax Court for review. In so doing, he also disavowed his initial appraiser's valuation, which he claimed was too high, alleging the first appraiser had failed to use the proper valuation method and had improperly classified the subject interest. To support his claims, he attached a new appraisal report to his petition.

As the court's opinion describes it, the petitioner's second appraiser characterized the interest at issue as a lesser-value—assignee instead of member—interest. Using both an income and net asset value approach, weighting their results at 80% and 20%, and applying "the appropriate applicable discounts," the new appraiser arrived at a value of just above $1 million.

In a pretrial motion, the petitioner sought to compel the government to stipulate the second appraisal without making the appraiser available at trial. (The court's opinion suggests that, due to a fee dispute between the petitioner and the second appraiser, the latter refused to appear in court.) The government argued that the new appraisal should be excluded from evidence on various grounds, including the apparent failure of the petitioner to have the appraiser testify as an expert witness and make her available for cross-examination.

After the court denied the pretrial motion, the petitioner asked for reconsideration, contending that the new appraisal was admissible as expert testimony by way of stipulation and also arguing that the IRS expert's valuation was flawed. The court considered both evidentiary and valuation arguments in turn.

Missing expert witness. "As best we understand," the court said, the petitioner argued that, because the IRS could not dispute the authenticity of his petition, including the attached new appraisal, it had to stipulate both the petition and the attached appraisal. Both documents were in evidence. Any requirements under Tax Court rules regarding the admission of expert testimony no longer applied; in any event, the rules only applied if the petitioner were to call the appraiser to testify, which he did not.

The court dismissed the petitioner's argument as an attempt "to end-run our procedural rules ... or to prevent this Court from exercising its gatekeeper function with respect to expert testimony." Neither the Tax Court's evidentiary rules nor Fed. R. Evid. 702 allowed for admission and consideration of the new appraisal. The petitioner asked the court to consider the report as an expert opinion, without making the author available at trial. He failed to qualify her as an expert and meet the preconditions for receiving the appraisal into evidence; because the report was not in evidence, the court could not consider the opinion.

The court said the first appraisal, which the petitioner had attached to his estate tax return form, was in evidence, but it declined to rely on it as expert testimony.

'Redefining' character of subject interest. The petitioner next contended that both his first appraisal and the IRS expert's valuation were defective but that there was sufficient other evidence in the record to enable the court to determine a fair market value of the subject interest that was less than the $1.78 million he initially had reported.

The petitioner's valuation-related challenges broke down into two major components.

1. *Classification of interest.* The first appraisal and the IRS appraisal erroneously classified the subject interest as a member interest, when in actuality it was a nonfamily member, or assignee, interest, the petitioner argued. This was so because the applicable fair market value standard envisioned a hypothetical willing buyer, who in this case could only be a nonfamily member and, therefore, could only obtain an interest that had greater limitations and thus was of lesser value.

The court saw this argument as an improper attempt to "redefine" the character of the subject interest. The petitioner "collapse[d] the two steps of the valuation process" into one. First, the valuator must identify the nature and character of the interest to be valued, and second, he must objectively determine its value. Here, the decedent was a member of the LLC at the time she transferred her interest to the trust. Therefore, the interest was a member's interest.

Under the fair market value standard, the court said, the best way to account for restrictions on a member's lack of influence on decision-making was to apply a discount for lack of control (or minority interest), as both the petitioner's first appraiser and the IRS expert did.

2. *Valuation methodology.* The petitioner claimed the IRS expert erred in treating the LLC as a real estate holding company and, by extension, using the discounted net asset value approach to value the subject interest. Because it was in part an operating company, some weight should have been given to its earnings and distributions.

The court recognized that the LLC was a going concern even assuming its members "had in mind the future appreciation of the building." But, even if the IRS expert viewed the company primarily as a real estate holding company and excluded the market and income approaches for his valuation, he accepted the $20 million value the petitioner had offered regarding the LLC's principal asset, the building. The building's value, in turn, resulted from the building appraiser's use of the income approach. In some of its earlier decisions, the court said it had allowed a weighted approach to valuing a closely held real estate firm, combining a net value and an income capitalization approach. For all these reasons, the LLC's value before determining the value of the decedent's proportionate interest was $20.6 million.

The court also upheld the IRS expert's discounts, finding the petitioner had provided no expert testimony to support different rates. In sum, the decedent's interest was worth $2.3 million.

Taubman v. U.S. Bank, N.A.

Citation: 2014 Cal. App. Unpub. LEXIS 4303
Date of decision: June 17, 2014
Experts: Gordon Romine (trustee);
Judge: Perluss
State/Jurisdiction: California
Court: Court of Appeal
Type of case: Expert Testimony
SIC code: 6792 Oil Royalty Traders

Court Spotlights Lack of Control in Oil and Gas Interest Valuation

In a nasty battle over trust assets, the feuding beneficiaries focused their attention on the valuation of oil and gas interests the trust owned. A recent appeals court decision explores issues having to do with the proper methodology to establish the assets' fair market value and the appropriate way to account for indirect and fractional ownership and lack of marketability. The court's discount rate raises more questions.

In 1990, the decedent established a trust naming herself as the sole trustee and her two children as beneficiaries. Because she intended to divide the trust assets equally, the trust provided for an equalization payment at the time of final distribution of the assets. The assets were the decedent's interests in various business ventures—including a shopping center and interests in oil and gas leases. In essence, the daughter was to receive the shopping center trust assets and the son the oil and gas trust interests. After the decedent's death in 1999, a contentious litigation developed between the siblings, as well as between the siblings and the trustee. In January 2011, the trial court issued a judgment finding it had to modify the trust to effect the decedent's intent for various reasons. The trustee would make an in-kind distribution of all assets to the daughter, except for the shopping center assets, which were to be divided evenly between the siblings. Because the brother had been overpaid during the life of the trust by some $6 million, the daughter had an equitable lien on the brother's pro rata interest in the assets; the brother, on the other hand, would receive credit against the debt in the amount of one-half of the current fair market value of the oil and gas interests. The court would terminate the trust and discharge the trustee after a final accounting. The court's findings positioned the siblings such that the brother would benefit from a higher valuation and the sister from a lower valuation of the oil and gas interests.

The interests consisted of "royalty interests, working interests [interest in oil wells and producing facilities] and minerals in place not currently being extracted" in properties located in various states. They were owned through the family trust or an oil company that owned interests in the mineral leases.

In March 2011, the daughter asked the court to instruct the trustee on how to value the interests. She argued that, since there was no identifiable market for buying the fractional interests, the court should use the value the estate had stated in its 2000 federal and state tax returns. The amount was approximately $1,248,000 and was based on an appraisal the estate had obtained from a petroleum engineering company in 1999.

In a subsequent filing in May 2011, the daughter urged the court to value the interests at twice the amount of the gross annual royalties generated by the oil and gas interests in the past 12 months. Since the royalties amounted to "approximately $630,000," the interests' fair market value was $1.26 million, she claimed.

Futures market vs. spot prices. In June 2011, the trustee said he had retained an expert, a "registered professional petroleum engineer," because the trustee believed that "a more informal method, such as an informal survey of the industry's use of multiples of 'trailing cash flow' will not provide the certainty" necessary to "satisfy the adverse interests of the beneficiaries." An informal survey would not put an end to the controversies that "have plagued this Trust for the last 11 years." The seven-page appraisal valued the interests at over $4.4 million and included 250 pages of charts, schedules, and other supporting documentation. The appraiser used 36-month strips of futures contracts quoted on the New York Mercantile Exchange (NYMEX strips) and a 10% discount rate to account for inflation. He also assumed a 50-year time line for future oil production from the properties.

The daughter did not hire her own expert. But, in a preliminary response to the trustee's position, she attacked the appraisal contending the appraiser used a flawed methodology. His valuation was based on a speculative futures market, and it failed to consider a temporary spike in oil prices in June 2011 owing to the political unrest in Libya and other oil-producing countries in the Middle East. She claimed the valuation date was January 2011, the date of the final judgment, rather than June 2011, and she contended that the interests should be valued at twice their annual earnings. In the alternative, if a multiple of gross annual earnings was not an appropriate basis, the court should use an average of the historic closing prices for oil and gas interests over the life of the trust. This method yielded a value of $2.32 million.

Meanwhile, the son maintained the assets were worth $10 million but did not formally object to the trustee's fair market valuation.

At an evidentiary hearing, the appraisal firm's representative said he had "conducted more than 1,000 valuations of similar properties." He explained that he relied on future contracts because they were "the closest publicly-traded reference point" for oil and gas reserves to be produced in the future and were widely used in the industry for valuation purposes. When cross-examined by the daughter, he admitted that the 50-year life of production he estimated was unsupported. The daughter also pointed out that he failed to include a discount to account for the fractional and indirect nature of ownership in the properties and its effect on the property's marketability. She did not propose a discount rate.

The court agreed that the appraisal failed to discount for "the fact that ownership of that oil and gas is indirect. It is not ownership of the oil and gas, but ownership in [the family trust] or [the oil company]." Subsequently, the court put it to the trustee that the "problem is there is no control" over the oil company or the trust's interest in the oil and gas. The court suggested that the Internal Revenue Service "routinely discounts for lack of control" and asked the trustee whether he knew anything about it. The trustee replied that to his knowledge for estate tax purposes the fair market value was "usually reduced by 20 to 35 percent to reflect the indirect nature of the ownership interests," but he was unable to cite to the applicable code section.

The trial court, sustaining the sister's objections, reduced the fair market value to $3.9 million, which was a 12.5% reduction of the appraiser's value.

Improper deviation from expert valuation. The brother attacked the valuation in his appeal, arguing the trial court lacked the evidence necessary to justify the additional discount or to deviate from the appraiser's value in other ways. After all, there was only one valuation expert.

The state Court of Appeals disagreed. It noted that there was no requirement that the trial court accept the testimony of the sole expert witness. The trial court had the authority to rely on all, part, or none of the testimony the trustee's expert gave. More importantly, there was evidence in the record contesting the expert's valuation. For one, the sister offered the early appraisal and estate tax returns reflecting the $1.2 million valuation from 1999, which was based on multiples of cash flow. She also submitted written objections to the expert's methodology and challenged numerous aspects of his calculation during cross-examination. The trial court sustained the objections, even if it did not specify which of the various objections it considered significant for its calculation. The appeals court concluded that the trial court's valuation was within the range of values in evidence and affirmed the valuation.

In re Tronox Incorporated

Citation: 2013 Bankr. LEXIS 5232
Date of decision: Dec. 12, 2013
Experts: Prof. Grant Newton (plaintiffs, solvency analysis), Prof. Daniel Fischel (defendants, solvency analysis); Prof. Jack Williams (plaintiffs, REV analysis), Jeffrey Balcombe (defendants, REV and damages analyses); Dr. Neil Ram (plaintiffs, environmental liabilities analysis), Neil Shifrin and Richard Lane White (defendants, environmental liabilities analysis)
Judge: Gropper
State/Jurisdiction: Federal/New York
Court: U.S. Bankruptcy Court
Type of case: Bankruptcy
SIC code: 1311 Crude Petroleum & Natural Gas, 2800 Chemicals & Allied Products

Expert's Market-Based, 'Self-Contained' Solvency Analysis Crumbles

Valuation experts of various stripes took center stage in a recent fraudulent conveyance suit regarding a parent company's decision to spin off its chemical manufacturing business from its highly profitable oil and gas exploration and production business. The transaction left the former with billions of legacy environmental and tort liabilities and ultimately led to bankruptcy. The litigation trust sued to recover from the defendants the value of the transferred oil and gas assets. The court's 82-page decision explored claims as to reasonably equivalent value, business enterprise value, and environmental and tort liabilities.

Liberating assets from liabilities. The plaintiffs and defendants started as a many-tentacled enterprise that included an oil and gas exploration business as well as a uranium mining business and various chemical plants. By November 2005, only two businesses remained: the oil and gas exploration and production (E&P) business and the chemical—titanium dioxide—business. The E&P business was dominant, with operating profits of about $1.8 billion for that year; in comparison, the chemical business brought in about $106 million. The conglomerate's enormous environmental and tort liabilities represented a major problem: Since 2000, it had incurred more than $1 billion in environmental response costs and was spending more than $160 million a year on remediation. This made it an "unattractive" acquisition candidate. In 2002, the eventual buyer of the E&P business rejected a merger, reasoning that future environmental liability would be "$BILLIONS" and could last for "at least 30 more years." (After the spinoff, it paid more than $18 billion for the nearly liability-free E&P business.)

As early as 2002, the parent company's top management hired Lehman Brothers to pursue a corporate reorganization. Essentially, it meant transferring the E&P business—the oil and gas assets—to a new holding company (one of the defendants in the suit) and transferring the ownership interests in the E&P subsidiaries to a new company; the old company was refashioned into the stand-alone titanium dioxide company.

In preparation for an IPO/spinoff of the chemical company, management prepared projections but, at the direction of its CFO, abandoned its customary methodology. Until February 2005, it had forecast titanium dioxide pricing using a mean treadline based on decades of historical pricing data, but the March 2005 forecast that was the source of the IPO numbers showed dramatic increases. Specifically, projected results increased by $99 million in 2008 (to a total of $228 million) and $128 million in 2009 (to a total of $325 million).

In November 2005, the split culminated in a master separation agreement in which the parent company dictated the terms. The chemical business would assume every legacy liability of every discontinued business the original company had owned in the prior 75 years. The E&P business would only assume liability based on "currently conducted" E&P operations. The net cash proceeds from the spinoff were $537.1 million, after expenses, but the chemical business was made to pay everything but $40 million in cash to the E&P entities. Last, but not least, it was to assume $442 million in pension obligations and $186 million in unfunded "other post-employment benefits."

At one point in 2005, Lehman Brothers prepared for a possible sale of the chemical business, but most potential purchasers balked at taking on the large legacy liabilities. Only one of the four finalists, Apollo, made a "final offer," which envisioned a purchase price of $1.3 billion, $300 million in indemnities from the new entity for the environmental liabilities the buyer would assume, and an additional $200 million indemnity for breaches of representation and warranties. The contract contained numerous open items and terms the new, E&P company previously had rejected. The sale did not go through. As part of doing due diligence, Apollo also hired an environmental consultant to value the legacy liabilities; the latter calculated them to be $556.1 million on an undiscounted basis.

A one-product business, the chemical company floundered almost immediately after the spinoff. From November 2005 through the third quarter of 2008, it lost $199.7 million. As it was struggling with poor cash flow, it had to fund legacy liabilities. It only was able to fund $90 million per year, net of reimbursements, but even that reduced amount was 56% of its 2006 EBITDA and 95% of its 2007 EBITDA. A financial analyst involved in the negotiations leading up to the spinoff summed up the situation in a picture that showed a flower (the chemical business) and a weed (the legacy liabilities) strangling the flower.

In January 2009, it petitioned for bankruptcy. The litigation trust sued in Bankruptcy Court (S.D.N.Y.) on behalf of a number of plaintiffs, including the three debtor entities that made up the estate of the chemical company and public and private entities that had claims against the debtors for environmental cleanup costs and tort liabilities. The defendants were the parent company and the entities making up the E&P business. The plaintiffs' principal claim for relief was that the transaction that removed substantially all of the parent company's assets from the legacy liabilities was an actual or constructive fraudulent conveyance. It left the debtor insolvent. The defendants characterized the transaction as an attempt "to unlock the value inherent in each of [the businesses]."

Actual fraud beyond dispute. Whether the transfers were actually fraudulent was a question of whether they "hinder[ed] and delay[ed] creditors," the court explained. In this case, it was beyond dispute that [the defendants] acted to free substantially all its assets—"certainly its most valuable assets"—from decades of historic liabilities, said the court. By the defendants' own admission, the assets represented 86.4% of the old entity's assets and accounted for 83.2% of its revenue and 112.6% of its net income as of December 2001. As a result, the legacy creditors would be left with a minimal asset base on which to recover in the future; accordingly, they were "hindered or delayed" as a direct consequence of the transaction, the court I concluded.

REV expert undergirds constructive fraud claim. Whether the transfers were constructively fraudulent was a question of whether the chemical business received "reasonably equivalent value" for distributing the E&P assets and other property as part of the spinoff, said the court. Both sides used REV experts.

The plaintiffs retained a reputed bankruptcy analyst to show there was no REV. He determined that the debtor companies conveyed property worth approximately $17 billion (including the E&P assets) and received in return $2.6 billion, a $14.5 billion reduction in value. To calculate the market value for the conveyed E&P assets, he compared the company's oil and gas business to seven independent, comparable E&P companies and determined it was worth approximately $12 billion as of November 2005. He then added a 30% control premium, concluding that the value of the transferred oil and gas assets was approximately $15.8 billion as of that date. His valuation aligned with valuation estimates from Lehman Brothers and Salomon Smith Barney and the actual price the future buyer paid only a few months after the spinoff, he said.

The defendants did not question the calculations, but their REV (and back-up damages) expert, who, the court pointed out, testified for the first time in a fraudulent conveyance suit, objected that the REV and solvency analyses should be on a strict entity-by-entity basis. This would mean that two of the debtor companies did not receive REV, but one did receive REV with the transfer of interests in an Australian titanium dioxide plant. The court dismissed that argument, finding that "the 'market' dealt with [the entities] on a consolidated basis." They appeared as one entity for purposes of the spinoff, and every one of them was liable on the debt issued as either a borrower or guarantor. It adopted the conclusions of the plaintiffs' REV expert.

Solvency experts with 'sterling credentials.' The critical next question was whether the transfers left the chemical company insolvent. The answer lies in a "balance sheet test," which requires a determination of whether the debts in the aggregate are greater than assets in the aggregate, said the court. In this case, the parties called insolvency experts with "sterling credentials," it added. In commenting on the experts' qualifications, it explained that the defendants' expert was well known for his view that "market prices typically are more reliable evidence of a company's value than ex post analyses prepared by experts in the context of litigation." For his solvency opinion, he said he did not rely on any of the defendants' other experts but strove for a "completely self-contained analysis."

To determine the chemical company's business enterprise value (BEV) as of November 2005, both experts used a three-prong approach: a discounted cash flow (DCF) analysis, a comparable company analysis, and a comparable transaction analysis. The plaintiffs' expert computed a BEV of $1.03 billion, whereas the defendants' expert said it was $1.7 billion.

1. *DCF analysis.* The major difference in the experts' DCF analyses related to the use of cash flow projections. The plaintiff's expert believed the company's internal projections required a downward adjustment. As he saw it, they were "sell-side" projections based on overly optimistic assumptions and key numbers "were imposed at the direction of [the parent company's] chief financial officer." For this reason, the expert used the February 2005 projections.

In contrast, the defendants' expert adopted the management projections without independent analysis or view to the chemical business's historical performance. He said his BEV aligned with the BEV that would result from using the projections of future cash flow of third parties "who were either potential bidders or banks that served as advisors and/or lenders" to such bidders.

The court strongly rejected the defendant expert's approach. The use of "sell-side" projections was "particularly insupportable," it said, because titanium dioxide prices began to erode in April 2005, as the defendants' industry expert admitted. They also far exceeded the chemical business's "peak" and "very strong" years of 2000 and 2005. And they were "particularly unreasonable" given uncontroverted evidence that the company's titanium dioxide business peaked in early 2005 and "was on the downturn" by November 2005. Further, use of the third-party projections would result in a BEV of only $1.5 million—almost $200 million lower than the defendants' expert had calculated. Moreover, it was clear that nearly all of the third-party projections used the company's inflated IPO forecasts or outdated data as their starting point, the court added.

For all of these reasons, the plaintiffs' expert was correct to use the earlier projections.

The court found little disagreement as to other inputs. The plaintiffs' expert determined 11% was an appropriate weighted average cost of capital, while the defendants' expert used one that was slightly lower (not specified). The plaintiffs' expert calculated the terminal values based on the Gordon growth model and applied a constant growth rate in perpetuity of 2.5%. The defendants' expert agreed that this was an accepted method but proposed a slightly higher 2.87% rate, which, he said, was based on a market approach.

The plaintiffs' expert concluded the DCF-derived BEV was $1.01 billion; the defendants' expert arrived at $1.7 billion. The court credited the value the plaintiffs' expert proposed.

2. *Comparable company analysis.* The plaintiffs' expert chose 10 commodity chemical companies, calculated EBIT and EBITDA for each, and added a reasonable control premium of 5%. His selection resulted in a LTM EBITDA multiple of 6.2. Based on this method, he arrived at an IPO value of between $770 million and $1.23 billion, with a midpoint value of $1.0 billion.

The defendants' expert selected 15 companies based on whether potential buyers or industry analysts considered the company comparable to the subject company. He admitted he had not performed an independent analysis of the comparables. He calculated a substantially higher LTM EBITDA multiple of 7.63 and concluded the subject company's BEV was between $1.48 billion and $1.6 billion.

The court found the defendant expert's comparables were not sufficiently similar to the subject company. They included DuPont, which was much larger and more diversified; some other diversified companies; and some specialty companies that "typically trade at a higher multiple than commodity chemical companies like [the subject company]." Consequently, his LTM EBITDA was too high, and his BEV was not persuasive.

3. *Comparable transactions.* The plaintiffs' expert identified seven comparable transactions, calculated EBITDA and EBIT for each, and applied the median to the subject company's adjusted LTM September 2005 operating results. Based on this approach, the company's BEV was between $960 million and $1.24 billion, with a midpoint of $1.1 billion.

The defendants' expert used three data sources (Capital IQ, FactSet, and Thomson SDC) to select comparable companies and included a transaction if it involved chemicals, took place during the three years prior to the IPO, and had a value greater than $50 million. The resulting LTM EBITDA multiple was 8.0, which again was significantly higher than the 6.6x the competing expert determined. Applying it to the management projections, he arrived at a BEV of $1.7 billion.

The court noted that the defendant expert's selection process included transactions involving an Indian fertilizer company, a Swiss company that manufactured waterproofing materials and parts for car manufacturers, and a company making foam-related products for diapers and adult incontinence products. Applying the multiple to the "overstated" internal projections added another flaw to the analysis.

Averaging his three BEVs, the plaintiffs' expert arrived at a BEV of $1.03 billion. Adding the value of nonoperating assets, he calculated a total of $1.22 billion. In contrast, the defendants' expert determined the total asset value was $1.81 billion. The court found the latter value "not persuasive."

Only one in-depth liabilities valuation. The second component in the solvency analysis was the amount of debt that the chemical business faced at the time of the IPO. There was little argument over many of the liabilities, including the company's financial debt, tax liabilities, liabilities for discontinued operations, and unfunded retiree liability. Instead, the parties' disagreement concentrated on the amount of environmental and tort liabilities, "which, again, is what this case is all about," said the court. Expert testimony figured prominently in this part of the trial, as well.

The plaintiffs' expert had decades of experience in environmental engineering, site remediation, and cost accounting. He concluded that the present value of the future response costs of environmental remediation at over 2,740 sites related to the parent company's activities was between $1.5 billion and $1.7 billion as of November 2005.

The defendants recruited two experts, but, as the court noted, the latter made it clear that the resulting 8,000-page report was not a comprehensive analysis, just a rebuttal. The final expert report estimated costs to be approximately $376 million.

"It is significant that [the plaintiff expert's] analysis is the only comprehensive valuation in the vast record of this case of [the chemical business's] environmental liabilities," the court said at the outset of its analysis. The defendants' failure to come forward with a comprehensive analysis at any point represented a "major failure of proof."

In keeping with his principle to rely on contemporaneous market information, the defendants' solvency expert "built his solvency analysis around" the findings in Apollo's 2005 environmental study. However, the court found this analysis unreliable because it only considered "known environmental sites," where a third party actually had filed a claim and even the solvency expert admitted on cross-examination that it did not measure the enterprise's "total environmental footprint."

The 2005 "Standard Guide for Disclosure of Environmental Liabilities" described four cost-estimating approaches: expected value, most likely value, range of values, and known minimum values. The plaintiffs' expert used a "most likely value" approach because, he said, he concluded that "the sites were either sufficiently well-developed to conclude that one remedy was likely or information was insufficient to assign reliable probabilities to remedial outcomes."

The defendants contended that the "expected value" approach was a probabilistic approach and the preferred methodology for estimating future environmental costs. The plaintiff expert's approach "fail[ed] to address future uncertainty, particularly the question of whether any environmental response action would be required at a site."

The court found the plaintiffs' expert had used his judgment and reasonably decided to adopt another acceptable methodology. Also, it explained, the object of a solvency analysis was "to assign a 'fair valuation' to all debts, with the term 'debt' defined as a liability on a claim, and 'claim' defined in the 'broadest possible sense' to include contingent, unmatured and unliquidated claims." The resulting solvency analysis often accompanied a bankruptcy filing, "where all debts are accelerated and debtors are obligated to send notice of the requirement of filing a proof of claim to every known potential environmental creditor." Ultimately, the court used the plaintiff expert's lower figure, valuing the environmental liabilities at $1.5 billion.

The value of the chemical company's other liabilities, it said, was not disputed and totaled approximately $803 million. Accordingly, the fair value of its liabilities was nearly $2.1 billion. These findings meant that the chemical business was insolvent as of the IPO/spinoff date "in that its liabilities at a fair valuation exceeded the value of its assets, even if we use Defendants' highest and most aggressive value for the assets," the Bankruptcy Court concluded.

Still awaiting final conclusion. Resolution of the fraudulent conveyance claim did not spell the end of litigation. The Bankruptcy Court recognized the defendants' right under the Bankruptcy Code to pursue claims against the debtors for, among other things, their failure to adhere to the terms of the spinoff generally and the MSA in particular. The defendants argue that damages the debtors owed would offset the damages the debtors were allowed to recover.

Editor's note: The court's discussion of what methodology to use in assessing environmental liabilities brings to mind a session at the November 2013 AICPA that explored the issue of how to deal with uncertainty in a conceptually correct way but did so in a different context: projecting and discounting future lost profits. According to the presenters, only the "expected value" was statistically valid, whereas the "most likely value" might "work by accident" but failed to account for the range of possible outcomes and ignored the possibilities of extreme outcomes.

Vega v. Fulcrum Energy, LLC

Citation: 2013 Tex. App. LEXIS 12323
Date of decision: Oct. 3, 2013
State/Jurisdiction: Texas
Court: Court of Appeals
Type of case: Contract
Experts: Gilbert Herrera (plaintiff); unknown (defendants)
Judge: Huddle
SIC: 4931 Electric and Other Services Combined (other electric power generation)

Expert's Disregard of ASB Guidelines Imperils Valuation

After a partnership dispute arose, the dismissed stakeholder sued, claiming the defendants breached an agreement that required them to buy back his interest, and retained an expert to value the business. Pretrial, the defendants unsuccessfully challenged the expert's valuation for failing to comport with the goodwill requirement in a controlling agreement. The jury adopted the expert's valuation, but the trial court subsequently set the verdict aside, prompting the plaintiff to appeal.

The defendants bought a retail energy business in which the plaintiff owned an interest. As part of the sale, he exchanged his old partnership interest for partnership units in the new company and also entered into an employment agreement. A related contract provided for a buyback of his interest (nearly 2%) if he was terminated without cause, and a provision in the partnership agreement specified that in appraising the interest "no value shall be placed on the goodwill or name of the Partnership." About a year and a half later, the plaintiff was terminated and sued in state district court, initially alleging the dismissal was without cause but subsequently adding a claim that the defendants also had breached the buyback agreement.

A $63 million value gap. The plaintiff retained an expert who used a market approach to estimate the business was worth $98 million. His affidavit stated that his value "did not include a value for the goodwill or name of the Partnership."

The defendants attacked the valuation in a pretrial motion, claiming the business's net, or book, value on the termination date was only $35 million and arguing that the partnership agreement mandated that the plaintiff's interest be calculated according to the book value under the asset approach. The expert's opinion, which sought to introduce evidence as to the overall business value, was inadmissible, they contended.

The court questioned the expert outside the presence of the jury to determine whether he had attributed any value to goodwill. The expert agreed that the company's book value was $35 million, resulting in a $63 million difference between its net worth and his calculation of value. He said that the "Sarbanes-Oxley Act of 2002" required that an appraiser accounted for a company's value in excess of net worth by ascribing value to its different intangible assets; whatever value remained after allocation of all the other intangibles represented the value of a company's goodwill. The expert added that there were guidelines from the Auditing Standard Board (ASB) to carry out the "allocation of intangibles." Even though his own firm had followed the ASB procedure in many cases, he did not do so in this case because not enough information was available to him and it was "a fairly exhaustive process." Since he did not follow the ASB guidelines, he could not say that doing so would have resulted in a $0 (zero) value for goodwill. Regardless, he stated that he had "placed no value on goodwill" and did not believe his $98 million estimate included goodwill; "service businesses don't tend to generate that sort of value in the absence of some intrinsic value," he said. In other words, the company's intangible assets were strong enough to account for "at least a significant part of the $63 million gap." The trial judge denied the defendants' motion and admitted the opinion into evidence.

At trial, the expert explained his methodology to the jury. In a first step, he considered "dispositive" historical transactions that involved the company to determine how much willing buyers and sellers paid for interests in the company. He emphasized that none of these transactions placed a value on goodwill or the name of the partnership.

In a second step, he performed a "confirmatory" analysis with two sets of comparables. The first included publicly traded companies that fell under the same standard industrial classification (SIC) code. The second set included three precedent comparable transactions. He admitted that, in terms of the precedent transactions, two of the three allocated a value to goodwill: Specifically, goodwill accounted for about 13.1% of the total purchase price for the three transactions. But, he claimed, there was no need for an adjustment in his valuation because that 13.1% rate was offset by the fact that the purchase price in the three transactions already reflected a discount to account for the sale of minority interests. At the same time, he noted that, if a goodwill-related adjustment were necessary here, it should be in the amount of no more than $60,000. By his calculation, the plaintiff's 2% interest was worth $1.98 million, he said.

He defined book value as a company's "assets less liabilities on a lower cost of market basis." Under this approach, the company was worth $35 million and the plaintiff's interest $780,000, he stated. But, he added, book value failed to value all of the company's assets and implied a value that was lower than the one the partnership agreement described. The correct value under the contract was market value.

On cross-examination, he admitted that he had done no analysis to explain the makeup of the $63 million valuation gap. But he stated that he did do an analysis to determine whether there was any value of goodwill or the company's trade name and concluded there was no goodwill. Yet, he also admitted that considering his use of three precedent transactions that included some goodwill, his $98 million value had goodwill "embedded."

The jury decided the plaintiff was terminated without cause and accepted his expert's $1.98 million valuation.

In a post-trial motion, the defendants argued the expert's opinion was unreliable. The expert failed to explain the $63 million difference in value ("because he did not do the work") and, therefore, lacked any basis on which to conclude that no portion of the difference represented goodwill. The trial court agreed and set aside the jury's damages finding. Contrary to the partnership agreement, the expert had not applied "the generally accepted method for allocating intangibles" to show his calculation did not contain goodwill. His assertion that there was no goodwill was "the type of *ipse dixit* opinion which is prohibited in the case law," said the court. The testimony could not support the jury's verdict.

In his appeal to the Texas Court of Appeals, the plaintiff argued the trial court's damages ruling was error. For one, the partnership agreement did not require the expert "affirmatively" to assess a value for the company's goodwill and subsequently deduct it from the $98 million enterprise value. All he had to do was state that his valuation did not include goodwill. This he did.

Contradictory goodwill statements. The appellate court agreed that the partnership agreement did not prescribe a method with which to value the interest without adding in goodwill. It merely required that the valuation not include goodwill. But, the court continued, "[t]he relevant question here is not what method is generally accepted or reliable ... but rather, what is a generally accepted and reliable method by which to arrive at the conclusion that one's valuation does not attribute value to goodwill." In this case, the expert identified a generally accepted process—following the ASB guidelines—but decided not to use it. Although this failure to adhere to it was not conclusive as to the reliability of the valuation, the expert failed to show that an alternative method could achieve the same objective.

Specifically, he asserted that the valuation did not include goodwill, but he could not explain the basis for his conclusion. His testimony wavered. First, he asserted that he determined the factors that suggested an existence of goodwill were not present in this case. Next, he said the company's unspecified intangible assets had "significant value," as if to suggest they could have made up the entire $63 million difference leaving nothing for goodwill. Finally, said the court, at trial the expert admitted that the precedent comparable transactions he had selected included goodwill and in response proposed, without doing more, a $60,000 deduction to compensate for any goodwill embedded in his valuation.

For all these reasons, his opinion was unreliable and was not legally sufficient evidence. At the same time, the appellate court refused to issue a take-nothing judgment for the defendants. The parties had agreed that the company had a book value of $35 million, and the plaintiff's expert had testified that, using that value, the plaintiff's interest was worth $780,000. Therefore, there was evidence to support some damages. Because liability also was a contested issue, the appellate court reversed and ordered a new trial on all issues.

VirnetX, Inc. v. Cisco Systems, Inc. (VirnetX v. Apple)

Citation: 2014 U.S. LEXIS 17748
Date of decision: Sept. 16, 2014
Experts: Roy Weinstein (plaintiff); unknown (defendant)
Judge: Prost (Chief Judge as of May 2014)
State/Jurisdiction: Federal
Court: United States Court of Appeals for the Federal Circuit
Type of case: Intellectual Property
SIC code: 4899 Communications Services N.E.C.

EMVR Must Not Swallow Apportionment, Federal Circuit Says

In appealing a $368 million jury verdict to the U.S. Court of Appeals for the Federal Circuit, Apple succeeded in eviscerating the various reasonable royalty calculations VirnetX's expert performed. The Federal Circuit's ruling explains what the limitations of the smallest salable unit approach are and why the court rejects the Nash bargaining solution.

In spring 2010, VirnetX Inc. sued multiple leading technology companies in federal district court (E.D. Tex.), including Cisco and Apple, alleging infringement of several patents related to creating secure protocols for virtual private networks. The court severed the cases. In the Apple suit, VirnetX claimed that Apple's FaceTime and VPN On Demand products violated four of the plaintiff's patents. Apple servers run FaceTime on iOS devices such as the iPhone, iPod, and iPad and on Mac computers. FaceTime allows secure video calling between select Apple devices. VPN

On Demand is a feature in the iPhone, iPad, and iPod Touch and allows users to establish secure virtual private networks.

Three reasonable royalty theories. In fall 2012, a jury trial took place at which VirnetX presented expert damages testimony. The expert offered three reasonable royalty theories to which Apple unsuccessfully objected under *Daubert.*

Under the first approach, for the royalty base, the expert used the lowest sales price of each model of the iOS devices containing the infringing components, ranging from $199 for the iPod Touch to $649 for the iPhone 4S. He only excluded costs for additional memory for which Apple charged extra. But for the use of FaceTime on Mac computers he determined a royalty base of $29, which was the cost of the software upgrade. Since Apple does not charge separately for FaceTime on other iOS products, he said he could not use a lower figure for them. He then applied a 1% royalty rate to the base relying on six comparable licenses, as well as VirnetX's policy of licensing its patents for 1% to 2% of the entire value of products sold. Damages under this approach amounted to $708 million: $566 million for products featuring FaceTime and VPN On Demand and $142 million for products featuring only VPN On Demand.

Under a second approach, the expert calculated damages for FaceTime alone relying on the Nash bargaining solution. NBS is a mathematical theorem that has received mixed reviews in patent cases. In essence, the model claims there is a mutually beneficial outcome for a two-party bargaining scenario. "After identifying the profits each party could expect without a deal and the surplus created by their cooperation, the Nash model allocates the value of the deal in two steps: each party first receives the same profits it could expect without a deal, and then the remaining surplus is divided evenly between them." See *Oracle America, Inc. v. Google Inc.*, 798 F. Supp. 2d 1111 (N.D. Cal. July 22, 2011)

VirnetX's expert claimed that the parties would split the incremental or additional profits stemming from the use of FaceTime. He used the front-facing camera on Apple's mobile devices as a proxy for the FaceTime feature to calculate the incremental profits that he thought were attributable to the addition of the camera feature. Invoking NBS, he first assumed the parties would split the additional profits 50-50 but decided to adjust the split by 10% based on "the relative bargaining power of the two entities." VirnetX, he assumed, would have received only 45% and Apple would have received 55% because VirnetX was in a weaker bargaining position in 2009. This approach yielded $588 million in damages for infringement related to FaceTime.

Under a third approach that also relied on NBS, the expert claimed that FaceTime "drove sales" for Apple iOS products. He drew on a customer survey to assert that 18% of iOS device sales would not have occurred but for the inclusion of FaceTime, Based on that figure, he determined the amount of Apple's profits that he believed were attributable to the FaceTime feature and again apportioned 45% of the profits to VirnetX. He arrived at damages of $5.13 per unit, for a total of $606 million in damages related to FaceTime.

The jury found Apple liable and awarded VirnetX approximately $368 million in reasonable royalty damages. In February 2013, the district court denied Apple's post-trial motions and upheld the award.

Erroneous jury instruction. Apple subsequently appealed the verdict, most importantly the damages aspect. It attacked both the district court's jury instruction on the applicable law related to the entire market value rule (EMVR) and the calculations VirnetX's expert performed.

(a) *Smallest salable unit.* At issue was the district court's instructing the jury not to use the entire market value rule (EMVR) unless either:

> (1) the patented feature creates the basis for the customers' demand for the product, or the patented feature substantially creates the value of the other component parts of the product; or (2) the product in question constitutes the smallest saleable unit containing the patented feature.

Apple claimed the instruction effectively allowed the patent holder to use the entire value of a multicomponent product as long as that product was the smallest salable unit containing the patented feature. Whereas under the controlling case law EMVR is the exception, the court's instruction created another—smallest salable unit—exception, Apple contended.

The Federal Circuit sided with Apple. According to the court, the purpose behind the smallest salable unit concept is to determine a royalty base that is much more closely related to the claimed invention than the entire value of an accused product, the court explained. Determining the smallest salable unit is only a step toward meeting the apportionment requirement. However difficult, when the smallest salable unit is a multicomponent product that has numerous noninfringing features that have no relation to the patented feature, the patent holder must attempt to identify the portion of value that is attributable to the patented feature. Under the district court's jury instruction, VirnetX's expert could simply claim the iOS devices were the smallest salable unit. The instruction was legally erroneous, the Federal Circuit said. "To hold otherwise would permit the entire market value exception to swallow the rule of apportionment."

(b) *Expert's royalty base.* In a related argument, Apple claimed the district court abused its discretion when it admitted the expert's royalty base. He used the entire market value of Apple's products without establishing that the protected components drove customer demand.

In defense of the expert's approach, VirnetX said that "software creates the largest share of the product's value" for the iOS products. The court dismissed that argument. The expert did not even attempt to subtract the value of unpatented elements—touchscreen, camera, processor, speaker—to which VirnetX "indisputably" had no claim, the court pointed out. Also, he failed to separate software from hardware, "much less to separate the FaceTime software from other valuable software components." Use of the software upgrade cost, $29, as the royalty base for FaceTime on Mac computers proves that the expert could have apportioned a smaller unit figure for the component.

The court dismissed the expert's statement that Apple did not charge separately for FaceTime on the iOS devices as an attempt to hide behind Apple's sales model to avoid the task of apportionment. Precedent is clear that there is no "necessity-based exception to the entire market value rule." The court found that the district court should have used its gatekeeping role "to ensure that only theories comporting with settled principles of apportionment were allowed to reach the jury."

(c) *Expert's royalty rate.* Apple also contested the expert's royalty rate. It was inadmissible because the expert relied on dissimilar comparable licenses, Apple claimed. Two of the licenses predated the patents in suit; three of the remaining four licenses came into being three years after a hypothetical negotiation between the parties would have taken place. By then, VirnetX was in a much better bargaining situation than it was in 2009, Apple said. The remaining, sixth, license covered 68 VirnetX patents, whereas a license with Apple would have covered only four patents. Scaled to size, the royalty rate equated to 0.24%, in contrast to the 1%-to-2% rate the expert applied.

This argument had no traction with the Federal Circuit. Four of the licenses related to the actual patents in suit and two of them covered related technology, the court found. Also, the jury heard about the alleged dissimilarities and was able to evaluate them. "No more is required in these circumstances."

(d) *Nash bargaining solution.* Apple's objection to the expert's second and third approaches focused on invocation of the Nash model. It claimed that using a 50-50 split as the starting point for calculating damages due to VirnetX was akin to using the 25% rule of thumb that the Federal Circuit soundly rejected in *Uniloc* because it insufficiently tied to the facts of the case.

The court agreed with Apple. It explained that in recent years various courts have confronted experts who invoked NBS in determining reasonable royalty damages. The courts' reactions have been mixed. The Federal Circuit said it aligned itself with courts that rejected the use of NBS where the expert failed to establish that the facts of the case—the real world—fit the model's premises. Here the expert did not show the fit. His "thin" attempts to adjust the 50-50 split to the real world by way of a 10% deviation could not save a flawed methodology.

The court dismissed the expert's statements that a 45-55 split adequately accounted for Apple's greater bargaining power as "conclusory assertions" and proof "how this methodology is subject to abuse." More importantly, the court said, even if the expert could explain the deviation from the 50-50 split, the method was defective because it ran the risk of "inappropriately skewing the jury's verdict." Using an inappropriate 50-50 starting point "provides a baseline from which juries might hesitate to stray, even if the evidence supported a radically different split."

For all these reasons, the Federal Circuit struck down the $368 million award against Apple and remanded for further proceedings in line with its ruling.

Editor's note: A digest of the related VirnetX suit against Cisco, *VirnetX Inc. v. Cisco Systems, Inc.*, 2013 U.S. Dist. LEXIS 28223 (March 1, 2013), as well as the district court's opinion, is available at *BVLaw*. Digests and court opinions of the other cases mentioned above are also at *BVLaw*.

Vision-Park Properties v. Seaside Engineering

Citation: 2014 U.S. Dist. LEXIS 41923
Date of decision: March 27, 2014
Experts: John Reuben Bice (appellants); Robert McCullar (debtor)
Judge: Walker
State/Jurisdiction: Federal/Florida
Court: United States District Court
Type of case: Bankruptcy
SIC code: 8713 Surveying Services

Debtor's Challenges Justify Bankruptcy Court's Emergence Risk Premium

In appealing the Bankruptcy Court's plan confirmation, the appellants took particular issue with the court's rejection of their expert's valuation of the debtor company. In their opinion, the court overrated certain risk factors surrounding the debtor and as a result determined an improperly low value. Ultimately, the discussion boiled down to the applicable discount rate.

The debtor was a small, closely held engineering and surveying company that specialized in hydrographic surveying and navigational mapping—a niche business. Based on their unique mapping and people skills, the company's five principal shareholders established a special rapport with the U.S. Army Corps of Engineers. Eventually, 90% of the company's revenues came from projects for the Corps. Because the government contracts were qualification contracts, not awards based on the lowest bid, the principals' experience was critical to securing the contracts and to the company's survival.

The company historically maintained three months' worth of operating capital on hand, but its financial situation devolved as a result of the economic downturn in late 2000, a change in its way of doing business, and the principal shareholders' unsuccessful real estate ventures. The ventures received funding from the appellants in the case, and the shareholders guaranteed the debt. Once the company and the individual shareholders filed for bankruptcy, the appellants acquired an equity interest in the company.

The debtor succeeded in obtaining approval from the Bankruptcy Court of its reorganization plan, which envisioned keeping its structure as a small business—and not allowing the appellants to acquire a majority interest in it—and continuing to employ all of its 23 workers. The Bankruptcy Court's approval turned on its valuation of the debtor.

'Way understated' discount rate. The Bankruptcy Court considered valuation testimony from the appellants' expert and a rebuttal opinion from the debtor's expert.

The appellants' expert valued the company under the going concern standard, using an income approach. He considered "the earning capacity of the business" and used "a discount rate that is reflective of the risk associated with the business [which] determines what the value of a future stream of income would be utilizing such a discount rate." He arrived at a "build-up" discount rate of 18.44%, allocating only 1.5% of it to the company-specific risk. He did not believe the departure of any one of the five principal employees would seriously affect the company's ability to preserve its contracts with the Corps. He concluded that the debtor was worth $960,000.

When testifying on direct, the debtor's expert advanced a liquidation analysis, which showed a negative $628,000 value. The appellants objected, and the Bankruptcy Court rejected that analysis as inappropriate. Consequently, the debtor's expert critiqued the appellant expert's opinion, particularly the latter's selected discount rate. That element, he said, was perhaps the most subjective factor of the analysis and critical because "just a few tweaks in the discount rate that is used can make a huge difference in the valuation that you end up with." By way of example, he explained that increasing the 18.44% rate used by the rival expert by just seven points would reduce the value of the company from $960,000 to $575,460.

He called the 18.44% rate "way understated" and said the company-specific risk in this case was "major." In his view, the appellants' expert "failed to separate the value of the business from the value of the professional owners of the business." The opposing expert did not adequately appreciate the debtor's difficulty of replacing key personnel given the principals' unique technical skills. The rebuttal expert believed the company would "not have the resources to withstand any sort of interruption of its services and to go through the process of finding key personnel."

Also, he said his review of the debtor's financial statements revealed an $80,000 liability for back wages and taxes to its employees that the appellants' expert had not considered. He projected a loss of approximately a quarter million for the most recent year, whereas the appellants' expert only recorded a loss of $57,000. According to the rebuttal expert, a financial analysis should account for a loss of that magnitude for the most recent year when the company historically had operating profits.

He noted that one of the authorities the rivaling expert used to support his analysis had proposed an 80% discount rate for a company in financial distress. Were he asked to state an applicable rate for this case, he would say it should be in the range from 40% to 75%.

Bankruptcy Court homes in on 'willing buyer.' The Bankruptcy Court noted that there were "two different experts talking about what each of them viewed as a discount rate" and acknowledged the impact of the discount rate on the valuation number. The court found it "extraordinary" that the value the appellants' expert had computed was only $40,000 less than the value the principals had placed on the company several years earlier, in 2008, 2009, and 2010. Yet, in 2011, the record showed a loss of almost $240,000. This factor indicated that the expert failed to give adequate consideration to the fact that the company was in bankruptcy—which "not only affected their value, it affected their credit rating, borrowing power and potential for obtaining new business," said the court.

It also emphasized that there were considerable other risk factors that a willing buyer would weigh in assessing the company. These related to the key role the principal shareholders played in dealing with the Corps and the company's deriving 90% of its revenues from contracts with the Corps. In the court's view, "if you don't have the employees and you don't have the contracts, what have you got left?"

Ultimately, the Bankruptcy Court arrived at a value of $200,000, without identifying the discount rate it applied or specifying the adjustments it made to the appellant expert's valuation. Based on its valuation, the court approved the debtor's reorganization plan.

No undue focus on risk factors. The appellants appealed the decision at the district court (N.D. Fl.), spotlighting the valuation issue. They alleged a host of errors resulting in the Bankruptcy Court's undervaluation of the company and its erroneous approval of the plan.

First, the appellants contended that the Bankruptcy Court's focus on the risk of losing certain key employees meant it valued something other than the entity that was featured in the plan, which contemplated retention of all employees.

The district court disagreed. The Bankruptcy Court simply took note of the unique circumstances in the case: The value of the company depended on "the human capital of a small number of employees with a unique skill set and a relationship with the U.S. Army Corps of Engineers." In this case, the district court added, the company's value did not lie in tangible assets. To consider the risks arising from the nature of the company did not mean the Bankruptcy Court "valued something other than the plan proposed."

Second, the appellants claimed the Bankruptcy Court was wrong to reject the only competent going-concern value—their expert's $960,000 valuation—in front of the court. They suggested that, since the court did not articulate its adjustments, it "effectively pulled a number out of thin air or merely split the difference between the two experts' valuation figures."

This argument also got no traction with the district court. "The Bankruptcy Court was free to accept the testimony of any witness, including an expert witness, in whole or in part." Here, it rejected the liquidation analysis that the debtor's expert proposed. At the same time, it relied on evidence discrediting the valuation that the appellants' expert advanced and particularly his discount rate. The district court found the rebuttal expert's testimony about the drastic effects of a change in discount rate on the overall valuation was particularly relevant. Using a discount rate in the suggested range of 40% to 75% "would produce results as reached by the Bankruptcy Court or a lesser value." Therefore, the Bankruptcy Court's valuation had support in the record.

Three, the appellants objected that the Bankruptcy Court's focus on a prospective buyer's concern over the alleged risks of a company coming out of bankruptcy reflected a market analysis and its attendant undervaluation of the company.

The district court found this claim unconvincing as well. The Bankruptcy Court's observation about the appellant expert's failure to consider the effects of bankruptcy did not mean it valued the company "strictly on a market analysis," rather it was analogous to the court's applying an emergence risk premium to reflect the challenges the company faced as it emerged from bankruptcy.

For all these reasons, the district court upheld the Bankruptcy Court's valuation and its confirmation of the reorganization plan.

Volterra Semiconductor Corp. v. Primarion, Inc.

Citation: 2013 U.S. Dist. LEXIS 163970
Date of decision: Sept. 24, 2013
Experts: Michael J. Wagner (Expert 1); Dr. Christine Siegwarth Meyer (Expert 2) (plaintiff); Dr. Matthew R. Lynde (defendants)
Judge: Spero
Country: US
State/Jurisdiction: Federal/California
Court: United States District Court
Type of case: Intellectual Property
SIC: 3674 Semiconductors and Related Devices

Expert's 'Dollar-for-Dollar' Damages Theory Short of Factual Support

In a patent infringement suit, the plaintiff by way of expert testimony advanced a unique price erosion theory under which it sought damages to the U.S. parent company based in part on lost revenues related to sales its foreign subsidiary made outside the United States. In a pretrial motion, the defendants attacked both the damages theory and calculations. The plaintiff failed to show a causal link between the price reduction that allegedly resulted in economic injury and any domestic misconduct by the defendants, and neither of its two experts gave an opinion that was admissible under *Daubert*, they said.

The plaintiff was a "fabless" semiconductor company that designed and manufactured mixed-signal integrated circuits used in power management applications. "Fabless" means that a company outsources the fabrication of the devices to a foundry abroad, i.e., China, because of lower labor costs. Similarly, the defendants designed, manufactured, and marketed digital power integrated circuits for computing, graphics, and communication applications. The plaintiff alleged infringement (N.D. Cal.) of two of its patents and obtained a jury verdict in its favor on liability. The case originally was headed toward a trial on damages in November 2013.

Defendants forced plaintiff to cut prices. The plaintiff maintained it sustained damages because the defendants took steps to obtain design wins with IBM and HP as to specific power switch products that compelled the plaintiff to lower its prices to stay competitive. The defendants' efforts included testing their infringing products at their U.S. facilities and meeting with IBM and HP representatives at numerous locations in the U.S. to persuade them of the superior performance and price of their products. These actions caused the plaintiff to lose revenue related to its own sales to the two clients and to sales that the plaintiff's wholly owned Asian subsidiary made. (The plaintiff was the sole owner of a third, international, entity that was the sole owner of the Asian subsidiary.)

To quantify the losses, the plaintiff retained two damages experts. Expert 1 first determined whether there was price erosion after a specified date and, if so, how much in additional revenue the plaintiff and its Asian subsidiary each would have made "but for" the price erosion that the defendants' infringing conduct caused. He reconstructed a hypothetical market that would have existed but for the infringement, considering "all the factors that could reasonably be expected to have influenced the pricing for [the plaintiff's] products, including general and economic and market factors and the nature of competition from discrete manufacturers." He also conducted an analysis of elasticity of demand. He concluded that the plaintiff could have received an additional $99.34 million in lost revenue (including projections as to future lost revenue). He attributed nearly $12,300 to price erosion related to the plaintiff's direct sales to IBM and HP and the remainder to sales the Asian subsidiary made to those clients.

Expert 2 addressed a different issue. She determined whether the plaintiff suffered any economic harm because of the effects of price erosion on past sales and anticipated future sales by the Asian subsidiary and, if so, what the amount of appropriate compensation should be. She relied on the first expert's report as to the amount of lost profits. In her view, the plaintiff sustained injury because of the lost value of its assets. Had the defendants not caused price erosion, the plaintiff's assets—i.e., the Asian subsidiary and the international entity that owned it—would have had more cash and would have been worth more. This increase in cash and value would have put the plaintiff in a significantly better economic and financial position, the expert stated.

She set down three hypotheticals to illustrate her conclusion. First, if the plaintiff wanted to sell both or one of the assets to a third party, it would "likely" obtain a much higher sales price. Second, the plaintiff would be able to use the additional cash to invest in or acquire other entities. Third, it could declare dividends to itself from the subsidiaries stemming from the additional cash. Whether the plaintiff in fact would have availed itself of the options was "irrelevant," the expert said. "Simply being deprived of these options constitutes a form of economic harm." She did not perform a valuation of the subsidiaries but concluded that the harm to the plaintiff equaled dollar-for-dollar the amount the offshore subsidiaries lost.

The defendants retained their own expert to respond to the plaintiff's price erosion theory and the corresponding testimony from Expert 1. According to the rebuttal expert, many factors other than the defendants' conduct prompted the plaintiff's price reductions. These included the worldwide recession, "cost pressures from customers and constant standard price drops expected in the industry," a need to compete with noninfringing alternatives, the plaintiff's desire to expand market share, and its decision to replace existing products with ones that cost less to manufacture and had more features. He based his conclusion as to causation on a review of select documents he had obtained from counsel. At times, he expressly questioned the credibility of the plaintiff's witnesses, noting, for example, that documents did not support a witness's testimony or ran counter to what he, the expert, had seen in the record. He did not do a hypothetical reconstruction of the market to determine the profit from sales that would have taken place but for the infringement.

Twofold attack on damages theory. In pretrial motions, both sides argued for exclusion of the expert testimony under *Daubert*. The defendants contended that the testimony by the plaintiff's Expert 1 on price erosion was inadmissible because he failed to consider other market factors to account for the price reduction, "cherry-picked" data to increase the amount of damages, and did not conduct the required elasticity analysis. For her part, Expert 2 made legal conclusions as to direct harm that were unjustified and that she was not qualified to offer; moreover, her valuation did not accord with widely accepted economic principles.

The plaintiff, meanwhile, claimed the defendant expert's opinion was unreliable because he failed to reconstruct the market to show hypothetically the lost profits. He unlawfully commented on the plaintiff's "motivations" in discussing what caused the decrease in prices and on the credibility of the plaintiff's witnesses. He "subjectively interpreted" the plaintiff's documents and deposition testimony and improperly spoke to the thinking of corporations and customers, instead of performing an economic analysis.

Moreover, the defendants claimed the plaintiff's price erosion theory was not sustainable as a matter of law for a number of reasons. The plaintiff was trying to capture damages for injuries to separate corporate entities. To the extent it claimed injury to itself, it had to rely on the scenarios Expert 2 developed, which were speculation, as she herself admitted. Most importantly, the plaintiff was unable to show the necessary link between the claimed price erosion, causing lost revenues, and "any domestic infringing acts by Defendants." The latter sold only $2,500 worth of infringing products in the U.S. and the plaintiff could not point to a single domestic sale that compelled it to lower its pricing in response.

The plaintiff responded that Expert 2's theory was not exactly a lost profits theory but addressed the lost value of assets. Also, by the time the court heard the motions, the plaintiff said it in effect had received a third-party offer to buy the parent company and the subsidiaries. Further, under its theory of causation, prices had to come down, not because the defendants sold infringing products that competed directly with the plaintiff's devices, but because actions vis-à-vis IBM and HP forced the plaintiff and its Asian subsidiary to lower prices. This conduct took place in the U.S.

Missing causal link? Before ruling on *Daubert*, the court discussed the challenges to the plaintiff's damages theory. A patentee generally tries to fit its case into the lost profits framework or else seeks a reasonable royalty under the statute, the court said at the outset. To qualify for lost profits, the plaintiff must show there is a reasonable probability that "but for" the defendant's infringing actions it would have made the sales that it lost to the infringer and that the lost profits were reasonably foreseeable. Also, under Federal Circuit precedent, a patentee corporation cannot claim lost profits of a related corporation even if both entities share an interest in the manufacture of the invention.

This, said the court, is precisely what the plaintiff was attempting to do by relying on the opinion of Expert 2. As she would have it, the harm to the plaintiff aligned dollar for dollar with the decrease in cash its asset entities had as a result of the infringement. This view of harm, the court concluded, was indistinguishable from an impermissible claim for the lost profits of a subsidiary.

What's more, the damages were speculative. The plaintiff's point about a tender offer to buy was untimely. Other evidence showed it was unlikely for any of Expert 2's hypotheticals to turn into real possibilities. In discovery, the plaintiff had admitted its international entity had not declared a dividend during the damages period. It also stated it "never attempted to market, advertise, or otherwise sell its shares of the international entity." Its Form 10-K stated that "[a]s of December 31, 2012, the cash and short-term investments held by our foreign subsidiaries was approximately

$72.1 million." Assuming "these funds were repatriated to the U.S., under current tax law we could be required to accrue and pay U.S. taxes on a portion of these funds," and "[o]ur current plan is to permanently reinvest these funds outside the U.S." For all these reasons, the plaintiff could not recover damages based on relying on the theory Expert 2 advanced.

At the same time, the court refused to dismiss entirely the plaintiff's claim to damages related to its foreign subsidiary's sales. Contrary to the defendants' arguments, the plaintiff was able to show that the infringing acts took place in the U.S., and there was no legal requirement that lost profits were only available if the plaintiff could show price erosion was the result of direct competition with the defendant.

The court next moved to the *Daubert* challenges and found another basis on which to exclude Expert 2's opinion. Her approach to valuation was not based on accepted economic principles. She failed to cite any scientific authority that supported her valuing the parent's harm on a dollar-for-dollar basis.

At the same time, the court determined that there was no reason to exclude the damages calculation that Expert 1 offered. He reconstructed the market and properly addressed the prices and sales that would have occurred in this hypothetical market focusing on the specific IBM and HP server projects. He considered other factors operating on pricing; his reaching a different conclusion than the defendants' expert did not justify exclusion of his opinion under *Daubert*. Contrary to the defendants' claim, he also performed the legally mandated analysis of elasticity of demand.

Finally, the court admitted most of the testimony the defendants' expert gave. It recognized that when it came to an expert's addressing the many factors that prompted the plaintiff to reduce its prices, there was a blurred line between causation and subjective intent. The plaintiff was correct in arguing that an expert must not discuss the subjective intent of a corporation or an individual. But, said the court, the rule did not prohibit him from opining on causation. At the same time, the plaintiff's claim that the expert impermissibly had commented on the credibility of witnesses had weight. "It is well-established that an expert may not invade the province of the jury by testifying about the credibility of witnesses." Therefore, on direct examination, the expert could not express an opinion that suggested the plaintiff's witnesses were not credible; however, on cross-examination, he would be able to explain his reasons for doubting the testimony of a witness if the plaintiff "opened the door."

Editor's Note: Following the court's pretrial ruling, there was no trial on damages.

Ward v. Ward

Citation: 2014 W. Va. LEXIS 128
Date of decision: Feb. 14, 2014
Experts: Ross Dionne (wife); Dan Selby (husband)
Judge: Per Curiam
State/Jurisdiction: West Virginia
Court: Supreme Court of Appeals
Type of case: Marital Dissolution
SIC code: 0811 Timber Tracts

Court Pans Valuation Based on Expert's Fiction, Not Fact

In a divorce case, the husband appealed to the state's highest court, arguing that the lower courts accepted a valuation of his business interest that did not reflect the company as it was on the valuation date. Rather, he said, the valuation was set by the wife's expert to increase its value and, thus, the wife's award.

The husband owned a 25% interest in three businesses. While he and the wife agreed to the value of two, they vigorously contested the value of his stake in the third company, which managed a 625,000-acre timber tract for a single client and which had four owner-managers in all. At trial, both sides presented expert testimony from CPAs who also were certified valuation analysts. Both experts agreed to use the capitalization of earnings method to assess the business's fair market value and also agreed that this method allowed for normalizing officer compensation where compensation was excessive.

Experts differ on need to normalize. The wife's expert explained that "normalization" of income served to "add back to the income of the company expenses that are discretionary to the owner and not reasonably necessary for operation." The point was that in a sale the buyer would ask: "Okay, what would we have to pay somebody to run this operation for us?" the expert added. He determined that the company paid the four owners a total of over $388,400 in 2008 and nearly $394,000 in 2009. The national average for officers and directors of corporations in the timber industry was between 1% and 5.2% of net sales, he said. This amounted to between $20,000 and $115,000 per year. Moreover, he found that, in West Virginia, average compensation for that type of position was just under $70,000 per year. He decided, "for purposes of valuing this company, that the four owners could step aside and somebody for $120,000 a year could drive this company." Making this adjustment, the company's actual expenses for officer compensation dropped and its net profits rose. The expert concluded that the husband's minority interest was worth $310,000.

As for goodwill, without interviewing any of the company's officers, he accepted as fact that the company basically had one customer. Therefore, he concluded that whether the husband left the business did not affect the work the company did or was able to do. For this reason, he did not adjust for personal goodwill in his valuation.

The husband's expert found that there was no need to normalize compensation since it was not excessive. The husband's 25% interest was worth just over $114,000. At the same time, the expert adjusted for personal goodwill based on his interview with the company's president. The latter explained that the husband maintained significant personal relationships with loggers working for the company and possessed a degree of personal integrity that created valuable rapport with the government regulators who scrutinized the company's operations. If the company lost the husband, it would lose loggers and a degree of ease and efficiency in dealing with the regulators. As a result, the husband's expert used a 33 1/3% "personal" goodwill discount to reduce the husband's interest from $114,000 to $76,000.

The family court (trial court) adopted the value that the wife's expert had proposed—$310,000—but reduced it by the one-third personal goodwill discount that the husband's expert determined. Accordingly, it found the husband's share was worth about $207,000, half of which belonged to the wife.

Both parties appealed to the circuit court: the husband to contest the family court's valuation and the wife to claim error as to its finding on personal goodwill. The circuit court affirmed both aspects of the decision.

Unjustified compensation decrease. Next, the parties appealed to the state's high court for review. The husband argued that both lower courts failed to value the business as it existed at the date of separation, that is, as a company owned and run by four individuals, all of whom received income from it. Instead, the courts accepted the fiction that the wife's expert created: that one executive forester being paid $120,000 per year could replace the four owners. The wife responded that the family court had discretion to adjust officer compensation in determining the fair market value.

For her part, the wife claimed that the lower courts erred when they adopted the personal goodwill discount that the husband's expert proposed.

The Supreme Court considered the parties' claims in turn. As for the valuation, it agreed with the husband. The wife's expert did not simply use the acceptable capitalization of earnings method. Rather, he transformed the business from one run by four people to one managed by one person; this fiction greatly decreased its compensation expense and greatly increased its profitability. True, the wife's expert could have adjusted the owners' compensation if it exceeded the national and state average compensation for the same work, but that is not what he did. Rather, said the high court, "he valued a hypothetical business that did not and does not exist." In approving of his valuation, both lower courts abused their discretion. Therefore, the Supreme Court remanded.

As for the valuation, the high court dismissed the wife's argument. It found that the husband proved that the business would lose one-third of its revenue if he left the company. Therefore, it was not error for the family court to discount the husband's interest based on personal goodwill and for the circuit court to affirm the goodwill adjustment.

Washington Mutual, Inc. v. United States

Citation: 2014 U.S. Dist. LEXIS 17553
Date of decision: Feb. 10, 2014
Experts: Roger Grabowski (plaintiff/taxpayer); Steven Mann (defendant/government)
Judge: Rothstein
State/Jurisdiction: Federal/Washington
Court: U.S. District Court
Type of case: Federal Taxation
SIC code: 6035 Federal Saving Institutions

DCF Model Proves Unreliable Tool for Ascertaining Cost Basis

In a case arising out of the savings and loan debacle, the successor-in-interest to a "healthy" thrift that agreed to take over a number of failing ones sued the government for a tax refund based on tax deductions and losses for certain intangible assets, specifically branching and RAP rights. The case hinged on whether the plaintiff could establish a cost basis for those rights. The plaintiff turned to a leading valuation expert who used an income approach to determine the fair market value of a specific group of branching rights. The government's expert attacked the valuation model's key assumptions and also tried to undercut its validity with a market analysis.

Another outgrowth of the S&L crisis. This case, said the court in its introduction, was yet another chapter in the "continuing saga that has its genesis in the savings and loan crisis of the late 1970's to early 1980's." In late 1981, a "healthy" Southern California thrift agreed to a supervisory merger with three failing thrifts: Two of them were in Missouri and one in Florida. Under the transaction terms, the acquirer assumed the liabilities of the failing institutions in return for a set of incentives from the government, including cash contributions, indemnities related to covered assets, and other payments that went through a special reserve account. Moreover, it received branching rights in Missouri and Florida. And it received the RAP right, meaning it was permitted to count the excess of the failing thrifts' liabilities over their assets as "supervisory goodwill" and apply it to its minimum regulatory capital requirement. Finally, it was able to structure the transaction as a tax-free "G" reorganization such that it could carry over the tax basis of the acquired assets and realize substantial built-in losses by selling the loans of the acquired thrifts.

In 1998, Washington Mutual (WaMu) acquired the healthy thrift and subsequently filed an amended income tax return claiming refunds for 1990, 1992, and 1993 related to the thrift's branching and RAP rights. After the Internal Revenue Service denied the requests, WaMu sued in federal court (W.D. Wash.) There, the government argued that the claim failed as a matter of law because WaMu was unable to show that the thrift had a tax basis in the rights. The court agreed, which triggered the plaintiff's appeal with the 9th Circuit. The Court of Appeals "return[ed] to the very basics of tax law" and began by defining the term "basis," which was "a taxpayer's capital stake in an asset for tax purposes." Here, the branching and RAP rights were part of the consideration the thrift received in exchange for taking over the three failing thrifts. The cost to the acquiring thrift "was the excess of the three failing thrifts' liabilities over the value of their assets." The 9th Circuit found the thrift's cost basis in the branching and RAP rights was "equal to *some part* of the total amount of that excess liability." (emphasis in original)

After the Court of Appeals found the plaintiff, in theory, had a cost basis, it sent the case back to the district court where the plaintiff had to show with reasonable certainty what the cost basis was before qualifying for any refund. To determine how much the thrift paid for the incentive package, the plaintiff had to ascertain: (1) the total value of the three failing thrifts' liabilities; and (2) the total value of their assets. As the district court put it: "While one may expect that this calculation would be straightforward (at least relatively speaking), the parties dispute each variable in the calculation."

The plaintiff claimed that the purchase price did not represent the fair market value (FMV) of the incentive package the thrift received as part of the supervisory merger. This claim, the district court emphasized, meant the plaintiff conceded that the value of the incentive package was *more* that its purchase price. It explained that, under case law, where one lump sum buys a conglomeration of assets, the plaintiff had to determine the cost of each asset "by apportioning the purchase price among the assets according to each asset's relative fair market value at the time of the acquisition." If the plaintiff was unable to establish the FMV of one of the assets in the package, it would be impossible to calculate the package's total FMV and by extension to determine the pro rate share of each asset, the court went on to say.

At trial the focus was on valuing the Missouri branching right. The plaintiff presented expert testimony as to its fair market value to a hypothetical buyer; the government offered an expert to critique the valuation and present a counteranalysis.

Five-step analysis to determine excess earnings. The plaintiff's valuation expert used an income approach and specifically "a discounted cash flow model known as the 'excess earnings' approach." He determined the excess earnings or cash flows a hypothetical buyer would expect from the branching right beginning in late 1981, excluding charges for the use of contributory assets, and discounted to present value by performing a five-step analysis. The steps include:

Step 1. Determine the projected net operating income for the Missouri branching right by projecting the Missouri deposit market growth rate and calculating the hypothetical buyer's expected share of that market. The expert projected Missouri's new deposit market would increase 47% in 1982, 39% in 1983, 32.3% in 1984, 26.5% in 1985, and 21.85% in 1986. He suggested the increase was due to inflation, which meant there was no actual growth in real-dollar terms. He described the hypothetical buyer as a "well-capitalized thrift" that would take control of part of the market by advertising and offering new products and a sense of "safety."

Because thrifts at the relevant time were not allowed to operate branches outside their home market, the expert drew on the acquiring thrift's actual expansion into Northern California in the 1970s to predict what the hypothetical buyer could expect to accomplish. With its headquarters in Southern California, the thrift originally was limited to opening branches within 100 miles of there. The expert believed Northern California was a new market in the way Missouri would be a new market for the hypothetical buyer. He concluded that the buyer would capture a market share equal to the institution's capture of 7% of the Northern California market after 10 years.

He also assumed that the buyer would use all the new deposits to originate new adjustable rate loan mortgages (ARMS). He assumed interest rates would remain flat but did not believe this would prevent the hypothetical buyer from generating new loans because ARMS would be attractive to consumers. He acknowledged that the rate could "impact" the "deposit market" and "tone down the amount that was available for new loans."

To project the "spread" the buyer would make on the new mortgage loans, he calculated the difference between the interest charged on the mortgage loans and the cost to the thrift for obtaining and processing the deposits. He assumed the buyer would obtain deposits from Missouri (it's less expensive than getting them from California) and make ARMS in California to achieve "a little bit more than the contract spread." From the cost of funds in San Francisco and Des Moines, Iowa, in 1981, he assumed a spread of between 2.25% and 2.75%. He adopted a midrange of 2.5% and arrived at net revenues of nearly $2.8 million.

Step 2. Determine the projected net income of the right. He determined that the tax rate applicable to the incremental income would be 36% and subtracted the corresponding amount from the operating income.

Step 3. Determine the cash flow attributable to the branching right. To isolate the cash flow, he separated income that was attributable to assets from the acquired thrifts. For this purpose, he subtracted capital charges from the projected income.

Step 4. Determine the value of the branching right prior to adjustments. Acknowledging that developing projections was a "risky business," the plaintiff's expert used a 22% discount rate to compute the present value of the right. He then calculated the residual period cash flow and converted it to present value, concluding it was $37 million before adjustments. He considered this figure conservative.

Step 5. Determine the FMV of the branching right. Recognizing that a hypothetical buyer had to make two "upfront investments" to capitalize on the Missouri branching right, the expert calculated $1.2 million in transaction costs to take over existing branches and acquire new branches in the state. The costs went toward advertising, signage changes, and training the workforce. There also was "assemblage value" related to the buyer's ability to buy the acquired thrifts' existing branches and not to have to find branch locations and assemble and build the infrastructure necessary to operate the business. This value was $5 million, he concluded. After subtracting the transaction costs and assemblage value, he arrived at an FMV for the branching right of $28.8 million.

Government attacks four 'value drivers.' The government contended the valuation model was unreliable. Broadly speaking, it failed to account for the gloomy economic situation that existed in late 1981. In particular, there were four "value drivers," or key assumptions, underlying the expert's cash flow projections that did not square with reality and together inflated the value of the right. Moreover, the government expert's market analysis brought into relief the model's lack of reliability.

The court considered the arguments and counterarguments in turn.

1. Unrealistic deposit market growth rate. The government's expert claimed that the opposing expert's projected high rate of deposit growth did not align with the dire situation in which the thrift industry found itself in 1981. As a result of high interest rates and regulations as to the rates thrifts could pay depositors, deposits actually were diverted from the thrift industry—a development known as "disintermediation." The acquiring thrift in fact lost about $720 million in deposits in 1981. The situation only improved due to Congressional action in late 1982.

The plaintiff argued that a product called "All Savers Certificate" justified the expert's "robust" deposit projections. Also, its expert's model actually indicated nominal deposit growth when adjusted for inflation. Finally, the hypothetical buyer would be able to attract depositors from other thrifts because, unlike them, it suggested "safety."

The court found the growth rate problematic. It credited the testimony of the government's expert about disintermediation and noted that the allure of the "All Savers Certificate" was nonexistent. The product, it said, "was quickly labeled a dud." Further, the plaintiff's inflation adjustment argument was only true for the model's statewide deposit projections. Multiplying the projections by the hypothetical buyer's projected share of the deposit market showed the model "more than compensates for inflation." And it was likely that depositors willing to move funds would have moved them to banks that not only were just as "safe," but also were able to offer a product with a higher rate of return—something the hypothetical buyer was not able to do until late 1982.

2. Unrealistic 7% market share. The government pointed out that the rivaling expert's growth rate analysis was based on the acquiring thrift's expansion into Northern California, which took place before disintermediation, in the 1970s. Then the thrift industry operated in a much more favorable environment.

Also, in terms of the thrift's Northern California expansion, much of the growth was the result of its buying existing institutions. In contrast, the plaintiff expert's model relied on an "organic expansion," assuming the hypothetical buyer would grab market share solely by opening new branches.

The plaintiff tried to downplay this conceptual difference by claiming it did not matter in terms of outcome whether the buyer opened new branches or bought up existing branches. Either way, the buyer would have had the same market share at the 10-year mark.

The government also introduced a letter from the acquiring thrift's then CFO to the Securities and Exchange Commission (SEC) written three days before the transaction and projecting the thrift would have $638 million in new Missouri deposit funds by the end of 1986—whereas the plaintiff's expert forecast the hypothetical buyer would have $1 billion by then.

The court agreed that the projected 7% rate was unrealistic. The Northern California expansion was "a wholly unreliable indicator" of the hypothetical buyer's ability to capture a share of the Missouri deposit market in 1981, it said. The plaintiff's expert also "did not properly account for the expense" of the rapid growth he projected. Finally, the court pointed out that "lowering [the model's] market share rate in Missouri to a level that aligns with [the CFO's] projections for 1986 reduces the model's computation of the Missouri branching right fair market value by almost fifty percent."

3. *Unrealistic quantity of new loans.* The government claimed the record contradicted one of the most critical assumptions underpinning the model: that the hypothetical buyer would be able to use the new deposits to originate ARMS, particularly in California where, according to the plaintiff's expert, demand for loans remained high. To do so was important because a high influx of new deposits without the ability to generate new loans would have a negative effect on the thrift's earnings as it would have to shoulder the cost of the interest on the deposits without receiving mortgage payments to offset it.

As the government told it, in 1981 the thrift industry was unable to originate mortgage loans to any measurable degree. The thrift's own statistics indicated that it originated a mere $342.6 million in new mortgages in 1981, compared to $2.3 billion in 1976. This steep decline, said the government, was a direct result of "sky-high" interest rates and the inability of homebuyers to finance their purchases. Also, the thrift's CFO testified that the thrift industry was loan-driven: If demand for loans was weak, a high influx of deposits would bring down earnings.

The plaintiff justified the assumption by noting that thrifts "historically had been able to use all of their deposits to make mortgages."

The court found the plaintiff's argument unconvincing. Relying on the institution's prior ability to originate loans ignored the reality at the time of the transaction. Also, given the industry's loan-driven approach, it was not surprising that in the past the thrift managed to originate loans from all of its deposits. According to the court, "this simply meant [it] was good at judging its need for deposits." The court emphasized that the plaintiff expert's model was deposit-driven: The hypothetical buyer would try to capture as many deposits as possible and *then* try to originate mortgages from those funds. Based on this approach, the hypothetical buyer could well generate more deposit funds than it could turn into loans, the court said.

4. *Unrealistic 2.5% net interest spread.* The government claimed that, since the plaintiff expert's model was based on new loans with new deposits, the hypothetical buyer would have to pay a going rate for a new market rate CD instead of the lower costs indicated in the 11th District Cost of Funds Index, which informed the expert's calculation.

The plaintiff countered that the buyer would have been able to bring in new deposits simply by "marketing and [its] secure reputation" in line with the thrift's earlier experience in Northern California.

The court dismissed the argument, repeating that the Northern California experience was not a reliable indicator of what a buyer could accomplish in the 1980s.

Government expert rebuts with market analysis. Besides critiquing the plaintiff expert's model, the government's expert performed a market analysis of some 200 in-state thrift mergers that took place around the date of the transaction. The impetus was the plaintiff's claim that the acquiring bank paid a premium because it wanted the branching rights. By the government expert's reasoning, if that were the case, then the in-state mergers should not show a similar premium because they did not include branching rights. But since these mergers did in fact indicate that the acquiring thrifts paid a similar premium, it was for some other intangible asset. Therefore, the opposing expert erred when he attributed a significant percentage of the premium for the transaction to the Missouri branching right, the government's expert concluded.

The plaintiff disparaged the market analysis as "worthless." It included thrifts that were "qualitatively different" from the failing thrifts that the acquiring institution took over. The latter involved assistance from the Federal Savings and Loan Insurance Corp. (FSLIC), whereas the market analysis also considered unassisted mergers.

However, the plaintiff's expert examined 55 in-state mergers that were part of the market analysis to determine "why the acquiring thrifts in those cases might have been willing to pay a [premium]." He concluded they paid for "synergy," which would be "some trade name value or market positioning." The government's expert dismissed that conclusion, noting that his own study involved small and large thrifts paying similar premiums. Synergy would result in far less gain for the larger thrifts than the small ones, but they still paid a premium on par with the one in the transaction at issue.

The court found the plaintiff expert's explanation unsatisfactory and said the market analysis "significantly undercuts the trustworthiness" of his model.

Because the plaintiff had failed to establish the FMV of the Missouri branching right, the court found itself "unable to ascertain the cost basis for either the branching rights or the RAP right, or, for that matter, to the incentive package." Consequently, it dismissed the plaintiff's refund claim.

Zelouf Int'l Corp. v. Zelouf

Citation: 2014 N.Y. Misc. LEXIS 4341
Date of decision: Oct. 6, 2014
Experts: Kevin Vannucci, McGladrey (joint—neutral—appraiser); James T. Ashe, Marcum LLP, Anthony Saunders (fair value appraisal), Elliot A. Lesser (forensic accountant) (all for respondent); unknown (plaintiff)
Judge: Kornreich
State/Jurisdiction: New York
Court: New York Supreme Court (Trial Court)
Type of case: Judicial Dissolution
SIC code: 5000 Wholesale Durable Goods

Court Hitches DLOM Application to Probability of Sale

When valuing a closely held company, New York law allows for the application of a discount for lack of marketability, and courts have many times applied it. Readers may remember the 2012 *Giaimo v. Vitale* case in which the court found a DLOM for a real estate holding company was appropriate. But is it mandatory? This was one of the key issues a New York trial court recently decided in the context of a statutory appraisal proceeding arising out of a long and nasty family feud.

Backstory. In 1984, an Iranian immigrant started a very successful textile business. After his death, the business went to his sons, Joseph (45%), Rony (25%), and Emil (25%). Joseph's son, Danny, had a 5% stake. After Joseph died unexpectedly, Danny suddenly had a 50%, majority ownership stake, and, even though he had little experience in the business, he promptly appointed himself president and made Rony vice president of the company. The two began a feud with Emil, who shortly thereafter suffered a mishap and fell into a coma. Eventually, Emil's wife Nahal succeeded in her fight for Emil's shares. Meanwhile, Danny and Rony kept increasing their salaries. In 2004, Danny earned $44,400 and in 2013 over $1.7 million. Rony's pay went from a little over $100,000 in 2004 to nearly $420,000 in 2011. Also, for years both men took millions of dollars in interest-free loans from the company, which they began to repay after Nahal sued them. And, from 2006 to 2013, Danny paid his mother a six-figure "salary," which then decreased slightly, totaling over $900,000, not for doing work, but for providing "emotional support." Starting in 2007, Danny and Rony leased a fleet of luxury cars costing approximately $100,000 per year that was mostly for their personal use. Also, in 2008, Danny formed another company that he solely owned and that began to sell to four of the original company's clients. The new company used the resources of the original company.

In 2009, Nahal made a books and records request and subsequently sued Danny and Rony for waste and misappropriation. In discovery, she fought for access to the records in an inventory database to prove that Danny and Rony overstated the cost of goods sold and understated the value of the inventory to make the company look much less profitable than it was and "steal" large amounts without the risk of being detected. During pretrial proceedings, in 2013, the parties jointly hired a neutral appraiser to perform a valuation of the company for mediation purposes. But, instead of a settlement, Danny and Rony decided to pursue a freeze-out merger, that is, form a new company to buy out Nahal and render her unable to pursue her derivative claims. Ultimately the court allowed the merger based on the stipulation of the parties that the court would rule on Nahal's derivative claims as part of an appraisal proceeding and would allow for additional damages and legal fees if she won on those claims.

Court leans on neutral valuator. Nahal rejected the company's $1.5 million buyout offer, and the appraisal proceeding went forward. Both sides agreed that the neutral valuator's appraisal should serve as the starting point of their analyses of what the fair value of Nahal's shares was. Fair value represents "what a willing purchaser, in an arm's length transaction, would offer for the corporation as an operating business." The parties' own experts focused on critiquing and adjusting the neutral appraiser's report.

The report determined the value of the original company on a controlling basis based on the assumption that it would generate earnings into perpetuity. The neutral appraiser considered using the three standard valuation methods—market, income, and asset approach—but decided only the income-based approach made for a meaningful valuation. He used the capitalization, as opposed to the discounted cash flow, method. After normalizing adjustments to the company's net income, including adjustments to Danny's salary, he arrived at a value of approximately $8.9 million. This amount included the value of the business the company lost from the four customers Danny's new company had serviced.

In a separate appraisal, the expert calculated the value of the company based on a controlling, nonmarketable basis, using a 30% DLOM to arrive at a $6.2 million valuation.

The party experts' disagreements with the report focused on the following points.

1. *SEAM.* One point of contention was tax affecting—whether an S corporation equity adjustment multiple (SEAM) was appropriate and what the individual tax rate was. At the direction of counsel, the neutral appraiser calculated a SEAM but stated that in his opinion it was inapplicable in this case. SEAM is a premium added to a valuation of an S corp to reflect the pass-through tax benefits not available to C corps. But, as the expert explained, since he was not valuing a minority equity interest but the entire company, there was no justification for applying a SEAM premium. The court agreed this premium was inappropriate.

2. *DLOM.* The other flashpoint was the discount for lack of marketability (DLOM). According to the neutral appraiser, "typically, a [DLOM] is usually only applicable for valuations of minority interests in closely-held companies under the assumption that a controlling owner would be able to force the sale of the company." It was inappropriate in this case, he said, but he applied it at the direction of counsel.

The parties' experts argued over its application and the percentage it should take. In essence, Nahal's expert maintained that case law held that a DLOM was never applicable in this scenario; alternatively, if the court allowed for one, it should not be more than 15%. The company's expert contended New York law required a DLOM.

The court found Nahal's expert mistakenly referred to a case that dealt with a minority interest, which was prohibited in New York. But it agreed that a DLOM was inappropriate here, crediting the neutral appraiser's reasoning. The expert was correct, the court said, in determining that:

> [T]he assumptions underlying a DLOM, such as hypothetical impediments to sale and the actual likelihood that [the company] would be sold, are entirely irrelevant to the determination of the fair value of Nahal's shares, which is based on her pro rata share of the value of the entire company on a controlling basis.

The court rejected the claim that New York law mandated a DLOM. Although New York law does not allow a discount for minority status, it allows for a DLOM when there is sufficient evidence of a "risk associated with the illiquidity of the shares." See *Giaimo v Vitale,* 101 AD3d 523, 524, 956 N.Y.S.2d 41 (1st Dep't 2012) (available at *BVLaw*).

Although it recognized that many court opinions have found a DLOM was applicable, "no New York case stands for the proposition that a DLOM *must* be applied to a closely-held company," the court said with emphasis. The idea underlying a DLOM is that the recovery of a frozen-out, minority shareholder should be less to account for the difficulty of selling a closely held company in a niche business as compared to a publicly traded company, the court explained.

This rationale did not apply here, the court found. Specifically, Danny had testified that the premise of the business was personal relationships. Therefore, it was unlikely that the company would or could ever be sold. A liquidity risk in this instance was "more theoretical than real," said the court. Since its founding, the company had never been sold and there was no reason to believe that "Danny will walk away from a company providing him with millions of dollars in income, a similar low interest loan facility, personal and family perks and control," unless and until the company eventually would go to other family members. According to the court, even though New York law does not allow a discount for minority status, it allows for a DLOM when there is sufficient evidence of a "risk associated with the illiquidity of the shares." See *Giaimo v Vitale*, 2012 N.Y. App. Div. LEXIS 8706 (2012) (slip op.) (available at *BVLaw*).

Risk, the court went on to say, was "a function of probability times the threatened harm." Here, although there would be harm in the form of a lower net purchase price, the probability that it would actually occur was "negligible." In the absence of a risk, a DLOM was inappropriate, the court concluded. A DLOM would "artificially depress Nahal's recovery due to a hypothetical sale that will never occur." This approach, the court found, would result in imposing "the very sort of minority penalty that New York law prohibits."

3. *Control premium.* One of Nahal's experts proposed a control premium to account for the "myriad benefits of and powers associated with controlling a company." The court found arguments as to the benefits or disadvantages of majority and minority stakes were "wholly irrelevant" where, as here, the company was being valued as a whole. Neither Danny's nor Nahal's stakes were the subject of valuation. The court also noted that in this fair value proceeding it would be inequitable to apply a control premium while the law prohibits a minority discount.

4. *Lost corporate opportunity.* The company argued that there should be no damages arising from sales Danny's new company made to four of the original company's customers. The new company sold junior sportswear, a product that the original company did not sell, the company claimed. Even if the old company had never before sold that product, Danny at least had a duty to offer the original company the chance to get into that market, which he did not do, the court said. This was particularly true because he used the original company's resources. The court included the amount of lost business based on the neutral appraiser's calculation in its valuation.

5. *Financials.* Nahal's expert claimed that the neutral appraiser's valuation required an adjustment because it was only as of Dec. 31, 2012. However, under the law, the valuation date is the merger date, which was in August 2013. The expert claimed that in the interim eight months the company increased in value by $2.1 million, or 23%. The argument had no traction with the court. This claim was based on a "mathematical exercise of plugging in the 2013 numbers and applying various weighing schemes," it found. The company's financials did not show an actual improvement in the company's performance. Therefore, an adjustment was unnecessary.

In sum, the court valued Nahal's 25% interest in the company at over $2.2 million.

Additional damages available. The court found that, in addition to the fair value of her 25% interest in the company, Nahal qualified for an additional $2.2 million based on certain of her waste claims and her misappropriation claim. While Nahal did not prove that Danny and Rony's potentially excessive salaries were disproportionate to the benefit the two conferred on the company, the $1 million Danny paid to his mother represented "a textbook example of corporate waste," the court said. The leasing of luxury cars for the two men's personal use also was wasteful. Damages for these types of misconduct amounted to about $220,000.

As for the misappropriation claim, the court extolled the work of Nahal's forensic accountant, who, by analyzing the records from the company's inventory database, was able to establish that the company's financial statements omitted over $14 million in gross profits during 2004 through 2010. Relying on benchmark profitability margins for comparable companies from the Risk Management Association, the accountant assumed a 25% profit margin. The court awarded Nahal $2 million, after adjusting for restrictions based on statute of limitation consideration. Reasonable attorney's fees and prejudgment interest in line with the court's order were also available.

Editor's note: In a two-part discussion of the case, New York business attorney Peter Mahler raises some interesting questions about the wider implications of the court's position on DLOM. For example, he asks whether the court's reliance on the probability of a sale harmonizes with the fair value standard of value and whether "there exist any theoretical or empirical bases for applying DLOM at the control level of value."

BVR
What It's Worth

Where every trustworthy business valuation begins.

Any informed stakeholder in business valuation, performance benchmarking, or risk management turns to Business Valuation Resources (BVR) for authoritative market data, training, and expert opinion. Trust BVR for unimpeachable business valuation intelligence. Our clients include business appraisers, certified public accountants, merger and acquisition professionals, business brokers, lawyers and judges, private equity and venture capitalists, owners, CFOs, and many others. BVR's market databases and analysis have won in the courtroom—and the boardroom—for 18+ years.

Deal & Market Data:

- Pratt's Stats®
- Public Stats™
- BIZCOMPS®
- Economic Outlook Update™
- Factset Mergerstat/BVR Control Premium Study™
- The FMV Restricted Stock Study™
- Valuation Advisors Discount for Lack of Marketability Study™
- ktMINE Royalty Rate Data & License Agreements
- First Research Industry & State Profiles
- Butler Pinkerton Calculator™ Total Cost of Equity and Public Company Specific Risk Calculator™
- Mergerstat® Review & Mergerstat Review Monthly
- Risk Premium Calculator
- Valuation Handbook - Guide to Cost of Capital
- BizMiner Industry Financial Reports
- PitchBook Guideline Public Company Comps Tool

News & Research:

- Business Valuation Update™
- BVLaw™
- Business Reference Guide Online

Training & CPE:

- Webinars
- Web Workshops & Symposiums
- Desktop Learning Centers
- Self-study CPE

Guides, Books & Reports:

- Guides & Books
- Special Reports
- Legal Compendiums

Learn more at: bvresources.com

Business Valuation Resources, LLC • 1000 SW Broadway, Suite 1200 • Portland, OR 97205
Phone: (503) 291-7963 • Fax: (503) 291-7955 • Email: info@bvresources.com

www.ingramcontent.com/pod-product-compliance
Lightning Source LLC
LaVergne TN
LVHW062156300926
849161LV00010B/2679
* 9 7 8 1 6 2 1 5 0 0 4 7 6 *